India in the Interim

This book shows a slice of the governmental interregnum from August 1947 to the start of the first general election in October 1951, and is a narrative of some of its intermediate moments in the light of contemporary politics. It is a multi-track chronicle, which draws attention to its discrete, if not determining, impact on the following decade of consolidation. While it is also a map of Prime Minister Jawaharlal Nehru's words and actions, drawn as it is mainly from his papers, it is embedded in the government. It describes a time of transitional governance in independent India's early political history and gives a glimpse of its multiple individual traits, identity tensions and institutional trends. The Nehruvian gaze traced here shows what a constant flux governing in those unsettled post-partition years was.

Rakesh Ankit is a lecturer in history and international politics at Loughborough University, United Kingdom. He is the author of *The Kashmir Conflict: From Empire to the Cold War, 1945–66* (2016) and *India in the Interregnum: Interim Government, September 1946–August 1947* (2019).

Provincial premiers with members of the central government

Source: Album 623, no. 27958, at the photo section of Nehru Memorial Museum and Library, New Delhi.

India in the Interim

The 1947–1951 Nehru Government

Rakesh Ankit

Shaftesbury Road, Cambridge CB2 8EA, United Kingdom

One Liberty Plaza, 20th Floor, New York, NY 10006, USA

477 Williamstown Road, Port Melbourne, VIC 3207, Australia

314–321, 3rd Floor, Plot No. 3, Splendor Forum, Jasola District Centre, New Delhi – 110025, India

103 Penang Road, #05–06/07, Visioncrest Commercial, Singapore 238467

Cambridge University Press is part of Cambridge University Press & Assessment, a department of the University of Cambridge.

We share the University's mission to contribute to society through the pursuit of education, learning and research at the highest international levels of excellence.

www.cambridge.org
Information on this title: www.cambridge.org/9781009525268

First published 2024

Printed in India by Avantika Printers Pvt. Ltd.

A catalogue record for this publication is available from the British Library

ISBN 978-1-009-52526-8 Hardback

Cambridge University Press & Assessment has no responsibility for the persistence or accuracy of URLs for external or third-party internet websites referred to in this publication, and does not guarantee that any content on such websites is, or will remain, accurate or appropriate.

Contents

Acknowledgements

This book is based on research done in the manuscript room of the Nehru Memorial Museum and Library, New Delhi, and I remember fondly the helpful staff there, especially Jyoti Luthra and Soumya Mohanty. Qudsiya Ahmed, Anwesha Rana, Saniya Puri and Priya Das at Cambridge University Press, India, responded promptly to its proposal and reworked the subsequent drafts, after it had languished for more than a year elsewhere. I cannot thank the three anonymous reviewers enough, whose scrutiny has halved the size of the book and saved me from twice as many errors as there undoubtedly remain. Virinder Kalra gave me an early opportunity to present a portion of it at the University of Warwick in December 2019 and has been very encouraging of the project. Ian Talbot, supporting as before, read a chapter and invited me back to the University of Southampton for a talk in February 2020.

Francis Robinson kindly commented on the introduction and reminded me of the essential importance of clarity of exposition. Madhavan Palat, Vijay Singh and Mahesh Rangarajan have been benevolent correspondents while I put it together at Loughborough and Coventry, where I thank Marcus Collins, Michel Cornette, Peter and Moira Ackers, Robert Knight, Steven Parfitt, Anthony Kevins, Ali Shair, Andrew Lui and, above all, Pippa Virdee. From Delhi, Atishi Marlena, Pujya Trivedi, Amit Bindal, Latika Vashist, Chitra Mishra, Aditi Bhardwaj, Rohit Wellington and Ronil Chaudhuri have been concerned and caring. Wajahat Ahmad and Aaliya Anjum have been inspiring hosts, Krithika Ashok has been a stalwart pen pal and Aditya Basu has cheered me on. As ever, my parents and family have given me prayers, wishes and more.

This book comes too late for Dr David E. U. Baker (1932–2021) and Ravish Tiwari (1981–2022), but grateful and poignant memories of our interactions are all over it.

Prologue

At the end of my research on the 1946–47 interim government published as *India in the Interregnum* (2019), I had hoped to produce a second instalment, on its 1947–51 successor, given its relative neglect in published accounts and presence in primary sources, especially the now-accessible post-1947 Jawaharlal Nehru papers.[1] The last years of the 1940s and the first of the 1950s constitute an intermediate period between Partition/Freedom (1947) and Republic/Democracy (1950–52) that is often seen through either or both of these lenses. This was captured in a critical review of *India in the Interregnum* that considered 'this continuity … to be the root cause of the ills that plague the post-colonial nation….'[2]

Approaching its eighth decade, as independent India experiences its eighteenth government, this book seeks to remember its first predecessor, which functioned in a uniquely intermediate period. It is important to do so because, whether in public recall or in academic research, the first Nehru government has had a somewhat shadowy existence, which is compensated by the axiom that it stood for a transitional phase for the country. But, as the late D. L. Sheth wrote, 'historicization makes historical sense, only when made in terms of contemporary sensibilities….'[3] This intervention then surveys the 1947–51 government, liminally located between dominion and democracy, and subsumed between Partition and nation-building, in an 'academic no-man's land'.[4] It attempts an exercise of historical recovery crystallised from the post-1947 prime ministerial papers in the hope that this reconstruction might help in reading post-Partition Indian party politics. The standard conception of that multi-party government is that it is clustered around a *duumvirate*,[5] but this book tries to bring forth and intertwine its multiple individual traits, identity tensions and institutional trends.

This triangular pyramid was held together by provincial or princely politics, progressive or prejudicial passions and party pronouncements. The all-India whole that was forged in those first years, before being put to a popular test, was pivotal to subsequent state-building, and this book probes the performance of that pre-1952 government, whose political heritage continues to be dissected. As it has been said, 'nations themselves are narrations …', so a history of the first independent Indian government is one way to contextualise the contemporary by answering the 'need for links and connections'.[6] The subjectively selected material here presents the post-1947 trials through its governmental figures and their episodes, capturing some of the tussle between popular impulses and authoritarian imperatives.

'Our present problem is not so much what Pakistan does or does not do, but what many of our own people do', wrote Jawaharlal Nehru to Sarvepalli Radhakrishnan on 22 January 1948, while admonishing him for his encouragement of the Rashtriya Swayamsevak Sangh (RSS).[7] A year and a half later, on 15 June 1949, he would write to his foreign secretary K. P. S. Menon that 'we should not worry ourselves about the Russian bogey [but] about internal conditions in India, which give rise to Communism'.[8] The aim in this book is precisely this tracing of what many of Nehru's compatriots did or did not do across the country, for which purpose it seeks the privileged prime ministerial desk as a vantage. From there, it gazes into provinces and states, to show their political crises, like the 'big gap' between the government and the 'working classes', about which Nehru cautioned Bombay's premier Bal Gangadhar Kher on 5 January 1948.[9] Simultaneously, the book probes the Congress party, where the powers of Vallabhbhai Patel provide the institutional prism through which the light of its ministries fell upon the people.[10] Thus, in a way, it attempts a description of *India after Gandhi*,[11] but before it becomes *Nehru's India*.[12]

Each of the following five chapters and their sections reassemble some snapshots of the governance of that volatile time. After an extended prologue from August 1947 until the first Governor-General Louis Mountbatten's departure in June 1948, Chapter 1 presents the months until the next major state milestone of April 1949, when New Delhi joined the new Commonwealth, in three thematic sections covering provinces or states, the central cabinet and the left- and right-wing. Here, the older bureaucratic apparatus joined hands with the newer political regime to valorise constitutional structures in the face of countervailing socio-cultural sensibilities. Chapter 2 shows the rest of

1949 and its equivocal governmental play of partisan ideologies vis-à-vis the political status quo or centre.

Chapter 3 explores the government's work in the critical year of 1950, with its much written about emergence of the republic through the constituent assembly debates.[13] Chapter 4 is a portrayal of Patel who, arguably, was the most powerful minister in the 1947–50 set-up, holding the home and states ministries apart from his clout in the Congress organisation. With massive information at his disposal, Patel deployed people, denied Nehru and disbursed patronage. A long Chapter 5 traces the year of 1951, its dress rehearsal of the first general election and the delayed reversal of the previous year's minorities pact with Pakistan. Side by side, as the Congress party imploded, its presidentship and the prime ministership were fused together. An extended Epilogue shows the lead-up to electoral democracy, a period of transitional governance that oversaw 'a slow tearing apart of the fabric of a whole way of life'.[14]

This archival history of a government is ultimately an attempt to revisit a time, which the manner of Gandhi's death and the matter of Nehru's life overshadowed. It shows another slice of the governmental *interregnum* from August 1947 to the start of the first general election in October 1951[15] and aspires to be a history of moments of the state in between. It is a multitrack suggestive chronicle of the period, which is arranged chronologically and overlappingly. It draws attention to its discrete, if not determining, background to the following decade of consolidation (1952–62), and while it is also a map of the prime minister's words and actions, drawn as it is from his office's papers, it is embedded in the government, much like he was. Since then, the politics of representation has become a 'hegemony of the numerically larger', and it has become 'irrelevant' whether public claims are 'historically sustainable'.[16]

> In our present-day transitional politics [why should] the whole of India, share in the liability arising out of the defections of some of its parts? Why [should] other parts of the country be called upon to pay for the inefficiency or callousness of some local administrations?[17]

Thus, wrote C. H. Bhabha (member, works, mines and power) to Cabinet Secretary H. M. Patel, ten days before the Partition Plan's announcement, while objecting to a proposed scheme of insurance against civil commotion and riot risks. Bhabha's other objections were that it would hurt industry and trade and accelerate inflation, and, overall, the summer of 1947 seemed to him a 'particularly inopportune moment' for insuring the country. Seldom were more ironic sentiments expressed or the pitch of the imminent nation queried more inadvertently. Almost exactly a year later, Jawaharlal Nehru would admit to the governor of East Punjab that there were 'inherent difficulties' about riot insurance.[18] If it was limited to the partitioned provinces, it will be burdensome; if it was spread country-wide, it will be objectionable.

If this raises the curtain on the anticipated and acknowledged provincial nature of Partition, then the prime ministerial correspondence from the time comprises concerns about the other side of the coin too, that is, the princely states.[19] From asserting to the maharaja of Manipur that his future 'obviously' lies with India,[20] to arguing with the maharaja of Indore that all states should, 'for their own good', join the constituent assembly,[21] and from directing the Madras government to non-cooperate with the Travancore state, to demanding from his ministerial colleagues looking after defence, transport and railways and works, mines and power departments that 'no facilities are afforded' and 'no controls relaxed' vis-à-vis the Hyderabad state,[22] Nehru was not content to wait and watch. Together, these exchanges provide some of the themes recurrent throughout this Prologue, and what follows, namely (a) conflicts between the centre and provinces over a variety of identity politics and institutional issues, under the 1935 act, (b) tensions between the Congress and non-Congress members of the government, (c) what may be called the 'hang-over' of Partition,[23] (d) the prime minister's power relative to that of his peers, and (e) the strain in this not being a pure government, electorally or constitutionally.

Consequently, many people were starting to take matters in their hands, in ways unexpected and yet unsurprising. A week from the announcement of the Partition Plan, Abul Kalam Azad (member, education) wrote to Nehru that the All-India Radio (AIR) news bulletin was being delivered in a heavy Hindi lexicon. With Patel denying having issued any directions, the prime minister was reduced to conclude that some individuals 'may have introduced their own ways …',[24] which would become the 'standard' sound of a nation to come,[25] the furies of which were then being expressed in the micro-histories emerging from the nearby 'epicentre' of violence.[26] For instance, a leading lawyer of Hissar, J. D. Kureshi's house was attacked a fortnight from 15 August 1947, his family members were killed and his daughter Gul Rukh, along with eight other girls, was abducted. When, subsequently, Kureshi was arrested, Shaukat Hayat Khan approached Nehru, from West Punjab, to intervene, while in the east, Thakur Das Bhargava, brother of premier Gopichand, spoke highly of him. When the district collector of Hissar was telephoned, it resulted in the girls being murdered, and in mid-November 1947, Kureshi was still in prison, while Mrs Kureshi was in Lahore.[27]

By then, a spell of terror had been cast in the heart of the national capital. From 7 to 9 September especially, in a 'one-way traffic … Hindu and Sikh hooligans … assisted by the police and troops, staged every atrocity reported or believed to have been perpetuated in West Punjab'.[28] Dewan Chaman Lall, a member of the Punjab legislature (1937–45) and the constituent assembly (1946–48), urged Defence Minister Baldev Singh to let the Akali leaders, Master Tara Singh and Giani Kartar Singh, visit 'the disturbed areas' while requesting 'the Sangh ... to desist'.[29] When Gandhi himself addressed a gathering of about 500 RSS members in New Delhi on 16 September 1947, the *sarsanghchalak* M. S. Golwalkar replied that 'he could not vouchsafe for the correct behaviour of every member'.[30] While Nehru could scarcely believe all that was 'happening in the Punjab and in Delhi',[31] people in Calcutta, not to be left behind, were talking about population exchange with East Bengal. With newspapers like the *Amrit Bazar Patrika* and the *Hindustan Standard* freely fanning the communal fires and West Bengal's Congress government not feeling the 'necessity of controlling' them,[32] who could rule this out?

The central government's attitude towards the public sphere was also raising eyebrows. Shankarrao Deo, Congress' general secretary, had indicated that the party read 'friendly criticism' as hostility to the government, as its absorption of former opponents like Dr B. R. Ambedkar, Dr S. P. Mookerjee and Shanmukham Chetty into the cabinet had somewhat swept away the cupboard of challenge, and yet, 'the mistakes being made in Delhi and the Punjab' were bound to be costly.[33] This government had arrived through the 1945–46 elections, about whose limited and 'incomplete' electoral rolls, the chief commissioner of Delhi had admitted a 'complete apathy' as there was 'no alternative but to let the election proceed'.[34]

Be that as it may then, now Nehru was receiving information that preparations were afoot for trouble at the Garhmukteshwar fair in UP like in 1946, that armed groups from Rohtak would head there, looting Muslim villages along the way in Delhi, Shahdara, Ghaziabad, Hapur and Meerut. The RSS and 'the old Hindu and Sikh members of the Unionist Party, the Jat Mahasabha, Arya Samajist leaders ... INA men and ex-servicemen', all were reportedly involved in this.[35] What precautions could be taken against such rumours of considerable stirs, at a time, when Muslims of Delhi were forced to become refugees in their own city, at the camps in Humayun's Tomb and Old Fort complexes. Threatened by the 'new-comer ... refugees', who were either handed over or were occupying houses vacated by Muslims,[36] an exodus was taking place, notwithstanding wishes expressed by Gandhi and the All-India Congress Committee (AICC).[37] And, the beacon of Indian nationalist Muslims, Abul Kalam Azad was yet to become a member either of the constituent or of any provincial assembly as Nehru was scouting for a 'Muslim vacancy' for him.[38]

This irony was both individual and institutional, as in incidents typifying the times, Syed Sultan Ahmad, barrister-legislator from Bihar, and H. S. Suhrawardy, politician-minister from Bengal, were 'closely searched' at

Delhi's Willingdon aerodrome repeatedly in September 1947, despite 'clear and definite orders' to the contrary.[39] Shortly after, when the Indian envoy to Egypt, Syed Hossain, arrived there from Calcutta, he too was searched, and the subsequent enquiry revealed that all Muslim passengers were being regularly separated on 'orders from higher authority', leaving the holder of arguably the highest executive authority in the country surprised.[40] In another incident, Umar Abid Zuberi, son of Dr I. H. Zuberi (principal of Islamia College, Calcutta, and subsequently principal of M. C. College, Sylhet) and nephew of civil servant M. H. Zuberi (secretary, communications, in Delhi until August and subsequently at Karachi), was arrested in mid-December 1947 under the public safety ordinance despite being a minor. No charges were brought, and he was released in mid-February 1948, after interventions by Governor C. Rajagopalachari.[41] Little wonder then that an old acquaintance of Rajagopalachari would ask him bluntly:

> Can a Muslim travel from Delhi to Lahore, Ahmedabad, or Karachi without fear? Is there any propaganda in Brahman-Bania press for the removal of these wrongs? Hyderabad is the next target.... Why should [it] be left when it is the centre of remaining Muslim culture? Of course, it is anti-democratic that [a] small minority should rule a majority.... But [are Brahman-Bania] a majority? Such questions [would] be regarded disloyalty to State. My friend, the propagation of democracy in a land where the social constitution is undemocratic is pure hypocrisy....[42]

To his personal credit, in a special circular letter to provincial premiers, the prime minister stressed that their basic problems were economic: development schemes, *zamindari* abolition, social reform and price controls. Though, to help in tackling these, he also drew the premiers' attention to build up 'home guards [and] intelligent service'.[43] Among the latter, Pandit Ravishankar Shukla of Central Provinces and Berar had publicly 'hinted at the possibility of [Muslims] losing the rights of citizenship in Hindustan....'[44] This provincial world was also bestirred with demands for new provinces to be formed on a linguistic basis. A short-notice question had appeared in the constituent assembly by the peasant leader N. G. Ranga, forcing the government to accept the principle, concede the demand of Andhra, reserve judgement on the rest and bring up 'first things first, the security and stability of India'.[45]

By December 1947, only one in five Muslims had been left in the nearby region of Ajmer, and from Gandhi in Bengal to Malkani in Sindh, Nehru was urged to visit the area. He sent his secretary H. V. R. Iengar, who reported unflatteringly on the home department as well as on Shankar Prasad (chief commissioner, Ajmer). An 'upset' Prasad and his patron, Patel, looked upon Iengar's visit as an 'inquiry' behind their backs,[46] and a beleaguered Nehru was forced to explain to Patel.[47] Closer still was Alwar, where to the plight of Meos,[48] their homes, fields and graves, was added the attack on Fateh Jung Gumbad, and Nehru demanded to Patel that the maharaja be 'pulled up'.[49] This theme of demanding from or explaining to Patel, and his officials, was not limited to communal questions. A cabinet decision to appoint a temporary board to choose candidates to start the new cadre of the Indian Foreign Service, under Nehru's charge, was 'held up' in the Home Ministry for two months.[50]

The problem was that cabinet members themselves were not being able to meet informally or frequently. This was leading to complaints that other ministers knew little about the work of any ministry, and thus there could be no joint responsibility. This tendency was spiralling out of the cabinet into the constituent assembly, whose members were piqued that important bills were placed 'almost at the last moment'.[51] The position of provincial premiers was better given Nehru's fortnightly letters to them and there the issue was one of intention, especially on the relative spectres of different communalisms, refugee rehabilitation and industrial truce between labour and capital.[52] When the Madras government sought to ban public meetings of the Muslim League, it seemed wrong to the prime minister, not only because there was 'not the least chance of … major trouble' but also because there was a chance in such a meeting to get 'useful information' of what the party was 'thinking'.[53] On the East Punjab government, complaints were coming that it was not working 'impartially' on rehabilitation, and, when the Bombay government used force against students and workers, blaming the socialist and communist parties, it was reminded that if it 'has to indulge in repeated conflicts', then it has 'lost touch' with the people.[54] It promptly went ahead and, along with the Madras government, banned the left-wing Congress organisation Rastriya Seva Dal.[55]

The crux between sections of the state and those of the society seemed to be, as Governor Rajagopalachari in Calcutta summed up, how 'to restore confidence and courage among the people, who have to live under a government they do not like'.[56] As for the RSS, in a speech at Lucknow on 6 January 1948, Patel said that it should 'let the four crores of Muslims to remain in peace'; in turn, he asked the 'Congressmen in office [to] win them over….'[57] Amidst all this, when one of the two Indian governors from the pre-1947 regime wondered about the general election, Nehru answered ambitiously, 'the next cold weather' after the constitution is passed in July 1948.[58] As of now, in January, with 'millions displaced' in Punjab and another million expected from Sindh,[59] it made spiritual sense for him to go to the Kumbh Mela. More so as Jayaprakash Narayan (JP) and the socialists were about to leave the Congress.[60] Within a week though, let alone the cause of socialism, the cause of India itself appeared in peril as Gandhi was assassinated by Nathuram Godse on 30 January 1948.[61]

Despite the consequent ban on the RSS,[62] and other organisations, reports came from as far as Madras province of the violence against Muslims. A surprised Rajagopalachari wrote to its premier that 'something should be done to make minorities feel that government will protect them'.[63] The UP government led the way in demonstrating a reverse sense. In February 1948, a Hindi newspaper *Bharat* published an account of the arbitrary removal of M. Raza, a transport inspector in Allahabad. When the matter was taken up with Dr John Matthai, transport minister, he expressed helplessness vis-à-vis the provincial government. When the complaint reached the UP premier, Govind Ballabh Pant, he admitted that the regional officer had shown 'excessive zeal', and got Raza reinstated, but also wondered how Matthai was interested in 'these relatively trivial matters....'[64]

Meanwhile, an organisation called Durga Horse had emerged in Jodhpur, and Sikh private armies, from ex-INA General Mohan Singh's Desh Sewak Sena to Qadiani volunteers, were being indulged by the East Punjab administration.[65] At Patiala, the activities of some leaders of the All-India States Peoples Conference was producing complications with the princely family, now patronised by Patel's States Ministry. There were talks of absorbing this organisation,[66] but Nehru wanted to give his former colleagues like Pattabhi Sitaramayya, Hira Lal Shastri and Jai Narain Vyas a chance to adjust to the new order. Adjusting was what he himself was doing to, above all, Gandhi's death, as life demanded to be carried on with work on Kashmir, the budget, inflation, the food situation, especially in Madras, the petrol and oil shortage, falling production and purchasing power and strikes in Tata collieries. Against this backdrop, it was strange for the government to refuse an increase in the dearness allowance of government employees while giving tax relief to the industry.[67] It dismayed some veteran Congressmen, who preferred 'wilderness rather than to collaborate with people, who praise the patriotism of Feudal Barons and Money Bags, Maharajas and Business Magnates'.[68]

The prime minister too was worried about the government's industrial policy statement, stalling nationalisation and its budget. These might have been against the repeated professions of the Congress rank and file as well as the recent report of the party's economic programme committee, but then, this was not only a Congress government. Its finance minister was Shanmukham Chetty, industries were being looked after by Syama Prasad Mookerjee and anyway Patel's and Rajendra Prasad's closeness to the industrial elite requires little repetition.[69] The latter were complaining about labour's 'intransigence', and Nehru was left to care for the 'psychological problems [of] giving a square deal'.[70] The impression in fact was that 'self-aggrandizement' was 'the law of life', and while Patel, Rajagopalachari and almost all the provincial premiers could not be accused of being 'tolerant' towards the 'left', occasionally they were reminded from below that 'once upon a time, we were all in the "left"'.[71] Mookerjee though was becoming more invested in the interests of Hindus in East Bengal, with about a million of them having migrated west since August 1947.[72]

Nehru, on the other hand, was striving for a country where minorities could live normally, and creating such conditions also included producing rules about the national flag and discouraging the practice of playing publicly what people considered to be the national anthem, as the constituent assembly had not decided on either.[73] With Tagore's *Jana Gana Mana* yet to be formally chosen, Nehru wanted to popularise its musical rendering, as he was doubtful if *Bande Mataram* was 'wholly suited ... both because of its difficult language and the tune'.[74] In May 1948, weighing upon the matter in a lengthy note for the cabinet, he would highlight the 'simpler' *Jana Gana Mana* satisfying the 'musical tests' of being a national anthem, and the 'peculiarly difficult' *Bande Mataram* being a 'poignant memory'.[75] *Jana Gana Mana* was also a nod to Subhas Chandra Bose and the INA, but Nehru's sense of 'owing a duty to the large Muslim population of India'[76] was not always solo, as Rajagopalachari too stressed that 'freedom ... will be worthless if government servant ... fail to show impartiality [and] it is the duty of leaders in democracy to disregard popular passions....'[77]

For now, however, there was a substantial food crisis worsening across Madras, and Central Food Minister Jairamdas Daulatram had requested provincial premiers and states' *diwan*s to divert food there, and the external affairs ministry was overseeing efforts for imports from Pakistan, Egypt, Burma and Vietnam. In the meantime, the allotment for Madras was increased from 2 to 4 lakh tons,[78] from May to October 1948.[79] Another sensitive issue was the future of ex-INA personnel.[80] While drawing the line at their reinstatement in the army, for reasons both mechanical and of morale, the government was anxious to afford them opportunities, with the home guards, the armed constabulary, the police and the civil service 'subject to merit and suitability'.[81] But both these matters depended upon, among other things, the provinces taking a national view, and the tendency there remained otherwise.[82]

A representative instance comes from a circular letter of 15 January 1948 issued by the revenue secretary of the government of Bihar that said that no mining lease would be granted to any firm unless it appointed only *Bihari*s.[83] Another comes from the complaint that the maharaja of Bikaner made in mid-April 1948 that the East Punjab government did not intend to give any water to his state from the Bhakra dam project in contravention to the original proposal. With the central government 'largely financing the project', it wanted to have an 'effective voice' in distributing the water 'for the larger good'.[84] But such provincialism, related party factionalism and the departure of Congress socialists paled in front of the communal outbreak and the communist challenge that flared up in March 1948 from western and eastern parts of the country, respectively. Hindu refugees from Sindh went on a rampage against the local Muslims in Godhra, leading to major migration, while Calcutta, at the other end, saw a sustained spell of strike by both industrial workers and government employees, resulting in the West Bengal government banning the Communist Party of India (CPI) without consulting New Delhi. The northern provinces were also busy promoting 'Sanskritised words', leading to complaints ironically from the incoming Hindu and Sikh refugees in the Kurukshetra camp, who had 'taken to hearing the Pakistan Radio'.[85]

In south India, on the other hand, Rajagopalachari continued to seek an assurance for minorities from 'all institutions conferring secular benefits' in the memory of Gandhi. When the Pachaiyappas Trust refused to open their colleges to Muslims, Rajagopalachari conceded his 'difficult' plea,[86] which left no option but to legislate. Nationalism could be similarly narrow. When the East Punjab government stopped the flow of canal waters to Lahore, it also created a military difficulty. There was now too much of it around Pathankot, which was coming in the way of building a bridge there, urgently needed for Kashmir operations, and Nehru confessed to the chairman of the constituent assembly, Rajendra Prasad, that he was out of sympathy with the party in East Punjab, where the Akali Sikhs were 'masters of the situation'.[87] Equally nonplussed by Bengal Congress' factionalism, he requested Prasad to deal with both.[88] If the protagonists in Punjab were Bhim Sen Sachar and Gopichand Bhargava, then the party was split between Dr Bidhan Chandra Roy and Prafulla Chandra Ghosh in Bengal.[89]

Upon the socialists' break from Congress,[90] alongside a growing appetite for authoritarianism and aggrandisement, while absorbing Hindu refugees from Sindh and East Bengal and thwarting Muslim returnees from Pakistan,[91] the list of central challenges in April 1948 was considerably longer than central convictions, comprising, for instance, the inauguration of Hirakud dam's construction and the new capital city of Bhubaneswar in Orissa.[92] With Vallabhbhai Patel incapacitated since his heart attack in March, some cabinet colleagues like K. C. Neogy appeared quick to take offence on overlapping ministerial work, while Dr B. R. Ambedkar laid into the Congress in his speech at the UP Scheduled Castes conference.[93] The prime minister could not see how Ambedkar could carry on after his wide-ranging attack, which had included a reference to 'fifth columnists in our ranks [referring to the Congress minister Jagjivan Ram] and only when we expose them … will we be able to replace Nehru and Patel'.[94] Writing to him at length, Nehru illuminated his understanding of this government:

> When I invited you to join, I put forward no conditions ... [but] ... I am
> Prime Minister chiefly because of my position in the Congress ... My
> invitation therefore was on [its] behalf ... Inevitably, our working together
> ... means ... at least an avoidance of any attack on the Congress.[95]

While at the centre, the non-Congress members were attacking it, in the
provinces, Congress ministries were attacking the communists. On Labour
Day 1948, governments in the two partitioned provinces, West Bengal and
East Punjab, hit the CPI the hardest. While the former had declared it illegal,[96]
it was East Punjab that saw the largest number of arrests, strengthening
the feeling that governments used special powers too easily and too much
against the communists, at a time when reports were being received 'about the
recrudescence of the RSS'.[97] Private armies were more pervasive, and yet it
was the communists who were being arrested more.[98] As an effort to improve
matters, a cabinet coordination committee was considered, but difficulties with
staff were one thing, and more worrying was the distance among ministers.
In early May 1948, taking up a hard-line, Ambedkar and the East Punjab
government broke up the inter-dominion conference on the canal waters
dispute, overriding the attempts of N. V. Gadgil, minister for public works.[99]

   Around the same time, Bombay premier Kher was disregarding New
Delhi's suggestion of allowing agricultural implements and accommodation-
related goods to proceed to Hyderabad. An embargo had been put on military
material, but this non-military machinery too had piled up at Bombay customs,
and these developments left an impression of a government that functioned 'as
pure opportunists ...',[100] were 'prisoners of coercive administrative apparatus
[and] narrow-minded nationalists' and had a 'party living on the capital earned
long ago'.[101] This lament, however, was followed by letting Patel and the
Bengal Congress have their way in the appointment of Judge N. C. Chatterjee,
president of the Hindu Mahasabha in 1947, to the Calcutta High Court in
1948.[102] Likewise, in Punjab, Bhargava had taken Akali leaders like Giani
Kartar Singh into his cabinet, while others under Master Tara Singh carried
on in opposition.[103] And in Madras, partymen were appealing to ministers to
send police to suppress anyone asking for food and work.[104]

   Communalism, the comparatively newer scourge, was also worsening
casteism, the older blight. The fate of the 'untouchables' in East Punjab,
inside and outside the refugee camps, got tied to evacuee property transfers,
when they demanded land during rehabilitation.[105] Nehru had been one of
those who had hoped for an opportunity in the aftermath of the then-current
crisis for some land redistribution, and with anti-*zamindari* bills pending in
various provinces, he pleaded with Bhargava 'to allot some land at least to
the Harijans'.[106] East Punjab was posing peculiar problems. In the summer of
1948, reports emerged of the private manufacture of arms and ammunition

on a considerable scale in the *gurdwara*s in Tarn Taran and elsewhere in Amritsar district. The prime minister bypassed the provincial ministry and instructed army authorities to enter such premises. The news leaked and led to an uproar. Brushing aside Bhargava's protests, Nehru replied that the East Punjab government was being 'carried' by New Delhi, wondered how such abuse of places of worship happened behind the local police's back and warned that Bhargava and his ministry seemed bent on 'petty retaliation'.[107] This vicious cycle was, of course, not limited to East Punjab. From Assam, Premier Gopinath Bardoloi was simply opposed to any migration from East Bengal to Assam, opting instead for having 'powers to control' it on the ground, despite the agreement reached at the inter-dominion conference held in Calcutta in April 1948.[108]

These were more than mere spokes in the wheel of reorganising government machinery, coordinating the cabinet and rebuilding the nation state,[109] and in May 1948 they provided another occasion for a lengthy and affectionate letter from Nehru to the convalescing Patel. New Delhi's rumour mills were working overtime about the fate of Hyderabad upon the departure of Mountbattens in June, a milestone of sorts: 'We have now had 9 ½ months of this government…. It will have to be reorganise[d]'.[110] For the moment, fighting was going on in Kashmir and talking was going on in Hyderabad. Trade had started with Pakistan on raw jute, raw cotton and food grains from there and coal, cloth, steel, paper and mustard oil to there, while tensions remained high across Punjab and Bengal. The prices of essential commodities were up, as was profiteering and smuggling in these, and the government struggled to educate refugee students without domicile requirements.[111]

Four ministries were especially troublesome: commerce; industry and supply; works, mines and power; and railways. A classic case of elements from all of them conniving in corruption was that of cloth smuggling, wherein large quantities of cloth were moved in trains from Ahmedabad to north India and then to Pakistan, but Patel would not let a cabinet coordination committee be formed. On the more fundamental economic problems, he was similarly baulking at the creation of a ministry on economic affairs. The situation in the national capital itself was holding a mirror to the country. It was so because the local administration did not function as it should, for there were too many elements in it that neutralised each other, and, in the police, conflicts between Punjabis and Pathans were becoming marked.[112] It was in this 'disconcerting situation' in late June 1948 that the dominion of India got its first Indian governor-general in C. Rajagopalachari.[113]

NOTES

1   'Selected Works of Jawaharlal Nehru', Jawaharlal Nehru Memorial Fund, accessed 21 December 2023, https://nehruselectedworks.com/.

2   Saumya Gupta, 'India in the Interregnum: Interim Government, September 1946–August 1947, Delhi: OUP, 2019', *Indian Economic and Social History Review* 58, no. 4 (2021): 565.

3   D. L. Sheth, *At Home with Democracy: A Theory of Indian Politics*, ed. and intr. Peter Ronald de Souza (London: Palgrave Macmillan, 2018), 9.

4   Sekhar Bandyopadhyay, *Decolonization in South Asia: Meanings of Freedom in Post-independence West Bengal* (New York: Routledge, 2009), 1.

5   Michael Brecher, *Nehru: A Political Biography* (Oxford: Oxford University Press, 1959), 389–425.

6   Edward Said, *Culture and Imperialism* (New York: Vintage, 1993), xiii–xxiv.

7   New Delhi, Nehru Memorial Museum and Library, File No. 5, Jawaharlal Nehru (JN SG) (post-1947) Papers.

8   File No. 24 (Part II), JN (SG) Papers.

9   File No. 5, JN (SG) Papers.

10   For a biography, see R. Gandhi, *Patel: A Life* (Ahmedabad: Navajivan, 1990). For personal papers, see Durga Das, ed., *Selected Correspondences of Sardar Patel, 1945–50, Vols. I–X* (Ahmedabad: Navajivan, 1971–74).

11   Ramachandra Guha, *India after Gandhi: The History of the World's Largest Democracy* (London: Pan, 2008).

12   Taylor C. Sherman, *Nehru's India: A History in Seven Myths* (Princeton: Princeton University Press, 2022).

13   U. Bhatia, ed., *The Indian Constituent Assembly: Deliberations on Democracy* (Abingdon: Routledge, 2018).

14   Francis Robinson, *Jamal Mian: The Life of Maulana Jamaluddin Abdul Wahab of Farangi Mahall, 1919–2012* (Karachi: Oxford University Press, 2018), 364–65.

15   Rohit De, 'Between Midnight and Republic: Theory and Practice of India's Dominion Status', *International Journal of Constitutional Law* 17, no. 4 (2019): 1213–34.

16   Sheth, *At Home with Democracy*, 32.

17   21 May 1947, Bhabha to Patel, File No. 3, JN (SG) Papers. See Ian Talbot and G. Singh, eds., *Region, and Partition: Bengal, Punjab, and the Partition of the Subcontinent* (Oxford: Oxford University Press, 1999).

18   3 May 1948, Nehru to Chandulal Trivedi, File No. 9, JN (SG) Papers.

19   See Ian Copland, *The Princes of India in the Endgame of Empire, 1917–1947* (Cambridge: Cambridge University Press, 1997).

20   22 May 1947, Nehru to the Maharaja of Manipur, File No. 3, JN (SG) Papers.

21   21 June 1947, Nehru to the Maharaja of Indore, File No. 3, JN (SG) Papers.

22   9 June 1947, Nehru to Baldev Singh, Bhabha and John Matthai, 21 June 1947, Nehru to P. Subbarayan, and 30 June 1947, Nehru to Patel, File No. 3, JN (SG) Papers.

23   I thank Ian Talbot for this formulation.

24   9 June 1947, Nehru to Azad, File No. 3, JN (SG) Papers.

25   Isabel H. Alonso, *Radio for the Millions: Hindi–Urdu Broadcasting Across Borders*
     (New York: Columbia University Press, 2023), 85–105.

26   Ian Talbot and D. S. Tatla, eds., *Epicentre of Violence: Partition Voices and Memories
     from Amritsar* (Delhi: Permanent Black, 2006).

27   13 November 1947, Note on J. D. Kureshi's case, File No. 4, JN (SG) Papers.

28   13 September 1947, K. Santhanam (*Hindustan Times*) to Rajagopalachari, File
     No. 61, Rajagopalachari Papers (V Instalment), NMML. Rotem Geva, *Delhi
     Reborn: Partition and Nation Building in India's Capital* (Stanford: Stanford
     University Press, 2022), 82–125.

29   21 August 1947, Chaman Lall to Baldev Singh, Correspondences, Diwan
     Chaman Lall Papers, NMML.

30   File No. 94, R. M. Deshmukh Papers, NMML.

31   24 September 1947, Nehru to Rajagopalachari, File No. 56, Rajagopalachari
     Papers (V Instalment).

32   1 October 1947, Doulatram to Rajagopalachari, File No. 74, Rajagopalachari
     Papers (V Instalment).

33   7 October 1947, Jayakar to Jagdish Prasad, Correspondences, Jagdish Prasad
     Papers, NMML.

34   22 December 1945, India Office to V. P. Menon, 4 January 1946, Menon to
     Christie and 28 January 1946, Christie's reply, File No. F.90/2/45-R, 1946,
     National Archives of India (NAI), New Delhi.

35   18 November 1947, Nehru to Patel, File No. 4, JN (SG) Papers.

36   Vazira Fazila-Yacoobali Zamindar, *The Long Partition and the Making of Modern
     South Asia: Refugees, Boundaries, Histories* (New York: Columbia University
     Press, 2007), 19–44; and Geva, *Delhi Reborn*, 126–69.

37   21 November 1947, Nehru to Patel, File No. 4, JN (SG) Papers.

38   17 December 1947, Nehru to Pant, File No. 4, JN (SG) Papers.

39   4 October 1947, Nehru to T. Sanjevi, File No. 4, JN (SG) Papers.

40   18 October 1947, Nehru to Patel, File No. 4, JN (SG) Papers.

41   30 December 1947, Zuberi to Rajagopalachari, File No. 72, Rajagopalachari
     Papers (V Instalment).

42   Undated but before June 1948, Fakir Nazir Ahamad (Mosque Pension Line,
     Samancota) to Rajah Gopala Acharya, File No. 61, Rajagopalachari Papers (V
     Instalment).

43   22 November 1947, Nehru to provincial premiers, File No. 4, JN (SG) Papers.

44   26 June 1947, Nehru to S. A. Brelvi (*Bombay Chronicle*), File No. 3, JN (SG)
     Papers.

45   27 November 1947, File No. 4, JN (SG) Papers.

46   This incident would trigger a rift, and its Gandhian resolution, between Patel
     and Nehru, for details of which see Das, ed., *Sardar Patel's Correspondence 1945–
     50 Vol. VI* (Ahmedabad: Navajivan, 1973).

47   29 December 1947, Nehru to Patel, File No. 4, JN (SG) Papers.

48   Rakesh Ankit, 'In the Hands of a "Secular State": Meos in the Aftermath of Partition, 1947–49', *Indian Economic and Social History Review* 56, no. 4 (2019): 457–88.

49   3 December 1947, Nehru to Patel, File No. 4, JN (SG) Papers.

50   17 December 1947, Nehru to Patel, File No. 4, JN (SG) Papers.

51   10 December 1947, Nehru to cabinet members, File No. 4, JN (SG) Papers.

52   5 January 1948, Nehru to provincial premiers, File No. 5. For Patel's views. See Das, *Sardar Patel's Correspondence 1945–50 Vol. IV* (1972), xlix.

53   5 January 1948, Nehru to Subbarayan, File No. 5, JN (SG) Papers.

54   5 January 1948, Nehru to Bhargava and Kher, File No. 5, JN (SG) Papers.

55   11 April 1948, Nehru to Kher and 16 April 1948, Nehru to Reddiar, File No. 8, JN (SG) Papers.

56   25 January 1948, Rajagopalachari to Nehru, File No. 56, Rajagopalachari Papers (V Instalment).

57   File No. 94, Deshmukh Papers.

58   13 January 1948, Nehru to Chandulal Trivedi, File No. 5, JN (SG) Papers.

59   See Nandita Bhavnani, *The Making of an Exile: Sindhi Hindus and the Partition of India* (New Delhi: Tranquebar Press, 2014).

60   23 January 1948, Nehru to Vijayalakshmi Pandit, File No. 5, JN (SG) Papers.

61   See Dhirendra Jha, *Gandhi's Assassin: The Making of Nathuram Godse and His Idea of India* (New Delhi: Penguin, 2022).

62   See Walter Anderson and Shridhar Damle, *The Brotherhood in Saffron: The Rashtriya Swayamsevak Sangh and Hindu Revivalism* (New Delhi: Penguin, 2019).

63   11 February 1948, Rajagopalachari to Reddiar, File No. 68, Rajagopalachari Papers (V Instalment).

64   29 February 1948, Rajagopalachari to Matthai, 8 March 1948, Rajagopalachari to G. B. Pant and 17 March 1948, Pant to Rajagopalachari, File No. 68, Rajagopalachari Papers (V Instalment).

65   2 March 1948, Nehru to Patel and 9 March 1948, Nehru to Trivedi, File No. 7, JN (SG) Papers.

66   See V. P. Menon, *The Story of the Integration of the Indian States* (Bombay: Orient Longman, 1956); and Das, ed., *Sardar Patel's Correspondence 1945–50 Vol. IV* (1972).

67   3 March 1948, Nehru to provincial premiers, File No. 7, JN (SG) Papers.

68   27 February 1948, C. V. Rajagopalachari to C. Rajagopalachari, File No. 65, Rajagopalachari Papers (V Instalment).

69   Stanley A. Kochanek, *Business and Politics in India* (Berkeley: University of California Press, 1974), 78.

70   5 March 1948, Nehru to Mookerjee, File No. 7, JN (SG) Papers.

71   11 March 1948, C. V. Rajagopalachari to C. Rajagopalachari, File No. 65, Rajagopalachari Papers (V Instalment).

72   6 March 1948, Nehru to Liaquat Ali Khan, File No. 7, JN (SG) Papers.

73   Sadan Jha, *Reverence, Resistance and Politics of Seeing the Indian National Flag* (Delhi: Cambridge University Press, 2016), 178–206.

74   7 March 1948, Nehru to provincial governors, File No. 7, JN (SG) Papers.

75   21 May 1948, Nehru's note, File No. 9, JN (SG) Papers. See A. G. Noorani, 'Vande Mataram: A Historical Lesson', *Economic and Political Weekly* 8, no. 23 (1973): 1039–43.

76   11 April 1948, Nehru to secretary, I&B, and secretary, CR, File No. 8, JN (SG) Papers.

77   4 March 1948, Rajagopalachari to Reddiar, File No. 68, Rajagopalachari Papers (V Instalment).

78   'Lakh' is a unit followed in the South Asian numbering system, where 1 lakh = 100,000.

79   9 March 1948, Nehru to provincial premiers, File No. 7, JN (SG) Papers.

80   Maybritt Jill Alpes, 'The Congress and the INA Trials, 1945–50: A Contest over the Perception of "Nationalist" Politics', *Studies in History* 23, no. 1 (2007): 135–58.

81   11 March 1948, Nehru to Stracey and Nehru's note on the INA (undated), File No. 7, JN (SG) Papers.

82   17 March 1948, Nehru to provincial premiers, File No. 7, JN (SG) Papers.

83   25 March 1948, Nehru to Sri Krishna Sinha, File No. 7, JN (SG) Papers.

84   11 April 1948, Nehru to minister, WM&P, and Bhargava and Patel, File No. 8, JN (SG) Papers.

85   1 April 1948, Nehru to provincial premiers, File No. 8, JN (SG) Papers.

86   21 April 1948, Rajagopalachari to Reddiar, File No. 68, Rajagopalachari Papers (V Instalment).

87   26 April 1948, Nehru to Prasad and 28 April 1948, Nehru to Bhargava, File No. 8, JN (SG) Papers.

88   Patel's handling of factionalism can be seen in Das, *Sardar Patel's Correspondence 1945–50 Vol. IX* (1974).

89   27 April 1948, Nehru to Patel, File No. 8, JN (SG) Papers.

90   M. Weiner, *Party Politics in India: The Development of a Multi-Party System* (Princeton: Princeton University Press, 1957), 42–64.

91   5 May 1948, Nehru to Patel, File No. 9, JN (SG) Papers.

92   15 April 1948, Nehru to provincial premiers and 16 April 1948, Nehru to Reddiar and Nehru's note to PPS, File No. 8, JN (SG) Papers. See Rohan D'Souza, 'Damming the Mahanadi River: The Emergence of Multi-purpose River Valley Development in India (1943–46)', *Indian Economic and Social History Review* 40, no. 1 (2003): 81–105.

93   27 April 1948, Nehru to Neogy and Nehru to Patel, File No. 8, JN (SG) Papers.

94   27 April 1948, Nehru to Ambedkar, File No. 8, JN (SG) Papers.

95   30 April 1948, Nehru to Ambedkar, File No. 8, JN (SG) Papers.

96   Sekhar Bandyopadhyay, 'The Story of an Aborted Revolution: Communist Insurgency in Post-independence West Bengal, 1948–50', *Journal of South Asian Development* 3, no. 1 (2008): 1–32.

97   1–2 May 1948, Nehru to Bhargava and Patel, File No. 9, JN (SG) Papers.

98   3 May 1948, Nehru to Trivedi, File No. 9, JN (SG) Papers.

99   3 May 1948, Nehru's note of interview with Ghulam Mohammad, File No. 9, JN (SG) Papers.

100 3 May and 6 May 1948, Nehru to Kher and to Rajagopalachari, File No. 9, JN (SG) Papers.

101 6 May 1948, Nehru to Pant, File No. 9, JN (SG) Papers.

102 12 May 1948, Nehru to Patel, File No. 9, JN (SG) Papers.

103 16 April and 20 May 1948, Nehru to Bhargava, File Nos. 8, and 9, JN (SG) Papers.

104 22 May 1948, C. V. Rajagopalachari to C. Rajagopalachari, File No. 65, Rajagopalachari Papers (V Instalment).

105 Ravinder Kaur, 'Narrative Absence: An "Untouchable" Account of Partition Migration', *Contributions to Indian Sociology* 42, no. 2 (2008): 281–306.

106 20 May 1948, Nehru to Bhargava, File No. 9, JN (SG) Papers.

107 21 and 26 May 1948, Nehru to Bhargava, File No. 9, JN (SG) Papers.

108 29 May 1948, Nehru to Gopinath Bardoloi, File No. 9, JN (SG) Papers.

109 29 May 1948, Nehru to R. K. Shanmukham Chetty, File No. 9, JN (SG) Papers.

110 30 May 1948, Nehru to Patel, File No. 9, JN (SG) Papers.

111 5 June 1948, Nehru to provincial premiers, File No. 10, JN (SG) Papers.

112 6 June 1948, Nehru to Patel, File No. 10, JN (SG) Papers.

113 21 June 1948, Nehru to Mountbatten, File No. 10, JN (SG) Papers.

1

June 1948–March 1949

PROVINCES AND STATES

The dominant political pattern in India in the years between the attainment of independence and the articulation of the republic was one of provincialism, as Akbar Hydari, the governor of Assam, averred in July 1948.[1] Here, too, the corresponding historiographical paradigm has understandably been that of Partition, with a wealth of material generated on the partitioned provinces of British India.[2] Afterwards, from the early 1950s, the linguistic reorganisation of states provided the scholarly context.[3] Located in-between these frames, this chapter maps three arenas: first, surveying the provinces and the intentions at play there; second, exploring the party, the cabinet and their clashes; and, third, considering the ideological currents from the left and the right that intersected violently and were, in turn, confronted thus by the centre.[4]

Functioning under the federal Government of India Act 1935, an Uttar Pradesh (UP) minister was in England within a year of independence to procure capital equipment and stores, while the East Punjab government was preparing to send a purchasing mission to America, Czechoslovakia and Switzerland. Such international initiatives meant internal competition, which was, in the words of Finance Minister Shanmukham Chetty, bound to raise prices and stretch delivery. The minister for industries and supply, Dr Mookerjee, too warned against the 'tendency of provincial governments to operate on their own'.[5] When Premier Gopichand Bhargava showed an unseemly insistence on amalgamating East Punjab and its contiguous hill states, the prime minister restrained him by indicating that the culturally and linguistically 'distinct' people of the latter were apprehensive about 'exploitation' from the former. Unwilling to enforce any merger yet, Nehru consoled Bhargava that the presence of three administrative units in the Indian Punjab need not preclude their cooperation.[6]

Such cooperation was also necessary between East Punjab and the princely states next to its southernmost district. The Meos of Alwar and Bharatpur were forced to take shelter in Gurgaon from there, and now the East Punjab government was seeking to dispossess them again, under the inter-Punjab evacuee property mechanism, regardless of their status as 'Indian citizens who had temporarily vacated without going to Pakistan'.[7] With Gandhi's assurances to the Meos ringing in his ears and with the Gandhians Vinoba Bhave, Pandit Sunder Lal and Mridula Sarabhai on the ground, Nehru was worried. This worry grew into embarrassment when he was informed about the case of Chaudhury Yasin Khan, the Meo leader of Gurgaon, who had been interned by the Delhi Police. Khan had been arrested by those who had 'no business to' do so, while those who could had 'not got a good case', and so, when Bhargava's ministry insisted on the withdrawal of the military from Gurgaon in early June 1948, leading Vinoba Bhave to complain, troops were sent back.[8]

An in-between community, their illegally caught leader and invidious institutional decisions apart,[9] the unusual plight of Partition was borne by people like the 3,000 Muslim henna cultivators of Faridabad. Syed Bashir Ali, senior lecturer in chemistry at Aligarh, brought up their bizarre circumstances when, under pressure of events in September–October 1947, they had left for Delhi and elsewhere in India and Pakistan. A third of them were now anxious to return to their lands, except for those that had been allotted to Hindu or Sikh refugees from West Punjab, rendering them evacuees. Was it now possible to recognise their 'ownership', thereby enabling the returnees to subsist by entitling them to rent it, and could their 'specialised' *mehndi* cultivation with its foreign market be a calling card for a people caught in circumstances not of their making?[10]

How could it, when in further-away Bihar, vague sympathy shown by certain Muslims towards the nizam of Hyderabad was considered intolerable by the Dr Sri Krishna Sinha ministry? Quite taken up with chasing those favouring enemies of India, that ministry was also keen to offer lavish compensation to landlords in its Zamindari Liquidation Act. The finance department in New Delhi was especially concerned with the effect on 'money market' of any such step.[11] Next door Orissa was similarly proposing to 'guarantee' a *zamindar*'s income calculated after taking costs of collection and adding sums for estate improvement. A nonplussed Nehru suggested instead a 'cooperative' and proposed progressive taxation, but he could not know the ground situation and left it to the premiers to 'deal with it'.[12]

Paying too much attention to Muslims and too much compensation to landlords was a perfect symbol of provincial politics across north India in mid-1948. To give one example, the Bihar government objected to the Ministry of External Affairs taking Mahboob Ahmad into the newly formed Indian Foreign Service. Ahmad, a member of the Indian National Army (INA) (1943–46), had served as secretary to Bose and was tried afterwards at the Red Court in the famous trials.[13] A bigger variation on this theme was blurted out by collector Ambala to the departing Edwina Mountbatten at the Kurukshetra refugee camp when he boasted that 'thousands of Muslims were still being sent away to Pakistan against their wishes in accordance with some inter-dominion agreement'.[14] Displacement of persons seemed to happen that summer of 1948 everywhere. Alongside Bhakra and Hirakud, the Massanjore dam in Dumka, near the Bihar–Bengal border, was awaiting approval from these governments because of two complicating factors. First, the Santhals who would be dispossessed had to be adequately provided for, and second, schemes like these had to be kept away from any readjustment of provincial boundaries. And then, Hydari related the situation in Assam.[15]

Its capital Gauhati had been the scene of a quarrel between Assamese students and Bengali railway staff over ticketless travel, which deteriorated into a wider row in which Bengali shops were attacked, one Bengali was killed and one injured, while three Assamese, of whom one was Muslim, were also injured. Of the shops damaged, three belonged to Bengali Muslims, which was enough for the allegation of Bengali Muslims continuing to enter Assam, as well as the neighbouring Cooch Behar princely state. With the latter's relations with New Delhi being conducted then through the governor, Hydari visited it and found that the maharaja's interim council comprised the chief minister (Himmat Singh, a UP Hindu), two Hindu ministers and one Muslim minister, the latter being an old man of a family settled in Cooch Behar for generations and widely respected for his expertise in regional history and archaeology. The state administration was then preparing rolls based on adult suffrage for elections to be held in September–October 1948, and Himmat Singh informed Hydari that contrary to the propaganda by the West Bengal Provincial Congress and the Calcutta press, the percentage of Muslims in Cooch Behar remained at 38 per cent, like the 1941 census. Out of these, amounting to a population of 6–7 lakhs, there were 30,000 Bengalis, the rest being Rajabansis and Cooch Beharis.[16]

Back in Assam, Hydari was doing another balancing act for the Bengali officers serving there amidst rising anti-Bengali feeling. Two out of five senior secretaries were Bengalis (supply and development and food), one of whom also held the post of cabinet secretary. The deputy police chief was a Bengali, the inspector-general was an Englishman, while a UP man administered the railway. Perhaps the feeling of nervousness and alarm among Bengalis in lower bureaucracy was simply from the region's 1947 rupture, while a more structural reason seemed to be the systematic discrimination against Sylheti (Bengali) personnel opting for service in Assam. Led by the 'ironman' of Assam, Finance Minister Bishnuram Medhi, a section of the government seemed to avenge the Sylheti officials for alleged past unfriendliness between the Surma and Assam valleys.[17]

The fire of fear in Assam, in the opinion of the Bardoloi ministry, on the other hand, was being stoked from Calcutta, thus forcing the palliative of preventive action. As for the unpopularity of the Bengali in Assam, the reason was partly historical and partly contemporary.[18] During British rule, the sub-overlords of Assam were the former's Bengali officials, while the area's commerce was in Marwari hands. With the Congress coming into the legislature in 1938, the Assamese got political office and went about trying to break down this duopoly. The events of 1947 furthered this festering mood against Calcutta's arrogance as well as its acquisitive nature regarding the neighbouring territory. P. C. Ghosh had recently toured Assam, making demanding speeches in this regard, and with Drs Mookerjee and Roy to follow, Hydari worried that West Bengal's 'grievance at partition' would see it 'try to make up for it....'[19] Everyone was grappling with the sudden change that 1947 had brought, and, in an expectedly sensitive, but also unexpectedly pragmatic, letter to the *nawab* of Bhopal, Nehru wrote as follows:

> There can be no going back to India as it was.... Nevertheless ... there is no settling down to it ... I am entirely hostile to any communalism but is it surprising that those Muslims, who till yesterday were champions of Pakistan, should be viewed with suspicion? Certainly, I wish to help them to become parts of the new India. There are many Hindus who have no such desire....[20]

That shifting time made for strange bedfellows. There were reports of Rajput rallies against *zamindari* and *jagirdari* being changed, even with compensation, but these rallies also saw slogans raised in praise of Qasim Rizvi, the Razakars' leader in Hyderabad. After all, Muslims or Hindus, the elite of old, preferred 'to satisfy a private grudge'.[21] With the first anniversary of independence coming up, provinces across India were struggling with economic difficulties, where the removal of controls from essential items in late 1947 was biting back on the dissatisfying reality that various sections of society did not shoulder their burdens equally.[22] Paucity was not the only

problem; paradoxes were galore. While housing was a 'terrible headache' in all
the provinces, some provinces were housing an increasing number of detenues
without charges or trial but on the judgements of police officers.[23] As the
Madras ministry started to devote its police towards enforcing prohibition, a
sober prime minister urged them to keep 'hands as free as possible', given the
looming Hyderabad situation.[24]

In August 1948, the Assam ministry, labouring under the misunderstanding
that Bhutan would accede to India because the West Bengal government
had refused to transfer Darjeeling to it, declined to give concessions on the
Dewangiri tract, upon which Thimphu looked sentimentally. It was a largely
forested area of about 80 square miles of no value to Assam, but this refusal put
New Delhi in a fix. It looked after Bhutan's foreign affairs and defence, and in
the context of the Chinese presence in Tibet, it was necessary to have a friendly
Bhutan like before, albeit with a treaty of increased subsidies and concessions,
which is where Dewangiri came from.[25] A disappointed Assam ministry then
turned south to East Bengal and sought an ordinance to prevent the influx
of people, both Hindus and Muslims. Now, the Ministry of Home Affairs
demurred on this extraordinary promulgation and reminded the provincial
government of New Delhi's rights to regulate the movement of people.[26] And
when nearby Bihar wished to deal directly with the Nepal government for
the construction of irrigation works, New Delhi put a restraining hand on
Patna's Gandak scheme as it was negotiating the larger Kosi scheme. This
'confusion' of parallel lines was a feature of those times, when New Delhi was
not powerful enough to reduce the association of its provincial counterparts to
only 'when necessary'.[27]

Whether it was the Central Provinces and Berar, from where Pandit
Shukla was seeking the formation of 'provincial units' in the army replacing
the then-existing zonal basis of recruitment, or Madras, where the O. P.
Ramaswamy Reddiar ministry was giving forcing orders in the name of law,
there was a strong 'provincial spirit' prevailing.[28] In such a scenario, gubernatorial
appointments were fraught and tactful personas were needed. Here, to bring
the princes, and their states, closer to provinces, it was desirable to appoint
them as governors. An early example was the appointment of the maharaja
of Bhavnagar to Madras to succeed General Archibald Nye.[29] It was easier to
make provinces accept such appointments at the apex; it was more difficult
to prevail upon them to absorb refugees on the ground. Nehru pleaded with
Govind Ballabh Pant for UP to accept 5,000 families, nearly 25,000 persons,
from the Frontier Province, whom the East Punjab government wanted out of
their Kurukshetra camp. These Hindus and Sikhs from Peshawar and beyond
were special in the sense of their association with the 'Frontier Gandhi' Khan
Abdul Ghaffar Khan.[30]

While one powerful premier was being requested to take in Hindu and Sikh refugees, another was being urged to not push out Muslims and make them refugees. Two years before the Nehru–Liaquat Pact, Dr B. C. Roy wanted to evict from West Bengal an equal number of those entering from the east. Roy's suggestion was problematic, for above all it posed questions like did the fact that a person was Hindu make one an Indian national and did the fact that another was Muslim make one a non-Indian?[31] By September 1948, however, the biggest cloud on the Indian horizon was Hyderabad. The passing of its patrimony via a standstill agreement in 1947–48 and what that meant for its culture and capital have been extensively catalogued.[32] The then-accompanying, larger possibility was of communal trouble started by non-Muslims across the country in retaliation to the Razakars there, and what was needed was 'to educate' public opinion that India was 'not out to punish the Muslims in Hyderabad....'[33] This needed a patriotic press to perform its duty, and Nehru himself wrote the first draft of the history of India's military invasion of Hyderabad a week after the act. It is a document that has served its purpose as a master narrative of what happened in the Hyderabad state over those three days in mid-September 1948.[34] It enshrined India's 'police action' against a 'recalcitrant state', which was neither 'foreign' nor 'independent', so it could not be considered 'conquered'.[35]

Following this, while the prime minister wished to be characteristically generous, also because it was in the government's self-interest, his counterparts favoured narrow-minded revenge. Given the military situation, the nizam could be easily deposed, but he was accepting of New Delhi's directives and comparing him to the Japanese emperor after 1945, Nehru wanted him to hand over power to a council of Hyderabadis subject to a military veto. Any other approach amounted to reducing Hyderabad to a 'colony', which could not do internationally. Qasim Razvi, the leader of the Razakars, was to be arrested and tried. Major-General J. N. Chaudhuri's regime was to continue with, as far as possible, 'the internal functionaries of the state', except where these were considered 'harmful', and this was not so much a soft line to Patel's so-called hard-line; rather, together they made the national line,[36] on one side of which fell moderate nobles like Zain Yar Jung and Ali Yavar Jung, while on the other were left former lower-level administrators who had 'felt the same way but could do nothing about it'.[37]

Side by side, provincial skirmishes continued. West Bengal and Bihar ministries were engaged in their own opportune agitations. B. C. Roy was petitioning Patel to demand certain areas from Bihar, while Sri Krishna Sinha was complaining to Nehru about it[38] and refusing primary education of Bengali children in Purulia and surrounding areas in their mother tongue.[39] This Bihari–Bengali imbroglio paled in front of intra-Bengali infractions as, with 'over 1000 persons coming in daily' from East Bengal, Calcutta was getting tense, and the officials of border districts seemed to be 'instructed to pressure Muslims to go over to East Bengal'.[40]

As he was leaving for his maiden appearance at the United Nations and the Commonwealth, the prime minister was hamstrung by his provincial counterparts. He listed to one of them, Dr Gopichand Bhargava, all the worrying matters connected with Bhargava's ministry. To begin with, there was the Akali duo of Master Tara Singh and Giani Kartar Singh, who were being tolerated out of a desire to not make martyrs of them. But they were at the tip of the iceberg in East Punjab and Sikh princely states, where favouritism, corruption and wealth concentration in the land allotment policy were causing more destitution than alleviating it. Instead of rehabilitating as many refugees as it could, the ministry was giving as much as 400–500 acres to individuals from certain communities.[41] In Kapurthala state, land available for 4,000 families had been reserved for one, and those kept out were from the Scheduled Castes kept in Jalandhar camps. In Jind state, many people from Dera Ghazi Khan and Muzaffargarh were in camps for nearly a year, and the great bulk of them were from among the lowest castes. In any allotment of houses, shops or lands of the Muslim evacuees, the non-Punjabis from Pakistan got less, which contrasted with the situation of the Punjabis in Delhi.[42]

It was in Europe and England that Nehru's conviction in India's position regarding Hyderabad was challenged. Upon his return, he had talks with Qazi Abdul Ghaffar and Padmaja Naidu, who had been visiting Hyderabad since September 1948, which contained thousands of refugees from all over the state. The prime minister was forced to amend his impression about the army's functioning and accept 'the massacre of possibly some thousands of Muslims by Hindus, as well as a great deal of looting'.[43] His wish to confirm this led to the appointment of the (in)famous Sunder Lal Mission and the production of its (classified) report later in 1948.[44] Before Nehru left for England, the government held that any administrative changes in Hyderabad would be limited; by the time he returned, extensive changes had taken place 'to Hinduise the entire administration'.[45] He reminded Patel's States Ministry that much trouble in 1947 was triggered by a similar removal of Hindu officers from Pakistan and their Muslim counterparts from India, and he tried to reassert his proclaimed word against their policy. In the garb of security, changes were made, taking in their wake persons like the Congress' Dr Zakir Hussain's brother and Dr M. A. Ansari's nephew. Their and others' places were filled by officers from neighbouring provinces who were rapidly promoted and empowered. Returning to the motif of the Muslim culture in Hyderabad, with its milestones like the Osmania University, the publication department and the translation bureau, Nehru wished to carry on with these educational hubs, without issuing a first-order writ on the material conditions around them. He was taking up these causes while not quite taking to task the states and defence ministries for the then-ongoing massacres across Hyderabad state.[46]

However, insofar as the majority–minority question was concerned, it was hardly just Hyderabad that was benighted, for much nearer was the Sikh position in East Punjab. Baldev Singh, the defence minister, put together a note that questioned joint electorates and emphasised the question of weightage. This had been denied to the Muslims in the then-ongoing constituent assembly debates and thus could hardly be applied to the Sikhs. Next, Singh pitched the proposal of a Sikh *suba* by carving out the southern non-Sikh parts with or without Gurgaon (to be transferred to Delhi). East Punjab was now a frontier province, and so security considerations came into the picture, but all this was distressing to New Delhi above all because of its similarity with the pre-1947 Muslim League. In turn, Nehru brought up the speeches of Master Tara Singh, which dominated the Hindu press in Delhi and UP.[47] The situation across East Punjab in Hoshiarpur, Gurdaspur, Ferozepur and Ludhiana districts was seeing a deterioration in Hindu–Sikh relations. A group of Hindu refugees fled from a camp in Ferozepur to Kurukshetra, claiming that terror activities were taking place at the former. Nor was the Kurukshetra camp a heaven, for its bad conditions had seen rising mortality among refugees. Medical arrangements were lacking, and sufficient water was not available. Finally, it was feared that if, in response to Tara Singh's demands, a Sikh province was made, then it 'would be a barrier' between India and Kashmir.[48]

Governor-General Rajagopalachari too was concerned about East Punjab vis-à-vis the lassitude in the rehabilitation of Muslims, and Nehru wrote to the civil servant-governor Trivedi to transfer two officials from Ambala – Ashvani Kumar, police superintendent, and Sunder Singh, magistrate Jagadhari – as two mosques were occupied by non-Muslims in Buria, as the provincial government's reluctance saw Rajagopalachari's desire to send United Council of Relief and Welfare workers there. The East Punjab government refused 'any outsider …',[49] even as it was not always clear who was responsible for camps for non-Punjabis like the 5,000 Bahawalpuris in Rajpura: the East Punjab government, or the Patiala state ministry, or the centre.[50] In November 1948, a Sikh charter was produced by Giani Kartar Singh, which, in New Delhi's eyes, appeared as a replay of the national-communal blamegame for-and-against group weightage, separate electorate, seat reservation and a religiously and linguistically autonomous sphere. Then, there were the Sikh backward classes, which wanted 'to be with the Scheduled Castes [risking] a reduction in the Sikh population [for] voting'.[51]

Turning away from all this, Nehru visited Hyderabad two months and 10 days after his government's operation polo. By now, there was a peasant revolt in the Telangana countryside,[52] while its towns were becoming a test case for the treatment of Muslims after Hyderabad's surrender. There was a third concern too as very many people depended on state service and denied that, where else were they to go except to the communists? The impression in government circles was that the Arya Samaj based in the city and the RSS and Hindu Mahasabha functioning out of the Central Provinces were behind the continuing violence against Muslims, now in those areas that had not suffered under the Razakars. There was also a concern that Major-General Chaudhuri's caretaker military government should be replaced by or renamed as a civilian government.[53] This would see the appointment of civil servant M. K. Vellodi as the official chief minister in December 1949.

All governments needed capital though, whether it was the partitioned Punjab, needing a brand new scheme, or the youngest Orissa, which had been planning Bhubaneswar.[54] The trouble here was that any go-ahead required capital amidst the economic crisis of 1948–49.[55] All governments also needed clarity on their territorial boundaries, if not cohesion in their cultural composition, and the Congress' linguistic provinces committee of Patel, Sitaramayya and Nehru came down against linguistic provinces in spring 1949.[56] Considering strong public sentiment, they agreed that the case of Andhra should be taken up before others, while setting their stall firmly against any redrawing in north India.[57] Dr B. C. Roy was disappointed when told that with Bihar and Assam accepting Bengali refugees 'with difficulty',[58] if it got around that this acceptance was to be accompanied by 'certain districts of Bihar being merged in West Bengal', it could only 'create a howl....'[59]

PARTY AND CABINET

For a party that had spearheaded a movement, the Congress inside the government had a difficult relationship with its pronouncements, and policies as an 'extreme dilatoriness' occupied the space in-between.[60] This was neither entirely new nor unexpected, given its earlier experiences of office,[61] and this section explores party crises and cabinet contradictions. By June 1948, in Nehru's own province of UP, Congress affairs comprised a contest of the Tandon and Kidwai groups, presaging the famous 'factional politics' of the 1950s–60s.[62] This adversely affected elections to councils and cabinets[63] and ministerial meetings of the Congress Working Committee (CWC).[64] When the UP government's labour department issued a circular that only representatives of the Indian National Trade Union Congress, the party's trade union, should be taken into the factory workers' committee, veteran trade unionist G. L. Nanda from Gujarat felt that this 'went too far'.[65] The other side of this coin was the party's dragging of feet on land reforms, and Sri Prakasa, a quintessential UP-man who was then India's envoy in Pakistan, cautioned the revenue minister of the state with these biting words: 'if we examine our organisation ... it was the sons of zamindars ... that made it possible for the lawyer leaders at the top to get, what is now called, *Swaraj....*[66]

Nehru and Patel, the lawyer leaders at the top, had risen above this group-ism in the formation of the central cabinet in August 1947, with the inclusion of prominent anti-Congressmen, among whom Shanmukham Chetty got embroiled in a fiasco in March 1948 concerning the income tax investigation commission, when his finance ministry sought to withdraw some cases of people perceived to be close to Chetty.[67] Understandably, it was not considered 'proper',[68] and fearing further misinterpretation, the prime minister intervened 'to leave the matter to the commission' with the proviso that the latter could 'say that they do not wish to proceed with certain references because of lack of evidence'.[69] S. P. Mookerjee, on the other hand, was a critic in the socio-cultural arena, as when he objected to the Tagore-creation from the 1910s, *Jana Gana Mana*, in favour of the Bankim-poem from the 1880s, *Bande Mataram*.[70] Nehru played down the still-provisional preference for the former, against which only two provincial governments had objected, one being West Bengal, and his tonal-orchestral and past longing-future triumph arguments, seen earlier, were expanded upon when explaining the choice to Dr B. C. Roy 'in the present context' by bringing in linguistic difficulty.[71]

Anyway, there was no singing away the deteriorating economic situation in the country. The government's industrial policy had sought an ineffective 'truce' between labour, employers and the state, while its controls policy was ineffectually removed.[72] The prices of cloth and food were rising, as was their smuggling, alongside corruption. A state plant in Calcutta for the manufacture of penicillin and anti-malarial drugs by the Haffkine Institute at a cost of INR 2 crore were delayed by Mookerjee's ministry.[73] One of the key accompaniments of the industrial policy, about wages, to be overseen by a committee chaired by the banker A. D. Shroff, was being whittled down by some members of the committee who 'challenged the whole idea of profit sharing'.[74] Herein lay the first impulses of the eventual planning commission, arraigned between the party and the cabinet.[75] Among its prototypes were a central statistical organisation under Dr P. C. Mahalanobis, with a standing committee of departmental economists under Dr Gyan Chand,[76] and a ministry for social and economic affairs with its council of experts. The latter was to accumulate and advise, while the former was to consider and coordinate, but neither had any executive or administrative functions.[77] For whether it was tackling price rise or effecting land reforms, exercising economy or undertaking construction, generating employment or interning the unionised unemployed as well as vis-à-vis the permit system with Pakistan, rehabilitating refugees or even restraining espionage,[78] the central cabinet was constitutionally dependent on the provinces.

Across the provincial party, the national government and the sub-continental relations was the category of 'Congress Muslims'.[79] To Nehru, this description applied to 'a few hundred well-known persons who have been in the Congress and suffered for the cause of India's freedom'.[80] Bringing up the cases of persons like Abdul Ghani and Habibur Rehman, both from Ludhiana, Nehru asked his minister for refugee relief and rehabilitation to consider how to help them. It was a personal initiative by the prime minister, which relied on his friends like Azad and Rafi Ahmad Kidwai to know those in need, to be helped from the PM fund. Instead, what got highlighted were those cases 'who went to Pakistan for a brief visit to some relation, coming back to India with a temporary permit because they could not get any other', in the process jeopardising their 'home or family in India'.[81]

In August 1948, Shanmukham Chetty finally got caught between the party and the government. As he was preparing to answer in the constituent assembly that doubled up as central legislature, resolutions moved by Congressmen like Damodar Swarup Seth and Upendranath Barman to deal with the deteriorating economic condition in the country, Chetty read from Nehru that the general secretary of the Congress 'had received a requisition from [many] members for an emergent meeting to consider … the withdrawal of some names from … the IT enquiry commission'.[82] Adding that many agitated members had come to him too, Nehru requested Chetty to come to the meeting and answer questions, specifically about the withdrawal of four names.[83] Chetty obliged and, taking this as a lack of confidence in him, resigned on 15 August, to spare the prime minister 'any embarrassment',[84] simultaneously explaining himself at length in his resignation letter.

Reminding the prime minister that several cases had to be sent to the Income Tax (IT) investigation commission before 31 December 1947, he recalled that it was intended for the central board of revenue to examine them in detail afterwards and then withdraw those without any prima facie case. It was this examination that had resulted in the withdrawal of these four cases, with the 'full concurrence' of the cabinet. Chetty was surprised, therefore, that the issue still became a matter for the party's consideration as, in consultation with the chairman of the revenue board, he had issued oral instructions on 19 February 1948, with the official order following on 12 March. To Nehru, it was an 'error of judgement' for Chetty to simultaneously pilot a bill 'with the provision that no withdrawal should take place without the consent of the commission', which had led 'many members to think that ignoring the assembly ... was a discourtesy'.[85] To the provincial premiers, he would highlight the 'awkward' timing of this episode, as Chetty oversaw two important legislative measures, namely the nationalisation of the RBI and the banking bill. His departure meant that a non-party voice had left denting Nehru's wish to deal with the economic situation on a non-party basis. Some months later, when, from Ankara, Ambassador Chaman Lall regretted that Chetty had been 'unnecessarily sensitive',[86] the latter alleged that his resignation was 'brought about by the scheming of a small clique' but was philosophical in that this was not unusual in 'party-wire pulling....'[87]

More straightforward, in theory at least, was law and order, where civil liberty, especially habeas corpus applications and the freedom of association in trade unions, was at the centre of a tussle between the legislature and the judiciary, as the former moved steadily to deprive the latter of some of its protective powers.[88] Given how recently India had become free, it was peculiar to potentially unfree so many, but the prime minister was receiving reports that the activities of the banned RSS were on the rise, in the guise of *jana adhikar*. To provide a balance, reports also mentioned of a small-scale revival of pro-Muslim League feelings, and to triangulate the scenario, there were 'some leaders of the Sikhs ... delivering intemperate speeches....'[89] But there was little political opposition on the ground, for the recently parted Socialist Party was still fraternal while the CPI had gone underground, under the Ranadive Line.[90] So, when the news came in August 1948 that the Hindu Mahasabha, still on trial for Gandhi's assassination, had decided to return to the political field, the industries minister, Mookerjee, was asked to explain his 'connection' with it.[91]

But the bona fides of many members of the Congress party on this communal-national question was hardly a yardstick. When the Bihar premier Sinha alleged about 'many Muslims from Pakistan' employed in industries and services in his province, it was a case of exaggerating and misreading trivial or isolated incidents produced by a police apparatus that had been reporting on the Congress a year ago. If these Muslims had returned to India, then they could not be assumed as non-national or 'potentially disloyal'; rather the real problem was that 'once the majority gets out of hand it will be very difficult to deal with'.[92] For that matter, the oppressed within this majority – that is, the Scheduled Castes – were not faring better either. One year from post-Partition violence, the 'Harijan' section of the relief and rehabilitation ministry was being shut down by Minister Mohan Lal Saksena.[93]

Nor was a third fault-line, language, showing the party's leadership in a flattering light. While a Hindi translation of the draft constitution was being printed by the Rajendra Prasad-chaired assembly, its Hindustani counterpart was not being so despite a committee led by the Gandhian Pandit Sunder Lal working on it for months; the less said, the better about an Urdu copy. Nehru, who wished for copies of all three, in both Nagari and Nastaliq scripts, to be printed at government account, was arguing for this 'extra expenditure' as a 'hallmark of independent existence'.[94] This was to little avail, and so the prime minister cast around for other symbolic ways to compensate and found Gandhi's first birthday, after his death, suitable. There was support from Governor-General Rajagopalachari, who too wished to celebrate it by getting the various occupied 'mosques in Delhi [to] be given back to the Muslims',[95] especially the Mehrauli shrine of Qutub Shah.[96]

In the immediate aftermath of Hyderabad's incorporation into India, this was as much about fulfilling a pledge from Gandhi as it was about producing a desirous effect in the freshly deteriorating atmosphere in central India. Initially, the talk there was about the Razakars, first as perpetrators and then as prisoners, then it moved to disavowing the figures of casualties in Hyderabad alongside an acknowledgement that 'a number of Muslims were arrested ... on suspicion'.[97] Finally, in the immediate wake of the swift denouement of the *nizamat*, a reimposition of controls regarding essential items was slipped through, and an enforcement directorate was recruited from provincial machinery as well as party organisation, whose president that year was Dr Pattabhi Sitaramayya, a Telugu Congressman. Simultaneously, from Madras, O. P. Ramaswamy Reddiar sought 'to retire public servants ... Muslims having sympathies with Hyderabad',[98] while in New Delhi, M. L. Saksena took over the 'treatment of Muslims in India', a charge that was previously with N. Gopalaswami Ayyangar, who was moving to railways and transport, as John Matthai returned to finance.[99]

Their combined list of challenges in the north in that month of September 1948 read like this: '(1) Jodhpur railway dispute, (2) Kurukshetra refugee camp, (3) Delhi housing for refugees'.[100] None of these could detract attention from Hyderabad, about which notes-after-notes were arriving on the violent absorption of that state, as thousands of Muslim families lost 'everything' across districts, with 70 per cent of the public servants losing their jobs.[101] It was reasonably feared that if such conditions continued, they would be wiped out.[102] By late November, a chief administrator and an inspector-general of police had been appointed alongside all the district collectors and police superintendents, and hundreds of *tehsildars*, inspectors and constables, the chief surgeon, the engineer-in-chief, directors-medical and jail departments, legal advisors and others, nearly none were knowledgeable in either the languages or the ways of the locals. Then there were the Muslim refugees from Indian provinces who had been staying in different camps across Hyderabad state but now were ordered to go back. Nehru could not entirely discount these notes when meeting people like Akbar Ali Khan and M. Y. Saleem, whom he knew since the 1920s. As pictures of the Razakar past blurred into a present of the Indian army's behaviour, they varied from no complaint in Aurangabad to conniving with looters and rioters in Jalna and Bidar. If there was 'even a fraction of truth' in these reports, then the situation was 'much worse' than he believed, with the unmissable irony that 'if the test of a government servant is how he behaved in the past against a popular movement, then many officers, who opposed the Congress movement, would have no place'.[103]

Nehru's trouble was that he was not just reining in the state apparatus but also his party's pride. During his visit to Hyderabad in the second half of December 1948, the State Congress complained to him about being neglected by Chaudhuri and V. P. Menon, but he was not willing to function only as a Congressman.[104] Writing to Krishna Menon, India's envoy in London, Nehru elaborated on the 'ticklish' Hyderabad situation as follows: 'more damage was caused there to the Muslims by the Hindus, after our troops went in … the Hindus, who had suffered a lot under the Razakars'. While his estimate of casualties remained those of Chaudhuri's – that is, '2500–3000 persons', a tenth of what the soon-to-come Pandit Sunder Lal Report put it at – he gave a clean chit to General Chaudhuri and a conditional chit to the army. But, for Krishna Menon's presentation in England, he persisted that there was 'no alternative' to the caretaker government, which by the way was 'wrongly called a military government', as General Chaudhuri was the 'only soldier in it'.[105] By the last days of 1948, the spoils of Hyderabad were being picked and parcelled by Chaudhuri's government and the Ministry of States, as companies or businesses with Muslim directors were being taken over.[106]

Simultaneously, in December 1948, the last premier of united Bengal, Muslim League's H. S. Suhrawardy came to New Delhi to complain about certain IT assessments of his by the finance ministry, for the fiscal years 1945–47, to the tune of INR 50 lakhs, and Matthai was urged to see to Suhrawardy's peculiar case, for at that time he was 'an alien in Pakistan and hardly a citizen in India'.[107] How many such high-profile cases could be intervened in? From Badrul Islam, a Delhi barrister now in Karachi, whose trusteeship of a property was mistaken as proprietorship, leading to the said property being raided,[108] to M. A. Ispahani, another Calcutta Leaguer businessman now in Chittagong, being taxed 'at an exorbitant rate', such high-handed treatment was bad, because it also led to 'action in Pakistan'.[109] The Ahmadis at Qadian (Gurdaspur), Punjab, were similarly pitchforked as being unwelcome on both sides.[110] They were asked to vacate the residential accommodation at the centre of their religious existence for settling non-Muslim refugees therein. Zafrulla Khan, Pakistan's Ahmadi foreign minister, sought a 'sympathetic consideration',[111] for no more than hundred houses that had around 300 Ahmadis living in them without their families that were expected to be back.[112]

By now, as the former movement men settled into their ministries across India, their corruption had started to grow too. One of the cases, related to Kishen Chand, a legislator from Mathura and the chairman of Brindavan municipality, is an illustrative miniature. Chand had been publicly charged with corruption and black-marketing and while collector, Mathura was investigating these, he was appointed chairman of a committee of the UP government, leading to the enquiry being dropped. Meanwhile, a case of perjury had hit the public domain, in which a munsiff's court called upon Chand to show cause. Close on the heels of this notice came Chand's nomination as a member of the Agra university senate and from Mathura to New Delhi, people were puzzled as to why Premier Pant was showering such favours on Chand. Then, there were the two legislators from Bulandshahr, who were being prosecuted by a private complainant for drawing travelling allowances on false certificates in Lucknow and Bulandshahr courts, with the UP government silent. The Bulandshahr collector had received another complaint about them, that of 'collecting grains' for the Prantiya Raksha Dal but 'not crediting the sale proceeds to that account', and an enquiry done at the *naib-tehsildar* level had found this complaint to be correct, whereupon the MLAs threatened the *naib-tehsildar*, who 'withdrew his report'.[113]

If all this was portentous, then the present was one of decay too. The Ministry of Relief and Rehabilitation had malfunctioned enough for a hunger strike to begin at Kingsway camp and for calls to be made for a separate organisation like the United Council for Relief and Welfare. With Gandhi gone and JP and Vinoba Bhave, among the Gandhians left, withdrawing their cooperation, the prime minister worried about the purely 'official approach' in providing 'social welfare'.[114] Nothing, however, was more welfare oriented than the wide-ranging Hindu Code Bill,[115] on which the Congress party was dragging its feet. While Ambedkar wished to take on the party, Nehru did not have that luxury. His difficulties inside the constituent assembly started with the partisan speaker G. V. Mavalankar himself,[116] who allowed interminable discussions, which delayed and diluted them. One way to sidestep this trap was to have informal talks with select personnel on specific points, but it felt stealth-like to Ambedkar, who consequently also doubted Nehru's sincerity. Warning his law minister, the third of his prominent non-Congress cabinet colleagues, that 'any action taken now, which irritates a large section and makes them more obstructive ... will not pay in the long run',[117] Nehru set himself up for the long-run unlike the slash-and-burn approach of Ambedkar.[118]

LEFT AND RIGHT

Some strand of socialism had been prominent in the Congress party's programme since the 1931 Karachi session, and yet its substance, in practical terms, remained at the surface, when it came to provincial governments.[119] In the late 1940s, these were revelling in putting people behind bars on the pretext of, or in the context of, being socialists-communists, and the following section brings forth this duet of political response with popular mobilisations, which had interludes like the arrest of the son of Dr Syed Mahmud, partyman since the early 1920s and minister in Bihar since 1937, on vague charges of being a communist. With the CPI not declared illegal, except in West Bengal, nobody ought to be arrested for association with it, and the nationalists were 'now doing exactly what [they had] bitterly opposed in the past'.[120] As Nehru explained to the sympathetic British parliamentarian Reginald Sorensen, law and order remained largely the preserve of the provincial governments, and there was a 'natural tendency' for them in those fraught years 'to function autonomously'.[121] In such a scenario, individual liberty had little value, but there was also the wider political context across Southeast Asia,[122] and Sorenson was asked if he would like to see an upheaval in India like that in Burma?

In a sense, the prime minister was defensive to both his external friends and internal colleagues. To the Bengal premier, a hardliner against labour demands, Nehru countered with the unholy trinity of magnates, merchants and middlemen trying to pressurise the government,[123] in addition to the 'growing tension between the two Bengals'.[124] Away from the partitioned provinces, in Malabar and areas across Madras, there were parallel movements on a smaller scale by communist groups and allies.[125] The result was 'a continuous state of tension in the public mind and the provincial governments',[126] which saw former trade unionists like G. L. Nanda drafting strong ordinances against anti-social activities in Bombay.[127] An economic context to this social churn is provided by the two grim reports prepared in quick succession by the central government's economists in August 1948 about

> ... acute inflation ... pressure of effective demand on an inelastic supply ... capital markets stagnant ... speculative holding of commodities ... inadequate increase in production due to technical bottlenecks, transport difficulties, communal and political disturbances and conflicting policy ... decontrol converted a suppressed inflation into an open one ... remedial measures: (1) monetary and financial: (a) reduction of deficit expenditure, (b) taxation, (c) borrowing, (d) savings, (2) industrial and trade policy: (a) voluntary co-operation of labour ... wages and allowances should be adjusted, (b) capital equipment from Czechoslovakia, Sweden, Switzerland, Canada, Australia, (c) consumer goods should be imported,

(d) foreign private investment, (3) controls over essential commodities: (a) food grains, cloth, kerosene, charcoal, (b) higher procurement prices, (4) co-ordination of economic policy: (a) a permanent organisation under the Cabinet, (b) an Economic Policy Committee, (c) Standing Committees of Departmental Economists [and] Secretaries, (d) a section for data collection, (e) a non-official advisory council consisting of representatives of industry, trade and labour, (f) National Planning Commission.[128]

Ten days later, a similarly breathless report from a similar set of officials added to the aforementioned categories 'deficit budgets, migratory movements, black market, tax evasion' as 'imminent danger' and urged a war footing for the economy. Among the measures suggested were

> … supplementary budget, retrenchment, postponement of prohibition, IT investigation commission, surcharge (above income of Rs. 5000/-), business profits tax @ 25%, personal super-tax, death-duties, agricultural income-tax, graduated surcharge on payment of land revenue (above Rs. 200/-), treasury bills at higher rates of interest for 6/12 months, non-negotiable 3/5 years savings bonds at higher rate of interest for small savings, saving certificates 3/5 years, postpone repayment of government loans, industrial bonus (on incomes above Rs. 500/-) in the form of saving certificates, (2) monetary measures: Reserve Bank notes issue be limited, banks required to hold Government securities @ 25% of their demand liabilities, (3) controls: capital issues for industrial enterprises as free as possible, bilateral export controls, freeze all personal income, ceiling prices for food-grains, rural rationing, anti-hoarding/profiteering ordinance, production targets-rewards, tax rebate for new companies/small-scale/cottage industries.[129]

Out of these portals of power, JP penned a note of his own and passed it to the Labour Minister Jagjivan Ram. Expectedly, it added to the above by bringing up

> … bureaucratic bungling, unwillingness of the business community to work on smaller margins, unpatriotic Communist Party, [no] minimum wage/adequate housing/disputes settlement machinery, trade union rivalries, refugee expenditure, failure of decontrol … remedies: the character of the government, not radical … link-up of foreign policy with national requirements, state monopoly of foreign trade, [no] import of luxury goods, attention to agriculture, workers' participation in management, educational drive among labour, raising of the bank rate, control of bank credit, compulsory savings, capital levy, bearer bonds, registration of property, purchase tax on luxuries, import of food-grains should be discouraged.…[130]

Amidst this feverish production of policy suggestions to meet the rising passions from left, the prime minister received a curious letter, reminding him of the restive passions of right. It was from the recently released M. S. Golwalkar, leader of the then-banned Sangh, who had been detained between 1 February and 6 August 1948 in the aftermath of Gandhi's assassination. Golwalkar looked back at it as an 'unbalanced action', and he was released for lack of evidence with an accompanying order interning him in Nagpur. Hoping for 'rapprochement', Golwalkar's letter ended with an ode to his trinity of lodestars: 'the Great God ... the Mother Land and the ghastly dream of the past few months'.[131] Golwalkar's release was accompanied by restrictions on his public activities, and on 8 September 1948, Hansraj Gupta (*sanghchalak*, Delhi), Vasant Krishna (organiser, Delhi), Dharmavir (secretary, East Punjab) and Narendrajit Singh (*sanghchalak*, UP) published a pamphlet titled *Nivedan* addressed to Nehru requesting him to lift these restrictions, which were removed on 13 October 1948.[132]

Back then, however, none had quite a monopoly over nation, service and organisation, and in Punjab, the INA hero G. S. Dhillon was fasting for his *suba* alongside General Mohan Singh and their Desh Sewak Sena. It had been difficult to absorb them in government service, as in the case of another of Bose's associate Anand Mohan Sahay, who could not be sent to Japan, then-Siam or Indonesia.[133] With most provincial premiers, in this case, Dr Gopichand Bhargava, unwilling to distinguish between headstrong but straightforward acts of integrity, the 'question of private armies [brooked] no compromise'.[134] On 22 September 194, Master Tara Singh presided over an Akali conference at Bhatinda and delivered a speech on Punjabi language and *suba* demands. With the Hindi (Nagari)–Punjabi (Gurmukhi) controversy rising, the heart of the matter was, 'Could the latter be the/an official language in Punjab?' This question of linguistics, however, got linked to community leadership, where Giani Kartar Singh, inside the East Punjab cabinet, and Master Tara Singh, outside, appeared to New Delhi as having their 'cake and eating it too'.[135]

Even where this was not the case, any anti-government campaign was met firmly. In August 1948, millhands in Bombay were restive, and their outlets like the *Lokayug* copped 'more than fair share' of state surveillance.[136] It was the Marathi counterpart of the communist *People's Age*, and it had published an article under the heading 'Long Live Martyr Hari Narayan' in a February issue. The Kher ministry deemed it actionable under the Indian Press Act of 1931 and slapped a security of INR 3000 on the publisher and the keeper of the press. Before it could be executed, in an April issue, the *Lokayug* published another article entitled 'Campaign of Dismissal in the IAF – to resist Oppression Is a Crime'. Once again, a security of INR 1,000 was demanded and, when it was not deposited, the paper was temporarily seized. Meanwhile, in July, the communist press had reported on police firing on striking scavenger women, and the action on *Lokayug* was naturally linked to this.[137] The Kher ministry shrewdly did not stop the publication of the *People's Age* and the *Janshakti* (Hindi) but only the Marathi organ.

If this was a typical urban sketch, then the rural scene across provinces saw an anticipation of various *zamindari* abolition bills. The lip service that provincial ministries were preparing was expected to be paid for by the centre, which was thus nervous. There was the related concern of land reforms encouraging inflation and the political will was weakening in front of the financial requirements of a uniform effort across the country.[138] From Bihar, where some of the early proposals on this legislation were emerging, they treaded a cautious path between government seeking power to acquire all *zamindari*s or those yielding an income of INR 5,000 and above, with compensation paid in non-negotiable non-transferrable bonds, redeemable in 40 annual instalments. Whether these burdensome bonds were 'valid compensation' under Section 299 of the 1935 Government of India Act was the issue,[139] and both sets of governments were wary of the judiciary.[140] In November 1948, the Bihar *zamindari* abolition bill was delayed for financial reasons on the part of Patna and legal reasons on the part of New Delhi. This meant neglecting a pre-1947 pledge of the party, but with the draft constitution being unclear on this matter, a cabinet committee was created to confer with Patna on the following formula for agricultural land: until such acquisition as for cash/bonds, the 'government will realise rents, pay the zamindar's share minus collection charges. The land will not go back to the zamindar'.[141] This was easier said than done; in neighbouring UP, when the revenue minister Hukum Singh presided over the *zamindari* abolition committee, he took care that parts of partyman Sri Prakasa's estate in Jaunpur were safe. If and when the provisional proposals were to be applied to the rest, its revenue would entitle him to 'higher multiples of compensation',[142] and from Karachi, Sri Prakasa cynically defended it as a

> … quiet refuge in old age without any fear of the tenants … I will now send them straight to patwari who … will exact every pie from them on behalf of the Government and a little more for himself! We shall still be able to console ourselves that we have abolished Zamindari even if we have brought no relief to the tiller.…[143]

In New Delhi, meanwhile, Muslim tenants in the houses in Phatak Habash Khan, where they had been resettled by Education Minister Azad's staff and the custodian of evacuee property, saw non-Muslims break the government seals. Nehru had appointed a new chief commissioner, a new deputy, a new minister for refugee relief and rehabilitation and a well-known partyman as custodian, but if all these people were 'ignored', what else could be done?[144] From nearby Gurgaon and Malerkotla, the southernmost district and the most secular princely state in Punjab respectively, fearful Muslims were moving to Delhi over the merger on anvil, Patiala and East Punjab States Union (PEPSU).[145] Malerkotla was a small state, and, as there were almost no Muslims left in East Punjab except in Gurgaon, Sikh officers at least should not have been sent there,[146] but it was easier to send a 'harmonious combination of Hindus, Muslims, Sikhs … to Ankara' to project such an India outside.[147]

Equally, it seemed easier for ministers to disburse patronage to various industrial magnets, as in 1948 there was little coordination on public expenditure between the revenue division and relevant ministries. Plus, there was concomitant tax avoidance on the profits accruing regardless of the prime ministerial instruction for 'adequate liaison' with the IT department.[148] Meanwhile, capital generation for the defence of the accused in the Gandhi murder case was galloping with the amount reaching INR 120,279.[149] If such was the state's inability in front of social passions from the right, then, what about its understanding of the passions from the left? A representative confidential report on communist activities in Hyderabad state reflected vaguely, and in an elementary manner, on communist principles and 'evil' deeds, with little actual, and nothing factual in it, yet much 'menace' was 'said to have happened'.[150] Likewise, the Bombay premier's attention was drawn to one case, that of Nana Purohit, 'a Mahar from Colaba', who had been interned since May 1948 on the charge of 'trying to run a parallel government', but with his Habeas Corpus application rejected, there was little to do.[151]

It was in the rural parts of the Madras province that agitation broke out against controls and for procurement price, which, at the instance of the Reddiar ministry, had been kept in 1948 at 50 per cent more than that of 1947. This was not affordable in the prevailing economic scenario, and the choice between no controls and high prices was a rather false one, as both had contributed to inflation, and leaders like N. G. Ranga were urged to keep peasants 'on the right path'.[152] From the other end of this spectrum, industrialist J. R. D. Tata reached out to Finance Minister Matthai, who was a former director of his board and, pointing out risk to investments, argued for uniform compensation for land acquisitions, if any. Given the potential for 'agrarian upheavals and no-rent campaign', Tata was reminded that 'the tender susceptibilities of investors may create a position which might ultimately be more injurious'.[153]

Meanwhile, bad news continued to spread. Orissa, in many ways the most economically promising province, was reporting a worsening financial position due to, first, a reduction in the central government's development grants and, second, a deficit in revenue collection from its adjoining 23 eastern princely states area. The main reasons for this were the abolition of cesses, as well as the elimination of excise duties, alongside rising administrative expenditure. Thus, a hitherto surplus province was now seeking financial aid from New Delhi, at a time when urban rehabilitation in East Punjab was hanging between ministries.[154] The catalogue of Orissa's demands makes for a revealing reading:

> (a) The statutory subvention … will be increased to Rs. 120 lakhs; (b) a post-war development grant will be made [for] the States area [of] Rs. 27.06 lakhs; (c) for financing new backward classes welfare schemes, a grant of Rs. 16.52 lakhs … in the States area, Rs. 13.26 lakhs; (e) Following special loans during the next financial year 1949–50: (i) Rs. 55 lakhs for financing the grow-more-food schemes; (ii) Rs. 3 lakhs for Pakistan refugees and (iii) Rs. 133.27 lakhs for the new capital construction.[155]

This laundry list hinted at the scope of challenges in front of the central government in 1949, which saw strikes and sabotages, food problems, amidst the tussle between importing food, thereby draining foreign exchanges, and producing food, and a lack of cooperation within ministries and between provinces, notwithstanding the extolling of the visiting World Bank delegation that India was almost the only Asian state, 'which can be looked upon as firmly established'.[156] This foreign endorsement came with an expectation around the encouragement of foreign capital in the country. In the industrial resolution of April 1948, the aim had been to regulate it, but now, with deteriorating circumstances, it appeared prudent to utilise foreign capital. For British businesses, no conditions were placed on their continuance.[157]

While the government was thus welcoming foreign capital, some of its subjects were approaching foreign capitals on other matters. P. R. Das of the Civil Liberties Union was preparing a memorandum to be forwarded to the UN in spring 1949 and was persuaded to not do so only by Nehru's repeated personal communications. In Das's reckoning, the executive's power to detain individuals without trial, as was there in the draft constitution, was a sham upon the fundamental rights provided for. He argued that the draft constitution had 'deliberately departed' from British and American examples in favour of the Japanese constitution of 1946 and displayed tendencies to return to 'absolutism' via provincial security acts. Bringing up the example of the case of 107 so-called communist detenues placed before the Calcutta High Court under the Bengal Act, among whom the high court ordered the release of 68, Das was not shy of making a personal hit at the prime minister by reminding him as follows:

Before taking office, you would have been horrified to learn that a single individual has been detained in jail without trial for 6 months, but I do not know how you will react to this form of tyranny which is being practiced all over India today.[158]

As yesterday's 'lawless laws' became today's 'security acts', Das suggested an appointment of a minister of state to scrutinise detention at the hands of local officials, but it was an episode in late March 1949 that came at an early crossroads of such protests and state polls. The socialist Basawan Sinha's month-long hunger strike in Dalmianagar pitchforked the industrial plight in the state in front of the provincial ministry and the central government. On the one hand, a part of Dalmia's factory had been burnt in the agitation that necessitated legal proceedings; on the other hand, the Dalmias had a reputation for large-scale worker dismissals. The Congress' own trade union was involved among them, as were various left groups.[159]

How was one to isolate 'communists-terrorists' while getting 'cooperation from others', especially with the general election coming up either in 'the end of 1950 or the beginning of 1951'?[160] This looming timeline also made wrapping up the Hindu Code Bill imperative, where speaker Mavalankar was proving a formidable roadblock.[161] Pressed, as seen earlier, by an impatient Ambedkar, Mavalankar's responses were both sophisticated and subversive. While he declared that his sympathy was for social reform, his concern as speaker was when and how to justify a closure motion in the assembly on this debate, given the 'revolutionary character' of the bill and the consequent 'turmoil all over the country':

> Shall we give the dissentients an argument that we are rushing through a measure of this type? Would it be equitable to commit the House in the absence of dissentients? Are we not exposing ourselves to a further attack that we shut out an opportunity of a free expression of opinion by those who are entitled under the law as it stands (apart from party mandate) to be present to express their views?[162]

Continuing that the debate on a radical bill like this could not be timed, Mavalankar wanted to give members a chance to let off steam, in Delhi and among provinces, as it was there that the measure's legality would play out. Outweighing those whose attitude could be described as 'delaying' by those who were genuine discussants, Mavalankar recommended the bill to be moved to a separate special session, as it had matters of 'blind faith', and concluded with a politically timeless question: 'Why should we set people unnecessarily against us?' Each of these threads of namely official imperatives, majoritarian impulses and party-political implications came together most substantially, once again, in the arena of Hyderabad, where civil servant M. K. Vellodi took charge from Major-General Chaudhuri in December 1949 and faced the task of holding trials of the ex-ministers, who had been under arrest for 18 months now. This stalemate was spectacularly broken through when the former Premier Mir Laik Ali escaped, with his family, in early 1950. Home minister D. S. Bakhle, another civil servant, and the state police had been warned about safety arrangements by one or two similar escapes earlier. The prosecution of the case against Ali and others was sanctioned on 26 February, but the state lawyer handling the case, V. L. Ethiraj, the first Indian crown prosecutor under British Raj, was away in Madras. Vellodi and Bakhle, there to function as official ministers, were told by the police that 'every Muslim in Hyderabad who was approached for assistance' by Laik Ali gave it 'wholeheartedly [including] a number of officers of the Government', and Vellodi concluded that 'to administer a state knowing that an appreciable part of its population cannot be wholly relied upon is a difficult task'.[163]

The quarrelsome state Congress was availing itself of this opportunity to associate with the government and Vellodi had recommended to V. P. Menon the inclusion in his cabinet of two of their members. The Laik Ali incident brought Menon around this view given that the two Hyderabadis nominated, one Hindu and one Muslim, were mostly yes-men. Meanwhile, any enquiry into the escape was bound to throw an embarrassing light on Vellodi's position and might even make him a sacrificial lamb, although in mid-January 1950 he had sought a different police chief. In New Delhi, there was a sense of amazement at Laik Ali's escape, accompanied by a suspicion of preferential treatment and consequent anger. And while a reconstitution of the government was inevitable, could the factional Congress be relied upon? If they could not pull their weight together, how were they to 'pull their weight with the different sections of the population'[164] and be 'pseudo-apostles of strong government'?[165]

NOTES

1   6 July 1948, Akbar Hydari to Nehru, File No. 11 (Part I), JN (SG) Papers.
2   Ian Talbot and G. Singh, *The Partition of India* (Cambridge: Cambridge University Press, 2009).
3   G. Kudaisya, *Reorganisation of States in India: Text and Context* (New Delhi: National Book Trust, 2014).
4   For Patel, 'disciplining the Congress ministries ... and ... the Princely States', see Das, *Sardar Patel's Correspondence 1945–50 Vol. III* (1972), xlix.
5   14 July 1948, Nehru to provincial premiers, File No. 11 (Part I), JN (SG) Papers.
6   5 June 1948, Nehru to Bhargava, File No. 10, JN (SG) Papers.

7   10 June 1948, Nehru to Mohanlal Saksena, File No. 10, JN (SG) Papers.

8   10 June 1948, Note on 'the case of Yasin Khan' and Nehru to PPS, File No. 10, JN (SG) Papers.

9   Rakesh Ankit, 'Bureaucracy, Community, and Land: The Resettlement of Meos in Mewat, 1949–50', *Journal of Social History* 54, no. 1 (2020): 306–29.

10   14 June 1948, Nehru to Bhargava, File No. 10, JN (SG) Papers.

11   16 June 1948, Nehru to Sinha, File No. 10, JN (SG) Papers. For a contemporary account, see Konrad Bekker, 'Land Reform Legislation in India', *Middle East Journal* 5, no. 3 (1951): 319–36.

12   6 August 1948, Nehru to Mahtab, File No. 12 (Part I), JN (SG) Papers.

13   3 October 1948, Nehru to K. P. S. Menon, File No. 14, JN (SG) Papers.

14   16 June 1948, Nehru to Chandulal Trivedi, File No. 10, JN (SG) Papers.

15   6 July 1948, Hydari to Nehru, File No. 11 (Part I), JN (SG) Papers.

16   Biman Chakraborty, 'Political History of Merger of the Princely States: A Study of Cooch Behar' (PhD thesis, University of North Bengal, Darjeeling, 2001), 120–60.

17   Ashfaque Hossain, 'The Making and Unmaking of Assam–Bengal Borders and the Sylhet Referendum', *Modern Asian Studies* 47, no. 1 (2013): 250–87.

18   Sanjib Baruah, *India against Itself: Assam and the Politics of Nationality* (Philadelphia: PENN Press, 1999).

19   6 July 1948, Hydari to Nehru, File No. 11 (Part I), JN (SG) Papers.

20   9 July 1948, Nehru to Hamidullah, File No. 11 (Part I), JN (SG) Papers.

21   12 July 1948, Nehru to the Maharaja of Bikaner, File No. 11 (Part I), JN (SG) Papers.

22   Ian Duncan, 'The Politics of Liberalisation in Early Post-Independence India: Food Deregulation in 1947', *Journal of Commonwealth and Comparative Politics* 33, no. 1 (1995): 25–45.

23   3 August 1948, Nehru to provincial premiers, File No. 12 (Part I), JN (SG) Papers.

24   8 August 1948, Nehru to Varadachariar, File No. 12 (Part I), JN (SG) Papers.

25   9 August 1948, Nehru to Hydari, File No. 12 (Part I), JN (SG) Papers. See Manorama Kohli, *From Dependency to Interdependence: A Study of Indo-Bhutan Relations* (New Delhi: Vikas, 1993), 37–53.

26   10 August 1948, Nehru's note on Assam, File No. 12 (Part I), JN (SG) Papers. See H. Roy, *Partitioned Lives: Migrants, Refugees, Citizens in India, and Pakistan, 1947–65* (New Delhi: Oxford University Press), 56–86.

27   10 August 1948, Nehru to Sinha, File No. 12 (Part I), JN (SG) Papers.

28   10 August 1948, Nehru to Reddiar and 18 August 1948, Nehru to Shukla, File No. 12 (Part I and II), JN (SG) Papers.

29   10 August 1948, Nehru to Rajagopalachari and Reddiar, File No. 12 (Part I), JN (SG) Papers.

30   19 August 1948, Nehru to Pant, File No. 12 (Part II), JN (SG) Papers.

31   25 August 1948, Nehru to Roy, File No. 12 (Part II), JN (SG) Papers. Joya Chatterji, *The Spoils of Partition: Bengal and India, 1947–1967* (Cambridge: Cambridge University Press, 2007), 61–102.

32 See Margrit Pernau, *Passing of Patrimonialism: Politics and Political Culture in Hyderabad 1911–1948* (New Delhi: Manohar, 2000); and Lucien D. Benichou, *From Autocracy to Integration: Political Developments in Hyderabad State (1938–1948)* (New Delhi: Orient Longman, 2000).

33 1 and 9 September 1948, Nehru to premiers, File No. 13 (Part I), JN (SG) Papers.

34 Srinath Raghavan, *War and Peace in Modern India* (London: Palgrave Macmillan, 2010), 65–100.

35 17 September 1948, Nehru's note on Hyderabad, File No. 13 (Part I), JN (SG) Papers.

36 Sunil Purushotham, *From Raj to Republic: Sovereignty, Violence, and Democracy in India* (Stanford: Stanford University Press, 2021), 76–126.

37 Undated, Monckton to Nehru, File No. 14, JN (SG) Papers.

38 27 September 1948, Nehru to Roy, File No. 13 (Part II), JN (SG) Papers.

39 4 March 1949, Nehru to Sinha, File No. 21 (Part I), JN (SG) Papers. See Robert D. King, 'Language Politics and Conflicts in South Asia' in *Language in South Asia*, ed. Brij Kachru, Yamuna Kachru and S. N. Sridhar (Cambridge: Cambridge University Press, 2008), 311–24; and Arunabha Ghosh, 'Jharkhand Movement in West Bengal', *Economic and Political Weekly* 28, nos. 3/4 (1993): 121–27.

40 29 September and 29 November 1948, Nehru to Roy, File Nos. 13 (Part II) and 15 (Part II), JN (SG) Papers.

41 3 October 1948, Nehru to Bhargava, File No. 14, JN (SG) Papers. See Gursharan Singh, *History of PEPSU: Patiala and East Punjab States Union, 1948–1956* (New Delhi: Konark, 1991), 77–100.

42 Ravinder Kaur, *Since 1947: Partition Narratives among Punjabi Migrants of Delhi* (New Delhi: Oxford University Press, 2007).

43 14 November 1948, Nehru to States Ministry, File No. 15 (Part I), JN (SG) Papers.

44 See A. G. Noorani, *The Destruction of Hyderabad* (London: Hurst, 2014).

45 14 November 1948, Nehru to States Ministry, File No. 15 (Part I), JN (SG) Papers.

46 Sunil Purushotham, 'Internal Violence: The "Police Action" in Hyderabad', *Comparative Studies in Society and History* 57, no. 2 (2015): 435–66.

47 J. S. Grewal, *Master Tara Singh in Indian History: Colonialism, Nationalism, and the Politics of Sikh Identity* (New Delhi: Oxford University Press, 2018), Part II, ch. 15.

48 23 November 1948, Nehru to Singh, File No. 15 (Part II), JN (SG) Papers.

49 29 November and 14 December 1948, Nehru to Trivedi, File Nos. 15 (Part II) and 16 (Part II), JN (SG) Papers.

50 20 March 1949, Nehru to Saksena, File No. 21 (Part II), JN (SG) Papers.

51 8 December 1948, Nehru to Giani Kartar Singh, File No. 16 (Part I), JN (SG) Papers.

52 Purushotham, *From Raj to Republic*, 182–224.

53 27 December 1948, Nehru to Chaudhuri, File No. 17, JN (SG) Papers.

54   Ravi Kalia, *Bhubaneswar: From a Temple Town to a Capital City* (Carbondale; Edwardsville: Southern Illinois University Press, 1994).

55   7 March 1949, Nehru to Trivedi, File No. 21 (Part I), JN (SG) Papers.

56   Asha Sarangi and Sudha Pai, eds., *Interrogating Reorganisation of States: Culture, Identity and Politics in India* (Abingdon: Routledge, 2020), 1–25.

57   30 March–1 April 1949, Draft report, File No. 21 (Part II), JN (SG) Papers.

58   Anwesha Sengupta, "'They Must Have to Go Therefore, Elsewhere'": Mapping the Many Displacements of Bengali Hindu Refugees from East Pakistan, 1947 to 1960s', *Public Arguments* 2 (January 2017): 5–26.

59   11 April 1950, Patel to Nehru and Nehru to Roy, File No. 41 (Part II), JN (SG) Papers.

60   23 June 1948, Nehru to N. V. Gadgil, File No. 10, JN (SG) Papers.

61   See Rakesh Ankit, *India in the Interregnum: Interim Government Sep. 1946–Aug. 1947* (New Delhi: Oxford University Press, 2019).

62   Paul R. Brass, *Factional Politics in an Indian State: The Congress Party in Uttar Pradesh* (Berkeley: University of California Press, 1965), 34–62.

63   7 June 1948, Nehru to P. D. Tandon, File No. 10, JN (SG) Papers.

64   28 June 1948, Nehru to Rajendra Prasad, File No. 10, JN (SG) Papers.

65   5 July 1948, Nehru to Pant, File No. 11 (Part I), JN (SG) Papers.

66   26 March 1948, Sri Prakasa to Hukum Singh, File No. 35, Sri Prakasa Papers (V Instalment), NMML.

67   See Nilkan Perumal, *Economic Ambassador: The Life and Work of Dr Sir R. K. Shanmukham Chetty* (Coimbatore: Popular Publications, 1954).

68   25 June 1948, Nehru to Varadachariar (Chairman, Investigation Commission), File No. 10, JN (SG) Papers.

69   7 June 1948, Nehru to Chetty, File No. 10, JN (SG) Papers.

70   Tanika Sarkar, 'Birth of a Goddess: "Vande Mataram", "Anandamath", and Hindu Nationhood', *Economic and Political Weekly* 41, no. 37 (2006): 3959–69.

71   15 June 1948, Nehru to Roy, and 21 June 1948, Nehru to Mookerjee, File No. 10, JN (SG) Papers.

72   Vanita Shastri, 'The Political Economy of Policy Formation in India: The Case of Industrial Policy, 1948–1994' (PhD thesis, Ithaca: Cornell University, 1995), 54–86.

73   19 November 1948, Nehru to Mookerjee, File No. 15 (Part I), JN (SG) Papers. Also, 'crore' is a unit followed in the South Asian numbering system, where 1 crore = 10,000,000.

74   26 June 1948, Nehru to Mookerjee, File No. 10, JN (SG) Papers.

75   26 June 1948, Nehru's note for Cabinet, File No. 10, JN (SG) Papers. See Nikhil Menon, *Planning Democracy: Modern India's Quest for Development* (Cambridge: Cambridge University Press, 2022), 1–25.

76   27 November 1948, Nehru's note, File No. 15 (Part II), JN (SG) Papers.

77   4 August 1948, Nehru's note, File No. 12 (Part I), JN (SG) Papers.

78   15 July 1948, Nehru to provincial premiers, File No. 11 (Part I), JN (SG) Papers, and 1 August 1948, Nehru to Maulana Azad, File No. 12 (Part I), JN (SG) Papers.

79   Mushirul Hasan, '"Congress Muslims" and Indian Nationalism, Dilemma, and Decline, 1928–1934', *South Asia: Journal of South Asian Studies* 8, nos. 1/2 (1985): 102–20.

80   10 August 1948, Nehru to Mohanlal Saxena, File No. 12 (Part I), JN (SG) Papers.

81   9 September 1948, Nehru to Gopalaswami Ayyangar, File No. 13 (Part I), JN (SG) Papers.

82   10 August 1948, Nehru to Shanmukham Chetty, File No. 12 (Part I), JN (SG) Papers.

83   Gita Piramal, *Business Legends* (New Delhi: Penguin, 1998), 401–02.

84   15 August 1948, Shanmukham Chetty to Nehru, File No. 12 (Part I), JN (SG) Papers.

85   16 August 1948, Nehru to Shanmukham Chetty, File No. 12 (Part II), JN (SG) Papers.

86   18 October 1948, Chaman Lall to Chetty, Correspondences, Diwan Chaman Lall Papers, NMML.

87   13 November 1948, Chetty to Chaman Lall, Correspondences, Diwan Chaman Lall Papers.

88   For the pre-1950 period, see C. H. Alexandrowicz, 'Personal Liberty and Preventive Detention', *Journal of the Indian Law Institute* 3, no. 4 (1961): 445–58.

89   16–18 August 1948, Nehru to provincial premiers, File No. 12 (Part II) JN (SG) Papers.

90   G. D. Overstreet and M. Windmiller, *Communism in India* (Berkely: University of California Press, 1959), 252–308.

91   24 August 1948, Nehru to Mookerjee, File No. 12 (Part II), JN (SG) Papers.

92   2 September 1948, Nehru to Sinha, File No. 13 (Part I), JN (SG) Papers. See Mohammad Sajjad, *Muslim Politics in Bihar: Changing Contours* (New Delhi: Routledge, 2014), 235–73.

93   8 September 1948, Nehru to Saksena, File No. 13 (Part I), JN (SG) Papers.

94   11 September 1948, Nehru to Prasad, File No. 13 (Part I), JN (SG) Papers. See Alok Rai, *Hindi Nationalism* (Hyderabad: Orient Longman, 2001), 93–122; and Rama Kant Agnihotri, 'Constituent Assembly Debates on Language', *Economic and Political Weekly* 50, no. 8 (2015): 47–56.

95   21 September 1948, Nehru to Mehr Chand Khanna, File No. 13 (Part I), JN (SG) Papers.

96   13 December 1948, Nehru to PPS, File No. 16 (Part II), JN (SG) Papers.

97   21 September 1948, Nehru to provincial premiers, File No. 13 (Part I), JN (SG) Papers.

98   22 September 1948, Nehru to Sitaramayya and Reddiar, File No. 13 (Part I), JN (SG) Papers.

99   25 September 1948, Nehru to Mohan Lal Saksena, File No. 13 (Part II), JN (SG) Papers.

100 3 October 1948, Nehru to his PPS, File No. 14, JN (SG) Papers.

101 25 November 1948, Note by Akbar Ali Khan and M. Y. Saleem and 26 November 1948, Nehru to V. P. Menon, File No. 15 (Part II), JN (SG) Papers.

102 Taylor C. Sherman, *Muslim Belonging in Secular India: Negotiating Citizenship in Postcolonial Hyderabad* (Cambridge: Cambridge University Press, 2015), 19–54 and 90–118.

103 26 November 1948, Nehru's note to Menon and Chaudhuri, File No. 15 (Part II), JN (SG) Papers.

104 15 December 1948, Nehru to V. P. Menon, File No. 16 (Part II), JN (SG) Papers.

105 30 December 1948, Nehru to Krishna Menon, File No. 17, JN (SG) Papers.

106 30 December 1948, Nehru to PPS, File No. 17, JN (SG) Papers.

107 12 December 1948, Nehru to Matthai, File No. 16 (Part II), JN (SG) Papers.

108 S. Goel, 'Tales of Restoration: A Study of the Evacuee Property Laws', *Studies in History* 36, no. 2 (2020): 251–79.

109 13 December 1948, Nehru to PPS, File No. 16 (Part II), JN (SG) Papers.

110 A. U. Qasmi, *The Ahmadis and the Politics of Religious Exclusion in Pakistan* (London: Anthem, 2014), 1–10.

111 28 March 1949, Zafrulla Khan to Nehru, File No. 21 (Part II), JN (SG) Papers.

112 28 January 1949, Mirza Bashir Ahmad to Nehru and Bhargava, File No. 21 (Part II), JN (SG) Papers.

113 29 December 1948, Nehru to Pant, File No. 17, JN (SG) Papers. See William Gould, *Bureaucracy, Community, and Influence in India: Society and the State, 1930s–1960s* (London: Routledge: 2010).

114 16 March 1949, Nehru to Mohanlal Saksena, File No. 21 (Part I), JN (SG) Papers.

115 Eleanor Newbigin, *The Hindu Family, and the Emergence of Modern India: Law, Citizenship and Community* (Cambridge: Cambridge University Press, 2013), 1–27.

116 See Subhash C. Kashyap, *Dada Saheb Mavalankar, Father of Lok Sabha: His Life, Work and Ideas, A Centenary Volume* (New Delhi: Lok Sabha Secretariat, 1989).

117 20 March 1949, Nehru to Ambedkar, File No. 21 (Part II), JN (SG) Papers.

118 Reba Som, 'Jawaharlal Nehru and the Hindu Code: A Victory of Symbol over Substance?' *Modern Asian Studies* 28, no. 1 (1994): 165–94.

119 Masani, 'Radical Nationalism in India, 1930–42: The Role of the All-India Congress Socialist Party' (DPhil. thesis, University of Oxford, UK, 1976).

120 8 June 1948, Nehru to Sinha, File No. 10, JN (SG) Papers.

121 10 July 1948, Nehru to Sorensen, File No. 11 (Part I), JN (SG) Papers.

122 Das, *Sardar Patel's Correspondence 1945–50, Volumes V–VII* (1973).

123 2 August 1948, Nehru to Roy, File No. 12 (Part I), JN (SG) Papers.

124 3 August 1948, Nehru to Suhrawardy, File No. 12 (Part I), JN (SG) Papers.

125 Dilip M. Menon, *Caste, Nationalism and Communism in South India Malabar 1900–1948* (Cambridge: Cambridge University Press, 2008), 159–89.

126 4 August 1948, Nehru to Krishna Menon, File No. 12 (Part I), JN (SG) Papers.

127 9 August 1948, Nehru to Nanda, File No. 12 (Part I), JN (SG) Papers

128 9 August 1948, File No. 12 (Part II), JN (SG) Papers.

129 22 August 1948, Report on 'the economic situation in India', File No. 12 (Part II), JN (SG) Papers.

130   28 August 1948, 'A Note on Inflation Analysis', File No. 12 (Part II), JN (SG) Papers.

131   11 August 1948, Golwalkar to Nehru, File No. 12 (Part II), JN (SG) Papers.

132   File No. 94, Deshmukh Papers.

133   29 September 1948, Nehru to Prasad, File No. 13 (Part II), JN (SG) Papers. See Steven I. Wilkinson, *Army and Nation: The Military and Indian Democracy Since Independence* (Cambridge: Harvard University Press, 2015), 60–81.

134   16 August 1948, Nehru to Bhargava, File No. 12 (Part II), JN (SG) Papers.

135   26 and 29 September 1948, Nehru to Bhargava, File No. 13 (Part II), JN (SG) Papers.

136   4 August 1948, Nehru to Kher, File No. 12 (Part II), JN (SG) Papers. See R. Chandavarkar, *Imperial Power, and Popular Politics: Class, Resistance, and the State in India, 1850–1950* (Cambridge: Cambridge University Press, 1998), 266–326.

137   17 August 1948, Kher to Nehru, File No. 12 (Part II), JN (SG) Papers.

138   9 September 1948, Nehru to premiers, File No. 13 (Part I), JN (SG) Papers.

139   28 September 1948, Nehru to Sinha, File No. 13 (Part II), JN (SG) Papers.

140   F. T. Jannuzi, *Agrarian Crisis in India: The Case of Bihar* (Austin: University of Texas Press, 1974), 10–28.

141   21 and 24 November 1948, Nehru to Sinha, File No. 15 (Part II), JN (SG) Papers.

142   Peter Reeves, 'The Congress and the Abolition of Zamindari in Uttar Pradesh', *South Asia: Journal of South Asian Studies* 8, nos. 1/2 (1985): 154–67.

143   19 and 26 March 1948, Singh–Sri Prakasa exchange, File No. 35, Sri Prakasa Papers (V Instalment).

144   12 September 1948, Nehru to Sarabhai, File No. 13 (Part I), JN (SG) Papers. Geva, *Delhi Reborn*, 126–69.

145   Singh, *History of PEPSU*; and Pippa Virdee, *From the Ashes of 1947: Reimagining Punjab* (Cambridge: Cambridge University Press, 2018), 77–101.

146   25 September 1948, Nehru's note to States Ministry, File No. 13 (Part II), JN (SG) Papers.

147   5 November 1948, Oliver Franks to Bajpai, Correspondences, Diwan Chaman Lall Papers.

148   23 September 1948, Nehru's note, File No. 13 (Part II), JN (SG) Papers.

149   26 September 1948, Nehru to Kher, File No. 13 (Part II), JN (SG) Papers.

150   2 October 1948, Nehru to Ramaswamy Reddiar, File No. 14, JN (SG) Papers.

151   17 November 1948, Nehru to Kher, File No. 15 (Part I), JN (SG) Papers.

152   24 November 1948, Nehru to Ranga, File No. 15 (Part II), JN (SG) Papers. See B. Siegel, *Hungry Nation: Food, Famine, and the Making of Modern India* (Cambridge: Cambridge University Press, 2018), 50–85.

153   30 December 1948, Nehru to Matthai, File No. 17, JN (SG) Papers.

154   8 March 1949, Nehru to Matthai, File No. 21 (Part I), JN (SG) Papers.

155   5 March 1949, Note by A. C. Mukarji, File No. 21 (Part I), JN (SG) Papers.

156   9 March 1949, Nehru to provincial premiers, File No. 21 (Part I), JN (SG) Papers.

157 March 1949, PM's statement on foreign capital in India, File No. 21 (Part II), JN (SG) Papers. See M. Misra, *Business, Race, and Politics in British India, c.1850–1960* (Oxford: Clarendon, 1999), 182–209.

158 27 March 1949, Das to Nehru, File No. 21 (Part II), JN (SG) Papers. See M. Jha, 'Nehru and Civil Liberties in India', *International Journal of Human Rights* 7, no. 3 (2003): 103–15.

159 Rita Sinha and Ramu Manivannan, eds., *Basawon Sinha: A Revolutionary Patriot (1909–1989): A Commemorative Volume* (New Delhi: Kamala Sinha, 1999), 58–62; and Shivangi Jaiswal, 'Labour Ministers, State and the Prism of Law, 1942–52', *South Asia Chronicle* 8 (2018): 233–56.

160 31 March 1949, Nehru to Sinha, File No. 21 (Part II), JN (SG) Papers.

161 Guha, *India after Gandhi*, 226–41.

162 28/30 March 1949, Mavalankar to Nehru, File No. 21 (Part II), JN (SG) Papers.

163 22 March 1950, Vellodi to Ayyangar, Correspondences, Gopalaswami Ayyangar Papers, NMML.

164 25 March 1950, Ayyangar to Vellodi, Correspondences, Ayyangar Papers.

165 20 March 1950, Ayyangar to Nehru, Correspondences, Ayyangar Papers.

2

April–December 1949

To 'Break Through the Bottlenecks ...'

Despite its lack of electoral imprimatur, there were no troubles for the Nehru government after it decided to remain in the remodelled British commonwealth in April 1949.[1] On the day that the constituent assembly ratified this decision, the only dissenting voices were those of the Khilafatist Hasrat Mohani, the UP socialist Shibbanlal Saxena and the Bombay liberal K. T. Shah. Chapter 2 chronicles the threefold challenges of 1949, refugees–food–economy[2] and the bottlenecks therein, and then interrogates the attempted breakthroughs by a still-contingent state, whose presentation of the new constitution ushered another age of establishment.[3] It demonstrates the tumult before any transformation within the administrative apparatus of a neither too strong nor yet fully centralised state. With the communists 'isolated', some peasant proprietorship could be attempted, along with control of key industries before the election, but it was the food situation that proved the biggest headache, and the provinces needed to initiate on the troika of intensive cultivation–procurement–rapid yields.[4]

On the other hand, some initiatives were unwelcome. When Indian army's chief General K. M. Cariappa made a press statement congratulating the prime minister for the Commonwealth conference and the country's 'all-round progress', he was told to not get 'mixed up ... with politics....'[5] Inside a week, Lt General Nathu Singh made comments on law and order in Lucknow,[6] as well as on 'step-motherly army pay scales....'[7] In this context, it was not surprising that in Hyderabad, where communism, food production and land reform came together, the Ministry of States outlined a fantastic proposal of the abolition of *jagirdari* over 60 years. Going this slow might lead to a 'rapid shift-over to Communism'.[8]

Across the southern peninsula, there was also a linguistic tussle simmering, and educationist Ali Yavar Jung suggested that like Banaras and Aligarh,[9] central centres like Andhra university (Telugu), Madras (Tamil), Mysore (Kannada) and Osmania (Urdu) could be created to spread the 'national language'.[10] Another academic, John Boyd Orr, the Scottish polymath who would win the Nobel Peace Prize later in the year, came visiting in April 1949 and left India having grasped the prime difficulty of decision-making in New Delhi and actioning them across the country. He too suggested a sort of planning commission, but one that was more active and less advisory so as 'to break through the bottlenecks in administration', given uncertain imports, large deficit areas and lack of implements as well as foreign exchange. His second suggestion was to make a commercial deal with America, and a third was about encouraging 'every family to grow … food' for India needed 4 million tons of food grains by 1951.[11]

Meanwhile, since the Jawaharlal–Vallabhbhai–Pattabhi committee had indefinitely postponed the consideration of linguistic provinces in northern India, voices were being raised against it, but none as loudly as that of Master Tara Singh, jailed in Banaras. Writing to Nehru, he asked for Sikhs to have the 'power to practice' their religion and language, and added, why should the Congress yield to the Hindu press when it wrote that they could not live in a province with the Sikhs in majority? When the Hindus had a majority at the centre and yet they could not accept staying in a Sikh-majority province, how could the Sikhs stay in a 'Hindu-majority province' when they are in 'minority in the centre also'? Continuing that it was 'easy' for the 'majority to pose as purely nationalists …', Tara Singh asked why 'if a Hindu of a depressed class embraces Sikhism, he is deprived of privileges and if a Sikh of a depressed class embraces Hinduism, he gets [them] … '? He knew the answer, namely that with 'that distinction removed, depressed class Hindus would embrace Sikhism', and made his intent plain thus:

> The Khalsa panth is not communal … most Hindus do not realise it … I do believe in the fundamental oneness of the Hindu and Sikh religions, but I do not call myself a Hindu … I make the following two demands: 1) Sikhs and Hindus of the depressed classes should have the same concessions; 2) a Punjabi-speaking province shall be created … I have never demanded and do not demand now an independent Sikh State….[12]

With the constituent assembly's advisory committee on minorities yet to consider these questions, the prime minister's response was framed around faith in institutions like it and individuals like Bhimsen Sachar, whose humane approach to administration saw him replace Gopichand Bhargava in East Punjab. Sachar, though, had a difficult time forming his cabinet as well as finding a house,[13] while his ministers were neither very obliging nor very courteous to him as there was an East–West Punjab fault-line at play.[14] Little wonder that New Delhi took away from them the planned Faridabad rehabilitation township.[15] Sachar's ministers were keen on having a majority in the board for this township, but with the army, representatives of four central ministries and the United Council for Relief and Welfare involved, this was not possible. With Dr Rajendra Prasad becoming the chairman of the board, the final authority was central, albeit with three representatives of the East Punjab government, and it was decided to accommodate '40,000 persons', half from NWFP and half from Dera Ghazi Khan.[16]

On the other side, in West Bengal, it was an external, ideological group that was the bone of contention between New Delhi and Calcutta. Even as the rest of the provinces agreed to not ban the CPI, it remained banned in West Bengal.[17] In Calcutta and nearby, incidents recently happened that elicited public sympathy for it, as the Roy ministry decided to sanction firings, worrying Nehru by this 'slippery slope'.[18] When Roy declared that communists had to be driven beyond the pale of society, Nehru argued that if 'present action' against them did not produce effect, 'an additional banning will not do it'.[19] The CWC was putting up a candidate against Sarat Chandra Bose in the upcoming South Calcutta by-election, and given the reactions in the city to incidents of police firing and charges of corruption or nepotism in the administration, it was going to be a tough task. Communist violence had to be separated from their ideology so as to not only 'rely on the repressive state'.[20]

This was easier said than done, elsewhere too. To give but one example, for the last 18 months, Nehru had been personally interested in the conditions of Muslims of Buria, Ambala, carrying this torch passed by Gandhi, and was assured about their rehabilitation by the Bhargava government. Now, in the summer of 1949, he learnt that few orders passed there were followed up; instead, their fruit gardens had been 'sold' to refugees, but the proceeds were withheld. In October 1948, when one of these Muslims was murdered, no action was taken by the police, while soon after when 'a (Harijan) was murdered, several Muslims unconnected [were] arrested'.[21] The problem was wider. In Delhi, with its administrative 'overlapping', in a similar set-up in Ajmer-Merwara and the not-so-similar Bhopal,[22] any place where 'the Muslims who went away temporarily … came back, [found] that their houses had been occupied or allotted', and some, in turn, were 'allowed to occupy other Muslims' vacant houses …' as the state was limiting its 'help to non-Muslims only'.[23]

The problem was wider still. In Assam, Premier Bardoloi found himself facing an 'influx of Muslims', which he claimed was after they had accepted 2.5 lakh Hindu refugees from East Bengal and warned about a demand for a census of displaced persons, with Bishnuram Medhi, the finance minister, being a strong opponent of 'any further refugees'.[24] This, combined with administrative leaks and procedural vagueness, was creating roadblocks for provincial dealings and central deliveries by all-India services.[25] In Bombay, a strike was organised by its municipal Kamgar Sangh, and the Kher ministry characteristically met agitation with arbitration, followed by repression. Kher had another axe to grind, as Dr Ambedkar was president of this union and demanded that he should either 'resign [or] exercise influence to end the strike'.[26] The latter checked the union's correspondence with the municipal commissioner and the relevant labour acts and considered the strike to be legal.[27] The chief cause was the municipal commissioner's failure to award the pay sanctioned in 1948, and the law minister concluded, therefore, that 'the union had become bitter'.[28]

Bombay workers' union was hardly alone in feeling thus, as from Kashmir to Hyderabad, problems in the state's functioning plagued societies.[29] While the former had become an international dispute, the latter too garnered international attention, when eight communists were sentenced to death by a special tribunal.[30] The prime minister preferred the terms 'terrorists or anti-social elements' and wished to 'avoid talking about communists as such', given foreign enquiries.[31] But India then was producing incidents at a rate difficult to keep up with. At the All-India Congress Committee (AICC) meeting at Dehradun, delegates from the borders of Hyderabad state had spoken about 4,000–5,000 Muslim refugees from Gulbarga and Osmanabad in Sholapur, who refused to return. In those two districts, there had been at least two big cases of indiscriminate shooting, one at the Aland Sharif *dargah* and the other at the Ganagapura village. These killings had yielded arrests, including of some Afghans, who were innocent and from whom money was extorted. Meanwhile, Dr Paul Ruegger of the International Red Cross had brought up the matter of prisoners in Hyderabad and was told that among them 'there were Razakars [and] Hindu prisoners … charged for committing similar offences against the Muslims….'[32] The problem was that Nehru did not 'quite know how things' were there, as he complained to Vallabhbhai Patel in a long note:

> It will be a good thing for a full report on Hyderabad for the cabinet. I wonder if you have seen Jaisoorya's (Sarojini Naidu's son) letter to the press…. The Muslims continue to be apprehensive. The State Congress are equally unhappy…. Who do we reply upon in Hyderabad … J. N.

Chaudhuri expects an intensification of communist activities.... There is
widespread criticism of officials.... [33]

Patel, who was convalescing in Dehradun, was getting concerned too as his
officials had not produced a report since March 1949 and the next stock-taking
was due only in September. This did not mean though that the spring-wells
of his worries were the same as Nehru's. He dismissed Jaisoorya's letter and,
citing a shortage of police, justified bringing in officers from neighbouring
provinces while refusing to accept them as communal or corrupt. For him, it
was the 'Muslim population' that was 'at best uncooperative, distrustful and
... patently communal', but even he admitted to the 'disturbing disappearance
of important persons such as the family members of Kasim Razvi', as well as
to the 'hopelessly divided State Congress', whose ranks had 'taken to crime'.
Therefore, Patel wanted to continue the Chaudhuri regime, especially vis-
à-vis the defying communists in the two forested districts of Nalgonda and
Warangal and the 'disloyal' local administrative machinery. [34] Their party
there, under Swami Ramanand Tirtha, was unable 'to win over the Muslims',
but Patel did not see why the Red Cross should be concerned, and instead,
invoking the 'Communist–Razakar alliance', he was not going to risk a
'popular administration' without having first brought about a 'popular verdict'
in its favour. [35]

For this question of loyalty and its attendant amoral economy, one need
not keep going to the Deccan, as Rafi Ahmed Kidwai brought to light the
'normal' fact that in Kanpur, UP, following Lucknow, many long-serving
Muslim railway officers were being dismissed as police 'suspects'. [36] Every
other day, some deputation came to New Delhi with accounts of such large-
scale dismissals based on fuzzy police reports. The thin end of this wedge
was provided by a Home Ministry circular issued against the communists but
used against Muslim employees, and a Jamiat-ul-Ulema delegation had gone
to Patel in April 1949. While the latter held that it was 'not the intention to
deal with Muslims' thus, by the end of May, 'many hundreds of people, more
specially in the Railways' had been dismissed. [37]

This is not to say that the intended target of this circular or their fellow-
travellers were spared. In June 1949, several members of the Socialist Party
were sent to prison. Many of these had been Congressmen a year ago and
now found themselves with various kinds of political prisoners. Some of them,
most prominently Dr Rammanohar Lohia, were agitating about Goa, the
Portuguese enclave in India, and for a Maharashtra province to include it.
Nehru, concerned about another communal flare-up with the Catholic part
of Goa, doubted 'the result of the plebiscite' there, but he was unimpressed by
his legislators 'talking about strong action being taken all over the world....' [38]

Patel, on the other hand, was apt to employ the motif of 'the cause of Indians' in the Portuguese and French settlements, where reportedly 'the International Court of Justice [was] sending observers'.[39] When the Home Ministry nevertheless 'dealt severely' with Lohia 'taking a procession to [Portuguese] Ambassador's House', members of the constituent assembly felt that this was excessive.[40] Simultaneously, from Assam, Governor Sri Prakasa was writing, after visiting Jorhat jail, where he met communist prisoners, that many were being detained 'unnecessarily'.[41]

In Delhi, the trouble was that the chief commissioner was caught between the Home Ministry and the relief and rehabilitation department, and the position of Muslims in the capital was now being categorised into those who (a) left their homes during the September 1947 disturbances and went to another part of India, and those who (b) went to Pakistan but with families left behind. About (a), there was a cabinet decision for them to be taken care of. That it was not being implemented was an indictment on the departmental organisation being built with a view to help the incoming refugees from Pakistan, with little sympathy for Muslim evacuees. As regards (b), there was the spirit of Gandhi from November 1947 making the Congress decide that Muslims should be encouraged to return, and many did. By May 1949, governments got stricter with permits, but Partition had split up families and people were being asked to 'go to Pakistan'. The custodian, lest it be forgotten, was only for property, but there was 'so much feeling against Muslims …'[42] that social workers like Mridula Sarabhai were much needed.[43]

In fact, the Mohan Lal Saksena-led ministry did not reckon that any special officer was needed to be appointed for 'uprooted' Muslims, technically neither a refugee nor yet a citizen. And, as one moved away from the capital, such cases multiplied. Those 'who had not gone out of India but had to leave their homes …' lost them as 'evacuee property' and sent applications, often to the prime minister.[44] In June 1949, the United Council for Relief and Welfare neared its end, despite Governor-General Rajagopalachari's patronage and Nehru's protests, as Saksena refused it financial assistance. It coordinated with other set-ups like the All-India Women's Conference in Calcutta,[45] and Nehru was angry that 'the approach to the Muslim refugees is on a par with the approach to [United Council]'.[46] Yet, when Mridula Sarabhai called on Saksena in June 1949 to seek aid, Saksena refused, as his ministry's funds were 'meant only for refugees coming from Pakistan'.[47] Stonewalled, the prime minister reached out to provincial premiers about the organisation's work on abducted women asking if its 'cost might be shared'.[48]

Along with Saksena, Mehr Chand Khanna, a rich refugee from Peshawar who had been the finance minister in the Congress' pre-1947 ministry there, also raised the matter of Muslim property in Delhi being dealt with 'leniently', with the owners 'allowed to return' and their temporary permits made permanent. In response, the prime minister sought a special officer for a closer scrutiny of individual cases, but for the permits, 'the instances cited were of women whose husbands [had] been here ... the number involved was about 50', and Nehru asked, 'how [did] these few concessions affect the problem ...?'[49] Interestingly, Khanna was also 'not in favour of including Harijans in the people registered for resettlement in Delhi'.[50] Such examples and similar were a matter of routine, and in such circumstances, state secularism boiled down to Muslims having 'no particular rights except what we, out of our grace, might grant them', with refugees like Khanna 'irritated by even a single instance of a Muslim being given any ... facility'.[51] Anyway, with Patel still convalescing in Dehradun, key matters such as these were being reserved, including whether a commission should be appointed for the backward classes,[52] differentiated into tribes, Scheduled Castes and Other Backward Castes.[53]

In a sense, finalising the constitution itself was slowing down, with Prasad putting on record the assembly's inability to finalise it before 15 August 1949 and turning to 2 October as the next appropriate date. A related issue was regarding the Nagari version, Prasad's favoured draft that he was so keen to have produced side by side that he desired to have a day in the week set aside for it, as the draft in English was to the 'authoritative' version for a decade and a half, after which he anticipated Hindi to be the centre's language and expected that 'people from south will get an opportunity of adjusting themselves'.[54] Nehru doubted the feasibility of both Prasad's timeline and his language proposal. If the constituent assembly went on as it was, then it would complete its discussions by the end of July whereupon drafting could begin, which was expected to take six to eight weeks. Another reading would happen then, by when they would be nearer November and, so, he thought 26 January 1950 as suitable. As regards the simultaneous adoption of a Hindi version, that would be highly contestable, as much for semantic as for social reasons.[55] Turning to the Irish parallel, Prasad's preferred comparison, Nehru pointed out that despite having a Gaelic draft, 'they found it very difficult to carry on'.[56]

While they waited for the new constitution, elections continued under the old. In South Calcutta, a prestigious battle dawned when the Forward Bloc's Sarat Chandra Bose took on the Congress candidate Suresh Chandra Das in a by-poll. Sarat Bose had been a member of the interim government of September 1946, and, of course, he was the brother of Subhas, but, in the 1940s, the Bose brothers had chosen to walk away from Gandhi and Congress.[57] The prime minister's electoral rhetoric was strong as he asked, 'Under which flag does Shri Bose stand?'[58] The voters of South Calcutta answered by giving Bose a comfortable victory against a faction-ridden party, and afterwards premier Roy explained away the result as under:

There were 74 boxes filled with Sarat Babu's ballot papers and 67 boxes for [Das] … inefficient Congress committee…. They were given Rs. 40,000/-…. Surendra Mohan Ghosh had thrown up their sponge … and [blamed government's] unpopularity … two messages came to me from Ghosh – one that as voting in female booths had been unfavourable, we should stop the polling … second that we should replace the ballot boxes….[59]

Others were giving their accounts too. Sucheta Kripalani reported a morally bankrupt party, unable to turn up at 'election booths dominated by organised communists', whose chief slogan was 'who kills our women?'[60] The passive party/aggressive ministry was risking much, and an anonymous worker who had joined it in 1905 and had voted for Bose despite his dislike for the 'brothers' ideology and vanity' wrote to Rajendra Prasad that South Calcutta did not as much vote for him as it voted against the Roy ministry, which had given them 'high prices, heavy taxation, black-marketing, profiteering … firing upon a procession of young girls in the street and young men inside the jail', while half the provincial party committee 'desired the defeat of Das'.[61] Vallabhbhai Patel was getting his own reports, and ultimately, the central leadership agreed that both organisation and spirit were lacking. Neither the INR 40,000 set aside nor the 210 motor cars with petrol were fully used, and the verdict was 'to show their dislike for the Bengal Congress, the provincial government [and] the Central government'.[62]

Six months into 1949 then, there was communal anguish in Hyderabad and UP, agitation elsewhere by socialists and communists, ambivalence towards the Congress and its provincial governments, lack of uniformity whether in evacuee property or in food procurement, tenants' agitation against ejectments by ordinance in Punjab and insufficient appreciation of the 'necessity for austerity'.[63] Among those dragging their feet was the assembly-as-legislature on the Hindu Code Bill, and given the timeline of the constitution's promulgation, it was now clear that there would not be a special session for it. It was also clear that without an informal, general agreement, the bill would be drawn out. Nehru was willing 'to give in on a point or two rather than take the risk of having the whole thing sabotaged'.[64] What was also getting sabotaged was Urdu, determined by the Pant ministry 'in opposition to Hindi', as the language of Muslims only, and thus 'drying up' across primary schools,[65] but it belonged 'more to the UP than to Pakistan'.[66] And across the Yamuna, in East Punjab, the officialdom was facing Sikh demands to make Punjabi and Gurmukhi the official language or script. With the language policy being a work-in-progress, it amounted to an entitlement to primary instruction in their mother tongue provided there were enough numbers. In Punjab, this

meant Hindi/Nagari or Punjabi/Gurmukhi at the primary stage, with English
or Urdu, as they were 'in common use'.[67]

As a rare consolidation in that time of transition came with the
union between Travancore and Cochin states, achieved on 1 July 1949,[68]
more common were the channels seemingly brought together against the
Congress, like in South Calcutta, 'revolutionary socialists, communists,
Hindu communalists, elements of the old INA ...' even as labour and capital
were 'sullen', land reforms were stuck, there was an 'inquisitorial' state and
there were 'inept, narrow-minded provincial governments'.[69] There were
many manifestations of this combined decline. In Delhi, Muslim returnees
continued to be evicted from their houses in the Pusa area. Their condition
on the road with 'houses lying empty in front of them' was too much, even for
crusty assembly members, to assuage whose conscience Saksena outsourced
these evictions to sensitive social workers.[70] Meanwhile, a small committee
was mooted to coordinate rehabilitation, comprising the home secretary (H.
V. R. Iengar), chairman, Saksena's ministry representative (M. C. Khanna)
and chief commissioner, Delhi.[71] Relatedly, when, from Bangalore, the police
reported on the former *diwan* of Mysore state, Mirza Ismail's letters in the
foreign press discussing the state of Muslims in India, Nehru, who had seen
these, acerbically put it for Patel that 'many of us know Sir Mirza Ismail far
better than the undisclosed source....'[72]

Across the islands of territory that was PEPSU, tenant ejectments
were being accompanied with cases of firing and deaths, in one of which in
Kishangarh (Patiala) 'the Superintendent of Police himself was the proprietor
of that land'.[73] In Bihar, the 'oldest Congressmen' Ram Narayan Singh,
Mahamaya Prasad Singh and Giridhar Narayan Singh were lamenting the
ministry's 'corruption', namely the molasses affair and the Bettiah estate
affair.[74] In Bombay, the Kher ministry was going after horse-racing, while
'black-marketing, anti-social industries, evasion of taxes, illegal profits'
continued, after its anti-prohibition drive, this being another 'desire to
improve private morals by legislation'.[75] This at a time when reports relating
to the firm of Dalmias and their brokers in Bombay were circulating, claiming
'colossal fraud'.[76] In Madras, the provincial government was proposing 'a tax
on advertisements in newspapers'.[77] In UP, appointments of Chief Justice
Malik and Justice Agarwala of the High Court were clouded by charges of
corruption.[78]

At the heart of all this was the fact that the fulcrum of the country, the
constituent assembly had stagnated as a parliament. It had been elected
for a different purpose over 1946–47, but with the first general election
sometime away, the dominion's regime from 1946 was staring at the prospect
of continuing as the republic's state in 1950. If this changeover had to have

some meaning, then changes of form, if not content, like a new cabinet were needed. One possible option was for fresh provincial elections in late 1949, for the assembly or parliament, after it had passed the constitution. Nehru was keen enough on this idea to have it 'included in the transitional clauses'.[79] Patel too agreed and suggested holding these elections in December 1949– January 1950 for the new legislature to meet after 26 January 1950, but their cabinet colleagues bar one shot down the proposal. The one central minister who agreed was the non-Congressman Dr Mookerjee.[80]

The shadows of 1945–46 lengthened in other ways too. East Punjab and West Bengal remained a source of distress for New Delhi, with their governments of 'rival groups', resettlement and removal of refugees, both now being border areas, civil machinery in both seeking military assistance while side-lining politically astute and administratively experienced governors at Simla and Calcutta, rising corruption and response to it on 'party lines' and with 'third degree methods' and different 'quota scandals', whether in rehabilitation or in imports.[81] This sense of 'drift' was personified in the changing of premiers: in one between Bhargava and Sachar, in the other between Roy and Sarkar.[82] Nehru decided to pay Calcutta a visit in mid-July to address the public directly, over and above his partymen and his security apparatus, who were busy collecting copies of communist circulars, which were then being used by enterprising home ministers like D. P. Mishra of the Central Provinces to highlight the CPI's real programme in India, that is, 'violence and sabotage'.[83]

Amidst all this, by June 1949, it was becoming clear that Vallabhbhai Patel would not 'ever regain his old standard of health'.[84] Nehru had been visiting his deputy in Dehradun, and much of their conversation that summer centred around 'Golwalkar and Tara Singh … Lohia and socialists' – all of whom were or had been detained or banned. While in agreement that there was little point in prolonging this situation, Patel sought the freedom of Golwalkar and Tara Singh, and Nehru that of Lohia and the socialists. He held the latter as 'impractical but good intentioned people' and did not wish to embitter them; Patel termed the former simply as 'prominent people' to be 'let out'.[85]

IN SEARCH OF 'SOMETHING "SPECTACULAR"'

In the summer of 1949, Jawaharlal Nehru was keen to re-connect with the public, starting with those in Calcutta, and this section reconstructs such interactions, albeit followed by routine reactions, thereby widening the chasm between individual words and institutional actions. For instance, when a worried West Bengal ministry suggested a 'conference', the prime minister,

who had thrived among crowds since the early 1930s, warned them that
if his audience were too distant, in the name of security, then he would go
towards them, for he was more concerned that there was an increasingly 'inert
or passively hostile' population, and he had 'no desire to continue governing
people who do not want us....'[86] Institutionally speaking, this certitude was
difficult to replicate, whether on falling food production or conversely rising
food imports across UP, Delhi, or East Punjab.[87] In the Etawah district of UP,
an American planner Albert Mayer had begun his experiments in cooperative
farming.[88] This pilot development project had started in late 1948 across 64
villages, and now it was proposed to extend it to about 600.[89]

In East Punjab, meanwhile, Sikh rehabilitation was being overshadowed
by demands for service representation and court or administration language.
New Delhi was refusing both and arguing that before Partition, Ambala
division, excepting Ropar and Kharar *tehsils*, spoke Hindustani, while
Punjabi was spoken in the rest of the (East) Punjab, barring Kangra (hill)
district.[90] After Partition, as millions (Hindus and Sikhs) entered the east
from West Punjab, they moved into the Ambala division and towards Delhi,
thereby reinforcing this distinction. With the official diminishing of Urdu
and a disavowal of English, the controversy was as much about the language
as about the script. The Sikh and Hindu demands were in head-on collision
here, especially in the Ambala division and Kangra district. In July 1949, the
best solution appeared to be two 'linguistic regions', with each being a second
language for the other and with English and Urdu continuing. The Hindu
groups did not agree to girls' schools with these options, while the Sikhs did
not agree to differentiate between girls' and boys' schools on this question.
Moreover, the Sikhs wished for 'the whole Jullundur division and the whole
of Ambala district',[91] whereas the Hindus wanted to exclude Ambala town,
Naraingarh and Jagadhari.

Simultaneously, at the business capital of the country, Bombay, events were
occurring, which too foreshadowed a certain future. The industrial court there
had awarded mill workers a bonus of INR 4.5 crores payable in two instalments
at the end of May and June 1949. The Kher ministry organised, instead, a
'saving campaign', leaving the communist unions 'hostile' and the socialist
union (Mill Mazdoor Sabha) 'non-cooperative'. Of the INR 2.25 crores paid
on 25 May, barely 10,000 were put in savings though, leading to an ordinance
from the central finance ministry on 11 June. Thereupon, the Kher ministry
that had initially suggested 2/3 of the second instalment for conversion into
savings, advised a reduction of this quantum to 1/5. Congress' own union,
the only one supporting compulsory saving, had urged a reduction to 1/3.
The finance minister declined and instead offered to render cash certificates,
a revision that was closer to the socialist union's position. Towards the end

of June, the press reported that Dr Matthai would be meeting Asoka Mehta and other socialist leaders to discuss this matter. This meeting took place on 1 July, and a concerned Kher resented Matthai 'giving so much importance to Mehta',[92] and sought to draw a line in the triangular relationship between the party, its labour constituency and the government's industry expert (Matthai).

This triangle was making administration tangled in other ways too. In July 1949, Food Minister Jairamdas Doulatram asked Krishna Menon to help with the purchase of fertilisers in England. Menon approached the Stafford Cripps and got an offer, whereupon S. Bhoothalingam, secretary in the industries and supplies ministry, sent a telegram to London criticising its price and the deal fell through. This correspondence to Menon, sanctioned by Bhoothalingam's minister, Dr Mookerjee, was sent without any reference to Doulatram.[93] That summer another correspondence involving another non-Congress figure was also reaching its climax. The Home Ministry had been communicating with M. S. Golwalkar, and by mid-July, Golwalkar had 'accepted some suggestions' that 'relevant provisions of the [RSS] constitution will be worked in the spirit contemplated' by the government, for a reassured Patel to feel that 'NO reasonable opposition now [existed] to the Sangh' and to decide 'to withdraw the ban'.[94]

While Patel was thus dealing with the Sangh, Nehru was visiting a tense Calcutta for a violent public meeting, which he termed a combination of 'terrorism and communism' exacerbated by a seething 'middle-class or lower' with a 'fascist' outlook, against a background of huge unemployment. With industrial workers from neighbouring Bihar and UP taking part in these troubles, the Bengalis were astir, and he was welcomed with garlands as well as stones, bullets and a bomb.[95] The South Calcutta debacle, after all, had many lessons, in addition to the major policy demands of 'food problem, refugees' rehabilitation, land reform, dollar expenditure [and] housing'.[96] As for Golwalkar, the prime minister agreed because 'repressive legislation has a bad odour' but remained concerned about a 'cult of violence'.[97]

In West Bengal, another tension was around language as the government ruled in favour of the use of mother tongue in both primary and secondary education, pending demand and feasibility. For non-Bengali children, this made Bengali compulsory, as too many variables rubbed against each other: mother tongue or official central languages or official provincial languages. When this formula was applied to East Punjab and its two linguistic areas, Master Tara Singh argued for Punjabi's primacy. His associate Giani Kartar Singh averred that following an agreement between ministers, Trivedi had agreed to the following formula: 'Punjabi in Gurmukhi compulsory from 1–5 standard in Punjabi area, Hindi/Nagari vice-versa … from 4th standard, the other language should be compulsory'.[98] In Hyderabad, there was a similar quarrel, centring on the future of Osmania University, to be 'based on the national language in the South'.[99]

Nehru was keen on most of the aforementioned, but little of it happened, and this left him asking for 'something "spectacular"' in the CWC meeting in July 1949, to which B. G. Kher responded rhetorically: 'How can we secure this when we support the rich and turn our machinery against the poor? The rich employ newspapers [for] propaganda, lawyers who defend them.... Could we publicly disown them? Is that "spectacular"? What is?'[100] What was spectacular was that the houses erected for refugees by the central Public Works Department (PWD) had 'collapsed' under rains, that a by-election was going ahead in the Amritsar seat reserved for labour despite the central government's unease about it, given the regrettable showing in South Calcutta,[101] that T. Prakasam and his Telugu group had made wide-ranging charges in the Madras governments of Ramaswamy Reddiar and his successor Kumaraswamy Raja,[102] and that Relief and Rehabilitation Minister Saksena had announced that all refugee camps 'will wound up by 31 October and all supply of free food would be stopped'.[103]

What was not spectacular was another note prepared by the Home Ministry on communist activity across the country. It was more ideological and less informative, instead of focusing on incidents like the outrages in Jessop & Co.'s factories in Calcutta 'when some Europeans were thrown into the furnace', and 'major incidents of attacks on police stations' across Bengal, Central Provinces, Hyderabad and Madras.[104] The prime minister remained keen to criminalise either the communists or the Razakars, as opposed to the former being categorised as political opponents and the latter being classified as prisoners of war.[105] Around this time, the first intimation of the upcoming currency and trade crisis was felt when London nudged New Delhi on its import policy within the sterling area. Delhi or Bombay shops were full of imported luxury articles at a time when, unlike food, there was cloth aplenty in the mills, but the mill owners rarely played the trade game as patriots but as profiteers.[106] An especially acute question was the sugar position where the government appeared 'powerless', allowing first an import of 50,000 tons at a cost of INR 3 crores, consequent to which came a seeming scarcity.[107] While provinces were being impressed upon about this shortage, in the national capital, sugar had a thriving black market. The chief commissioner confessed being 'beaten', and premiers were reduced to seeking cooperation from 'unscrupulous' traders.[108] By the end of 1949, sugar had become 'an acid test' for the government, with 'neither any faith in the industry nor any sympathy'.[109]

But the talk in the corridors of power still centred around corruption, factions, administration (appointments, transfers, licences), public works (in Delhi, 13 inches of rain in two days saw many refugee houses washed away), insufficient food and a sullen labour, combining to whittle away foreign exchange and sterling reserves. Side by side was the reality of Delhi's refugee rations being discontinued after 31 October, with their discontent checked by their hope.[110] The central government knew that it was near-impossible to stop free rations and turn refugee camps into work centres notwithstanding the many township plans. Nehru even 'thought of conscription of able-bodied refugees from 15 to 40 [in] some semi-military formation ... to weed out persons who do not want discipline or work'.[111] With little food, housing and education, 'a period of technical work', for matriculates or graduates, was another template to be tested but for the prominent 'service mentality'[112] and 'old rut' ministers.[113]

For a fortnight in August 1949, a crowd of refugees staged a *dharna* in front of the prime minister's house, though most of them were better off than those in provinces, and the township in Faridabad was coming up for them, largely from the Frontier Province. Afterwards it was reported that M. C. Khanna had 'engineered these demonstrations'.[114] With 'alarming unemployment', Nehru was repeatedly stressing 'a year of manual work, social service....'[115] In August 1949, a report into the workings of the West Bengal ministry came comprising 17 allegations, from 'improper favouritism/nepotism, unconscious influence, irregularities [to] partiality in civil supply, cooperative & industrial procurement and distribution'.[116] Within the ministry, a non-cooperating group-of-six had been formed, which deplored some CWC decisions on the province as 'unjust', namely, those related to Cooch-Behar princely state and Manbhum district.[117] This group desired Cooch-Behar's amalgamation with the province and as regards Manbhum, wanted New Delhi to 'issue decrees against Bihar'.[118]

By now, the constituent assembly's work was approaching a climax, and it was the language question that remained a livewire right to the end. There was some talk about putting in a proviso that 'Hindi numerals can be used wherever the President considers necessary', while UP's Purushottamdas Tandon proposed that 'provinces using one language may communicate with each other in that language'.[119] In the canvassing for the Amritsar by-election, it had emerged as an electoral point for the Akalis as also for the Namdharis, led by Maharaj Partap Singh, a co-worker of Gandhi. The Namdharis[120] loyal to the Congress before 1947 were being neutral, while the party's allied Akalis had 'decided to oppose' its candidate.[121]

With the end of constitution-making in sight, the proposal to dissolve the assembly and have a general election based on the existing provincial assemblies was floated again. This time it met with the powerful opposition of Rajendra Prasad, who began with the technical reason that all the states did not have legislatures before moving to the representational, namely, 'difficulty regarding Muslims, Christians and Sikhs', as with separate electorates gone, 'these communities will have a just grievance that this general election is being resorted to in order to get rid of their representatives … mostly independent from Congress Party'.[122] The chairman ended with a significant observation that back in 1945–46, Congress could have prominent and helpful non-party men elected, but not now, thereby making the new house a yet more one-party assembly. If Nehru's object was 'to bring some fresh blood', Prasad thought that it could be served by replacing 'those members who are also provincial [legislators]'.[123]

Such regular reminders about the nature of the state came most starkly from Nehru's own UP, where in August 1949, Kanpur and Jhansi saw possession being taken of houses of Muslims because a member of the family had left for Pakistan. Premier Pandit Govind Ballabh Pant held that with the ordinance passed, one needed to accept the fact that Partition had split up families, and while he was urged to interpret the ordinance 'reasonably', what took place on the ground was 'a competition in more and more severe action'.[124] September 1949 broadened the scope of this severity as the economy suffered the shock of the British devaluation of the pound sterling by over 30 per cent vis-à-vis the American dollar, with India forced to follow suit.[125] It necessitated cabinet meetings on three successive days, with Dr Matthai stressing cutting down public expenditure for the next two financial years and making the following proposals:

> [In] the revenue budget for 1949–50, each ministry should surrender 10% of TA … 5% of pay and DA and 20% of development expenditure. [For] the capital budget for 1949–50, each ministry should surrender 20%.… Schemes sanctioned … should be re-examined.… Additional demands should … be met out of savings. [In] the capital budget for 1950–51, the total outlay [to] be Rs. 100 crores.[126]

To overcome any disagreements, Matthai also suggested formation of a committee consisting of Nehru, Patel and himself. On cuts in government salaries, Matthai preferred 'a 10% reduction all round, reducing procurement price, incidental charges, ex-factory price, distribution cost'.[127] In the third meeting, Jairamdas Doulatram stated that while it was possible to achieve a 5 per cent reduction by reducing incidental changes, for the other 5 per cent he suggested granting subsidy as provinces opposed any reduction in procurement prices unless accompanied by a price reduction of essential commodities. Following him, Dr Mookerjee opined the possibility of reducing the price of cloth by 10 per cent, and so the cabinet decided to instruct provincial food ministers accordingly. This third meeting was also attended by S. Varadachariar (chairman, IT investigation commission) and two of his commissioners, who claimed that they might recover from all the cases 'about 50 crores' in about 2–3 years and sought the 'power of search in [princely] states',[128] apart from additional staff. A statement on the activities of anti-corruption departments in the provinces for the quarter ending 30 September 1949 is a telling survey here:

> *Madras*: number of case investigated (79), number of government servants involved (4), number of members of public involved (0), number of cases sent up for trial (37), number of cases ending in conviction (1), number of cases ending in acquittal (45), sums of mercy involved (33,795/-), remarks: either no evidence or false accusations in 42/45 cases; *Bombay*: (172), (95), (212), (96), (43), (5), (77,538/-), besides 25 cases under enquiry, 39 cases pending, 7 cases dealt with departmentally, 1 case closed; *West Bengal*: (182), (194), (40), (25), (4), (10), (68,195/-), besides 4 cases ending in conviction, 21 cases sent for departmental action. Of these, 9 punishments; *Punjab*: (31), (18), (1), (0), (3), (3), (3000/-), besides this, departmental actions against 14 officials; *UP*: (7), (21), (0), (0), (0), (0), (7889/-); *Bihar*: *Report from this state is never received*; *MP*: (92), (67), (14), (7), (5), (4), (48851/-), out of 92 cases, 25 black-marketing, 40 bribery, 22 criminal misappropriation and 4 cheating; *Assam*: (19), (15), (1), (2), (0), (0), most enquiries on anonymous petitions and pending; *Orissa*: (8), (3), (6), (1), (0), (0), (28,435/-), besides these, enquiries made in 17 cases; *Ajmer*: (9), (12), (0), (3), (0), (0), (2910/-), enquiries made in 14 cases.[129]

In October 1949, a Delhi business deputation, headed by Lala Hans Raj Gupta and Jaipal Mal Gupta, met the prime minister and gave a memorandum, which conveyed their feeling that the IT department worked on the assumption that every businessman was guilty. In the investigation commission, the integrity of its chairman and commissioners apart, 'many of the junior officers employed were making money', and 'while large number of cases were started, very few succeeded', suggesting that 'the only successful method would be to seek the cooperation of the trader'.[130] Indeed, even Chairman Varadachariar suggested the appointment of a judge on the commission to give an option for voluntary declaration of undisclosed profits. All these matters would wait until Nehru returned from his maiden prime ministerial visit to America in November 1949, but underneath them was his gathering insistence on planning[131] for his equally reluctant finance minister, not to mention the deputy prime minister. Keenly however he felt its 'necessity'; he could not 'take a step in a hurry'.[132]

Instead, he informed Matthai about S. A. Trone, an engineer-economist, and suggested extending his stay in India as a roving advisory-expert, listing Trone's work experience in America, China, Japan and the Soviet Union. On Gandhi's 80th birthday, the celebrations of which were overshadowed by Britain's devaluation, and Pakistan's refusal to do so, as 90 per cent of India's trade was with these two countries, this meant that either its value fell, as in the former case, or it came to a standstill, as with the latter. Meanwhile, the remorseless questions of evacuee property were being answered by intended evacuees making 'remittances [to Pakistan] in preparation', showing that 'talk of a secular state had no reality in fact'.[133] This enforced economic downturn, and the existing social unrest saw the Madras government emulating West Bengal in banning the CPI even as three deputations came to New Delhi demanding a Telugu-speaking Andhra area.[134] If this matter was dragging, then so was that old question of the national anthem, with many assembly members insisting that 'the Constitution should not contain any reference' to it, in a way leaving a revolving door.[135]

Away from all this, Orissa was seeking to restructure its cultivating land by getting the eastern states' princes, local feudals and big farmers to contribute on a 50:50 basis, thus circumventing land reforms. But the Asaf Ali and Harekrushna Mahtab combine in Cuttack needed loans from New Delhi, and Matthai was requested to consider these 'from the political point of view'.[136] Simultaneously, when Jairamdas Doulatram cautioned against stopping all rice import, irrespective of the foreign exchange crisis, Nehru demanded an attempt to replace rice with wheat. India's food crisis has been on and off since 1939, and while the overall annual crops were 'good' since 1946, the non-rice-eating areas did not get much of it, whereas in rice-eating Bengal, the ration allowed, 12 ounces, had not been fully consumed. As 'a concession … 100,000 tons of rice … as a reserve' was to be imported from Southeast Asia, and the rationing was to be reduced, given that 'in Delhi only about 80% [was] consumed'.[137]

This economic downturn did not mean, however, that the existing socio-political fault-lines somehow receded. The prime minister's old concerns about the army not mixing with the press and politics grew anew when he was told by Premier Kher that General Cariappa had agreed to attend a function connected with a *vyayamshala* around Poona. This institute was 'connected with the [Sangh]', and a nonplussed Kher had asked for Cariappa to consult governments in the future 'before drawing up a programme in their province'.[138] Cariappa continued to be a fly in the civilian leadership's ointment and gave a message to journalist D. F. Karaka's newspaper, 'a most undesirable type' from the other end of the ideological spectrum.[139] Meanwhile, East Punjab continued to see personal rivalry in its ministry, when Premier Sachar found it difficult to continue and his predecessor Bhargava (1947–49) returned to be his successor (1949–51). Nehru could not interfere but conveyed his concerns to Patel that 'the services are demoralised, schemes like the Bhakra dam [will] suffer [and], the new capital will remain in the air'.[140]

This was also often the case in the application of the evacuee property ordinance,[141] where people like the jurist Abdur Rahman and Mrs M. A. Ansari, 'the widow of one of the greatest fighters for India's freedom',[142] were treated shockingly. The former's case was not so straightforward. From 1915, he had been attached to Dr Ansari in Delhi, and later, he became a High Court judge in Madras, being transferred to Lahore afterwards. In 1947, Nehru's ministry nominated him as India's representative on the UN's Palestine Commission, and while he was there, Partition took place. He wished 'to opt for India', but by the time he returned, there was no place for him in East Punjab. After serving for a brief period in Lahore, he retired to London, from where he sought his movable property, requiring an exception to be made.[143]

From the other partitioned end, Dr B. C. Roy was firing back at New Delhi. Disagreeing with the prime minister that the central government gave Bengal a big grant for refugee rehabilitation, Roy distinguished the grant of INR 3 crores in 1948–49 and 1949–50 from the INR 5 crores given as a loan and contrasted them adversely against what was spent for 16 lakh refugees at about INR 20 per person over this time. Warming up to his theme, Roy claimed that his ministry's expenditure for 1949–50 was an estimated INR 47,500,000 in which INR 1.75 crores was grant and the rest loan. Further, he had requested a loan for the dispersal of students from Calcutta. Recalling that Partition left West Bengal with a deficit of INR 2.5 crores, he reminded Nehru that in March 1948, Calcutta's share of income tax receipts was brought down from 20 per cent to 12 per cent (INR 6 to 3.5 crores), while Bombay's share was enhanced. This despite both making similar contributions to the tax pool, with the reason offered being the small size of West Bengal, but the East Bengal areas had contributed only 5 per cent of undivided Bengal's revenues, while now the former was a border state, requiring infrastructure. Then there was the movement of 1.5 million people,[144] and Roy charged the centre with 'vacillating policies' and demanded a loan in 'a gentle warning'.[145]

Nehru accepted that the expenditure on those coming from West Pakistan had been much greater than those coming from East Pakistan, but so was the scale and pace of this movement, and the CWC was 'convinced that West Bengal required a psychological approach'.[146] Roy did not let up, and despite Patel, Rajagopalachari, Abul Kalam Azad and Bengal's governor K. N. Katju discussing assembly elections or personnel changes in Roy's ministry and in Bengal Congress, with the economic downturn and a sluggish constituent assembly, New Delhi was urging 'consensus',[147] especially as Katju confirmed that there was 'unanimity of not having elections in the middle of 1950'.[148]

In the big middle between Punjab and Bengal, the sugar business in UP and whether to control or decontrol it was the key dilemma on which provincial premiers and the sugar syndicate preferred the latter, raising concerns about their reciprocal relationship. This sugar question and the 'vocal middle classes' on it were something of a puzzle for the prime minister.[149] Apart from sugar and services, the third big lobby, economically significant in this serious financial situation, was around defence expenditure. Before Nehru went to America in November 1949, he had met with Cariappa, Baldev Singh and H. M. Patel, when Singh had hoped to reduce the then-defence expenditure of INR 157 crores, amounting to more than half of the government's revenue, by 5 crores. By the time Nehru returned, the defence expenditure had instead increased to INR 171 crores. Now, a reduction of INR 20 crores was sought, with the accompanying necessity to demobilise[150] 150,000 soldiers from an army of 500,000.[151]

With the army going to be reduced thus, any reinstatement of ex-INA men was out of the question. As one of them, Major-General J. K. Bhonsle, was reminded, 'vast numbers of our comrades who lost their all in the 30 years struggle for India's freedom have not been helped'.[152] Meanwhile, despite these attempts at economising, the finance minister was feeling sidelined, and, in light of the differences on the upcoming planning commission, he urged Nehru to reconsider his position.[153] But this was no time to exit the government when there was a contentious 'ejectment of cultivators and tenants from their holdings' in the border districts of Ferozepur and Amritsar.[154] And so, ushering in the new year of 1950 with the coming of the republic, the prime minister set out the government's, the party's and the provinces' challenges:

> We become more and more governmental.… After January 26th, we shall have an old-new Parliament and about a hundred new members will come.… Might I encourage the return of members of the Scheduled-Castes.… I remind you of the 'grow-more-food' campaign but please do not look to the Centre always…[155]

NOTES

1   See R. J. Moore, *Making the New Commonwealth* (Oxford: Clarendon, 1987); and Sunil Purushotham, 'Jawaharlal Nehru, Indian Republicanism, and the Commonwealth', in *Commonwealth History in the Twenty-First Century*, ed. Saul Dubow and Richard Drayton (London: Palgrave Macmillan, 2020), 143–59.
2   17 May 1949, Nehru to Pandit, File No. 23 (Part II), JN (SG) Papers.
3   Rohit De and Ornit Shani, 'Assembling India's Constitution: Towards a New History', *Past and Present* gtad009 (2023).
4   1 April 1949, Nehru to provincial premiers, File No. 22 (Part I), JN (SG) Papers.
5   24 May 1949, Nehru to Cariappa, File No. 23 (Part II), JN (SG) Papers.
6   Anit Mukherjee, *The Absent Dialogue: Politicians, Bureaucrats, and the Military in India* (New Delhi: Oxford University Press, 2019), 38–96.
7   31 May 1949, Nehru to Cariappa, File No. 23 (Part II), JN (SG) Papers.

8   8 April 1949, Nehru to V. P. Menon, File No. 22 (Part I), JN (SG) Papers. See A. M. Khusro, *Economic and Social Effects of Jagirdari Abolition and Land Reforms in Hyderabad* (Hyderabad: Osmania University Press, 1958).

9   10 April 1949, Nehru to J. N. Chaudhuri, File No. 22 (Part I), JN (SG) Papers.

10   K. Datla, 'A Worldly Vernacular: Urdu at Osmania University', *Modern Asian Studies* 43, no. 5 (2009): 1117–48.

11   2 May 1949, John Boyd Orr to Nehru, File No. 23 (Part I), JN (SG) Papers.

12   19 April 1949, Tara Singh to Nehru and Patel, File No. 23 (Part I), JN (SG) Papers.

13   10 May 1949, Nehru to Tara Singh and 13 May 1949, Nehru to Trivedi, File No. 23 (Part I), JN (SG) Papers.

14   See G. S. Bhargava, *Bhim Sen Sachar: An Intimate Biography* (New Delhi: Har Anand, 1997).

15   L. R. Vagale, B. M. Bhuta and M. S. V. Rao, 'Faridabad: A Critical Study of the New Town', *Ekistics* 10, no. 59 (1960): 156–65.

16   13 and 25 May 1949, Nehru to Sachar, File No. 23 (Part I and II), JN (SG) Papers.

17   Sekhar Bandyopadhyay, 'Freedom and Its Enemies: The Politics of Transition in West Bengal, 1947–1949', *South Asia: Journal of South Asian Studies* 29, no. 1 (2006): 43–68.

18   13 May 1949, Nehru to Roy, File No. 23 (Part I), JN (SG) Papers.

19   19 and 23 May 1949, Roy–Nehru exchange, File No. 23 (Part II), JN (SG) Papers.

20   14 May 1949, Nehru to provincial premiers, File No. 23 (Part I) and 22 May 1949, Nehru to Roy and Prasad, File No. 23 (Part II), JN (SG) Papers.

21   15 May 1949, Nehru to Sachar, File No. 23 (Part I), JN (SG) Papers.

22   S. M. Haider, 'Social Organisation of the Refugees in Bhopal State', *Sociological Bulletin* 6, no. 1 (1957): 61–71.

23   19 May 1949, Nehru to Saksena, File No. 23 (Part II), JN (SG) Papers.

24   18 May 1949, Nehru to Bardoloi, File No. 23 (Part II), JN (SG) Papers.

25   18 May 1949, Nehru to Matthai and other ministers, File No. 23 (Part II), JN (SG) Papers.

26   18 May 1949, Nehru to Ambedkar, File No. 23 (Part II), JN (SG) Papers.

27   Santosh Suradkar, '*Mukti Kon Pathe*? Caste and Class in Ambedkar's Struggle', *Economic and Political Weekly* 52, no. 49 (2017): 61–68.

28   17 May 1949, Ambedkar to Kher, File No. 23 (Part II), JN (SG) Papers.

29   21 May 1949, Nehru's note on Hyderabad and Kashmir, File No. 23 (Part II), JN (SG) Papers.

30   Rohit De, 'Rebellion, Dacoity, and Equality: The Emergence of the Constitutional Field in Postcolonial India', *Comparative Studies of South Asia, Africa and the Middle East* 34, no. 2 (2014): 260–78.

31   22 May 1949, Nehru to J. N. Chaudhuri, File No. 23 (Part II), JN (SG) Papers.

32   23 May and 2 June 1949, Nehru to PPS, File Nos. 23 (Part II) and 24 (Part I), JN (SG) Papers.

33   4 June 1949, Nehru to Patel, File No. 24 (Part I), JN (SG) Papers.

34   I. Thirumali, 'The Political Pragmatism of the Communists in Telangana, 1938–48', *Social Scientist* 24, nos. 4/6 (1996): 164–83.

35   13 June 1949, Patel to Nehru, File No. 24 (Part I), JN (SG) Papers.

36   25 May 1949, Nehru to Ayyangar, File No. 23 (Part II), JN (SG) Papers.

37   27 May 1949, Nehru to PPS, File No. 23 (Part II), JN (SG) Papers. See L. Bear, *Lines of the Nation: Indian Railway Workers, Bureaucracy, and the Intimate Historical Self* (New York: Columbia University Press, 2007).

38   5 June 1949, Nehru to PPS and Patel, File No. 24 (Part I), JN (SG) Papers. See S. S. Mendes, 'Jawaharlal Nehru and the Liberation Struggle of Goa', *Proceedings of the Indian History Congress* 67 (2006–07): 549–55.

39   4 June 1949, Patel to Nehru, File No. 24 (Part I), JN (SG) Papers.

40   13 June 1949, Nehru to Patel, File No. 24 (Part I), JN (SG) Papers.

41   6 June 1949, Nehru to Sri Prakasa, File No. 24 (Part I), JN (SG) Papers.

42   31 May 1949, Nehru to Saksena, File No. 23 (Part II), JN (SG) Papers.

43   Aparna Basu, *Mridula Sarabhai: Rebel with a Cause* (New Delhi: Oxford University Press, 1996), 100–34.

44   3 June 1949, Nehru to Saksena, File No. 24 (Part I), JN (SG) Papers.

45   Maria Framke, 'The Politics of Gender and Community: Non-Governmental Relief in Late Colonial and Early Postcolonial India', in *Gendering Global Humanitarianism in the Twentieth Century Practice, Politics and the Power of Representation*, ed. E. Moller, J. Paulmann and K. Stornig (London: Palgrave Macmillan, 2020), 143–66.

46   6 June 1949, Nehru to Saksena, File No. 24 (Part I), JN (SG) Papers.

47   8 June 1949, Nehru to Saksena and 10 June 1949, Nehru to PPS, File No. 24 (Part I and II), JN (SG) Papers.

48   13 June 1949, Nehru to Kher, File No. 24 (Part I), JN (SG) Papers.

49   6 June 1949, Nehru to M. C. Khanna, File No. 24 (Part II), JN (SG) Papers.

50   8 June 1949, Nehru to Khanna, File No. 24 (Part II), JN (SG) Papers.

51   13 June 1949, Nehru to Bajpai, File No. 24 (Part I), JN (SG) Papers.

52   2 June 1949, Nehru to Patel and 5 June 1949, Nehru to A. V. Thakkar, File No. 24 (Part I), JN (SG) Papers.

53   5 June 1949, Nehru to Home Ministry, File No. 24 (Part I), JN (SG) Papers. See Nomita Yadav, 'Other Backward Classes: Then and Now', *Economic and Political Weekly* 37, nos. 44/45 (2002): 4495–4500.

54   4 June 1949, Prasad to Nehru, File No. 24 (Part I), JN (SG) Papers.

55   See Robert D. King, 'The Poisonous Potency of Script: Hindi and Urdu', *International Journal of the Sociology of Language* 150 (August 2001): 43–59.

56   5 June 1949, Nehru to Prasad, File No. 24 (Part I), JN (SG) Papers.

57   See S. K. Bose, *Sarat Chandra Bose: Remembering My Father* (Kolkata: Netaji Research Bureau, 2014). 5 June 1949, Nehru's statement, File No. 24 (Part I), JN (SG) Papers.

58   7 June 1949, Nehru to Kala Venkatarao, File No. 24 (Part II), JN (SG) Papers.

59   14 June 1949, Roy to Nehru, File No. 24 (Part II), JN (SG) Papers.

60   14 June 1949, Nehru to Patel, File No. 24 (Part II), JN (SG) Papers. See Arun K. Jana, 'Confronting the "Congress System" in West Bengal: Electoral Strategies

of the CPI in the 1950s', *Journal of Political Studies* 12 (March–October 2016): 1–20.

61 14 June 1949, Anonymous letter from Calcutta to Prasad, File No. 25 (Part I), JN (SG) Papers.

62 17 June 1949, Nehru to Patel, File No. 25 (Part I), JN (SG) Papers.

63 5 June 1949, Nehru to premiers and 8 June 1949, Nehru to Sachar, File No. 24 (Part I and II), JN (SG) Papers.

64 8 June 1949, Nehru to Ambedkar, File No. 24 (Part II), JN (SG) Papers. See Chitra Sinha, *Debating Patriarchy: The Hindu Code Bill Controversy in India (1941–1956)* (Oxford: Oxford University Press, 2012), 133–77.

65 See David J. Matthews, 'Urdu Language and Education in India', *Social Scientist* 31, nos. 5/6 (2003): 57–72; and Sudha Pai, 'Politics of Language: Decline of Urdu in Uttar Pradesh', *Economic and Political Weekly* 37, no. 27 (2002): 2705–08.

66 10 June 1949, Nehru to Pant, File No. 24 (Part I), JN (SG) Papers.

67 14 June 1949, Nehru to Sachar, File No. 24 (Part II), JN (SG) Papers.

68 Holden Furber, 'The Unification of India, 1947–1951', *Pacific Affairs* 24, no. 4 (1951): 352–71.

69 15 June 1949, Nehru to provincial premiers and Krishna Menon, File No. 24 (Part II), JN (SG) Papers.

70 15 June 1949, Nehru to Khanna, and 18 June 1949, Nehru to Saksena, File No. 24 (Part II) and File No. 25 (Part I), JN (SG) Papers.

71 21 June 1949, Nehru to Patel, File No. 25 (Part I), JN (SG) Papers.

72 15 June 1949, Nehru to PPS, File No. 24 (Part II), JN (SG) Papers. See Björn Hettne, *The Political Economy of Indirect Rule: Mysore 1881–1947* (London: Curzon Press, 1978).

73 18 June 1949, Nehru to States Ministry, File No. 25 (Part I), JN (SG) Papers.

74 18 June 1949, Nehru to Sinha, File No. 25 (Part I), JN (SG) Papers.

75 19 June 1949, Nehru to Kher, File No. 25 (Part I), JN (SG) Papers.

76 21 June 1949, Nehru to Mookerjee, and 27 June 1949, Nehru to Desai, File No. 25 (Part I and II), JN (SG) Papers.

77 21 June 1949, Nehru to Matthai, File No. 25 (Part I), JN (SG) Papers.

78 27 June 1949, Nehru to Kidwai, File No. 25 (Part II), JN (SG) Papers.

79 21 June 1949, Nehru to Patel, File No. 25 (Part I), JN (SG) Papers.

80 23 and 29 June 1949, Patel–Nehru exchange, File No. 25 (Part II), JN (SG) Papers.

81 23 June 1949, Nehru to Sachar, File No. 25 (Part II), JN (SG) Papers.

82 22 and 28 June 1949, Nehru to Roy, File No. 25 (Part II), JN (SG) Papers.

83 27 June 1949, Nehru to Sarkar, and 28 June 1949, Nehru to Home Ministry, File No. 25 (Part II), JN (SG) Papers.

84 29 June 1949, Nehru to Krishna Menon, File No. 25 (Part II), JN (SG) Papers.

85 29 and 30 June 1949, Nehru to Patel, File No. 25 (Part II), JN (SG) Papers.

86 1 and 2 July 1949, Nehru to Sarkar, File No. 26 (Part I), JN (SG) Papers.

87 1 July 1949, Nehru to Jairamdas Doulatram, File No. 26 (Part I), JN (SG) Papers.

88 See A. Mayer and R. L. Park, *Pilot Project, India: The Story of Rural Development at Etawah, Uttar Pradesh* (Berkeley: University of California Press, 1958);

and Deepa Ramaswamy, 'Making a Self-Reliant Citizen: Technocracy, Rural Redevelopment and the Etawah Pilot', *Journal of Planning History* 22, no. 1 (2022): 68–82.

89   2 July 1949, Nehru to premiers, File No. 26 (Part I), JN (SG) Papers.

90   Baldev Raj Nayar, *Minority Politics in the Punjab* (Princeton: Princeton University Press, 1966), 57–119.

91   9 July 1949, Sachar to Nehru, File No. 26 (Part I), JN (SG) Papers.

92   11 July 1949, Kher to Nehru, File No. 26 (Part I), JN (SG) Papers. See Harold A. Crouch, *Trade Unions and Politics in India* (Bombay: Manaktala, 1966), 78–96.

93   10 July 1949, Nehru to Mookerjee, File No. 26 (Part I), JN (SG) Papers.

94   12 July 1949, Home Ministry to provincial governments, No. 40623, File No. 26 (Part I), JN (SG) Papers.

95   16 July 1949, Nehru to Krishna Menon, File No. 26 (Part I), JN (SG) Papers.

96   20 July 1949, Nehru to Kher, and 21 July 1949, Nehru to Rajagopalachari, File No. 26 (Part II), JN (SG) Papers.

97   20 July 1949, Nehru to provincial premiers, File No. 26 (Part II), JN (SG) Papers.

98   21–22 July 1949, Nehru to Patel, File No. 26 (Part II), JN (SG) Papers. See Satya M. Rai, *Partition of the Punjab: A Study of Its Effects on the Politics and Administration of the Punjab (I) 1947–56* (Bombay: Asia Publishing House, 1965), 218–51.

99   Kavita Datla, *The Language of Secular Islam: Urdu Nationalism and Colonial India* (Honolulu: University of Hawaii Press 2013), 106–37.

100   25 July 1949, Kher to Nehru, File No. 26 (Part II), JN (SG) Papers.

101   25 July 1949, Nehru to Gadgil and to Sachar, File No. 26 (Part II), JN (SG) Papers.

102   27 July 1949, Nehru to Raja, File No. 26 (Part II), JN (SG) Papers. See J. G. Leonard, 'Politics and Social Change in South India: A Study of the Andhra Movement', *Journal of Commonwealth Political Studies* 5, no. 1 (1967): 60–77.

103   27 July 1949, Nehru to Saksena, File No. 26 (Part II), JN (SG) Papers. See Ian Talbot, 'Punjabi Refugees' Rehabilitation and the Indian State: Discourses, Denials and Dissonances', *Modern Asian Studies* 45, no. 1 (2011): 109–30.

104   27 July 1949, Nehru to H. V. R. Iengar, File No. 26 (Part II), JN (SG) Papers.

105   30 July 1949, Nehru to Paul Ruegger (International Red Cross), File No. 26 (Part II), JN (SG) Papers.

106   31 July 1949, Nehru to Neogy, File No. 26 (Part II), JN (SG) Papers.

107   26 August 1949, Nehru to Doulatram, File No. 28, JN (SG) Papers.

108   29 September 1949, Nehru to Doulatram, File No. 30, JN (SG) Papers.

109   4 December 1949, Nehru to Doulatram, File No. 32 (Part I), JN (SG) Papers. See Sanjaya Baru, *The Political Economy of Indian Sugar: The Political Economy of Sugar in India—State, International and Structural Change* (Oxford: Oxford University Press, 1990).

110   1 August 1949, Nehru to premiers, File No. 27 (Part I), JN (SG) Papers.

111   13 August 1949, Nehru to Saksena, File No. 27 (Part II), JN (SG) Papers.

112 7 August 1949, Nehru's notes for fortnightly letter, File No. 27 (Part I), JN (SG) Papers. See David C. Potter, 'Jawaharlal Nehru and the Indian Civil Service', *South Asia Research* 9, no. 2 (1989): 128–44.

113 24 August 1949, Nehru to Krishna Menon, File No. 28, JN (SG) Papers.

114 12 August 1949, Nehru to Krishna Menon, File No. 27 (Part II) and File No. 28, JN (SG) Papers. See S. Kana, 'Voluntarism in Partition's Aftermath: The Faridabad Story', *Contemporary South Asia* 31, no. 1 (2023): 1–18.

115 15 August 1949, Nehru to premiers, File No. 27 (Part II), JN (SG) Papers.

116 21 August 1949, Nehru's note, File No. 28, JN (SG) Papers.

117 M. F. Franda, *West Bengal, and the Federalizing Process in India* (Princeton: Princeton University Press, 1968), 8–61.

118 25 August 1949, Nehru to Nalini Ranjan Sarkar, File No. 28, JN (SG) Papers.

119 23 August 1949, Nehru to Gopalaswami Ayyangar, File No. 28, JN (SG) Papers.

120 B. Maingi, 'Politics of Minority Communities of Punjab: A Case Study of the Namdhari Sikhs', *Proceedings of the Indian History Congress* 69 (2008): 1243–53.

121 24 August 1949, Nehru to Sachar, File No. 28, JN (SG) Papers.

122 29 August 1949, Prasad to Nehru, File No. 28, JN (SG) Papers.

123 29 August 1949, Prasad to Nehru, File No. 28, JN (SG) Papers. See Stanley Kochanek, *The Congress Party of India: The Dynamics of a One-Party Democracy* (Princeton: Princeton University Press, 1968), 3–26.

124 29 August 1949, Nehru to Saksena, File No. 28, JN (SG) Papers.

125 Rakesh Ankit, "De-linking "the Two Rupees": Devaluation Dilemma and Economic Divergence in the Decolonised Subcontinent, September 1949–February 1951', *Modern Asian Studies* 57, no. 3 (2023): 918–39.

126 26 September 1949, Cabinet meeting (330/44/49), File No. 30, JN (SG) Papers.

127 27 September 1949, Cabinet meeting (331–6/45/49), File No. 30, JN (SG) Papers.

128 28 September 1949, Cabinet meeting (337–9/46/49), File No. 30, JN (SG) Papers. See N. Tyabji, *Forging Capitalism in Nehru's India: Neocolonialism and the State, c. 1940–1970* (New Delhi: Oxford University Press, 2015), ch. 4.

129 Emphasis in original; File No. 37/61/49-PII, 1949 (MHA, Police II), NAI.

130 3 October 1949, Nehru to Matthai, File No. 30, JN (SG) Papers.

131 See Medha Kudaisya, '"A Mighty Adventure": Institutionalising the Idea of Planning in Post-colonial India, 1947–60', *Modern Asian Studies* 43, no. 4 (2009): 939–78.

132 29 September 1949, Nehru to Matthai, File No. 30, JN (SG) Papers.

133 2 October 1949, Nehru to provincial premiers, File No. 30, JN (SG) Papers.

134 2 October 1949, Nehru's note on linguistic provinces to Patel, File No. 30, JN (SG) Papers.

135 2 October 1949, Nehru's note on national anthem to Patel, File No. 30, JN (SG) Papers.

136 3 October 1949, Nehru to Matthai, File No. 30, JN (SG) Papers.

137 3 October 1949, Nehru to Doulatram, File No. 30, JN (SG) Papers.

138 17 November 1949, Nehru to Cariappa, File No. 51 (Part I), JN (SG) Paper.

139   On Karaka, see Rotem Geva, 'Torn Between the Nation and the World: D. F. Karaka and Indian Journalism in the Second World War', *Modern Asian Studies* 57, no. 5 (2023): 1459–94. See also Lloyd I. Rudolph and Susanne H. Rudolph, 'Generals and Politicians in India', *Pacific Affairs* 37, no. 1 (1964): 5–19.

140   19 November 1949, Nehru to Patel, File No. 51 (Part I), JN (SG) Papers.

141   1 December 1949, Nehru to premiers, File No. 32 (Part I), JN (SG) Papers.

142   M. Hasan, *A Nationalist Conscience: M. A. Ansari, the Congress, and the Raj* (New Delhi: Manohar, 1987).

143   2 December 1949, Nehru's note, File No. 32 (Part I), JN (SG) Papers.

144   Chatterji, *The Spoils of Partition*, 105–58.

145   1 December 1949, Roy to Nehru, DO No. 757/C, File No. 32 (Part I), JN (SG) Papers.

146   2 December 1949, Nehru to Roy, File No. 32 (Part I), JN (SG) Papers.

147   25 December 1949, Nehru to Roy (copy to Rajaji, Patel, Katju and Azad), File No. 33, JN (SG) Papers.

148   7 January 1950, Nehru's note on West Bengal elections, File No. 34, JN (SG) Papers.

149   27 December 1949, Nehru to Pant, File No. 33, JN (SG) Papers.

150   28 December 1949, Nehru to Cariappa, and 30 December 1949, Nehru to PPS, File No. 33, JN (SG) Papers.

151   4 January 1950, Nehru to PMS, File No. 34, JN (SG) Papers. See Mukherjee, *The Absent Dialogue*, 97–136.

152   7 December 1949, Nehru to Bhonsle (copied to Patel), File No. 32 (Part I), JN (SG) Papers.

153   29 December 1949, Nehru to Matthai, File No. 33, JN (SG) Papers.

154   30 December 1949, Nehru to Bhargava, File No. 33, JN (SG) Papers.

155   31 December 1949, Nehru to provincial premiers, File No. 33, JN (SG) Papers.

3

1950

Figure 3.1 Union cabinet ministers with the president, January 1950
Source: Historic Collection/Alamy Stock Photo.

A 'BALANCE SHEET ...'

Until the start of 1950, the interim government was carrying all within and before it. That critical year though, as this chapter shows, was the crucible that saw non-Congress members leave the cabinet, while the party's turf war came to the fore, outlining the upcoming electoral battle. These ideological tussles and individual contests inside the party and the cabinet are explored here, with the India–Pakistan Minority Pact providing an analogy to wider socio-cultural tensions. That year was also climactic for Nehru–Patel differences on Congress organisation and China, which this time 'were papered over' by Patel's death.[1] Within a week of the new year, there were ominous signs when the Faridabad township project was effectively trifurcated between cooperatives (1,000 houses), contractors (2,000) and East Punjab public works (1,000). These houses were meant to be ready by June, but now, there were apprehensions all around.[2] There was some ambiguity around the coming of the republic, which had been passive and somewhat inert in its immediate substance. After all, the premiers, with their ministries, were to continue under a new name – chief minister – and under a different oath of allegiance. In the old-new central parliament, very few women and Scheduled Caste members had come in and the Akalis had refused to accept this constitution, while the Hindu right-wing groups had 'declared their condemnation'.[3]

Moreover, the challenges coming in the last days of the old constitution cast a shadow over the first days of the new. From London, D. N. Pritt, the lawyer-legislator, was making representations on the summary death sentence by a military court in Hyderabad to '108 peasants and communists'. Pritt held that the said trial was rather a court martial, as the advocate-general acted for both the prosecution and the defence, while mercy petitions did not reach the nizam's privy council. Their executions were arranged for 23 January, so as to prevent the appeals from reaching the Supreme Court, and Pritt requested the central government to stop any executions before 26 January. Especially highlighted were the death sentences for two children, one of whom was 11-year-old Dina Lingayya. Pritt and his allies had their own channels of information, including British nationals returning from Hyderabad, who brought forth scandalous snippets like '30 [prisoners] were sentenced to death in November, 78 more recently, 50 others to imprisonment up to 50 years [and] 13 are to be executed on 22nd [January]'.[4] Dismissing most of Pritt's objections as 'unreliable',[5] Nehru declined to oblige.

The last few days leading up to 26 January 1950 were indeed rather extraordinary. On the one hand, refugee camps in Kurukshetra and Delhi were grappling with the medical treatment of patients before they were shut down.[6] On the other hand, Patel's Home Ministry was wondering when and whether to cut the umbilical cord of the Telugu-speaking districts of Madras province, given a lack of agreement on its financial implications, especially the Tungabhadra river scheme.[7] On the administrative side of things, superannuation was hanging over many officials, but with little talent 'to lose' at a passage of 'great need', the cabinet decided to extend some age limits, accepting the 'danger of patronage being exercised improperly'.[8]

Then, with the princely integration into the Indian union more or less over bar the outstanding cases, it was time to reward their *rajpramukh*s in terms of allowances, with the rates being fixed as follows: 'Saurashtra: 6.16 lakhs per annum, Madhya Bharat: 2 ½ lakhs, PEPSU: 5 lakhs, Rajasthan: 5 lakhs [and] Travancore-Cochin: 3 lakhs'.[9] The ruler of Kashmir was out of this, while the nizam of Hyderabad was above such handouts.[10] And, at the new-old Federal Supreme Court, Chief Justice H. J. Kania sent down a shocker by taking up an attitude of resistance to Justice Bashir Ahmed's appointment at the Madras High Court. An agitated Nehru wondered if Kania deserved his own post, and in Bashir's case, he had support from Rajagopalachari. Nehru even wrote to Patel to 'ask Kania to resign' and, while this did not happen, the outgoing governor-general and the incoming prime minister overruled Kania and elevated Bashir Ahmed as 'a permanent judge of the Madras High Court'.[11]

The Rajagopalachari–Nehru relationship was rather strong at this time, and the former was approached to be the first chairman of the planning commission (with C. D. Deshmukh and G. L. Nanda as its members), a fact ironic in light of Rajagopalachari's later critiques.[12] Once India became a republic, the prime minister 'drew up a balance sheet' of work since August 1947 in which the integration of the states was a considerable credit, while the debit side had the major entries of no food nor general election. However, the mere fact of carrying on was 'no mean achievement'.[13] As for the general election, it depended on provincial preparations of electoral rolls and others. An election commission with an autonomous chief commissioner was yet to be appointed, and another complication was the census that was due for early 1951. It was clear that the election would be postponed until winter 1950.[14]

Anyway, from London, Krishna Menon was sending cautionary notes to remind that underneath mass enthusiasm for elections was the matter of careful candidate selection; otherwise, 'most countries have had to have a dictatorship in their transitions'.[15] For him, as for Rajagopalachari in New Delhi, selection by Patel and Nehru was the only possibility, since these candidates would be winning in the latter's name, as previously they had done in Gandhi's. They knew that it was as the government that the party would be contesting, for non-party ministers like Gopalaswami Ayyangar were struggling in the existing parliament. On the immigrants (expulsion from Assam) bill, the socialist N. G. Ranga challenged the government, and Babu Ram Narain Singh told Ayyangar that in such emotive matters, 'reasonableness [was] interpreted as cowardice', and if still the restraining bill was passed, it was because the vociferous opposition was also most anxious 'to continue' in the house.[16]

On the other hand, in the largest provincial assembly, that of UP, every question was being viewed from the 'party angle', in the 'tug-of-war' between Pant and Kidwai factions,[17] in which Nehru could make little difference. Meanwhile, New Delhi continued to be the scene of the old skulduggery around the working of the evacuee property ordinance. Maulana Hifz-ul Rahman gave many instances for officials Dharma Vira and Uma Shankar Dikshit around two specific points: first, Clause 1 of Section 2 (d) of the ordinance defined evacuee as a person who because of Partition or 'civil disturbances, leaves or has, on or after the first day of March 1947, left … for outside India'. The words 'has left' were intended for persons who left India 'permanently', but the interpretation accepted by the custodian's officers enveloped even temporary absences. When such persons, upon their return, managed to get their properties, these were re-gazetted as evacuee property, leaving little 'finality' in the matter.

Second, notices were issued on the assumption that all Muslims are evacuees and were even issued to persons who had been long dead under the formula *to whom it may concern*. There were cases of 'blank notices', signed by assistant custodians, being given to field inspectors for discretionary use, and an especially egregious instance was when 'one Assistant Custodian held in one case that the onus to prove that no property had been allotted in Pakistan to the person to whom notice ... was issued, would be on [that] person'.[18] Relations with Pakistan, on the other hand, had deteriorated since India's devaluation and Pakistan's demurral to do so in September 1949. While a formal trade deadlock emerged, neither government wished to turn it into a war, with their economies bleeding, armies being reduced, mounting unemployment and worsening budgetary positions.[19] This latter also related to Matthai's taxation proposals, and while reassuring him that he wanted to 'encourage commercial classes',[20] Nehru rued that they wanted more and 'meanwhile condemn government'.[21]

In the first fortnight of February 1950, all of this was momentarily overshadowed by a recrudescence of large-scale communal riots in Calcutta, even as from East Punjab, Bhargava was resolving to give Master Tara Singh 'a fight',[22] by, among other things, expanding the cabinet so as to have 'a representative each of the Congress Sikhs, the [Udham Singh] Nagoke group, and the Giani Kartar Singh group'.[23] Patel was keen, with East Punjab being a frontier state,[24] whereas it was Azad who delved into the Calcutta riots, which had started in the Bagerhat district of Khulna division in East Bengal between the 'Namasudra' community and the government there over 'revenue payment' in December 1949.[25] When they reached West Bengal, the Calcutta press, especially the Bengali newspapers *Dainik Basumati*, *Ananda Bazar Patrika* and *Yugantar*, reported it provocatively, leading to the first instances of violence against Muslims in Berhampur, followed by Calcutta. On 6 February 1950, the Hindu Mahasabha held a meeting in which ex-major general A. C. Chatterjee of the INA 'incited people to avenge Bagerhat', and the next day, there was a meeting in Maniktala, where Ashutosh Lahiri of the Mahasabha led an inflammatory procession demanding that in Calcutta '13,000 local Muslims [should] hand over their houses to the 13,000 refugees from East Bengal'.[26]

Dr B. C. Roy then contacted Dr S. P. Mookerjee as he admitted that 'communalism had affected sections of the [police]', and, after 10 February 1950, two police officers were transferred from Maniktala and three were suspended in Howrah, even as complaints started coming about the army. Azad felt that if Roy himself or some other minister with the police commissioner had visited Maniktala, the situation could have been different. In total, 70,000–80,000 Muslim artisans of Calcutta lived in Maniktala, Raja Bazar, Narkeldanga, Ultadanga and Entally. They were attacked, their houses were burnt and property was looted. In Howrah, there were four large Muslim localities, out of which three were attacked. As ever, it was impossible to be precise and the local estimate was that about 1 lakh had left, while Azad's own view was 50,000–60,000, excluding Howrah. Azad's report was followed by Mohan Lal Saksena's letter that called for 'an exchange of populations'.[27] Herein was the emergence of that 'insoluble' problem, which would lead to the Bengal- and Assam-specific Nehru–Liaquat Pact, right up until the signing of which major incidents continued. Attacks on Muslim villages in Assam were renewed on 8 April, 'when 5 villages in Barpeta were burnt and inhabitants simply butchered'. Incomplete casualty figures amounted to 70-plus deaths as raids continued in 'open daylight for about 2 hours [with] armed guards posted at distance of 3 miles'. Thousands started leaving 'in small boats and tree rafts' in Brahmaputra, and like in Bengal, the state government 'failed' to cope with the situation, worsened by its own land revenue policy that deepened the insider–outsider divide,[28] and an estimated 2.5 lakh Muslims migrated.[29]

But away from the deaths of that partitioned region too, the die was getting cast. For instance, it was declared that all translations of the constitution will be in Nagari script with a glossary of Hindi terms, giving the impression that 'only persons knowing the Devanagari script should read [it]'.[30] Another seed of discord was sown in December 1949 in an Ayodhya mosque (Babri Masjid) when the UP government 'did little' about their district magistrate who 'misbehaved', while the regional Congressmen gave their approval to what happened and 'Pandit Govind Ballabh Pant refrained from taking action for fear of a riot'.[31] Nehru admitted that 'many Congressmen [had] become communal....' and accepted that he did not know 'what [to] do.... Merely to preach goodwill irritates people when they are excited. Bapu might have done it, but we are too small for this kind of thing'.[32]

Those who did something, like Dr S. P. Mookerjee and K. C. Neogy, were at the other end of this spectrum. Neogy was getting restive regarding Bengal, for as the union commerce minister, he also felt somewhat guilty for the happenings there by linking it to the cabinet's decision to stop coal supplies to Pakistan that led the latter to oppress Hindus. Neogy's concerns had only annoyed Patel, 'who perhaps thought that Pakistan would fall at his feet'; instead, as the trade deadlock continued and murder and migration carried on, Neogy sought to resign and 'proceed to Bengal [as] expiation'.[33] In his reply, Nehru contrasted the 'positive superstructure' in the country with 'a negative feeling' in the states, which led to many things happening,[34] which included issues that he was intimately associated with like Kashmir. The conflict there had produced refugees and camps, not least in the Jammu region, which were 'not considered as anybody's responsibility'.[35]

And this certainly included his own province of UP, where the IT investigation commission was unable to make any headway. On 10 September 1949, a request was made by the commission to Lucknow for some information. No reply was received, and a reminder was sent on 28 September and another on 13 October. Ultimately, a reply came on 4 November, asking for a copy of the letter of 10 September. This copy was sent, and its receipt was acknowledged, but no reply came to its substance. On 7 December, the commission enquired again, and on 20 January 1950, the UP government replied asking the commission again for a copy of the letter of 10 September. With the commission's patience stretched, they complained in New Delhi, following which the UP secretariat replied on 8 February by claiming that all this delay had occurred because the commission's letters 'had been addressed to a wrong department' even though they had been sent to the chief secretary. This led to 'another investigation as to who [was] responsible for these obstructive tactics....'[36] Simultaneously, the UP government was jailing any youth 'attracted to communism', and the case of the Zaidi sisters of Panipat, expelled from Aligarh Muslim University and arrested in Banaras, became symbolic. The sisters, granddaughters of scholar Altaf Husain Hali (1837–1914), were handled badly by the police, and they responded by a hunger strike. Thereupon, they were put in 'solitary confinement', following a 'lathi charge', which sent two of them to the hospital.[37]

UP, however, took a backseat in April 1950, with all the attention on Bengal, on which Nehru and Syama Prasad Mookerjee exchanged nine letters in three days, leading to Mookerjee's resignation from the cabinet over the minorities pact with Pakistan. Before that, Mridula Sarabhai was reporting from Calcutta about the wider implications of this intra-Bengal issue 'such as *Akhand Hindustan*....'[38] The prime minister wanted the agreement with his counterpart, Liaquat Ali Khan, 'to be recognised',[39] and for that, he agreed to accept Mookerjee's resignation. In his replies, Mookerjee articulated his own conviction, which was that the pact was 'no solution' as it kept the minorities on both sides as they were, instead seeking guarantees from the majority state apparatus. Once the pact was announced, Mookerjee wanted the ministerial 'right to make a statement' and distance himself from it.[40] Nehru accepted this but continued to argue that 'the alternative was war'.[41] Mookerjee's problem was that while his intent to resign had been announced and the agreement had been placed before the parliament, his resignation had not been formalised, thus leading to speculations. Seeking immediate relief and pledging out-of-office cooperation, he asked Nehru to handover his portfolio to Patel, whereas the prime minister persisted in suggesting Mookerjee postpone his resignation, pending a reconstitution of the cabinet.

On 11 April 1950, they met for a discussion in which Nehru hoped that Mookerjee would 'reconsider', adding that 'the Bengal and Assam members of parliament desire that you and Neogy should withdraw', and that both Prasad and Patel wished similarly.[42] This appeal came to no avail and Mookerjee left the cabinet,[43] alongside Neogy, leaving Nehru to his agreement with Liaquat, for which the next steps were to appoint a central minister to oversee it and, as a confidence-building measure, a Muslim minister to the Roy cabinet.[44] In Assam, the situation was more delicate with the Assam Expulsion Act involved. While the prime minister had not agreed to his Pakistani counterpart's request to include this act in their agreement, he accepted the need to investigate it, as he had come across a case from Dibrugarh, where an old resident had been told to leave within three days, and he was also concerned about jute and rice cultivation in Goalpara, whose 'vast Muslim population' had left it with 'very few' Hindu refugees to substitute.[45] On the other hand, many more Hindu refugees had come to the Cachar district, from where fewer Muslims had left, and so he suggested sending Hindus from Cachar to Goalpara. But the epicentre of the problem remained in Bengal and, after conferring with Patel and Prasad, Nehru requested Rajagopalachari to go to Bengal as a goodwill ambassador. When UP, without any major incidents, was seeing 'almost a mass movement among Muslims to migrate to Pakistan – peasants, artisans, metal workers, locksmiths, domestic servants ...',[46] the Delhi Pact risked certain failure in Calcutta.

With Rajagopalachari reluctant, as he was not considered 'sufficiently Hindu-minded' for Bengal, the prime minister was desperate, especially as Chief Minister Roy was seeking Mookerjee as central minister, which could only mean leaving 'West Bengal under Hindu Mahasabha'.[47] Even Patel opined that it was undesirable to have Mookerjee as New Delhi's envoy, and Nehru repeatedly urged Rajagopalachari, but people were also alleging that Roy's own 'affiliations were with people who ... incline towards communalism'.[48] Dr B. C. Roy, in turn, wrote that given the tension among the Hindus nobody but Vallabhbhai Patel was welcome. Unlike Nehru, his people questioned 'the sincerity of Liaquat' and Roy, having received reports of 'harassment by the Ansars at the customs', urged the prime minister to 'inform Karachi [that] re-requisitioning of houses [and] fear of arrest leads many to avoid going back'.[49] Dr Radhakrishnan, ambassador in Moscow, cautioned Nehru that 'people's anxiety is due to their lack of confidence in Pakistan ... in your case they would argue it is a triumph of hope over experience'.[50]

The wily Rajagopalachari was understandably wary, but apart from being unwell, his main objection was that as a former governor in Calcutta and governor-general in New Delhi, he should not be equated with his Pakistani counterpart. He suggested Dr Prafulla Chandra Ghosh, Neogy or the Assam governor Sri Prakasa.[51] Amidst all this, it was agreed that Patel, who had been 'a brick during these days' and supported Nehru inside and outside the party in 'a very moving' manner, would go to Calcutta.[52] Simultaneously, P. C. Ghosh was urged to 'give the lead' by 'going back' to East Bengal (Ghosh was born in Dhaka), as a Gandhian gesture.[53] Home secretary H. V. R. Iengar also was of the view that Patel's visit would be decisive, as Iengar understood from Patel that he wanted to give Nehru's agreement with Liaquat 'a fair trial'.[54] Overall, of course, Patel held the view that 'brutalities in Pakistan have brutalised even the mild Hindu of West Bengal'.[55] Nehru, on the other hand, was always keen to emphasise that this was not in isolation but that the 'Hindu Mahasabha and the RSS's objective [was] the Muslim League's objective in reverse'.[56] This also alienated friends, an example of which were the Quakers in the country, who after all their good work in Punjab and Bengal and friendliness with Gandhi were being treated suspiciously and worse in the Central Provinces 'because of tendentious police and CID reports'.[57] Meanwhile, Saksena's ministry's rigid legalisms on the evacuee problem and permits too were spotlighted under the Delhi agreement, as with 'large numbers of Muslims leaving the UP, Rajasthan and Delhi', the government had to undertake some relief, at least for those who were dispersed within India.[58]

Patel's interventions and steadfast support in April 1950 were the crucial cornerstone of inter-governmental correspondence with state chief ministers, on whose actions rested the implementation of the Delhi Pact. Anyway, some population exchange was 'inevitable' and 'automatic',[59] but the fact remained that Hindus in East Bengal were now Pakistani nationals, and the government was moving ahead with passing a new evacuee property law, as well as the all-important representation of the people bill, for the first general election now expected in April 1951, after the census. Despite its intent, this new evacuee property bill contained clauses that brought within their scope of suspicion 'any person who may have business or private dealings in Pakistan', as the desire 'to prevent large scale transfers of property' enlarged the custodian's discretion to retrospective judgement for actions taken before October 1949.[60] These provisions were suspect as much from the substance of fundamental rights as from the spirit of the Delhi agreement, and three cases from one day in mid-April 1950 showed this:

> 1) Masha Allah Jan 2) Khan Sahib Obaidullah Khan, 3) Darya Khan ... Obaidullah Khan at a most critical moment in Lyallpur towards the end of 1947 [was] of enormous help in saving the Hindu-Sikh population. The Pakistan/West Punjab government ... made it impossible for him to

continue.... Now for some technical consideration, all the permits issued to him, his parents are to be cancelled.... The word of a Prime Minister ought to have some importance in this country.[61]

This last was quite an admission, but not an isolated one. Just after the signing of the Nehru–Liaquat Pact,[62] in their shared province of UP, in the district of Shahjahanpur, there were Holi riots accompanied with migrations and their justifications, and the UP Congress committee was now dominated by the Tandon group, whose partisans like Bishambar Dayal Tripathi outdid members of the Mahasabha.[63] There were routine instances of street harassments of Muslims,[64] but there was also a feeling that migrations continued because of certain pull factors too, namely 'that people could earn big wages there ... artisans and others'.[65]

But to a protesting Karachi, which the prime minister visited after the agreement, New Delhi had to deny any Muslim exodus from UP, Central India and even West Bengal, where the numbers had reportedly gone down, from about '10,000 a day' to '1500 or less', while the number of Hindus coming in was still around '10,000 a day'. Referring to Patel's effect in Calcutta, Nehru passed on to Liaquat his observation that for those who wished to return to East Bengal, their houses had been 'requisitioned', while among those who stayed back, there were prominent arrests made. With both bureaucracies busy hammering out an ad hoc trade agreement,[66] facilities were also sought for the Quakers and the Red Cross to work at customs and camps.[67] Nehru returned from Karachi confident, but the problem lay lower down the chain of command – in Dhaka, Calcutta and along the *borderlands* between them.[68] Then there was the press on both sides, with the Bengali press in Calcutta not even printing the numbers of Hindus returning to East Bengal.[69] And then there were anomalies like the families of about 3,000 officers and men serving in Indian defence forces but with 'families in East Pakistan'.[70] Above all, there was the realisation that 'mere police and army methods [were] not adequate'.[71]

Pending public support, the need of the hour lay in a better kind of administrative apparatus to help rein in the scenario. The scholar-diplomat K. M. Panikkar penned a note at this time on the new combined all-India services, having served as a member of the viva voce board. He felt that the candidates needed training on the lines of defence services, with the first object to produce an 'Indian type', which could then function as 'the steel frame of a new social democracy'. For this, they needed to know the whole of India, by texts as well as by touring and training in different regions, but above all by ensuring that 20 per cent of officers in a province should not belong to it. All this was with an aim to stem an already 'marked deterioration of educational standards', wherein UP (and Bihar) was 'the worst'. Panikkar found Mirabai and Kabir, receding in the memory of young recruits, and one crucial point that he made was that 'with a tradition of a central autocracy, it is not easy for people to understand the complicated constitution [nor] the idea of parliamentary responsibility'.[72]

Until then, ejectment of old tenants, a majority of whom were from the Scheduled Castes, in the name of displaced persons and ownership compensation, at the hands of relief and rehabilitation officials would continue across East Punjab. Almost 6,000 such families were under notice, and the political leadership, which in pre-1947 UP had successfully fought 'against such ejectment', could not stop these.[73] They themselves were a changed class, with Jagjivan Ram having to issue an apology, when in April 1950, a document came to light of his having received INR 10,000 in cash from the Dalmias in November 1947. There was little point in moving against Ram, for the Dalmias went around with a 'freely opened purse'.[74] Anyway the cabinet was to be reconstructed in terms of the new constitution; indeed, it should have been done around 26 January. Now, three months later, it was imperative, in the aftermath of the departure of Mookerjee, Neogy and in anticipation of the departure of Doulatram and Matthai. The prime minister wanted Pant, Sri Prakasa, Mahtab and Rajagopalachari, but he did not have an entirely free hand in the matter.[75]

It would also now be a more Congress cabinet as Nehru wrote to Govind Ballabh Pant, on successive days, to join as finance minister, given also that they thought on 'different lines' in their province, although 'Sardar Patel was rather doubtful'.[76] Suggesting Dr Sampurnanand as his successor, Nehru shared that Dr Matthai was not in harmony with the planning commission, with which Pant 'would fit in'.[77] But neither Pant, nor Rajagopalachari and not Sri Prakasa were keen to come to New Delhi in the summer of 1950. Patel, Prasad and Nehru all thought that Sri Prakasa could leave his gubernatorial post in Assam for Doulatram, who fitted more to governorship (Bihar) than ministership (food),[78] and requested Chief Minister Bardoloi.[79] Simultaneously, Gopalaswami Ayyangar was offered finance, who cited his rustiness vis-à-vis 'the money market' and suggested the Madras businessman-legislator T. T. Krishnamachari. The latter's acerbic personality however was not popular, especially with Patel and Rajagopalachari. Moreover, Krishnamachari's inclusion meant that there would be 'four Brahmins from South' in the cabinet, and Ayyangar then sought bureaucrat C. D. Deshmukh, governor with the Reserve Bank of India since 1943, as his financial advisor.[80]

The prime minister was reluctant for Deshmukh to come in 'immediately after Matthai',[81] and so tentatively conveyed to the president that his reconstructed cabinet will have Rajagopalachari as minister without portfolio and chairman of economic committee, Sri Prakasa (commerce), Ayyangar (finance), K. Santhanam (transport and railways), Deshmukh (financial advisor) and Ajit Prasad Jain (rehabilitation).[82] However, as was usual at the time, the last word did not belong to Nehru. Rajagopalachari refused and Patel, in addition to disliking Krishnamachari, did not approve of Ayyangar while accepting Deshmukh.[83] So, Ayyangar remained at transport and railways, Deshmukh got finance and Mahtab replaced Mookerjee at industries and supplies. While this personnel changeover was going on, political challenges too continued:

> Bengal & Assam: Hindu migrations from East to West about 12,000 a day; Hindus going back between 3000 to 4000 a day. Exodus of Muslims from the UP and Rajputana almost as big as Muslim exodus from West Bengal.... Elections must be held early next year.... Some states do not quite appreciate this urgency.[84]

On the economic side, the trade embargo with Pakistan persisted, control–decontrol dilemma endured, the food–famine binary spread and agro-based industries started to suffer, with an imbalanced export–import policy since devaluation and loss of markets like Britain adversely impacting 'weavers and spinners'.[85] Almost three years from Partition, it was clear that neither of the two countries formed, nor the communities forced could 'injure the other without injuring itself'.[86] Another example from UP showed this situation. Nisar Ahmed Sherwani, one of the few who had left the coveted colonial civil service to join the national movement, found himself at the mercy of his secretary, Har Govind Singh, over 'some incident of a cow or several cows', on which Singh made unspecified charges and left Sherwani's ministry, demanding, and getting, an enquiry against the minister, leaving the only possible 'inference that Sherwani [was] not wanted'.[87] Nehru, concerned lest he lose another of his stalwart nationalists from UP, Rafi Ahmed Kidwai, urged him to 'keep out of this business....'[88]

ELECTIONS 'FREE AND FAIR ...'

On 5 May 1950, Prime Minister Jawaharlal Nehru and his ministry resigned so that President Rajendra Prasad could appoint a new council of ministers under the new constitution. There was a new flavour in foreign exchange reserve too, which remarkably in the financial year ending 30 June 1950 closed with a credit balance. And there was a new current in the air about the management of the upcoming general election, as the following section starts by situating their administration within the politics around them. This was being spearheaded by JP, whose critique is important, given the usual reception of elections. From the UP by-elections of 1948, it had been evident that the

Congress would spare no means in winning, and in the recent by-election in the university constituency of Bihar council, there were 325 voters, of whom 145 were government or semi-government servants. The socialists were supporting Awadesh Nandan Sahay, while the Congress had put up Awadh Bihari Jha. Sahay lost the election by 95 votes, and JP minded not the result so much as 'the methods used by the ministry', which filled him with 'fear' about the forthcoming general election. In this by-election:

> DMs, DCs and other officers were used to canvass and to collect ballot papers from the voters. Ministers, including the CM, personally telephoned government servants advising them to vote for the Congress candidate.... How could a minister in his 'individual' capacity instruct a magistrate to go about collecting ballot papers for a party candidate? Muslim voters were intimidated by government officers to vote for the Congress candidate under the threat that it was only the Congress which could protect the Muslims.... 3 officers were asked to explain why they acted against the service rules in canvassing [for Sahay].... This kind of double standard cannot but raise grave doubts about the fairness of the coming elections....[89]

Next to elections on the faith–fairness scale was the new Supreme Court, which got jurisdiction of the privy council from about October 1949 and emerged on 26 January 1950. It had six judges to begin with and, under the constitution, a bench of five judges was required on any issue involving its interpretation. The experience from the inauguration of the republic was that 'the Court [was] inundated with applications' to uphold Fundamental Rights because litigation was 'cheap' and 'for appeal in criminal matters'. It was decided in March 1950 that the 350 pending appeals at the Hyderabad privy council too would be handled by the Supreme Court. The records of these appeals were in Urdu and translators were being arranged for them. The result of all this was that since October 1949, the court had disposed of over 110 appeals and 130 petitions, and Chief Justice Kania wanted to appoint at least three more judges from September 1950, to form one bench of five, another of three and leave one judge on the Hyderabad appeals. Simultaneously, he requested the government 'to reduce the work of the Court' by making suitable amendments in the constitution,[90] which was rebuffed, in this instance, by citing the difficulty to change it at this early stage.[91]

In the meantime, in May 1950, the rehabilitation ministry in Delhi and its custodian in Bombay were faced with a tricky situation, when upon taking over, as evacuee property, some mills belonging to Messrs Ahmed Abdul Karim Brothers Ltd, they found that Abdul Karim had entered a deal with Dayabhai Patel, son of Vallabhbhai, to exchange Dayabhai's pre-Partition shares of the Karachi electric supply company. Dayabhai approached the minister concerned as the custodian in Bombay moved to allot the mills to a newly floated company of refugees upon their collection of the capital necessary to run them. Keeping in mind the triangle of rescuing Dayabhai's assets in Pakistan, the requirements of refugees from Pakistan and the legal position, Saksena suggested that:

> Abdul Karim may be permitted to exchange his mills with the shares of Dayabhai Patel on the condition that the latter will transfer [it] immediately to the Bombay government for a sum of Rs. 50 lakhs. The latter would transfer the same to the new refugee company for Rs. 80 lakhs of which Rs. 35 lakhs would be paid in cash and the balance recovered in instalments. As the mills are said to be worth nearly a crore, the transaction, while rescuing Dayabhai's capital, would save Rs. 30 lakhs for the evacuee property pool and be favourable to the 30 refugees who have formed the new company.[92]

This neat transaction, however, had a non-refugee salvaging his capital from Pakistan, while the property of thousands remained inaccessible, and Saksena turned to Nehru for advice. The prime minister too wished to 'proceed warily' in ascertaining the value of the two properties, while avoiding 'any cash payment' to Dayabhai Patel. Instead, the Bombay government could take charge of the mills and give Dayabhai shares in them.[93] This was a family matter to oblige, but industrialists like R. K. Dalmia were an altogether different case. When reproached about the lack of cooperation from his firms with the IT investigation commission, Dalmia pointedly reminded Nehru of his 'contributions' to the Gandhi Memorial Fund and 'purchase' of *National Herald* shares before taking on Patel and his letter, 'the language [of] which [did] not befit the Deputy Prime Minister'.[94]

Meanwhile, the new cabinet was grappling with old problems. The Delhi Pact was an irritant in West Bengal, and the movement from UP too continued. Indeed, by the last week of May 1950, without any major incidents since March, 'about 200,000 Muslims' had left.[95] At the same time, the Roy government had spent INR 4 lakhs on the relief of Muslims in Calcutta, with New Delhi contributing a quarter of this sum and West Bengal being the one state where Muslims' 'reinstatement' was now policy. By early June 1950, the 'official' figures of movement in Bengal were as follows: '(1) Hindus arriving in West Bengal from East – 49880, (2) Hindus leaving West Bengal for East – 31516, (3) Muslims arriving in West Bengal from East – 17692, (4) Muslims leaving West Bengal for East – 20899'.[96]

From the other side of Bengal was the newly consolidated state of Rajasthan, across parts of which, from Ajmer-Merwara to Alwar-Bharatpur, between 1947 and 1949 there had been major displacements in what have been termed as the 'further shores' of Partition.[97] Now, in May 1950, with the Hiralal Shastri government in office, a deputation of Muslims from Tonk, led by Syed Zahir Ahmed, who had been connected with the old States Peoples organisation, came to New Delhi. At least a fifth of the Muslims from this former princely area had recently left for Pakistan, and the cause seemed to be a pushing out of Muslims from the services. In February 1950, appearance of notices stuck on Muslim houses telling them to 'go to Pakistan' was followed by arson and stone-throwing, and in an incident in late April, 'some [Sangh] members went to buy a watermelon from a Muslim seller [and] said something offensive about Muslim women', leading to a fracas and arrests. This led to a *hartal* by the local Sangh and Mahasabha elements, and Muslims were asked to leave Tonk. Interestingly, over 1947–49, when many Sindhi refugees had arrived, there had been little trouble, but now, the district magistrate there was Himmat Singh from Udaipur, and the police superintendent was a Sikh named Niranjan Singh, previously at Bundi, where he had earned a partisan reputation. Nehru had pushed for the transfer of several officials in UP earlier and wanted Shastri to enquire whether Niranjan Singh's 'objective is different from ours'.[98] In a rather extraordinary sequence over two days in late May 1950, Nehru showed how determinedly he could pursue his objectives when officials in his government were being petty:

> Hakim Nisar Ahmed & Masha Allah Jan (Delhi), Dr. Majid-ud-din Ahmed (Aligarh, UP), Messrs. Fakir Mohammed Shamsuddin & Allaudin (Rajasthan), Abdul Wahab (Punjab), Anwaruddin (MP), Haji Zakaria (Bangalore), Miss Fathima Kanu (Bombay).... People who had gone before the permit system was introduced should not be punished. In view of the [Delhi] agreement, we proceed generously [or] face a huge exodus of Muslims from the UP and Rajasthan.[99]

To Maulana Azad, he admitted that many such cases were 'complicated and [he] can do nothing except to draw attention to them'.[100] In others, he ensured a permit (Masha Allah Jan), insisted on a humane scrutiny (Fathima 'went to see her sister-in-law in Pakistan, who was ill and fell ill herself; because she could not get a permit to return, she was declared an evacuee'), restrained from any disentitlement (Haji Zakaria) and rebuked on judging people's loyalty without any evidence, in face of previous recommendations (Fakir Mohammad Shamsuddin and Allaudin and Dr Majid-ud-din Ahmed).[101] These five odd exceptions only prove the rule affecting scores of such cases, one of which was that of Hakim Nisar Ahmad's, and Ajit Prasad Jain, the new relief and rehabilitation minister, was urged to look closely into it. It was a peculiar case, and it illustrates well the predicament of someone who, though an Indian national, was considered a non-national. The departmental position was that defined as an evacuee, he was treated as such, but the question was whether a person, who is defined thus, also automatically becomes a non-national. After all, the evacuee laws applied to persons who abandoned their nationality by evacuating for Pakistan, and to that extent an evacuee and a non-national were concentric categories. But as the law was both intricate and vague, when applied randomly, it rendered nationals as evacuees.[102]

Occasionally a case came that tugged at the heartstrings more than usual, for it would be a reminder of a bygone time. Saimullah Beg of Lucknow, a leading member of the UP Liberal Party back in the 1910s and a friend of Motilal Nehru, had gone on to be ennobled as Nawab Zoolcadur Jung in Hyderabad and had fallen foul of the state. He reached out for relief, recalling that Motilal Nehru had sponsored him for the legal practitioners' *sanad* from Justice Knox of Allahabad High Court. Beg, over 70 years of age and with K. M. Munshi (now food minister, earlier agent-general in Hyderabad) as his witness, took recourse to how he did his 'best' to advice the nizam, but his problem was that he had transferred the house in which he was then living to his daughter Sultan Bano Begum. This house was declared to be an evacuee property by the custodian as she left for Pakistan and Beg was asked to pay its rent from when she left. Beg wrote to the administrator-minister Vellodi that the question of migration did not arise because after August 1947, when the army was partitioned, her husband Brigadier M. H. Hussain opted for Pakistan and thus she remained there with him. The evacuee property ordinance, on the other hand, was promulgated two years later, on 22 August 1949. Further, Major-General Chaudhuri's regime had tried to purchase the house from Beg, who had informed them that it was in his daughter's name, but he lived in it and paid the taxes. Now the law had augmented his anxieties unless the house could be exempted from the evacuee property pool and instead be purchased by the government.[103] Here was another tale of partitioned lives, and the Congress satrap from Orissa, H. K. Mahtab, threw light on its causes:

> The popular mind was not prepared for independence.... The effects of war ... the calamities of partition.... Congress as an organisation [and] the present administration stands really on the political reputation of ... Nehru and Patel [who] cannot afford to be too big for the country.[104]

Otherwise, Mahtab warned the party's general secretary Shankarrao Deo, decisions made by the rank and file would be 'foisted' on them unless 'a Supreme High Command' of Nehru, Patel and the party president would look after electoral issues.[105] In his own way, Nehru agreed with this assessment, when he assured Krishna Menon that the main difficulty in the government was not the continuing influence of colonial civil service[106] but the ministers themselves allowing them 'greater scope' with their deficiencies or differences.[107] By the summer of 1950, several cases of evacuee property were those belonging to Muslim civil or military officers who had opted for Pakistan in 1947, as Beg's aforementioned situation had prompted a survey.[108] The irony was that foreigners could hold property and visit but not a forced migrant. A second question was still more sardonic: could these persons be 'permitted to settle in India after retirement ... because they [had] their homes here',[109] given plentiful ministerial advice to 'take advantage' of the trade deadlock with Pakistan?[110]

An equally corrosive crisis was that of corruption. In June 1950, H. P. Mody, the governor of UP, informed New Delhi that the Pant government had accepted penalty money from industrialist Padmapat Singhania as settlement of charges against him because of insufficient evidence.[111] They proposed to deal similarly with industrialist Ram Ratan Gupta and accept a penalty of INR 2,50,000.[112] Understandably, the Varadachariar-led commission had a different view. Gupta and his partners had admitted to INR 129 lakhs as their undisclosed income between 1940 and 1948, INR 75 lakhs as the assessable amount of profit and INR 55 lakhs due as tax.[113] To this, Finance Minister Deshmukh added that this penalty without law amounted to 'amnesty' for a 'felony' and smacked of state 'defeatism'.[114] It also appeared that the UP government's case against Gupta would be 'dropped', much as the Bombay government's case against Singhania 'in which all the witnesses were bought over',[115] and following a precedent set by the central textile commissioner in 1948, in the case of Singhania's swadeshi cotton mills. Mody also reminded New Delhi that 'during ... the war and immediately thereafter ... the government of the day ... gave the big operators a free run'.[116] A month later, a denouement of sorts of this drama was achieved when Varadachariar, taking his cue from G. D. Birla, reiterated a 'bearer bond proposal' (initially rejected by the cabinet), which 'will indirectly give the Commission an indication ... of concealment'.[117]

Obviously, this scheme depended on the cooperation of the captains of industry even as some new members of the cabinet were firming up their own incomes and allowances. There was some feeling about cabinet minister's salaries being held apart from other income, which did not stop Sri Prakasa from arguing that those 'who hold temporary political offices at the whim of the electorate ... must be treated as a class apart'.[118] Anyhow, this vagueness was an endemic feature affecting evacuee property law, IT investigation commission as well as the language policy of AIR broadcasts. Prepared by the department of information and broadcasting, under the charge of R. R. Diwakar, which came under the Home Ministry,[119] the new guidelines were rather 'indeterminate'. Insofar as the radio was concerned, the question was largely 'territorial', although the prime minister was still fighting the lost causes of Hindustani and Urdu. He wanted to encourage both, even as he knew that 'Hindi will have predominance' and therefore batted for 'the simplest language [with] the greatest intelligibility'.[120]

Meanwhile, trade with Pakistan remained in official abeyance. In June–July 1950, a Pakistan traders' delegation visited Delhi, while Bhim Sen Sachar led a delegation to Lahore. Pleading for a relaxation of the permit system and resumption of road–rail traffic, the delegation narrated the roundabout nature of existing trade that saw 42,000 bales of cotton being sent 'from Pakistan to [French] Pondicherry and from there [to] India', with spices making the journey in reverse.[121] By now figures, even if inaccurate, were starting to give some idea of post-Partition and post-devaluation (1949) economic deterioration of the country in terms of falling food production, continuing petrol rationing, decontrolled paper, rising (controlled) sugar import and collectivised cotton crop.[122]

This international economic decline went hand in hand with the deterioration in inter-communal relations, a point that was reinforced when Akshaya Brahmachari gave an account of what had happened at Ayodhya in late 1949 with the accompanying concern that the trouble 'may spread to Mathura', supported as it was by prominent Congressmen like Raghav Dass and Bishambar Dayal Tripathi. Brahmachari narrated how 'a hotel called the star hotel, owned by a Muslim, was vacated in December last under section 144. Next day, its possession was taken up by some Hindus, and, four days later, they renamed it as Gomati'. It had become 'almost impossible for Muslims to be buried' there, and Muslim graves had been 'dug up',[123] which was also why several Muslims in East Punjab province and states, who had been forced to convert in 1947 and now desired to reconvert, were being objected to by 'their neighbours'.[124] In Ajmer, Muslim railway employees, whose families had to leave for Pakistan and were trying to return now, were being targeted, and in the Lucknow railway workshop, Muslim employees were being forbidden to pray inside the factory, as well as being told to pray during the mid-day lunch break. In Jhansi and Bombay railway workshops, going for Friday prayers in the local mosque was being audited 'as half a day's absence', and Hafiz-ur-Rahman of Jamaat-i-Hind suggested to Railway Minister Ayyangar to reduce the period for *namaaz* to 15 minutes if this would save Muslim employees from wage reduction.[125]

Another variation on this theme was the case of Abdulla Haji Ismail from Godhra, where in March 1948 much destruction of Muslim houses took place, leading to people fleeing to Bombay and Karachi. Among these, some were able to return before the permit system was introduced. Abdulla Ismail did not leave Godhra but sent his wife and children, who now wished to return but could not do so because the permit system moved them from officer to officer. Instead, Abdulla, a Gujarati, who could not even sign his name in Urdu, and others like him were pressured to leave and were given temporary one-way permits to Pakistan. The Indian envoy in Karachi did not help nor did his deputy in Lahore, where they went next, having collected their families on their way back to India. Some left their families there and returned to India, lest they lost their homes too if they remained away for long. From Bengal to UP, thousands of Muslims who left after 1 February 1950 had been permitted to return and, the property question aside, could not the Saurashtra state and Bombay province 'allow separated families to come together'?[126]

Meanwhile, Punjab was seeing a fresh campaign of Master Tara Singh, and when Bhargava reported to Patel that the Master had asked members of the old Panthic Party to leave the Congress, Patel warned them that whoever obeyed 'Masterji's fiat' risked 'expulsion'.[127] Nehru, Patel and Governor Trivedi wrote to Baldev Singh warning him that in the midst of the trade blockade with Pakistan, it was 'the duty of Sikh leaders to dissociate themselves' from Tara Singh.[128] In his reply, Baldev Singh pointed out that 'the responsibility' for this rested with the East Punjab government and the provincial Congress, as in the recent by-election in the labour constituency of Amritsar, Baldev Singh had helped the party win against the combined opposition of Akali Dal and Forward Bloc, only to see it lose in a Sikh constituency in Ferozepur to the Akali candidate. For Baldev Singh, 'the evil of partition, delays in rehabilitation and scramble for office' made Master Tara Singh's actions unexceptionable, but for New Delhi, 'whatever the sins' of the government/party,[129] this tension was also exacerbating the 'indiscipline in the army'.[130]

Simultaneously, the government was wrestling with delays in executing major schemes like the fertiliser factory at Sindri. The parliament's estimates committee was scrutinising its progress, from the original capital investment in 1944, INR 10.79 crores, to which subsequently 0.5 crore was added for water supply and 1.5 crores for additional power plant. By March 1950, INR 15 crores had been spent on the project, and this figure was expected to rise to INR 23 crores because of 'a delay of nearly 2 years in the acquisition of land'. The construction was expected to be completed by 1 March 1951, one-third production capacity was aimed for by 1 May 1951 and full production of ammonium sulphate by the end of 1951. This was expected to save INR 60 per ton of ammonium sulphate, as it could be produced at INR 200–210, while its import price was INR 270. But the characteristic feature was the number of agencies responsible, the central PWD, Bihar public health and engineering departments and the Eastern Indian Railway.[131]

There was neither a nodal officer nor a coordinating authority within the three central ministries involved and between them and the Bihar government. The latter was anyway struggling with Kosi River, and Nehru was seeking alternative ways to engage the labour force in the state for digging up canals,[132] pending the huge dam, dependent on scarce foreign exchange. The Bihar government was dragging its feet on many matters. Out of its quota of 50,000, it had taken half that number of displaced persons. A set of 1,600 houses in Dhanbad, constructed by the central labour ministry for coal miners, had seen occupancy in only 200 – those with water supply and sanitary arrangements, and the relief and rehabilitation ministry was keen to have temporary control of others. But these houses had been built out of a coal cess and were being kept 'exclusively for colliery labour'.[133] The Bihar ministry was also struggling with *zamindari* abolition, and Nehru was concerned enough to urge Patel, Ambedkar and Prasad to help 'find some way out'.[134] Meanwhile, in neighbouring West Bengal, Dr B. C. Roy now had a Muslim minister alright, but he had not given him adequate work.[135]

Over July–August 1950, as the food situation in Bombay and Madras deteriorated, the refugee situation in Bengal and Assam remained 'unsatisfactory', and from Punjab came allegations about an 'unpatriotic' Master Tara Singh.[136] What was also coming to a critical point was the communist challenge, following the unsuccessful line of armed resistance since February 1948.[137] In mid-July 1950, the CPI issued a public statement followed by a press conference by general secretary S. A. Dange that the party had decided to 'work on constitutional lines', but an unconvinced Home Ministry cautioned the states that there was 'irrefutable evidence' otherwise, and this was a mere 'shift in tactics'.[138] Zamindari abolition was important for this reason too as was the ongoing appeal 'to industrialists to increase production'.[139]

So was getting the planning commission going for the prime minister at least, for which he has had expertise brought in from near and far in the form of Trone and Dr P. C. Mahalanobis.[140] However, the latter had a feeling of 'marking time' in Delhi,[141] and the former was proving expensive to retain. While Nehru persuaded Deshmukh to 'reassure' Mahalanobis otherwise, he could not convince him to pay Trone's admittedly expensive terms,[142] whose approach to planning for Deshmukh was 'fundamentally totalitarian'.[143] Trone's service was hardly the most important thing that the central government could not afford in 1950. The economic committee of the cabinet recommended to reduce defence expenditure to eventually 'Rs. 140 crores [in] 1953–54', alongside estimating a reduction in the army 'to 200,000 from 516,000'. As K. M. Munshi offered to employ those released for land development projects in Madhya Bharat,[144] Dr B. R. Ambedkar expressed concern that 'this reduction … may affect the Scheduled Castes in the Army',[145] and 'proportionate reductions of various classes' ought to be calculated.[146] Persons, albeit of another kind, were also on the mind of the parliament, where H. V. Kamath demanded a statistical statement on the Delhi Pact. The Home Ministry's reply began by claiming that of the 22,000 Muslim industrial employees in the Great Calcutta area, who had left, 9,000 were re-instated, and then gave figures thus:

> (1) Before the agreement (from 7 February to 8 April 1950) (a) from East to West: 5,47,049 Hindus, 6,847 Muslims; (b) from East Bengal to Assam: 1,90,530 Hindus, negligible Muslims; (c) from East Bengal to Tripura: 1,20,000 Hindus, not available for Muslims; (2) Before the agreement (from 7 February to 8 April 1950) (a) from West to East: 65,537 Hindus, 5,54,715 Muslims; (b) from Assam to East Bengal: negligible Hindus, 1,24,063 Muslims; (c) from Tripura to East Bengal: negligible Hindus, figures not available for Muslims; (3) After the agreement (from 9 April to 18/25 July 1950) (a) from East to West: 9,99,290 Hindus, 2,18,708 Muslims; (b) from East Bengal to Assam: 1,91,751 Hindus, 46,617 Muslims; (c) from East Bengal to Tripura: 93,582 Hindus, 32,083 Muslims; (4) After the agreement (from 9 April to 18/25 July 1950) (a) from West to East: 5,03,273 Hindus, 4,09,741 Muslims; (b) from Assam to East Bengal: 32,561 Hindus, 37,578 Muslims; (c) from Tripura to East Bengal: 5417 Hindus, 2649 Muslims. Grand Total: After the agreement from East Bengal to India: 12,84,623 Hindus, 2,97,408 Muslims; After the agreement from India to East Bengal: 5,41,251 Hindus, 4,49,968 Muslims. Difference in Statistics of movement by train between East and West from 12 April 1950 to 11 July 1950: according to East Bengal: from East to West, 5,70,755 Hindus and 1,12,180 Muslims; from West to East, 4,49,192 Hindus and 2,42,939 Muslims; according to West Bengal: from East to West, 8,51,119 Hindus and 1,77,387 Muslims; from West to East, 4,15,287 Hindus and 3,52,707 Muslims.[147]

The Nehru–Liaquat Pact may thus have stemmed somewhat this migration, but it could not stop the trend of thinking among West Bengal leaders like Dr Roy about the situation in the east. Beginning with the 1941 census, Roy recalled that there were about 1.12 crores of Hindus in East Bengal then, of which '45–50 lakhs' had come since 1947. Their departure had created space for the growth of a 'Muslim middle-class' there, and Roy argued that 'whatever decision might have been arrived at by Liaquat', this group would not be 'helpful' in its implementation, leading to a return of the Hindu middle class there. Second, the latter had a considerable number of dependents in rural areas, many of whom were now 'returning without their leaders', and Roy was pessimistic about them. All this led him to conclude that it was just

not desirable to induce the Hindu middle-class ... to go back.... The
Muslim middle-class ... are inclined to look more complacently to the
presence of people of a lower status.... There is no longer any attempt
at forcible conversions, which proves that [it] was merely a method of
frightening the middle-class.... This leads me to think that the remaining
[rural] Hindu population of East Bengal would adjust themselves....[148]

This class–caste bias was joined by regional resistance, and C. C. Biswas and
A. Malik, central ministers for both the Bengals appointed by New Delhi
and Karachi respectively, reported that the two state governments nearly
ignored them.[149] Undercut by those 'on the spot', the central governments
were having difficulty in first estimating the figures of migrations, then
categorising them as 'travellers', 'refugees', 'migrants' and 'smugglers', and
thus talked 'vaguely of over 20 lakhs of persons having come'.[150] By 15
August 1950, the relief and rehabilitation ministry had reached a figure of
41.5 lakhs, out of which '26.5 lakhs came to India', but, according to the
Intelligence Bureau, this figure could 'go down to 10 lakhs', while 'about 6
½ lakhs' had gone back to East Bengal. Plainly, all figures were 'wrong',[151]
much like those relating to the 'inadequate' food grains and 'rising' prices.[152]
In the latter case, President Prasad was asked to enable the parliament to
issue an order under Article 392, as the council of states was yet to be,[153]
because the general election was yet to be.

Another, and more intimate, election was on the anvil in mid-August
and that was for the Congress presidency, for which P. D. Tandon and J.
B. Kripalani were squaring off,[154] pitching the Congress *duumvirate* in
opposite camps. Tandon, propped up by Patel, hoped that Nehru would
support him, given their quasi-familial ties, but Nehru wrote to Tandon
that he was 'encouraging communalism, revivalism, intolerance [and]
narrow-mindedness' by voicing the 'excuse that Pakistan behaves badly'.[155]
Before Tandon could, Patel replied to this letter (that was copied to him)
and engaged in a spirited defence of Tandon.[156] Recalling Tandon's 'high
position' in the UP Congress for over three decades, Patel reminded Nehru
that as recently as January 1950, Tandon had contributed to and presented
an *Abhinandan Granth* to him. Given that the refugees were 'undoubtedly
bitter and disillusioned' and prone to 'extremism', Patel refused to hold
Tandon accountable for their views.[157]

On his part, Nehru did not underplay his affection for Tandon 'for
at least 50 years', but nor did he mince words on their mutually accepted
differences after 1947 and listed these: Tandon's pro-Hindi attitude, his
condemnation of the Delhi Pact and his public association with 'this new
turn being given to the Congress'.[158] When Patel requested him to rethink,

Nehru upped the ante by threatening to resign, but in deference to Patel, he re-considered his statement. Given Tandon's popularity among the AICC, Patel wanted Nehru to save it for after Tandon's election. Reassuring his apprehensions on the CWC, Patel reminded him that the party president 'has either to conform or to quit', and Tandon was 'too good a disciplinarian', but was Nehru equal to him, and would he be mature in the event of his election?[159] Tandon responded to Nehru's anguished letter with a sorrowful reply of his own, agreeing that past affections notwithstanding, they differed on Hindi's position and the refugee question. What Tandon took exception to was Nehru attributing 'communalism and revivalism' to him. Outlining his position on this, Tandon expounded on an 'all-round unity' with the expansive proviso that 'diversities be kept within proper limits' and agreed, in the abstract, that he 'would revive some of the spiritual standards [of] the past'. On the concrete 'question of refugees', Tandon suggested 'a capital levy for rehabilitation', for 'there were men who wished to use the refugees for discrediting the Congress'.[160]

With lines thus drawn for the party showdown; the prime minister got back to governing the country where nothing was as vexing as the food situation. With the centre being hamstrung, and the states seeing 'hoarding', Nehru worried enough about 'peasantry voters ...' to threaten 'emergency in any badly affected area....'[161] In Gwalior, protesting students were met with police firing, with Patel lamenting this that could be 'exploited by ... the Communists, the Jagirdars and Hindu Mahasabha', for he remembered that 'Parachur, whose revolver was used for Bapu's murder, came from there [with] the RSS and the Mahasabha quite powerful because of the ruling circles....'[162] On 15 August 1950, the Hindu Mahasabha organised a meeting in the national capital, in which speeches were made 'for the undoing of the Partition'.[163]

A day later, the prime minister, his deputy, Rajagopalachari and Rajendra Prasad engaged in a lengthy exchange on the appointment of the central government's first special officer for the backward classes under the new constitution. Their officials had suggested, with Patel's approval, the name of I. M. Lall, a senior civil servant from 1922 of the Punjab cadre. Nehru was inclined towards a non-official like Thakkar Bapa.[164] Lall's service record contained a dismissal and unfavourable comments between 1925 and 1934 and then in 1950 by H. M. Patel.[165] Patel put this down to Lall not getting on with certain cliques, and they had to find a place for him. As Patel was usually against non-official appointments,[166] Rajagopalachari entered the exchange with his suggestion of Shavax Lal, who had been his secretary and was serving President Prasad in the same capacity. Otherwise, Rajagopalachari suggested

Kaka Kalelkar, like Thakkar Bapa, a non-official 'associated with Bapu'.[167] Patel now sought Prasad's counsel, while dismissing Kalelkar as 'a complete misfit', and reiterated his anxiety to have a 'preference for an IAS, amenable to persuasion, cognisant of administrative difficulties and embarrassment'.[168] Prasad, however, refused to let go of Shavax Lal and instead suggested L. M. Shrikant, in-charge of Bhil Seva Mandal (Gujarat) and one of Thakkar Bapa's men. Rajagopalachari endorsed Shrikant,[169] and, for once, Patel was outmanoeuvred.[170]

Shrikant's appointment was not without some late drama though. Labour minister Jagjivan Ram did not want him and came up with his alternatives (Malik of Bengal or B. P. Varma from Bihar), and his canvassing left Patel rather upset.[171] This was far from an isolated case, and the inability to appoint the chief engineer for the Damodar Valley project shows deeper difficulties. Starting in July 1948, the project was without a chief engineer for two years and two months. Its board of consultants had members from Chicago and Madras, but candidates on its wish list for this major post were either indisposed or unwilling or engaged otherwise.[172] Let alone such individual dilemmas, the 'desperate' financial situation around how 'to economise'[173] delayed the setting up of the central statistical organisation, and while the Preventive Detention Act, 1950, was being resorted to for 'black-marketeers, hoarders', Nehru wanted it also for those 'who shout too much about war with Pakistan'.[174] He instructed his state counterparts thus,[175] keeping in mind intelligence reports, which showed Moulichand Sharma (Jan Adhikar Samiti) and Lala Yudhraj (Punjab National Bank) meeting Dr Mookerjee and communicating with P. B. Dani (RSS) for a Golwalkar–Mookerjee meet.[176]

The pact for which Dr Mookerjee had left the cabinet had, however, not left Nehru at peace. The new-old permit system refused to consider 'persons who left India for Pakistan before 19 July 1948 and returned to India before that date' as Indian citizens, leaving Nehru to ask how they could 'presume migration by travel'. Furthermore, persons who went to Pakistan before or after 19 July 1948 but returned before 26 January 1950 saw their citizenship simply disappear. Consequently, the then-ongoing preparation for voter rolls was becoming a litmus test for citizenship. While the old permit system did not apply to Bengal, its new variant had a clause making travelling to East Bengal enough to lose nationality. Then, there was a separate clause 'for Muslims who migrated from UP between 1 February and 31 May 1950', notwithstanding the fact that many of them subsequently returned,[177] and the prime minister wanted to know how many such old cases the government would be carrying into the new republic.

NOT ENOUGH 'FIRST-RATE MEN'

In the autumn of 1950, priorities of the central government were seriously impacted by the contest for Congress presidency, and this section charts its course while, side by side, showing the consequences of this turnover of men and material. When a party worker came to seek clarification from Nehru, he answered thus, setting the tone for the events of September:

> There were three names, Kripalani, Shankarrao Deo and Tandon. I felt that I should support Deo ... I do not trust [Tandon's] judgement.... There may be some trouble [with] Kripalani.... There would be no difficulty in Shankarrao's case.... Then Mahtab said that Kripalani had larger support ... [so he] should be supported....[178]

But, when Krishna Menon wrote from London to be upfront about it, Nehru demurred, while being franker in his portrayal of the candidates as 'negatively good' (Deo), 'cantankerous and frustrated' (Kripalani) and a 'reactionary symbol' (Tandon). Menon wanted his friend to hold three offices at least, 'PM-ship, the Foreign Office, Congress leadership', something that would happen from September 1951, but for now, with Patel around, Congress presidency amounted to 'responsibility without power', while most of his colleagues wanted to have general elections no sooner than May 1951.[179] Still, prime ministers must administer simultaneously, and around the time that battlelines were being deepened in the party, the government was delineating the salient features of the Bhakra-Nangal dam-canal project.[180] Its estimated cost was INR 133 crores, with an expected return of 3.87 per cent, 10 years after completion, and a prescribed productivity test rate of 3.75 per cent. This return, however, was subject to optimistic technicalities like (a) a betterment levy of INR 75 and INR 50 per acre of perennial and non-perennial irrigation area, payable in 15 annual instalments, and (b) a 50 per cent increase in the current water rates per acre of irrigated area. The Nangal dam and power plant, followed by the Bhakra canal system, were expected by 1954, thereby utilising Sutlej waters.[181] With contracts awarded to the French, it was imperative for Punjab province and states and Rajasthan to make the project self-sustaining, even as the Sikh situation in the state was heating up again, with 36 Akalis being arrested in a message to Master Tara Singh.[182] He too would be arrested at Amritsar on 7 September, as the East Punjab government accused Gian Singh, chief minister of PEPSU, for having thrown 'his weight behind Tara Singh'.[183]

Other parts of the country were similarly restive. From Hyderabad, Chief Minister Vellodi was reporting the 'violent propaganda' of the Socialist Party and of the Mazdoor Sangh exploiting the 'food situation', which he had met by 'preventive detention'.[184] The food situation was causing anxiety across the country, from Bihar to Madras and Bombay to Assam, which also suffered from a powerful earthquake on 15 August. From importing rice from then-Burma to issuing ordinance to check price rise and enable bank advances to agriculturalists, there was a policy frenzy in response.[185] In between was Bengal, and here, a lack of security for the Hindu minority in the east was being met by Dr Mookerjee's sweeping proposals like 'transfer of territory or a separate bloc for minorities or a compulsory exchange of populations'.[186] Even as the upcoming party election started to vitiate the atmosphere between Congress stalwarts,[187] they were putting their heads together on the 'terrific housing problem'.[188]

Nehru's note of 30 August 1950 tried to sketch yet another statistical picture of the still-fluid scenario in Bengal. It claimed that 15 lakh persons had come over from East Bengal to India from August 1947 to December 1949, while over 25 lakhs had come from 1 January 1950. These were the relief and rehabilitation ministry's figures. Nehru's Ministry of External Affairs, on the other hand, gave the following numbers: from East Bengal, August 1947–January 1950, 13 lakhs; February–April 1950 (Delhi Pact), over 7 lakhs; April–August 1950, over 11 lakhs; so, the grand total was 32 lakhs. This total was arrived at after deducting the number of Hindus who returned to East Bengal in 1950: over 7 lakhs. Then, the Muslim exodus from India to East Bengal was estimated at 5.5 lakhs and subtracting this from 32 gave a figure of over 26 lakhs. Since Delhi Pact, over 8 lakh Hindus had come in and over 4 lakh Muslims had gone out from India. In the second half of August 1950 itself, the Hindu migration from east to west was 82,102, while the Hindu return from west to east was 73,842. In the same period, Muslims coming from east to west were 35,184, and Muslims going from west to east 27,798.[189] Thus, four months after the much-heralded Nehru–Liaquat Pact, mass migration in Bengal continued while the country at large faced a drought in south India, floods in the east and the earthquake in Assam.[190]

It was against this miserable background that the general election was being mooted, and the administrative measures needed were starting to be outweighed by electoral considerations. By now, the Chief Election Commissioner Sukumar Sen had confirmed that it was 'difficult' to hold elections before October 1951 as some state governments had 'not functioned' well.[191] They were distracted, like the Kher ministry by the strikes in textile mills in Bombay, as well as by R. J. Pringle, chief controller of imports, offering to resign because he was forced to issue licences, for which the commerce ministry had a 'bad name'.[192] Pringle was soon joined by members of the estimates committee, who were similarly displeased about either the favouritism showed by the ministry or the time taken by it. From Bombay, there was one case making its way to the prime minister, in which a firm had paid a bribe of INR 5,000. It was about a Dr Cooper, who had waited for months to import some instruments, before mentioning it to Birla, and 'within 3–4 days the license came'.[193] Some months later, he was officially informed that his application had been rejected. Sri Prakasa's officials were now forced to enquire, and Commerce Secretary C. C. Desai's weak reply cited an absence of previous papers. Desai passed the parcel to G. R. Kamat (economic affairs secretary), who, as the chief controller of imports in 1947–48, could not remember any representation from any quarters. As for the uncoordinated action, it was due to the extraordinary conditions from June 1947 onward that is first, 'all the Muslim employees opted for Pakistan' and then 'the riots in Delhi … for nearly a week' in September.[194] Kamat had, towards the end of 1947, issued a public notice giving these extraordinary conditions as the reason for not dealing with applications, now regarded as lapsed. This sounded reasonable enough, and there was no more to enquire around this matter from 1947 to 1950, when governments were struggling to procure food, and the food ministry wanted certain areas in Bihar to be 'put under the central government.…'[195]

From corruption in import licencing to hoarding in food procurement,[196] effective working was at a premium and K. M. Munshi was ready with a desperate plan of action for 72 rice mills and their estimated 78,000 *maunds* in north Bihar. Claiming that some of these stocked across the open border in Nepal, Munshi sought a levy of paddy and rice from cultivators with 25 acres of land or 200 *maunds* as in central Bihar, from where 20,000 *maunds* had been obtained. With 3/4th of the agricultural year gone, Munshi sought a general notice that every cultivator with more than 50 *maunds* of paddy or 30 *maunds* wheat should report within a week to the district administration or risk 'detainment' under the Essential Supplies Act of 1946.[197] That year was also the last time Jawaharlal Nehru had been the Congress president. Now, in the first week of September 1950, J. B. Kripalani, his successor then, lost to P. D. Tandon in a close verdict. Unlike most premiers, Bhimsen Sachar supported Nehru, and he shared his reflections on Tandon's win in a way that echoed the Congress left's and the Socialist Party's reasoning:

> Was it right for Pandit Nehru to keep his personality out of the picture?
> … There is a general complaint that [he] does not provide any protection
> against victimisation.… If Sardar Patel had not won over the Rajasthan
> and PEPSU votes, Tandon could not have succeeded.[198]

Whether it was M. O. Mathai in his office or Mohanlal Gautam in his province, it was clear to all that Patel and Tandon wanted Nehru to continue as they could 'immobilise' him organisationally, and thus the upcoming Nasik

Congress session would (and did) pass whatever resolutions that he wanted so that he had no 'excuse to leave government'.[199] Even as he was exhorting his minister to extend the permit of, for example, Haji Syed Mohammad Hussain, 'an old Khilafatist and then a Muslim Leaguer [in] decrepit condition [to] die here where his forefathers lived',[200] his supporters were seeking to bolt the Congress door. Bhimsen Sachar drafted a resolution 'to authorise [the prime minister] to constitute a parliamentary board ... to select candidates', but it depended on whether the prime minister will 'assert' himself.[201]

This draft was met by another prepared by Harekrushna Mahtab and Shankarrao Deo, which suggested that the prime minister should be 'in consultation' with the Congress president, the chairman of the central machinery for conducting elections, and from the states, the chief ministers, provincial presidents and one nominee of the central board should recommend candidates.[202] When Patel and Tandon opposed this at the Nasik meeting on 19 September, Bombay's S. K. Patil suggested that the selection of parliamentary candidates should be done by a committee of Nehru, Patel and Tandon, and the selection for state legislatures by their nominee, along with the concerned chief minister and provincial president. While most minds had thus turned to the general election, Sucheta Kripalani, a member of the election sub-committee for Congress president, wanted a judicial enquiry into Tandon's victory, claiming reports of

> [w]idespread irregularities ... membership lists not maintained ... nomination papers tampered with, returning officers partisans ... special representatives sent to Rajasthan, Vidarbha, CP, UP, Nagpur.... In Bengal, election was set aside.... In Andhra, not possible to hold [it].[203]

From UP, K. D. Malaviya, among the few, 'isolated' people loyal to Nehru there, was reporting that Pant and his favourites were openly saying that 'because of Jawaharlalji's approach ... the Hindu officers of the UP are demoralised, unable to take drastic action against Muslims ... behaving mischievously'.[204] Pant's officers would have liked to (mis) use the widening scope of the Prevention Detention Law, while the same officers were working leisurely in the delimitation committees for the general election. Meanwhile, the Bengal migration statistics remained in flux. The Intelligence Bureau's note on the traffic between east and west for all of two days, 7 and 8 September 1950, was sobering:

> 12,373 Hindus from East to West: 3250 refugees, half migrating for first time; 10,894 Hindus from West to East: 2377 refugees, 815 going for resettlement, 1552 going to dispose properties; 6675 Muslims from East to West: 1605 refugees, 1456 coming back for resettlement; 5191

Muslims from West to East: 314 refugees, 35 migrating for first time. 4000 Hindus normal travellers, 2500 Muslims normal travellers.[205]

Its conclusion was that the migration of Muslims from west to east had mostly ceased as they considered the situation as normal, but the incoming Hindus outnumbered those outgoing by about 400 per day, and it appeared that more would come after the Pujo and the jute season. Meanwhile, disturbances across another border were rising, and this was in Pondicherry and the French settlements in South India.[206] It was not Patel but Nehru who wrote to the Madras chief minister about these 'gangster tactics' and suggested that his government could either 'quietly help pro-merger groups' and/or take away contracts/licences from 'merchants engaged in smuggling'.[207] Speaking of the latter, at the Congress' Nasik session, a pamphlet was distributed titled *The Mystery of the Birlas*, giving information about their tax transactions in Bengal and their preference for export–import licences in Bombay.[208] Even 'honest businessmen' like J. R. D. Tata, Ambalal Sarabhai and Purshotamdas Thakurdas were said to concur, and Sri Prakasa was asked to take 'very special care with the Birlas....'[209]

In September 1950, like the Cooper licence case from Bombay seen earlier, the Kesoram cotton mills case from Calcutta came under the public scanner for concealment of income, evading taxes, as well as for getting the investigating officer, N. C. Roy, transferred and suspended. The Kesoram cotton mills had pleaded in June 1948 that their books had been destroyed and then produced, in March 1949, statements of sales. In June, they submitted revised returns showing a higher tax liability, and Roy was transferred in September. Reportedly, he had detected 'the omission of the sale of certain "disposal goods" for Rs. 9 ½ lakh', and the impression strengthened that 'a desire not to hurt the susceptibilities of the assessee [came] in the way'.[210]

Dr B. C. Roy's defiant response laid out the case thus: in June 1948, the Birlas had complained of harassment from N. C. Roy and on that occasion the government had supported the official. A year later, however, his transfer was recommended because he did nothing for 15 months about the Birlas' claim that their manufacturing accounts were destroyed. His successor had proceeded to obtain the figures of production, filed by the firm, in which a large discrepancy of several lakhs of yards in the three years from 1944–45 to 1946–47 was found. Cautioning Nehru against being influenced by either public reportage or pamphleteering, Roy brought up 'similar papers concerning your government, and yourself ... circulated in thousands'; as for N. C. Roy, there was a police enquiry against him for divulging official secrets.[211] Thus checked, Nehru turned to the Attorney-General M. C. Setalvad who, after examining the case, suggested a judicial enquiry, but this was a matter primarily for the state government.[212] Finance Minister C. D. Deshmukh was equally shy of 'sitting in judgement',[213] with the Birlas active in many spheres, Food Minister K. M. Munshi wrote appreciatively of the way 'Mr. Birla secured 10,000 tons of rice from Burma', when the embassy in Rangoon was unable to.[214]

The prime minister gave up and turned towards the Bombay textile workers strike, now more than seven weeks old, with the Kher government arresting thousands and killing dozens and the arrest of Tilakraj Chadha, secretary of the Socialist Party in East Punjab, by the Bhargava government, which kept him as a criminal prisoner, instead of being 'as hard on the profiteers and the black-market....'[215] But, when the communist Shaukat Usmani, who had left for Pakistan, wished to come back, Nehru did not feel obliging. For this old, if 'unreliable', comrade, he was willing to help regarding 'the publication of his stories' but not in the rehabilitation of his life, given the recalcitrance, and worse, of officials from UP to Bengal.[216] A security ordinance that the Rajasthan government had promulgated in September 1949 had now made its way to New Delhi, with a clause on 'hatred or contempt or disaffection towards the government of any Indian province or state or any minister [thereof]'. In this newly merged state, there was no popularly elected assembly, and, because of an absence of a council of states, its government's actions could not be referred to in the central parliament either. Any appraisal was thus 'impossible', which was further suppressed by this ordinance, about which it was also unclear whether the States Ministry was responsible.[217]

In the autumn of 1950, coercion and clashes thus existed in a wide arc from Rajasthan to Assam, with its incoming Bengali immigrants, especially the 15–20 per cent Muslims among them. With no permit system in place, even as 200 Muslims were going to West Pakistan daily via the Sindh border, roughly 120 Muslims were coming from East Pakistan per day into Assam 'searching employment'.[218] It was in the Hyderabad state that this combination of scarcity and uncertainty clashed, specifically in Raichur, which saw food riots from 29 September 1950. Nehru received its report from Padmaja Naidu and forwarded it to Patel, who was visiting Hyderabad:

> ... 2000 people looted grain shops, lathi charge, firing, 1 woman killed, 6 injured ... low ration, resentment that 1 ½ lakh sanctioned for Sardar's reception in Hyderabad ... drawn-out trial of Kasim Razvi, delayed trials of the Laik Ali cabinet ... sent a list to Sardar at his request of Muslim officers arrested 2 years ago ... 2 have been sentenced to death and 1 to 25 years imprisonment ... ironical that they should get death sentence while Kasim Razvi gets away with life sentence and Laik Ali and Moin Nawaz with millions....[219]

Two days after Padmaja Naidu's letter, M. K. Vellodi sent the official account of looting and firing, injuring 12 and killing 2 persons. Vellodi had visited Raichur, interviewed people and disbursed INR 500 to the dead and INR 50–100 to the injured. Vellodi also sent to V. P. Menon a background sketch of the rioting. With much of the post-1948 Hyderabad state apparatus comprising officers from neighbouring provinces, civil supplies were under the control of such a troika, who had not imposed statutory rationing in Raichur, where there were cheap grain shops. During September, as 'off-takes' from government shops increased and food grains were distributed, the officials decided to close these shops and check ration cards, as there was grain available in the market in Raichur, though at higher prices. On 27 September, the first signs of discontent emerged among the 'Harijans regarding the high prices', following which the deputy superintendent of police directed merchants to sell '*jowar* at Re. 1/4/- for 2 *seers*: control price being 3 *seers* per rupee'. The merchants objected and closed their shops, leading to a panicky promise by the local food committee members that government shops will reopen on 29 September. That day, as the supply officer tried to collect labourers to shift grain from the godown to the shops, he was faced by a large crowd, which looted hundreds of bags and then proceeded to the cooperative sales society and looted it as well.

Their stone-throwing was met by police firing, with one woman killed on the spot. All this while, the civil administrator had been away, and the rudderless local administration charged the leader of the Depressed Classes for this trouble, which escalated, leading to more firing. Vellodi justified the closure of the cheap grain shops by claiming that these were meant for 5,000 people but three times more were drawing rations. In Raichur, like elsewhere in the state, there was a ban on the movement of grain between villages, and Vellodi felt that the administrator should have ensured supplies, especially as food was getting precious for the 'Harijans'. Finally, Vellodi turned his attention towards the conduct of the crowd, 'not much a hungry mob', which 'wanted the merchants to sell grain at a [reduced] price', this being a 'proof … of propaganda [led] by Mr. Basavarajappa, leader of Depressed Classes….'[220]

Against this background, when he reached Hyderabad, Vallabhbhai Patel met Vellodi, Padmaja Naidu and the state Congress leaders, while his secretary V. Shankar met the Jamiat leaders, the local press, and a chamber of commerce deputation. Where Nehru had found Padmaja's reports 'sensitive', Patel found her 'hysteric' as he set about answering her. Recalling that originally the number of Razakars detained was 15,654, he claimed that by September 1950, all but 12 had been released. Separately, out of more than 2,000 Razakars arrested for atrocities, 340 had been tried and sentenced to imprisonments or death, 28 were under trial and others released. As regards government servants, 'in one batch, 41 cases were registered, 14 persons arrested, 8 undergoing trials, 50 absconding; in another batch, 29 cases, 27 absconding; in third batch, 51 accused, 11 *chalanned*, 5 acquitted and 35 absconding'.[221] As for the ex-ministers, the matter was before the High Court, and he was meeting 'persons not directly affected by [Razakar] atrocities [but] anxious that these … should be dealt with' and that 'the Nizam should suffer too', and even three out of four Congress ministers were 'against any mercy'. Therefore, Patel awaited the completion of Qasim Razvi's case before considering any clemency, while reasoning that it was 'possible for government servants to avoid … atrocities' by reminding Nehru of considerate civil servants from their freedom movement days.

Giving examples, such as of Mir Asghar Ali, who was 'sentenced to death in a case in which he had some villagers shot, while they were escaping from a burning village, and Baqer Hussain, sentenced to life for similar atrocities committed on Hindus, because they … cut off the beard of a Mohammedan', he pointed out that in neither of these cases were there any ministerial orders. Then, Patel answered Padmaja Naidu's claim, based on press 'canard', about the cost of his reception in Hyderabad. Vellodi had told him that his reception cost was 'not likely to exceed Rs. 12,000', one-tenth of the figure quoted by Naidu. Lastly, he corrected the 'seizure' of properties by the custodian to these being 'frozen' and conceded that families of such government servants should not be left high and dry. By now, however, it was hard to avoid the impression that New Delhi appeared intent 'to make profit' from Hyderabad, with the latest example being the military hospital there, whose equipment was 'taken away to Poona'.[222]

Away from this profiteering, Jagjivan Ram's labour ministry was seeking common minimum wages for agricultural workers across states to the opposition of chief ministers like B. C. Roy. Back in November 1945, the then Ambedkar-led labour department had circulated a bill with provincial support for 'statutory protection against drastic reduction in wages' upon the return of peace. Later, Calcutta agreed that minimum wages could be fixed through industrial tribunals, and this law was passed on 15 March 1948, making it incumbent on provincial governments to fix them by 15 March 1951. Subsequently, there was a meeting of the central advisory board for minimum wages in July 1950. Roy's resistance, based on the following grounds, therefore was a surprise:

(i) fixation of minimum wages for agricultural workers employed seasonally would be unjustified; (ii) … will dislocate rural economy by introducing labour union; (iii) increase price of foodstuffs; (iv) if persons owing up to 5 acres or more are required to pay minimum wages, there will be reluctance to cultivate more, and (v) the cost of inspectorate will be high.[223]

In 1950, there were more than 40 countries across the world that had fixed minimum wages in cash or kind for annually employed workers in regular operations. In India, wages had not kept pace with inflation through the 1940s, especially for agricultural labour, and fixation of minimum wages was expected to induce labour to keep to village and contribute to the grow-more-food campaign.[224] It was hard to believe that given its revenue, the West Bengal government could not implement this step, but Roy was not the only reluctant one; Central Province's R. S. Shukla was another, and he addressed his counterparts in early October 1950.[225] At the Nasik Congress, Shukla had expressed his desire to postpone minimum wages until after the general election and to reconsider the size of holding 'exempted'. Shukla's disapproval extended from the Minimum Wages Act to the planning commission, wherein he demanded greater state representation. Assuring him that the 'actual work … will be done in a state', Nehru nevertheless insisted on 'a coordinated all-India view.…'[226] Issues with essential items illustrate this point. The crux of the sugar problem was effective price and cane movement from producer states like UP and Bihar. On the other hand, there was Bombay, a deficit state struggling with high prices of grains, cotton, oilseeds and tobacco.[227]

The prime minister's feeling of living 'in a state of siege',[228] at this time, was on multiple levels as he was prevailed upon to join Tandon's working committee by Maulana Azad, albeit with renewed misgivings.[229] But in mid-October 1950, Dr Sampurnanand, UP's education and labour minister, engaged him in a spirited correspondence about it. If Nehru felt compelled by circumstances in 1950 to stick together with Patel and Tandon, then Sampurnanand reminded him that in 1942, he had stressed similarly to Congress Socialists, and he bluntly challenged Nehru, 'Can you dismiss anyone?'[230] India had, unlike Russia and China, adopted the old government with its democratic 'trappings' and was being run by the same public servant with their 'pre-1947 mentality'. Concerned that they will all become either 'Communists or Communalists', Sampurnanand criticised Nehru about hurting his old friends in UP as 'we never had a leader in the sense in which CR Das, Lajpat Rai, Sardar Patel and Rajendra Babu were leaders in their provinces', on especially the Muslim exodus from it.[231]

In his reply, Nehru agreed that they needed to stick together but wondered what it was that they were sticking for, admitted that it was a mistake to continue the 'old government' but asked if that was not 'inevitable'. To Sampurnanand's revolutionary examples, he pitted 'Gandhiji's genius … peculiarly suited to India's passivity [and] conservative social structure'.[232]

As for the UP Congress, he was 'feeling ignored' since 1936–37, which had got stronger since 1946–47 with its 'weak handling' of the Ayodhya incident in 1949 and on 'over 200,000 Muslims quitting' in 1950.[233] To this could be added the perennial grievance against the new custodians of old property. Maulana Hussain Ahmed Madani of Deoband,[234] one of the staunchest supporters of the Congress since the early 1920s, ruefully mentioned to Nehru the cases in Delhi of formerly nationalists, now deemed evacuees: Haji Mohammad Din, Haji Ismail and Haji Pherosuddin. Madani then brought up the matter of his family's school in Medina since 1920, started by contributions from the subcontinent and looked after by his brother. By 1950, there were difficulties in sending money there, and Madani sought permission of the Reserve Bank of India for INR 25,000 (far less than the pre-1947 INR 60,000). Madani's own *Darul-Ulum* (est. 1867) was witnessing decline, from 1,700 to 1,100 students, of which 250 were from East Bengal but none from West Pakistan. The question now was about resuming contacts there, and Madani sought permits for certified students.[235]

Meanwhile, Patel was getting worried about the electoral rolls being prepared in East Punjab, which to him showed an 'inflated number of voters in the Sikh areas ... to secure more seats'.[236] There appeared to be an increase of 10 lakh voters from 1945, which required an addition of 10–12 seats, but Chief Minister Bhargava was insisting that this increase, based on temporary allottees who had since moved, was 'fictitious'. One of Bhargava's main worries was that if seats per district were allotted on the new rolls, Jalandhar division will get more seats than Ambala division, and he preferred following the figures of the 1941 census minus the Muslims plus the displaced persons. Bhargava had tried to convince Sukumar Sen unsuccessfully, as another of his fears was that if the new rolls were followed, 'in Jullundur division, the Sikh backward classes candidates may be able to secure 2–3 seats more'.[237] The other place where numbers were starting to matter similarly was Assam, where New Delhi had refused a permit system because it could harm the movement of Hindus from East Bengal. It was also opposed by the West Bengal government, where in a random week the official numbers looked thus:

> 8.10.1950: 4786 Hindus from East to West, 6078 Hindus from West to East, 3231 Muslims from East to West, 2480 Muslims from West to East ... 14.10.1950: 6983 Hindus from East to West, 9935 Hindus from West to East, 2186 Muslims from East to West, 2738 Muslims from West to East.[238]

So, if New Delhi could not have a permit system 'just for Assam' and action could not be taken under the undesirable immigrants act, then what could be done about the 'Muslim new-comers to Assam'?[239] Simultaneously, the Delhi

Pact was undercut powerfully by none other than Achhru Ram, the custodian-general, who called it a 'hoax', in just one of many such examples of senior officials holding 'strong views not in consonance with the government'.[240] It applied to each of the following statements of government policy: (*a*) 'the return of Hindu migrants to East Bengal', (*b*) 'Muslims going to West Pakistan via Sind', (*c*) '[food] supplies from abroad', (*d*) 'surplus provinces to loan less fortunate states', (*e*) continuing control on sugar/*gur*, potential control on newsprint and duty on hessian, and (*f*) 'the preparation for the general election [for] May 1951'.[241]

An immediate example was provided by the Bhargava government that expressed its regret in loaning quantities larger than 15,000 tons wheat and 5,000 tons rice by end-December 1950 and that too with a 'guarantee' that this loan will be returned from early-January 1951. East Punjab's estimated 2,00,000 tons food grains had 42,000 tons wheat earmarked for export and 18,000 tons for seed. Of the remainder, 1,25,000 tons were saved for the state to see through to end-February. With no procurement due until May 1951 and an expected delay in imports, Bhargava feared becoming a 'deficit state',[242] given the control of gram by the centre and the consequent withholding of *bajra* by producers. With 'direct government dealings' of this kind either sending 'the prices up or the stuff underground', Food Minister Munshi asked a Delhi merchant, Dhan Kanwar Jain, who was able to supply 50,000–1,00,000 tons at 'slightly above the control price', demonstrating thereby that food was 'available in private hands....'[243]

Checkmated thus by the 'cumbrous' officials, the prime minister was also checked by his colleagues, like N. V. Gadgil, who demanded that 'only in very rare circumstances should the PM speak in advance of cabinet decision. Even [then], he should consult the principal colleagues … where the cabinet works through sub-committees, the proceedings should be made available in time'.[244] Amidst all this, in November 1950, President Prasad demanded that 'previous knowledge', as against 'compulsory learning', of Hindi be required of new recruits to government service.[245] Dr Syed Mahmud from Patna could not help but muse that they were 'happy when striving for freedom but the fulfilment of that object brought its own punishment'.[246] A prime example was Dr B. R. Ambedkar's striving for changes in the proposed Hindu Code Bill on the major controversies in the matter, namely 'monogamy, divorce, joint family, succession, daughter's share and matriarchal systems'.[247] Another was Nehru drafting the planning commission's conciliatory reply to a recalcitrant Munshi promising non-interference,[248] when the latter complained of being made to feel 'like a delinquent child' by the overreaching commission.[249]

An organisation that was perpetually overreaching was the set-up of custodians of property across the country but especially in UP. Calling them a 'monster … above the government',[250] Nehru was anguished at their discrimination on a sequence of cases from Agra, whose facts were as follows.[251] On 2 June 1950, a representation was received by the relief and rehabilitation ministry from the Agra shoe market association for an allotment of shops to the Muslim shopkeepers, given the unsettled conditions. Next day, the ministry wrote to the UP custodian, and soon after, Ajit Prasad Jain, the rehabilitation minister, went to Lucknow to discuss this matter. It was agreed that in the atmosphere then prevailing in Agra, any allotment of shops to refugees was likely to create panic among the Muslims, but nor could Muslim 'pockets' be created. Accordingly, the association was asked to send its nominations and it suggested eleven names to the assistant custodian who, 'demoralised' at this diminution of his authority, allotted the shops to the nominees without making any enquiries. Subsequently, it was found that these nominees were those who either already had shops or were outsiders, and their allotment had the perverse effect of keeping Muslim shopkeepers in 'pockets' surrounded by displaced non-Muslims. The matter was reconsidered, and on 9 October, orders were passed to restrict allotments to only those in the shoe-making business, and the UP custodian came to Agra to oversee this but, instead, re-allotted 17 shops, including these 11, to the refugees. Now, the association appealed to Azad, who brought the matter to Jain, pointing out that six (Muslims) out of the 11 allottees had been given possession. Jain requested the UP custodian to consider restoration in these six cases, only to realise that evacuee property was the preserve of the judiciary. This led to his plea to the prime minister to notify exclusions from the purview of the law for such cases.

Nehru, Azad and Jain were getting agitated in a futile cause, for when the UP government did 'nothing about settling Brahmin agriculturalists from Rawalpindi',[252] who were associates of Subhas Chandra Bose, there was little hope for Muslim shoemaker-shopkeepers in Agra. And yet, the same UP government was proposing to create 143 two-member constituencies for its 430-strong legislative assembly,[253] of which 90 were to have a seat reserved for the Scheduled Castes, while the remaining 53 were for 'some Muslims if possible'. The central cabinet and Sukumar Sen were opposed to this proposal because two-member constituencies were for Scheduled Castes and Scheduled Tribes only. Sen had a connected question on 'the necessity to reserve' single-member constituencies for the Scheduled Tribes, as in certain areas in Orissa, Madhya Bharat and Bombay, the concentration of Scheduled Tribes was '70–80% or more', and Sen argued that even if two adjoining constituencies were combined, their percentage would remain 'above 60%'. Thus, though only one seat in that two-member constituency would be reserved, 'both the seats will go to the Scheduled Tribes', while the state would 'still be required to reserve another seat...', and Sen proposed that in such areas they should have two single-member constituencies. Such a 'contingency' did not arise in the case of Schedule Castes as their concentration was 'nowhere near 50% in any area'.[254]

All this calculation had been triggered by JP's protest at the government's favoured first-past-the-post-system of voting as opposed to proportional arrangements.[255] Nehru moved swiftly and checked the UP government's proposal and JP's protest simultaneously, while agreeing with Sen that 'there might occasionally be one reserved seat for Scheduled Tribes in a single-member constituency'.[256] Soon after, Dr Mookerjee wanted voting rights for 'migrants from Pakistan', with 31 December 1950 as the cut-off date, and Nehru assured Mookerjee that while 'the great number' of these migrants were on the electoral rolls, it was difficult to distinguish between permanent and temporary residents. Here, Dr Ambedkar agreed with the prime minister that it was not possible 'to bring these people in without upsetting all our work'.[257] These permutations confirmed that the general election had now been 'fixed for November–December 1951', although the food situation would push it further.[258]

JP continued with his challenging posers that first-past-the-post was 'a dishonest device to artificially multiply the strength of the majority party and to deny any representation even to a 49% minority'.[259] But, his remained a marginal voice, as was Chief Justice Kania an emerging problem. When N. V. Gadgil, central minister for works, said in the parliament that if the Supreme Court declares a particular legislation 'unreasonable, it is going beyond its jurisdiction',[260] Kania protested to Nehru, who affirmed that in their peculiar situation if an interpretation of the constitution given by the courts was 'not what the makers [had] intended', then the latter would 'amend' it.[261] All this was pushed into the background from December 1950, when India's food crisis saw 'the hand [did] not reach the mouth' in several states.[262]

A food ministers' conference was called on 11–12 December as the spirit of self-reliance gave way for import of 37 lakh tons of food grains in 1951, of which 27 were for Bihar, UP and MP, with Madras, Bombay, Saurashtra and Hyderabad being the other areas under strain. A *Hungry India* was 'living from ship to mouth', in the words of K. M. Munshi.[263] These 37 lakh tons would require 150 ships, stretching the 'forex', and with 'unreal' prices, despite existing controls, and freight charges rising (due to the Korean War), Madras gave up rural rationing and protest was in the air. In UP, C. B. Gupta was 'brick-batted' at Agra; in Bombay, *morcha*s were staged, and the only option was to seek grains and ships from America and Britain. Internally, it was time 'to shelve all expenditures [like] capital for Punjab', and what was the point in holding the general election at a time of 'grave national emergency', Munshi asked.[264]

Instead, Nehru took on prohibition, a topic with a Gandhian stamp,[265] having got his opportunity in a request from the Central Provinces home minister D. P. Mishra, who had sketched the financial position of his state vis-à-vis prohibition, wherein the expected surplus was nullified by crop failure, relief works, dearness allowance, price-rise, grow-more-food' and had turned into 'a deficit'.[266] With the abolition of state sales tax and *malguzari*, the revenue side showed loss and the political ground an 'agitation', and the one revenue-generator was to reconsider the policy of prohibition, introduced in the province in 1938, without any 'real decrease' in drinking, illicit liquor and crimes. On the other hand, the loss of revenue from prohibition was an estimated INR 156 lakhs in 1950–51. Armed with this information, Nehru was 'agreeable to any step' that Mishra might take.[267]

Around the time that state food ministers were conferring in Bombay, J. B. Kripalani was moving to inflict a possible political cost on his party, by announcing the formation of a Congress Democratic Front (CDF) as a 'watch dog'.[268] To Tandon, Kripalani wrote that it was natural to the 'game of democracy' between and within parties, that too in a broad outfit like the Congress, and the front was formed with a four-fold aim of challenging the party's 'malpractices', its 'partisan' president, seeking an 'impartial enquiry' in his election and putting an end to 'cliques'.[269] When Nehru admonished the 'ordinary man' in the parliament on 7 December 1950 for not putting up with a few more controls or a little less sugar, the Gandhian Kishorilal Mashruwala admonished him in turn, reminding him of these cliques and their 'corruption'; the prime minister could only reply that 'government functions through a vast number of functionaries....'[270] His admission was poignant for, two days before, on 15 December 1950, the government had lost one its most important functionaries, Vallabhbhai Patel. His death at the age of 75 was not only 'a heavy blow' for Nehru but also brought the curtain down on the post-Gandhi era of the *duumvirate* atop Indian politics. Much has been made about the Nehru–Patel equation, which will be under focus in the next part. It is sufficient to close this with one of Nehru's many tributes to his closest (at the time of death), longest (in their political life) and strongest (inside government since September 1946) colleague:

> There will always be a sense of emptiness for those who had the privilege of knowing and working with Sardar Vallabhbhai Patel ... a mixture of single-mindedness and many-sided activities.... He has left his powerful impress.... You will have to do without him.... Disciplined and co-ordinated action was [his] great strength and it is this that we must learn from him.[271]

NOTES

1   Das, *Sardar Patel's Correspondence 1945–50 Vol. X* (1974), lxxvi.
2   7 January 1950, Nehru to Rajendra Prasad, File No. 34, JN (SG) Papers.
3   18 January 1950, Nehru to provincial premiers, File No. 35, JN (SG) Papers.
4   19 January 1950, Krishna Menon to Nehru, File No. 35, JN (SG) Papers.
5   20 January 1950, Nehru to Krishna Menon, File No. 35, JN (SG) Papers. See De, 'Between Midnight and Republic', 1231.
6   21 January 1950, Nehru to Mohanlal Saksena, File No. 35, JN (SG) Papers.
7   21 January 1950, Nehru to Kumaraswamy Raja, File No. 35, JN (SG) Papers.
8   22 January 1950, Nehru to Gadgil, File No. 35, JN (SG) Papers.
9   23 January 1950, Note by V. P. Menon, File No. 35, JN (SG) Papers.
10   On this territorial, administrative and 'emotional integration' directed by Patel, see Das, *Sardar Patel's Correspondence 1945–50 Vol. VII* (1973), li–lvii.
11   23 January 1950, Nehru to Patel, File No. 35, JN (SG) Papers. See A. Sengupta and R. Sharma, eds., *Appointment of Judges to the Supreme Court of India: Transparency, Accountability, and Independence* (New Delhi: Oxford University Press, 2018), 3–17.
12   1 February 1950, Nehru to Kher, File No. 36 (Part I), JN (SG) Papers. See Aditya Balasubramanian, *Toward a Free Economy: Swatantra and Opposition Politics in Democratic India* (Princeton: Princeton University Press, 2023).
13   2 February 1950, Nehru to chief ministers, File No. 36 (Part I), JN (SG) Papers.
14   7 February 1950, Nehru to chief ministers, File No. 36 (Part II), JN (SG) Papers.
15   13 February 1950, Krishna Menon to Nehru, File No. 36 (Part II), JN (SG) Papers.
16   14 February 1950, Ayyangar to Nehru, File No. 36 (Part II), JN (SG) Papers.
17   14 February 1950, Nehru to Rafi Ahmed Kidwai, File No. 36 (Part II), JN (SG) Papers.
18   14 February 1950, Nehru to Saksena and Ayyangar, File No. 36 (Part II), JN (SG) Papers.
19   17 February 1950, Nehru to Matthai, File No. 37 (Part I), JN (SG) Papers
20   D. Tripathi and J. Jumani, *The Concise Oxford History of Indian Business History* (New Delhi: Oxford University Press, 2007), 144–81; and D. Lockwood, *The Indian Bourgeoisie: A Political History of the Indian Capitalist Class in the Early Twentieth Century* (London: Bloomsbury Academic, 2020), 174–94.
21   16 February 1950, Nehru to Matthai, File No. 37 (Part I), JN (SG) Papers.
22   14 March 1950, Bhargava to Patel, Correspondences, Gopichand Bhargava Papers, NMML.
23   Rai, *Partition of the Punjab*, 198–217.
24   22 March 1950, Trivedi to Bhargava, Correspondences, Bhargava Papers.
25   Sekhar Bandyopadhyay, with Anasua Basu Ray Chaudhury, 'Partition in Bengal: Re-visiting the Caste Question, 1946–47', *Studies in History* 33, no. 2 (2017): 234–61.
26   20 February 1950, Azad to Nehru, File No. 37 (Part I), JN (SG) Papers. The next para is based on this letter.

27   21 February 1950, Nehru to Saksena, File No. 37 (Part I), JN (SG) Papers.

28   10 April 1950, Syed Abdur Rouf to Azad, File No. 41 (Part II), JN (SG) Papers.

29   U. Misra, *Burden of History: Assam and the Partition-Unresolved Issues* (New Delhi: Oxford University Press, 2018), 141–62.

30   3 March 1950, Nehru to Mavlankar, File No. 38, JN (SG) Papers.

31   See Dhirendra K. Jha and Krishna Jha, *Ayodhya: The Dark Night—The Secret History of Rama's Appearance in Babri Masjid* (Delhi: HarperCollins, 2016).

32   5 March 1950, Nehru to Kishorilal G. Mashruwala, File No. 38, JN (SG) Papers.

33   4 March 1950, K. C. Neogy to Nehru, File No. 38, JN (SG) Papers.

34   4 March 1950, Nehru to Neogy, File No. 38, JN (SG) Papers.

35   8/9 April 1950, Nehru to Saksena and Bakshi Ghulam Mohammad, File No. 41 (Part II), JN (SG) Papers. See C. Snedden, 'What Happened to Muslims in Jammu? Local Identity, "The Massacre of 1947" and the Roots of the "Kashmir Problem"', *South Asia: Journal of South Asian Studies* 24, no. 2 (2001): 111–34.

36   3 March 1950, Nehru to Pant, File No. 38, JN (SG) Papers.

37   10 April 1950, Nehru to Pant, File No. 41 (Part II), JN (SG) Papers.

38   22 March 1950, Sarabhai to Ayyangar, Correspondences, Ayyangar Papers.

39   9 April 1950, Nehru to Mookerjee, File No. 41 (Part II), JN (SG) Papers.

40   10 April 1950, Mookerjee to Nehru, File No. 41 (Part II), JN (SG) Papers.

41   10 April 1950, Nehru to Mookerjee, File No. 41 (Part II), JN (SG) Papers.

42   12 April 1950, Nehru to Mookerjee, File No. 41 (Part II), JN (SG) Papers.

43   P. K. Chatterji, *Syama Prasad Mookerjee and Indian Politics* (Delhi: Foundation Books, 2022), 210–62.

44   10 April 1950, Nehru to Roy, File No. 41 (Part II), JN (SG) Papers.

45   10 and 11 April 1950, Nehru to Bardoloi, File No. 41 (Part II), JN (SG) Papers.

46   11 April 1950, Nehru to Rajagopalachari, File No. 41 (Part II), JN (SG) Papers. Chatterji, *The Spoils of Partition*, 159–208.

47   13 April 1950, Nehru to Rajagopalachari, File No. 41 (Part II), JN (SG) Papers.

48   12 April 1950, Nehru to Pandit and 13 April 1950, Nehru to Roy, File No. 41 (Part II), JN (SG) Papers.

49   17 April 1950, Roy to Nehru, File No. 42 (Part I), JN (SG) Papers.

50   14 April 1950, Radhakrishnan to Nehru, File No. 41 (Part II), JN (SG) Papers.

51   13 April 1950, Rajagopalachari to Nehru, File No. 41 (Part II), JN (SG) Papers.

52   14 April 1950, Nehru to Rajagopalachari and Prasad, File No. 41 (Part II), JN (SG) Papers.

53   19 April 1950, Nehru to Ghosh, File No. 42 (Part I), JN (SG) Papers.

54   See Das, *Sardar Patel's Correspondence 1945–50 Vol. IX* (1974).

55   12 April 1950, M. O. Mathai to Nehru, File No. 41 (Part II), JN (SG) Papers. See Subhasri Ghosh, ed., *The 1947 Partition in The East: Trends and Trajectories* (Abingdon: Routledge, 2022).

56   12 April 1950, Nehru to Kher, File No. 41 (Part II), JN (SG) Papers.

57   12 April 1950, Nehru to R. S. Shukla, File No. 41 (Part II), JN (SG) Papers. See G. Carnall, *Gandhi's Interpreter: A Life of Horace Alexander* (Edinburgh: Edinburgh University Press, 2010).

58 11 and 12 April 1950, Nehru to Mohanlal Saksena, File No. 41 (Part II), JN (SG) Papers.

59 15 April 1950, Nehru to chief ministers, File No. 41 (Part II), JN (SG) Papers.

60 14 April 1950, Nehru to Saksena, File No. 41 (Part II), JN (SG) Papers.

61 18 April 1950, Nehru to Saksena, File No. 42 (Part I), JN (SG) Papers.

62 Pallavi Raghavan, *Animosity at Bay: An Alternative History of the India–Pakistan Relationship, 1947–1952* (New York: Oxford University Press, 2020), 47–72.

63 Yasmin Khan, 'The Arrival Impact of Partition Refugees in Uttar Pradesh, 1947–52', *Contemporary South Asia* 12, no. 4 (2003): 511–22.

64 17 April 1950, Nehru to Pant, File No. 42 (Part I), JN (SG) Papers. See Pratinav Anil, *Another India: The Making of the World's Largest Muslim Minority, 1947–77* (London: Hurst, 2023).

65 3 May 1950, Nehru to Subimal Dutt, File No. 43 (Part I), JN (SG) Papers.

66 17 April 1950, Cabinet Meeting on India–Pakistan trade, File No. 42 (Part I), JN (SG) Papers.

67 19 April 1950, Nehru to Liaquat, File No. 42 (Part I), JN (SG) Papers.

68 Willem van Schendel, *The Bengal Borderland: Beyond State and Nation in South Asia* (London: Anthem Press, 2004), 256–96.

69 1 May 1950, Nehru to Roy, File No. 43 (Part I), JN (SG) Papers.

70 14 April 1950, Nehru to Liaquat, Correspondences, Ayyangar Papers.

71 3 May 1950, Nehru to Roy, File No. 43 (Part I), JN (SG) Papers.

72 18 April 1950, Nehru to chief ministers, File No. 42 (Part I), JN (SG) Papers. See David C. Potter, *India's Political Administrators: From ICS to IAS* (Oxford: Oxford University Press, 1996).

73 18 April 1950, Nehru to Bhargava, File No. 42 (Part I), JN (SG) Papers.

74 1 May 1950, H. K. Bhattacharjee to Nehru and Patel, File No. 43 (Part I), JN (SG) Papers.

75 2 May 1950, Nehru to Krishna Menon, File No. 43 (Part I), JN (SG) Papers.

76 1 May 1950, Nehru to Pant, File No. 43 (Part I), JN (SG) Papers. See S. R. Bakshi, *Govind Ballabh Pant: The True Gandhian* (Delhi: South Asia Books, 1991).

77 2 May 1950, Nehru to Pant, File No. 43 (Part I), JN (SG) Papers.

78 1 May 1950, Nehru to Sri Prakasa and 5 May 1950, Nehru to Bardoloi, File No. 43 (Part I), JN (SG) Papers.

79 6 May 1950, Nehru to Bardoloi, File No. 43 (Part I), JN (SG) Papers.

80 18 May 1950, Ayyangar to Nehru, File No. 44 (Part I), JN (SG) Papers.

81 18–19 May 1950, Nehru to Ayyangar, File No. 44 (Part I), JN (SG) Papers.

82 21 May 1950, Nehru to Prasad, File No. 44 (Part I), JN (SG) Papers.

83 23 May 1950, Patel to Nehru, File No. 44 (Part I), JN (SG) Papers.

84 2 May 1950, Nehru to chief ministers, File No. 43 (Part I), JN (SG) Papers.

85 29 April 1950, K. D. Malaviya, to Nehru, File No. 43 (Part I), JN (SG) Papers.

86 18 May 1950, Nehru to Lester Pearson, File No. 44 (Part I), JN (SG) Papers.

87 21 May 1950, Nehru to Pant, File No. 44 (Part I), JN (SG) Papers.

88   21 May 1950, Nehru to Rafi Ahmed Kidwai, File No. 44 (Part I), JN (SG) Papers. See R. Biswas, *R. A. Kidwai: Bridging Region and Nation: A Political Biography* (Chennai: Notion Press, 2020).

89   19 May 1950, JP to Nehru, File No. 44 (Part I), JN (SG) Papers.

90   21 May 1950, Kania to Nehru, File No. 44 (Part I), JN (SG) Papers. See George H. Gadbois Jr., *Supreme Court of India: The Beginnings* (New York: Oxford University Press, 2018), ch. 3.

91   21 May 1950, Nehru to Kania, File No. 44 (Part I), JN (SG) Papers.

92   22–23 May 1950, Saksena to Nehru, D. O. No. 1999/PSMR, File No. 45 (Part I), JN (SG) Papers.

93   23 May 1950, Nehru to Saksena, No. 651-PM, File No. 45 (Part I), JN (SG) Papers.

94   23 May 1950, Ramkrishna Dalmia to Nehru, File No. 45 (Part I), JN (SG) Papers.

95   23 May 1950, Nehru to Roy, File No. 45 (Part I), JN (SG) Papers.

96   14 June 1950, Subimal Dutt's report, File No. 46 (Part I), JN (SG) Papers.

97   Ian Copland, 'The Further Shores of Partition: Ethnic Cleansing in Rajasthan in 1947', *Past and Present* 160, no. 1 (1998): 203–39.

98   24 May 1950, Nehru to Hiralal Atal, File No. 45 (Part I), JN (SG) Papers.

99   25 May 1950, Nehru to Saksena, File No. 45 (Part I), JN (SG) Papers.

100   25 May 1950, Nehru to Azad, File No. 45 (Part I), JN (SG) Papers.

101   25 May 1950, Nehru to Dharma Vira, File No. 45 (Part I), JN (SG) Papers.

102   2 August 1950, Nehru to Ajit Prasad Jain, File No. 50 (Part I), JN (SG) Papers. See Uditi Sen, *Citizen Refugee: Forging the Indian Nation after Partition* (Cambridge: Cambridge University Press, 2018), 23–70.

103   20 May 1950, Jung to Nehru and 25 May 1950, Nehru to Pant, File No. 45 (Part I), JN (SG) Papers.

104   26 May 1950, Mahtab to Nanda, File No. 47 (Part I), JN (SG) Papers.

105   10 July 1950, Mahtab to Shankarrao Deo, File No. 48 (Part I), JN (SG) Papers.

106   Arudra Burra, 'The Indian Civil Service and the Nationalist Movement: Neutrality, Politics and Continuity', *Commonwealth and Comparative Politics* 48, no. 4 (2010): 404–32.

107   1 and 4 June 1950, Nehru to Krishna Menon, File No. 46 (Part I), JN (SG) Papers.

108   27 June 1950, Nehru to Ayyangar and Ajit Jain, File No. 46 (Part II), JN (SG) Papers.

109   4 July 1950, Nehru to Baldev Singh and Prem Krishen, File No. 47 (Part I), JN (SG) Papers.

110   29 June 1950, K. M. Munshi to Nehru, File No. 46 (Part II), JN (SG) Papers.

111   30 June 1950, Nehru to Deshmukh and Varadachariar, File No. 46 (Part II), JN (SG) Papers.

112   27 June 1950, H. P. Mody to Nehru, File No. 46 (Part II), JN (SG) Papers.

113   3 July 1950, Varadachariar to Nehru, File No. 47 (Part II), JN (SG) Papers.

114   7 July 1950, Deshmukh to Nehru, File No. 47 (Part II), JN (SG) Papers.

115 8 July 1950, Nehru to Mody, File No. 47 (Part II), JN (SG) Papers. See Gould, *Bureaucracy, Community, and Influence in India*, 104–36.

116 29 July 1950, Mody to Nehru, File No. 49 (Part II), JN (SG) Papers. See Indivar Kamtekar, 'A Different War Dance: State and Class in India 1939–1945', *Past and Present* 176, no. 1 (2002): 187–221.

117 28 August 1950, Deshmukh to Nehru, File No. 53 (Part I), JN (SG) Papers.

118 2–4 July 1950, Nehru–Sri Prakasa exchange, File No. 47 (Part I and II), JN (SG) Papers.

119 For Patel's position on both evacuee property and language policy, see Das, *Sardar Patel's Correspondence 1945–50 Vol. VIII* (1973).

120 1 July 1950, Nehru to Patel and Azad, File No. 47 (Part I), JN (SG) Papers. See Alonso, *Radio for the Millions*, 85–105.

121 3 July 1950, Nehru to Ayyangar, Jain and Prakasa, File No. 47 (Part I), JN (SG) Papers.

122 2 July 1950, Nehru to chief ministers, File No. 47 (Part I), JN (SG) Papers.

123 9 July 1950, Nehru to Shastri, File No. 48 (Part I), JN (SG) Papers.

124 9 July 1950, Nehru to Bhargava, File No. 48 (Part I), JN (SG) Papers.

125 9–12 September 1950, Nehru–Ayyangar exchange, File Nos. 48 (Part I) and 55 (Part I), JN (SG) Papers.

126 9 July 1950, Nehru to Ajit Prasad Jain, File No. 48 (Part I), JN (SG) Papers.

127 6–8 July 1950, Bhargava–Patel exchange, Correspondences, Bhargava Papers.

128 10–11 July 1950 Nehru to Baldev Singh, Patel and Trivedi, File No. 48 (Part I), JN (SG) Papers.

129 14 July 1950, Baldev Singh–Nehru exchange, File No. 48 (Part II), JN (SG) Papers.

130 25 July 1950, Nehru to Cariappa, File No. 49 (Part I), JN (SG) Papers.

131 Undated, early-July 1950, note by B. Shiva Rao, File No. 48 (Part I), JN (SG) Papers.

132 12 July 1950, Nehru to N. R. Pillai, File No. 48 (Part I), JN (SG) Papers.

133 8–15 July 1950, Ajit Prasad Jain to Nehru, File No. 48 (Part II), JN (SG) Papers.

134 25 July 1950, Nehru to Patel, Ambedkar, and Prasad, File No. 49 (Part I), JN (SG) Papers.

135 13–14 July 1950, Nehru to Roy, File No. 48 (Part II), JN (SG) Papers.

136 15 July 1950, Nehru to chief ministers, File No. 48 (Part II), JN (SG) Papers.

137 Javeed Alam, 'State and the Making of Communist Politics in India, 1947–57', *Economic and Political Weekly* 26, no. 45 (1991): 2573–83.

138 21 July 1950, Iengar to chief secretaries, File No. 49 (Part I), JN (SG) Papers.

139 22 July 1950, Azad to Nehru, File No. 49 (Part I), JN (SG) Papers.

140 26 July 1950, Nehru to Deshmukh, File No. 49 (Part II), JN (SG) Papers.

141 12 July 1950, Mahalanobis to Pitambar Pant, File No. 49 (Part II), JN (SG) Papers.

142 19 June 1950, Trone to Mahalanobis, File No. 49 (Part II), JN (SG) Papers.

143 25 July and 28 August 1950, Deshmukh to Nehru, File Nos. 49 (Part II) and 53 (Part I), JN (SG) Papers.

144 28 July 1950, File No. 50 (Part I), JN (SG) Papers.

145 24 August 1950, Ambedkar to Brigadier Misra, File No. 54 (Part I), JN (SG) Papers.

146 2 September 1950, Nehru to Ambedkar, File No. 54 (Part I), JN (SG) Papers. See M. S. A. Rao, 'Caste and the Indian Army', *Economic and Political Weekly* 16, no. 35 (1964): 1439–43.

147 1 August 1950, Nehru's reply to H. V. Kamath, File No. 50 (Part I), JN (SG) Papers.

148 1 August 1950, Roy to Nehru, No. 610-CM, File No. 50 (Part I), JN (SG) Papers. See Chatterji, *The Spoils of Partition*, 211–60.

149 5 August 1950, Cabinet Meeting, Case 318/52/50, File No. 50 (Part II), JN (SG) Papers.

150 13 August 1950, Nehru to Roy, File No. 51 (Part II), JN (SG) Papers.

151 20 August 1950, Nehru to Ajit Prasad Jain, File No. 52 (Part I), JN (SG) Papers.

152 5 August 1950, Cabinet Meeting, Case 314/52/50, File No. 50 (Part II), JN (SG) Papers.

153 11 August 1950, Nehru to Prasad, File No. 51 (Part I), JN (SG) Papers.

154 Weiner, *Party Politics in India*, 65–97.

155 8 August 1950, Nehru to Tandon, File No. 51 (Part I), JN (SG) Papers.

156 See Das, *Sardar Patel's Correspondence 1945–1950 Vol. X* (1974).

157 9 August 1950, Patel to Nehru, File No. 51 (Part I), JN (SG) Papers.

158 9 August 1950, Nehru to Patel, File No. 51 (Part I), JN (SG) Papers.

159 11–12 August 1950, Nehru–Patel exchange, File No. 51 (Part II), JN (SG) Papers.

160 12 August 1950, Tandon to Nehru, File No. 51 (Part II), JN (SG) Papers. W. Gould, *Hindu Nationalism, and the Language of Politics in Late Colonial India* (Cambridge: Cambridge University Press, 2004), 234–64.

161 14 August 1950, Nehru to Sinha, File No. 51 (Part II), JN (SG) Papers. See R. H. Mills, 'India's Food Crisis', *Far Eastern Survey* 28, no. 10 (1959): 145–49.

162 12 and 15 August 1950, Patel to Nehru, File No. 51 (Part II), JN (SG) Papers.

163 15 August 1950, Nehru to Patel, File No. 51 (Part II), JN (SG) Papers.

164 Saagar Tewari, 'Kasht-nivarak Thakkar Bapa: Samaj seva ko samarpit jeevan par ek vihangam drishti', *Pratiman* 5, no. 10 (2017): 278–96.

165 16 August 1950, Nehru to Patel, File No. 52 (Part I), JN (SG) Papers.

166 22 August 1950, Patel to Nehru, File No. 53 (Part I), JN (SG) Papers.

167 24 August 1950, Rajagopalachari to Nehru, File No. 53 (Part I), JN (SG) Papers. See M. Prasad, *A Gandhian Patriarch: A Political and Spiritual Biography of Kaka Kalelkar* (Bombay: Popular, 1965).

168 25 August 1950, Patel to Nehru, File No. 53 (Part I), JN (SG) Papers.

169 27–30–31 August 1950, Nehru–Rajagopalachari–Patel correspondence, File No. 53 (Part II), JN (SG) Papers.

170 11 September 1950, Patel to Nehru, File No. 55 (Part II), JN (SG) Papers.

171 9–11–14–16 September 1950, Nehru–Patel correspondence, File No. 55 (Part II), JN (SG) Papers.

172 16 August 1950, P. P. Varma to Nehru, File No. 52 (Part I), JN (SG) Papers. See D. Klingensmith, *'One Valley and a Thousand': Dams, Nationalism, and Development* (New Delhi: Oxford University Press, 2007), 190.

173 18 August 1950, Nehru to PMS, File No. 52 (Part I), JN (SG) Papers.
174 20 August 1950, Nehru to Patel and Jagjivan Ram, File No. 52 (Part I), JN (SG) Papers.
175 26 August 1950, Nehru to chief ministers, File No. 53 (Part I), JN (SG) Papers.
176 18/19 August 1950, IB report, File No. 53 (Part I), JN (SG) Papers, File No. 53-I. See Craig Baxter, *The Jana Sangh; A Biography of an Indian Political Party* (Philadelphia: UPenn Press, 1969), 31–53, 107–52.
177 20 August 1950, Nehru to Ajit Prasad Jain, File No. 52 (Part I), JN (SG) Papers.
178 23 August 1950, Talk between Nehru and G. Ramachandran, File No. 53 (Part I), JN (SG) Papers.
179 21 and 25 August 1950, Krishna Menon–Nehru exchange, File No. 53 (Part I), JN (SG) Papers.
180 See Henry C. Hart, *New India's Rivers* (Hyderabad: Orient Longman, 1956).
181 See D. Haines, *Rivers Divided: Indus Basin Waters in the Making of India and Pakistan* (Oxford: Oxford University Press, 2017).
182 23 August 1950, Trivedi to Nehru, and 26 August 1950, Deshmukh to Nehru, File Nos. 53 (Part I) and 54 (Part II), JN (SG) Papers.
183 9 September 1950, Trivedi to Nehru, File No. 54 (Part II), JN (SG) Papers.
184 27 August 1950, Vellodi to Buch, File No. 53 (Part I), JN (SG) Papers.
185 28 August 1950, Nehru to Munshi, File No. 53 (Part I), JN (SG) Papers.
186 28 August 1950, Nehru to Nellie Sengupta, File No. 53 (Part I), JN (SG) Papers. See Sengupta, 'They Must Have to Go Therefore, Elsewhere'.
187 29 August 1950, Mathai's note on Rajagopalachari–Amrit Kaur talks, File No. 53 (Part I), JN (SG) Papers.
188 31 August 1950, Nehru to Nanda, File No. 53 (Part II), JN (SG) Papers.
189 30 August 1950, Nehru's note, File No. 53 (Part II), JN (SG) Papers.
190 Berenice Guyot-Rechard, 'Reordering a Border Space: Relief, Rehabilitation, and Nation-building in North-eastern India after the 1950 Assam Earthquake', *Modern Asian Studies* 49, no. 4 (2015): 931–62.
191 1 September 1950, Nehru to chief ministers, File No. 54 (Part I), JN (SG) Papers.
192 2 September 1950, Nehru to Sri Prakasa, File No. 54 (Part I), JN (SG) Papers.
193 13 and 21 September 1950, Nehru to Sri Prakasa, File Nos. 55 (Part I) and 56 (Part I), JN (SG) Papers.
194 24 September 1950, Sri Prakasa to Nehru, File No. 56 (Part I), JN (SG) Papers.
195 2 September 1950, Nehru to Sinha, File No. 54 (Part I), JN (SG) Papers.
196 Sarah Ansari and William Gould, *Boundaries of Belonging: Localities, Citizenship and Rights in India and Pakistan* (Cambridge: Cambridge University Press, 2019), 103–34.
197 2 September 1950, Munshi to Nehru, File No. 54 (Part I), JN (SG) Papers.
198 7 September 1950, Bhimsen Sachar to Nehru, File No. 54 (Part II), JN (SG) Papers.
199 8 September 1950, M. O. Mathai's note, File No. 54 (Part II), JN (SG) Papers.
200 12 September 1950, Nehru to Ajit Prasad Jain, File No. 55 (Part I), JN (SG) Papers.

201 14 September 1950, Sachar to Nehru, File No. 55 (Part I), JN (SG) Papers. See Kochanek, *The Congress Party of India*, 27–53.

202 19 September 1950, Mathai's note, File No. 55 (Part II), JN (SG) Papers.

203 20 September 1950, Sucheta Kripalani to Tandon, File No. 56 (Part I), JN (SG) Papers.

204 1 October 1950, Malaviya to Nehru, File No. 58 (Part I), JN (SG) Papers.

205 14 September 1950, Nehru to chief ministers, File No. 55 (Part II), JN (SG) Papers.

206 See Jessica Namakkal, *Unsettling Utopia: The Making and Unmaking of French India* (New York: Columbia University Press, 2021).

207 25 September 1950, Nehru to Kumaraswamy Raja, File No. 56 (Part I), JN (SG) Papers.

208 27 September 1950, Nehru to chief ministers, File No. 56 (Part II), JN (SG) Papers. Rohit De, *A People's Constitution: The Everyday Life of Law in the Indian Republic* (Princeton: Princeton University Press, 2018), 77–122.

209 27 September 1950, Nehru to Mahtab and Sri Prakasa, File No. 56 (Part II), JN (SG) Papers.

210 28 September 1950, Nehru to Roy, File No. 56 (Part II), JN (SG) Papers.

211 13–14 October 1950, Roy to Nehru, File No. 59 (Part II), JN (SG) Papers.

212 31 October 1950, M. C. Setalvad to Nehru, File No. 61 (Part II), JN (SG) Papers.

213 11 November 1950, Deshmukh to Nehru, File No. 63 (Part I), JN (SG) Papers.

214 28 September 1950, Munshi to Nehru, File No. 56 (Part II), JN (SG) Papers.

215 28 September 1950, R. K. Varma to Nehru and Nehru to Bhargava, File No. 56 (Part II), JN (SG) Papers.

216 28 September 1950, Nehru to Mridula Sarabhai and S. K. Sinha, File No. 56 (Part II), JN (SG) Papers.

217 28 September 1950, Nehru to PPS, File No. 56 (Part II), JN (SG) Papers.

218 29 September and 1 October 1950, Patel–Nehru exchange, File No. 58 (Part I), JN (SG) Papers.

219 1 October 1950, Nehru to Patel, File No. 58 (Part I), JN (SG) Papers.

220 1 October 1950, Vellodi to V. P. Menon, File No. 58 (Part I), JN (SG) Papers.

221 13 October 1950, Patel to Nehru, File No. 59 (Part II), JN (SG) Papers. This and the next para are based on it.

222 11 December 1950, Nehru to Baldev Singh, File No. 67 (Part II), JN (SG) Papers.

223 1 October 1950, Nehru to Roy, File No. 58 (Part I), JN (SG) Papers.

224 T. C. Sherman, 'From "Grow More Food" to "Miss a Meal": Hunger, Development, and the Limits of Post-Colonial Nationalism in India, 1947–1957', *South Asia: Journal of South Asian Studies* 36, no. 4 (2013): 571–88.

225 N. A. Mujumdar, 'Minimum Wages in Agriculture', *Indian Journal of Agricultural Economics* 12, no. 4 (1957): 67.

226 2 October and 16 November 1950, Nehru to Shukla, File Nos. 58 (Part I) and 64 (Part I), JN (SG) Papers.

227 15 October 1950, Note by V. T. Krishnamachari and 20 October 1950, Kher to Nehru, File Nos. 59 (Part II) and 60 (Part II), JN (SG) Papers.

228   2 October 1950, Nehru to PPS, File No. 58 (Part I), JN (SG) Papers.

229   13 and 16 October 1950, Nehru to Tandon, File No. 59 (Part II) JN (SG) Papers.

230   19 October 1950, Sampurnanand to Nehru, File No. 60 (Part II), JN (SG) Papers.

231   Gould, *Hindu Nationalism, and the Language of Politics in Late Colonial India*, 160–233.

232   21 October 1950, Nehru to Sampurnanand, File No. 60 (Part II), JN (SG) Papers.

233   Ansari and Gould, *Boundaries of Belonging*, 67–102.

234   B. D. Metcalf, *Husain Ahmad Madani: The Jihad for Islam and India's Freedom* (London: Simon & Schuster, 2012).

235   23 October 1950, Nehru to PPS, File No. 60 (Part II), JN (SG) Papers.

236   23 October 1950, Patel to Nehru, File No. 60 (Part II), JN (SG) Papers.

237   Undated, October 1950, Bhargava to Patel (no. 4973-CMP), File No. 60 (Part II), JN (SG) Papers. See Ornit Shani, *How India Became Democratic: Citizenship and the Making of the Universal Franchise* (Cambridge: Cambridge University Press, 2018), 85–121.

238   23 October 1950, Nehru to Prasad, File No. 60 (Part II), JN (SG) Papers.

239   19 November 1950, Nehru to C. C. Biswas, File No. 64 (Part II), JN (SG) Papers. See Chetna Sharma, 'National Register of Citizens Assam, India: The Tangled Logic of Documentary Evidence', *Journal of Immigrant and Refugee Studies* 22, no. 1 (2024): 225–37.

240   14 November 1950, Nehru to Ajit Prasad Jain, File No. 63 (Part II), JN (SG) Papers.

241   1 November 1950, Nehru to chief ministers, File No. 62 (Part I), JN (SG) Papers.

242   5 November 1950, Bhargava to Nehru, File No. 62 (Part II), JN (SG) Papers.

243   19 November 1950, Nehru to Munshi, File No. 62 (Part II), JN (SG) Papers.

244   11 November 1950, Note by Gadgil (264/CF/50), File No. 64 (Part I), JN (SG) Papers.

245   7 November 1950, Nehru to Prasad, File No. 62 (Part II), JN (SG) Papers. See Abhay Kumar Dubey, 'Hindi and the Politics of Status: Official/National— Anatomy of a Double Sector Discourse', (2021), 1–73, accessed 12 May 2024, https://abhaykumardubey.com/wp-content/uploads/2021/08/Politics-of-Hindis-Status-latest-1.pdf.

246   14 November 1950, Mahmud to Nehru and Nehru to Patel, File Nos. 63 (I and II), JN (SG) Papers.

247   14 November 1950, Ambedkar to Nehru, File No. 63 (Part II), JN (SG) Papers.

248   16 November 1950, Nehru's draft for R. K. Patil to Munshi, File No. 64 (Part I), JN (SG) Papers.

249   8 November 1950, Munshi to Patil, File No. 64 (Part I), JN (SG) Papers.

250   19 November 1950, Nehru to Ajit Jain, File No. 64 (Part II), JN (SG) Papers. See Aishwarya Pandit, *Claiming Citizenship and Nation: Muslim Politics and State-Building in North India, 1947–1986* (New Delhi: Routledge India, 2022).

251   17 November 1950, Dharma Vira's note, File No. 64 (Part I), JN (SG) Papers. This para is based on it.

252 18 November 1950, Nehru to Pant, File No. 64 (Part II), JN (SG) Papers.
253 See C. P. Singh, 'A Century of Constituency Delimitation in India', *Political Geography* 19, no. 4 (2000): 517–32; and J. Ambagudia, 'Scheduled Tribes, Reserved Constituencies and Political Reservation in India', *Journal of Social Inclusion Studies* 5, no. 1 (2019): 44–58.
254 17 November 1950, Sukumar Sen to Nehru, File No. 64 (Part I), JN (SG) Papers.
255 Sherman, *Nehru's India*, 145–76.
256 18 November 1950, Nehru to Dharma Vira, File No. 64 (Part I), JN (SG) Papers.
257 Undated, November 1950, Nehru to Mookerjee, File No. 66 (Part I), JN (SG) Papers.
258 17 November 1950, Nehru to chief ministers, File No. 64 (Part I), JN (SG) Papers.
259 4 December 1950, JP to Mathai, JN (SG) Papers, File No. 66-II
260 3 December 1950, Gadgil to Nehru, File No. 66 (Part I), JN (SG) Papers.
261 2 December 1950, Kania–Nehru exchange, File No. 66 (Part I), JN (SG) Papers.
262 3 December 1950, Nehru to chief ministers, File No. 66 (Part I), JN (SG) Papers.
263 Siegel, *Hungry Nation*, 86–119; and David C. Engerman, *The Price of Aid: The Economic Cold War in India* (Cambridge: Harvard University Press, 2018), 1–18.
264 6 December 1950, Munshi to Nehru, File No. 66 (Part II), JN (SG) Papers.
265 David M. Fahey and Padma Manian, 'Poverty and Purification: The Politics of Gandhi's Campaign for Prohibition', *The Historian* 67, no. 3 (2005): 489–506.
266 10 December 1950, Mishra to Nehru, File No. 67 (Part II), JN (SG) Papers.
267 30 December 1950, Nehru to Mishra, File No. 69 (Part II), JN (SG) Papers.
268 Marcus F. Franda, 'The Organizational Development of India's Congress Party', *Pacific Affairs* 35, no. 3 (1962): 248–60.
269 10 December 1950, Kripalani to Tandon, File No. 67 (Part II), JN (SG) Papers.
270 11–17 December 1950, Mashruwala–Nehru exchange, File Nos. 67 (Part II) and 68 (Part I), JN (SG) Papers.
271 18 December 1950, Nehru to chief ministers, File No. 68 (Part I), JN (SG) Papers.

4

'Captain who ... steered India'

From August 1947 to December 1950, the 'Captain who ... steered India',[1] in the words of Jawaharlal Nehru, the outsized figure of the central government and the Congress party was Sardar Vallabhbhai Patel.[2] This part follows closely the trajectory of Patel's presence and significance between June 1948, Mountbatten's departure from India, and December 1950, Patel's death, and finds his influence beyond any inference, in a clear display of elite prowess against public power,[3] despite the fact that for much of this time Patel was periodically unwell, following the heart attack that he suffered in the wake of Gandhi's assassination. Nehru, who visited him in his periods of convalescence in either Dehradun-Mussoorie or Bombay, could not govern easily without him, and many matters remained delayed within the overall reorganisation of government machinery in this transitional stage.[4] When they were given, Patel's views were characteristically conservative and commanding, as can be seen from his note on the economic situation in the country from July 1948:

> Economic malaise [is] because we [are] not able ... to ensure co-ordination between ... government, industry, and labour.... A sense of frustration in industry ... [as labour] wields the big stick.... If we approach capitalists ... in the right manner, we shall achieve their cooperation.... Among them there are patriots ... what is required is a small committee of the Cabinet to supervise.[5]

Whether it was making judicial appointments to the then-Federal Court from provinces, where he prevailed upon Nehru to appoint Mehr Chand Mahajan from East Punjab in place of Ram Lal, whom the prime minister favoured, not only because he was senior to Mahajan but also because he had a reputation of being impartial, whereas Mahajan was a 'bit of rolling stone'.[6] Or, whether it was the doings of the Sangh, which held a meeting on Janmashtami 1948 at Ajmer, regardless of its ban since Gandhi's assassination, where Mukund Malaviya, nephew of Pandit Madan Mohan Malaviya, demanded a 'Hindu Raj' and warned that 'more blood will be shed in India soon than during the last 2000 years',[7] it was to Patel that Nehru deferred to. While complaints flooded that summer of 1948 on police behaviour, not leaving Rameshwari Nehru, whose secretary Masud was arrested on 'meagre evidence',[8] for Patel, it was best to leave the police alone and instead work 'cooperatively' between communities.[9]

The East Punjab High Court question was more than about the individual careers of Mahajan and Lal. Justice Achhru Ram, who had been touring the province, had found an organised attempt by Master Tara Singh, to dominate state administration including judiciary. At a meeting in Hoshiarpur, it was resolved to demand for a Sikh chief justice, as well as for sessions judge or police superintendents in each district to be a Sikh.[10] With Achhru Ram's and Ram Lal's departure, Sardar Harender Singh was the senior-most judge. Refugee rehabilitation and police coercion in the national capital, on the other hand, was related to the differences between minister Saksena and Delhi-in-charge Khanna.[11] This was yet-more pronounced in places like Hyderabad, where within a day of the nizam's surrender, the prime minister pressed for a cabinet committee because of the 'ticklish' constitutional position, whereas Patel wanted to absorb it first, without worrying about 'any appearance of conquest'.[12]

It was also thus in the party organisation, where in September 1948, Pattabhi Sitaramayya got Nehru's support for presidency after Prasad initially refused continuing. Then, he had second thoughts and thus, this first post-Gandhi election for Congress presidency became a shadowy battle between Patel, who was prompting Prasad, and Nehru, who brought up Prasad's ill-health and constituent assembly duties. Eventually, Nehru gave in to Patel's wish, while Patel gave in to Prasad's chairmanship and the need to have a president from south India, especially the restive Andhra region.[13] At the assembly too, Prasad's ill-health meant that in November 1948, the CWC seriously considered appointing a new chairman in Dr S. P. Mookerjee, who had been assisting Prasad. Here, given Mookerjee's ministerial load, Nehru preferred Mavalankar as 'the same person [to] preside over the two different aspects of the assembly'.[14] Underneath such personnel issues were systemic challenges like corruption of the kind that saw an allotment of several hundred acres of evacuee land in Chhatarpur, near Delhi, to government officials like M. S. Randhawa and Datar Singh, or the badly run relief work in Calcutta for which money was being sent from primarily the PM fund and central treasury.

Patel, who controlled party's relief fund, kept it for Punjab, as some donors had explicitly tied their donations thus, whereupon Nehru urged him to put out a public notice, given that most government resource had 'gone to helping people from Western Pakistan'.[15]

Congress party funds were neither the only nor the most opulent thing under Patel's control in September 1948. That was Hyderabad's treasury, now seized and thus were frozen any grants from it, like those to Aligarh, Banaras, Vizag, Shantiniketan and Deoband. First, the Razakars had stopped these payments over July–August and now Chaudhuri's military government, leading Nehru's request their continuance especially to the 'nationalist' Deoband, where roughly 1,400 students came from foreign countries.[16] And then as he left for Europe to make his maiden appearance at the world stage, Patel deputised for Nehru, similarly writing a fortnightly letter to provincial premiers. It is a little-heralded document that lays bare their differences amidst similarities. On Kashmir and Hyderabad, Patel hoped that Nehru would induce some 'proportion',[17] across East Asia, Patel looked at India and Japan as the two secure bastions amidst communism, while for Pakistan, his parallel was 'the Nazi disease of seeing enemies all round'. On the economic front, his anxieties were to enforce 'anti-inflationary measures … curtailment of government expenditure', and to deal 'drastically' with labour. Institutionally, they had set up a priorities committee (economic) of the cabinet and Patel desired a similar body in provinces. Overall, he demanded a 'ceaseless watch' of 'underground workers, communist cells [and] manifestations of class or communal consciousness'.[18]

Patel communicated with Nehru too and in response to the former's letter of 15 October 1948, the prime minister produced a 2000-word essay, which was complementary. Nehru began with the Cold War,[19] and went further than Patel in outlining India as a 'dominant power' in Asia and situating therein the Anglo-American 'desire to cultivate' it, as 'China cannot play an effective part for a long time' and 'Pakistan does not come into the picture'.[20] Turning then to the clouds on this horizon, Hyderabad and Kashmir, he called the former over internationally because the Indian army 'rapidly' disposed it, while on the latter, the plebiscite occupied people's minds, who could not 'get rid of the idea that Kashmir is predominantly Muslim and therefore likely to side with Pakistan'.[21] Nehru, like Patel, refused 'any intervention' and their position was similar: 'either a full acceptance of the UN's ceasefire or a partition … i.e., Western Poonch, Gilgit, Chitral, most of the Baltistan to go to Pakistan'. Where he differed was that he was mindful that Kashmir and Hyderabad were used to judge India and so, while he wished no radical change in Hyderabad pending an election, Patel, and his advisors, wished to remove the nizam and divide Hyderabad into its linguistic areas. Next, regarding the incoming

Hindu refugees from East Bengal, where Patel had followed premier B. C. Roy in writing that, 'we would … send out Muslims from West Bengal in equal numbers …', Nehru wondered as to how would one 'pick' them, which law 'would justify this' and asked was it not better to stop refugees coming from East Bengal?

The prime minister then turned to the RSS and the CPI, about whom the government was being criticised for preventive detentions.[22] But, how could they remove the ban on the former, as Patel had proposed, while continuing it on others? He concluded with the Bihar *zamindari* abolition bill, on which the legal view portended 'a major crisis' with its insistence on cash compensation. While external trouble could be refused invitation, like the time when Harry Pollitt, the British communist, was refused visa in November 1948 with Nehru agreeing with Patel and declining to meet Pollitt in London,[23] how long could the CPI be banned? Or, for that matter, the RSS, which was showing signs of activity. Nehru shared the intelligence that he was getting, about an RSS agitation, when the Congress session would be taking place in Jaipur. In February 1948, New Delhi's decision to ban the organisation had come without 'sufficient intimation' for provincial governments and, keen to avoid this, Nehru urged Patel to give them 'a certain latitude'.[24] Patel did not need to do that, for almost all provincial premiers were his camp followers and instead, he went ahead and attempted a trespass on Nehru's Ministry of External Affairs. His creation, the economy committee of the cabinet, had recommended that 'external publicity should be re-transferred to Information & Broadcasting'; under the Home Ministry.[25]

By spring 1949, as the lifting of the ban on the RSS came closer,[26] screws on the CPI in West Bengal were being tightened, after a violent attack on Jessops' factory near Dum Dum. The factory had seen the dismissal of some employees, and had sought state protection.[27] Patel had been refining the essential services (prevention of strikes) bill thereby dealing with strikes sponsored by the communist unions especially in the railways,[28] and, highlighting the events in Calcutta, he emphasised 'necessary' wider powers,[29] whose expanding definition enveloped ex-rulers, as Orissa claimed Mayurbhanj from Bihar,[30] and New Delhi feared that 'all kinds of forces' were behind it: from tribes to communists to industrialists.[31]

There was a similarly fluid situation further east in Assam, where the tension was between the people of hills and the people of plains and Premier Bardoloi desired for a greater say over the former, backed by the Assam Rifles.[32] At nearby Manipur, Patel was sending a new dewan, 'greatly worried' as he was about 'the communists', which Nehru thought as 'somewhat exaggerated'.[33] The one place where, after the shocking Sunder Lal report, Nehru tried to remain hands-on was Hyderabad. He was keen to change the narrative there from coercion to cooperation as quickly as possible and, during his December 1948 visit, he sought out individuals like S. M. Nawab, trained in Europe on cooperatives, who had prepared a scheme to check communist activities. Directing Major-General Chaudhuri to encourage Nawab, he emphasised such approaches in addition to Patel's preferred 'military and police action'.[34]

Security apart, property was the other paramount frame for Vallabhbhai Patel,[35] and he was worried over developments in this regard in the draft constitution. Convalescing in Bombay, he sent to K. M. Munshi a 4-page note to circulate among the party.[36] Starting with the fault-line between fundamental rights in property guaranteed in the Congress resolution of 1931, and its 1945 election manifesto,[37] when it promised 'the removal of intermediaries between the peasant and the state ... on payment of equitable compensation', Patel brought in the third angle of foreign enterprises, to be acquired upon 'fair compensation'. Compensation thus was the 'sacred obligation', one that Patel was not willing to forgo in fear of 'some distant upheaval'. Reminding the party that their socialist friends were no more with them,[38] Patel moved to his main point that before socialism, 'the country must have sufficient wealth', as he suggested a 'compromise between nationalisation and private enterprise'.[39] With state resources inadequate, he argued that 'you have to make it worth it's while' for private capital to do 'its bit'. On the other hand, with his grip on the security side of things, he was unwilling to accept that without acquisition of property, there would be 'a revolution'. Patel concluded with terming it his 'ardent desire while there is yet life in me'; personal words that rendered political opposition impossible.[40] Nehru, recognising the note's potency, tried to stop its circulation among assembly members, even as the chief whip Sinha distributed it,[41] and penned his own note in which he distilled the issue down to three possibilities, foreshadowing the tussle between the judiciary and the legislature:[42]

> Whether courts should have power [to] overrule the legislature [on] compensation [or] the legislature should be supreme [or] two types of property differentiated: zamindari and industrial plants. [For] the former, the legislature should be the authority ... the court should have the power to intervene [in] the latter....[43]

Related to this was the question of the privy purse to princely rulers,[44] a constitutional guarantee, which was applauded for the sovereignty (and savings) achieved by it, and Patel failed to understand 'the fears' regarding this 'solemn' undertaking that he had given, which too could not be left to future parliaments and had to be 'consecrated'. The same was true for princely privileges, whose 'self-respect and honour' was important, with their territories gone. Reminding Nehru of their assurances to the rulers accompanying the latter's accession and claiming that 'there was nothing to compel them', he recalled their 'capacity for mischief'. As against that, the amounts which they had settled for were liable to be reduced with each generation. Under the draft constitution, these prior covenants reached with rulers would not be justiciable and if his cabinet colleagues hesitated then Patel was prepared to come from Bombay, for making any 'transitional provision', as the cabinet had suggested, made Patel feel betrayed and he left Nehru in no doubt about his 'mental strain'.[45]

The cabinet's and Nehru's surprise was that these privy purses, free of income tax, were for 'perpetuity' and they were unsure if any government was able to guarantee thus. Nehru suggested the alternative of 'a specific article guaranteeing all obligations … without giving a list of these …' thereby eschewing publicity.[46] A relieved Patel accepted this and assured Nehru that he would help him 'face the party', while for the *zamindars* he was happy to concede that they were 'only intermediaries….'[47] This correspondence had spanned 15 August 1949, and an unwell and emotional deputy prime minister, 'away from' his comrades, was 'unhappy' to hear that a group of refugees had laid siege to Nehru's house and wished to be in Delhi to tell them that the prime minister had treated them with 'greater consideration than they deserved'. Someone whom Patel treated likewise was the recently released M. S. Golwalkar, who called on him on 16 August 1949. In their talk, Patel explained to Golwalkar 'the pitfalls which the RSSS should avoid', and 'warned him against the Savarkar group, of which Godse was the exponent'. Distinguishing thus between different strains of the Sangh, Patel found Golwalkar 'receptive', and conveyed to Nehru his conviction that the latter 'will not give us any trouble'.[48]

In turn, the prime minister communicated the draft compromise hammered on the right to property with Rajagopalachari, Ambedkar, Mookerjee, Ayyangar, Munshi and Krishnaswami Iyer, which privileged 'compensation….'[49] With the guarantees to princes not being a secret though, Nehru worried about 'trouble' especially with Govind Ballabh Pant, who too was unwell. While all this was going on, in Bombay, Home Minister Morarji Desai was withholding writer Mulk Raj Anand's passport since mid-April 1949, depriving him from travelling to Paris for World Intellectuals Congress. After the intelligence officers interrogated Anand at home, he was called in for an interview by Desai, who made it clear that he did not want anyone to go to this Congress and, as many of Anand's utterances 'helped' the government's opponents, Desai refused to release his passport as well as 'refused' to reveal the regulation invoked. Anand guaranteed that he would not speak otherwise, pointed that his wife was ill in France, and pleaded that he needed to visit London for publishing purposes, but Desai did not budge.[50]

Nor did Patel for, as his health recovered, his attention turned first to matters of party politics and next to economic problems. He was angry at the economist K. T. Shah for forming a party even as his membership of the assembly had been supported by the Congress,[51] over Patel's opposition. Above this was the worsening economic scenario across the country and Patel's advisor V. P. Menon had a report prepared by a committee of secretaries, which Patel endorsed as he worried about the upcoming devaluation crisis in which London would want India 'to cut down imports, increase exports and ... facilitate investment by dollar countries....'[52] Urging Nehru to take the assistance of the troika of Dr John Matthai, Rama Rau and C. D. Deshmukh, he turned his focused to the language and services question in East Punjab, without settling which he did not wish to release 'the quixotic' Master. The case with Golwalkar was 'different', for Patel was convinced that he had come 'round to our view ...' but Tara Singh clung to 'his faith in the return of Sikhs to West Punjab, in East Punjab being virtually a Sikh state [and] in Punjabi being the only language for [it]'.[53]

Soon, Nehru was travelling for his maiden visit to America in November 1949 and Patel was back in Delhi, writing to provincial premiers and reading from the prime minister.[54] For his part, Patel's 15-page uncharacteristically long letter contained their shared concerns around communism in China–Tibet and Burma–Indonesia, racism in South Africa, French and Portuguese possessions in India, Pakistan at the Security Council, compulsory savings, voluntary cuts, self-sufficiency in food grains, and the integration of Banaras, Tripura and Manipur princely states.[55] On 14 November, the 60th birthday of the prime minister, Patel wrote a second letter to the premiers that began with his 'blessings and prayers' for Nehru and ended with the news of the imminent hanging of Nathuram Godse and Narayan Apte for the murder of Gandhi.[56] By the time Nehru returned, the long-speculated merger of the state of Cooch Behar with West Bengal had been made by the States Ministry,[57] without any reference to the people of Cooch Behar, with much agitation in Assam, and, above all, while giving no information to the cabinet and to the prime minister, who had given public and private assurances otherwise. This was no isolated instance. When Govind Ballabh Pant visited Nehru on 25 December 1949 and the prime minister asked what had brought him to Delhi, Pant said a meeting on 'the future of Vindhya Pradesh', surprising Nehru and strengthening his impression that decisions were 'imposed without consultation' by the States Ministry.[58]

At the still-more powerful Home Ministry,[59] the situation was yet more sobering. At Rewa, there had been an incident that was metamorphosing into a multidimensional row involving police firing and preventive detention. The district magistrate there had made arrests, one of the reasons for which was participation in a deputation to give 'false information' to Nehru. The said deputation had come to the prime minister, and mentioned the Rewa firing incident, in terms of fear that 'action might be taken against them', which is what had happened. Patel's response was curious, terming the detention order 'stupid', on the one hand, and calling it 'right', on the other, given 'past misdeeds'.[60] The person detained was released, while the officer concerned was replaced, but this matter involving politician S. N. Mehta and official V. K. B. Pillai would not go away and was picked up by JP, who drew unflattering parallels with pre-1947, when the Congress used to demand judicial enquiry of executive atrocity and filled in some details that had not reached Nehru. The Rewa firing was in the lead-up to the inaugural conference of the Hind Kisan Panchayat to be held there on 26–27 February 1950. District authorities had jailed 'most of the local socialist and Kisan panchayat workers', as well as denied 'all the petrol, hotel and tent facilities ...'; as JP put it, 'to Sardar Patel, everything that we do appears to be creating disturbance'.[61]

Patel's reply was equally trenchant and began with the claim that since the mid-1930s, the Congress Socialists had propagated that Nehru was 'more sympathetic' towards them,[62] before arguing that 'Jai Prakash ... ignores that as against 2–3 persons killed and half a dozen wounded, 38 policemen were injured'. Patel then turned to the Hind Kisan Panchayat, who 'wanted 1000 gallons of petrol (were allotted 100) ... tents, shamianas, durries, stay in state bungalows [and] supply of water'.[63] This matter followed similar instances of firings over student and women demonstrators in Calcutta, with even Nehru agreeing that it was 'justified', but what he felt was not was a lack of enquiry. For this, Rajagopalachari suggested 'a convention' that a major firing should automatically lead to 'an enquiry' as such incidents rose: from Salem prison to Nasik and Sabarmati, across Rajasthan and at Rewa and Bareilly. There was a feeling that the police continued as pre-1947, and Rajagopalachari's suggestion was forwarded to Patel to show that it was not 'above criticism'.[64] For the latter, however, it was the public that was so 'used to firings' then that it was being slow in 'adapting itself to similar action taken by [its] representatives....' Instead of demanding accountability from the police, Patel demanded trust from the public and refused a convention for enquiry, calling it 'a slur on our ... capacity to judge'. Moreover, 'any weakening ... would slacken the pace of adaptation' and, referring to the Calcutta incident, Patel asked:

> Are we to surrender our government to hysterical women mischievously led [by] a subversive organisation? ... Are we to surrender [policemen] to a bewildering public inquiry? ... Administrative machinery is as sensitive as public opinion.... Public opinion is easier to handle because public memories are shorter ... the final judgment of justice must be that of the executive....[65]

Patel would only concede a magisterial enquiry, in 'any appreciable loss of life', and 'a judicial in-camera inquiry', and so were the chief ministers told in early March,[66] despite the counterarguments about winning 'people over'.[67] It was against this immediate backdrop that over 20–21 February 1950, Nehru wrote to Patel, Prasad and Rajagopalachari that he wished to 'get out of office'.[68] This was a culmination of rising refugee numbers in West Bengal and Assam and the risible attitude of the party and the rehabilitation ministry on the evacuee property bill. Then there was the reformed cabinet under the new constitution, where Nehru had wanted Krishnamachari for industries and supplies, Mahtab for food and agriculture and Ajit Jain for relief and rehabilitation, but Pant looked upon unfavourably to Jain's appointment, Mookerjee was difficult to dislodge, given the happenings in Bengal, while Patel's favourite Munshi was holding food. Thus thwarted, Nehru turned towards his pet project, the planning commission, where he wanted Ayyangar, as chairman, Deshmukh, Nanda, G. L. Mehta and Mahalanobis. But then, the CWC passed a resolution for him to be the chairman, and Nanda advised the desirability of having a representative each of industry and agriculture, with three partymen. And so, the reformulated group was Nehru, Nanda, Deshmukh, Mehta and R. K. Patil.

The Congress old guard responded immediately. A 'distressed' Patel urged him to 'do nothing which would make confusion worse'.[69] As did Rajagopalachari and to both, the prime minister reassured suitably, but he felt overwhelmed by Bengal and wished to emulate Gandhi by being 'on the spot'. Simultaneously, he felt 'exhausted' and alienated by the 'petty wrangles and jealousies'[70] in the party and the government. The socialist N. G. Ranga spoke for many when he told Nehru that both Patel and he should leave some ministries. In reply, the prime minister submitted that most of his time was 'spent in dealing with Pakistan, Kashmir and relief and rehabilitation', that 'no policy decision [was] made without the Deputy Prime Minister' and 'the proper way is for the party to have a leader who is in tune with its own views....'[71] Afterwards, writing to Rajagopalachari, Nehru mused over the party, especially in UP, the parliament and the public, chiefly in Bengal, given that

> [n]o Hindu in East Bengal has any feeling of security ... a vast number of them will come over. It is difficult to push them back and it is impossible to absorb them.... I have even thought that war is better than this.... And yet I know well that war can only make them worse.[72]

Between these exchanges in the second half of February and the second half of April, when the crescendo of crisis between Bengal(s) climaxed with the Nehru–Liaquat Pact and the resignation of both the Bengali ministers from the central cabinet, Mookerjee and Neogy, Patel stood by Nehru, and it was his immovable force that was deployed on the ground in mid-April 1950, in favour of the pact.[73] He camped in Calcutta for days, made a radio broadcast, gave a press conference to 'about 50 editors', met six prominent ones separately, as well as 'some leading refugees', and helped improve the 'hostile and bitter' atmosphere.[74] Taking a dim view of Mookerjee's and Neogy's resignations, Patel met prominent Congressmen like S. M. Ghosh and P. C. Ghosh, for B. C. Roy's administration needed party support as people were already eyeing the election with its refugee votes. With neighbouring Bihar and Orissa taking only 8,000 and 9,000 refugees, respectively, given their stand that Bengalis must be rehabilitated in Bengal and the Assam government refusing even that number, there was added pressure on a sullen officialdom and a sulking party in the state.

As regards the selection of a central minister, Patel reported that C. C. Biswas was considered the best man to parley with Pakistan. A grateful Nehru was agreeably relieved, as the latter was a college contemporary of President Prasad, over other names like those of jurist Radha Binod Pal of Tojo trial fame and Mitter of the minorities board. As for 'the differences among Congressmen ... if Patel [did] not succeed ... [who could]'.[75] By mid-May 1950, as the Bengal situation stabilised a bit, there was an emerging cloud on the cabinet's horizon, namely, the planning commission, which was making Dr Matthai unhappy. Patel was happy to have Deshmukh as Matthai's successor but was neither keen on Ayyangar nor on Krishnamachari, and Rajagopalachari was considered. Nehru preferred the latter to remain 'the chairman of the economic committee',[76] while Rajagopalachari himself wanted external affairs.[77]

By late May, clouds were parting, more by circumstances than anything else. With Patel insisting that the finance portfolio be held by someone 'in touch with business', and, simultaneously, warning Nehru about carefully defining the functions of the planning commission, Nehru was left with little option but to have the sympathetic bureaucrat Deshmukh move to finance, while assuring Patel that the commission will not 'come in the way of ... any ministry'.[78] While these changes were going on, the outgoing M. L. Saksena was reading from M. R. Bhide, home minister of PEPSU, about evictions of 23,000 tenants, some cultivating lands since 1944, under the new tenancy act. Bhide was anxious about the 'communistic' Kishangarh area and Faridkot district, with its 'Rai Sikhs' but, instead of absorbing them, he made 'a demand for land in the rest of India'.[79] Existing colonial tenancy laws were bad enough and were now laced with communalism and corruption, for 6,600 of these tenants were of Muslim landlords, who had to surrender possession of their lands to new allottees from West Pakistan. There were also some 16,000 landless persons from West Pakistan, with temporary allotments, who too had 'to make room for the new allottees'.[80]

As ever, one case stood for many, becoming a touchstone for policies and prejudices. In May 1950, the case of Hakim Nisar Ahmed of Jodhpur emerged as such. Ahmed had gone to Karachi on 7 July 1948 in the days when no permit was required. While he was there, the permit system was introduced, and he was given a temporary permit to return to Jodhpur. Here, the dewan and the district magistrate gave him testimonials as a permanent resident. Subsequently, the rehabilitation ministry extended his permit for three months, causing displeasure to the States Ministry, who added that Nisar Ahmed was 'an exceedingly undesirable person' and he should be removed. Faced with this, minister Saksena contended that it was not correct 'to mix up' his past activities with his right to remain, and over 23–24 May, Azad brought up Ahmed's case as the latter was arrested in Delhi, whereupon Nehru telephoned Iengar to suggest that Ahmed might be let out on bail. A conditional bail was granted and Iengar reported to the prime minister next morning with relevant papers, which allow a reconstruction of his story, albeit according to intelligence reports. As long ago as 1912, Ahmed had been sentenced for forgery and rape. In 1917, he was convicted for rioting and assault. By 1940, he had become the president of the Marwar state Muslim League and a confidant of the maharaja of Jodhpur. But this file was not without its discrepancies nor without all kinds of testimonials for his work in the city municipality, one of which was from the civil servant C. S. Venkatachar, administrator of Jodhpur. Then, there was the question of whether his visit to Pakistan was 'intended as migration', and thus this case impinged upon the permit system. Originally introduced to stop people from Pakistan coming (back) to India, the system had become a tool 'to keep out undesirables', and to Nehru, this change was not justifiable:

> There are plenty of Muslims who had played an objectionable part in the Muslim League.... We can proceed against Nisar Ahmed in any way we like if he has committed an offence.... But how can we say that he has lost his Indian nationality because he went to Pakistan before the Permit System was introduced and then came back, or because he committed some crimes in his youth [or] was an aggressive Muslim Leaguer?[81]

For the moment, Nisar Ahmed was to be under arrest in Jodhpur, where a bail-with-bond could be allowed as he received, until recently, a monthly stipend for running a state dispensary. If he left, like the large numbers of Muslims who were leaving via the railway line between Jodhpur and Sindh, that would be a solution in the eyes of some and a law-and-order situation for others. The Rajasthan government was asking New Delhi 'to induce Muslims to go back to their homes', as Karachi proposed 'to close the border', which only accelerated their movement. Pakistan was playing the permit game back, something that India was doing in Punjab, as the Delhi agreement applied only to East and

West Bengals and Assam. To Azad, Nehru recounted Ahmed's dismissal from Jodhpur police (1929), removal from the municipality (1938), externment from the city (1939) and travels to Pakistan (1947) in which he was said 'to have passed secret intelligence', with the conclusion that 'it is difficult to have much sympathy'.[82]

While all this was going on, John Matthai issued a statement accompanying his resignation in which he termed the Nehru–Liaquat Pact as 'appeasement' of Pakistan. Azad responded to this by stating that Matthai did not express such dislike when he was in the cabinet, which Patel termed 'inaccurate', and Munshi, Baldev Singh and Sri Prakasa deplored Azad. Patel himself was 'bitter', warning that 'Maulana will have to face public discomfiture', as Azad had decided to respond to Matthai against his advice and in case 'Mookerjee tries to make capital of the controversy'.[83] The prime minister was then onboard the naval ship *Delhi* to Indonesia and was not only sorry about Azad but also angry about Matthai's reference to cabinet proceedings.[84] But as he confided to Krishna Menon at this time, whether on Nisar Ahmed or John Matthai or Rajagopalachari, Nehru 'often differed with Sardar Patel, but [they] never had arguments about petty matters'.[85] In June 1950, Rajagopalachari's appointment as a minister without portfolio made some people 'disgruntled', enough for the proud Rajagopalachari to withdraw. This information had come from Patel and Nehru sought to reassure Rajagopalachari,[86] who saw that Patel was uneasy about it, the party cackled with 'old prejudices' and asked, 'Having been made to swagger as Head of the State, how can one go through this?'[87] The matter was discussed when Nehru visited Patel at Dehradun, where it came up that Mahabir Tyagi of UP and H. V. Kamath were among those who had objected.[88] Over and above such issues, both Nehru and Patel knew that they had so tied themselves up 'by all kinds of difficulties that most of [their] lives [was] to be spent in trying to overcome them'.[89]

None among these was knottier than Kashmir. Advised by Nehru's secretary-general G. S. Bajpai and his own mandarin Vishnu Sahay, Patel was becoming 'apprehensive' about Sheikh Abdullah. To him, Nehru's friend seemed to act 'independently' and was 'critical of, if not hostile to', New Delhi. Patel had in mind, first, Abdullah's efforts to have 'separate' talks with Chaudhury Ghulam Abbas in Azad Kashmir and, second, the UN-appointed Australian juror Owen Dixon's attempts at mediation. He feared that if they were not careful, once demilitarisation was done, a plebiscite would follow.[90] Nehru agreed that Abdullah's attitude was 'most unwise', but he was still preoccupied with the 'unhappy' situation in Bengal caused by 'the Calcutta press as well as Mookerjee'.[91] Patel had more to do on both and his worries from Abdullah were his 'failure' with communists, the 'dissensions' in his party and his feeling that Abdullah was 'losing hold on the Valley ... I agree with you that a plebiscite is … dangerous because we might be faced with an exodus [of] the non-Muslims....'[92]

As for Bengal, where he had worked so hard in April, Patel's main problem was that he could 'find no legal powers to deal with either press or Syama Prasad', given the Supreme Court judgement in 'Crossroads' and 'Organiser' cases.[93] He lamented the 'idealistic' constitutional provisions, and the often-repeated cliché of idealistic Nehru and practical Patel is no retrospective reflection, as Gulzarilal Nanda, hailing from Patel's state but an ally of Nehru, summed it up in July 1950: 'there are two urges at work – for safety and social justice. In the minds of the people, Sardar is identified with the [former], and you represent the [latter]....'[94] Around this time another small exchange took place between the prime minister and his deputy that throws a big light on their different emphases. In late July 1950, Nehru circulated a note on the post of deputy minister and appeared inclined towards having them, though without enhancing their salaries and varying their privileges.[95] Patel questioned the usefulness of this post, which could cost INR 4,000–5,000 per month and would lead to 'jealousies and scrambles....'[96] Rather, Patel was inclined to place state governors and *rajpramukh*s in the warrant of precedence above union ministers, reflecting his patronage of the princely rulers and provincial chieftains. Ultimately, both gave in to the other's preference on the superfluous post of deputy ministers and the special precedence of cabinet ministers.[97]

By early September 1950, Vallabhbhai Patel was again feeling unwell, and doctors advised him to move to Bombay. There he could also raise money for the victims of Assam's earthquake, where Nehru was travelling to. And from there, he could also control his two primary ministries via his trusted officials; the extension of one of whom – V. P. Menon – was expiring on 26 September 1950. Menon has been recalled recently as the 'unsung architect of modern India',[98] but any work that he did from 1947 hinged on his loyalty to Patel and, in turn, Patel's leverage with Nehru. By now, more than the big states, it was the *jagirdari* system in Part B and C states that had become the most important problem, and Patel wanted Menon to remain for the next year. From territorially large unions like Rajasthan and Madhya Bharat to smaller set-ups like Manipur and Tripura, none had elected representation, and all required 'supervision'. The ministry also claimed to 'abolish' *jagirdari* in Hyderabad, albeit 'attendant on abolition of *zamindari* in Bihar and UP', via 'a solution [whose] annual burden would be Rs. 114 ½ lakhs', which, to them, a rich state like Hyderabad could afford.[99]

Patel would now weigh in on matters mostly from Bombay; some with characteristic vigour and others with a weakening hand. In the former category came the Bihar Land Reforms Bill, on which President Rajendra Prasad had dissented on 8 September. The cabinet met the next day, read Prasad's note and reiterated its advise to sign the bill. This was despite the doubts of the relevant cabinet committee, and Prasad's note raising some constitutional issues. Patel felt otherwise and, instead of backing the Bihar government, he wanted to refer its bill to law and home ministries.[100] Patel was willing to put up with the delay involved, but Nehru went ahead and wrote to Prasad to certify this bill. Prasad sought the advice of Setalvad but conceded assent to spare any 'embarrassment'.[101] Another such issue arose when in early September Nehru argued against imposing 'restrictions' on Muslim government servants in India from visiting their relatives in West Pakistan. For Patel, this matter was about 'reciprocity', although there could be none because there were 'no Hindu or Sikh employees in West Pakistan', and he was willing to concede in East Pakistan. His feeling was that this was an avenue 'for disloyal government servants to pass on information'; his words were characteristic in that Pakistan 'cannot *liquidate* a problem [Hindus and Sikhs?] and then accuse us of action when we have to deal with a problem [Muslims?] which we cannot *liquidate*', and he wanted the states to refuse leave if they had 'any apprehensions'.[102] Over five successive days in September, this matter went back and forth, and Nehru too replied typically thus:

> The point is whether we should treat our Muslim employees differently from our non-Muslim employees. There are not very many Muslims in our Services…. Any attempt to discriminate against them indicates that we do not trust them…. There is no permit system in Bengal and people can come and go.[103]

Patel refused to budge. Claiming that he did not intend a 'general ban', and only desired 'discretion', he could not be oblivious that this discretion would work out in practice as discriminatory only against Muslims, but he dug his heels against West Pakistan, for which each case was to be viewed with 'regard to the position [of] the government servant, access to information and his reliability'.[104] But the prime minister too did not give up. For him it was 'not a question of government's right to stop anyone from going to Pakistan but a question of *exercise* of that right … everybody will understand that it is only for Muslim officers'.[105] There were more such officers in Nehru's UP than in any other state, as he argued that all governments have ways of 'judging conduct' and their state governments were, if anything, 'over-alive'; any person going to West Pakistan had to get a permit and a 'no objection' certificate. The prime minister knew that he needed support in this war of wills, and he mentioned that Rajagopalachari agreed with him, although the latter was his usual evasive self. In his first letter to Patel, he had written that he did not see 'anything unreasonable' in what Patel had said. In his second letter, after hearing Nehru, he wrote that 'when we trust persons belonging to a community and retain them in office, it would be improper to subject such persons to invidious treatment....' Patel replied that he had not taken up this question suo moto, that he would tell state governments that they had a 'right to refuse leave', and while he still felt that 'some general instructions should issue', he was 'prepared to drop the idea'.[106] By this time, both were in Nasik for the election of Patel's candidate Tandon over Nehru's ally Kripalani, and the prime minister accepted the compromise that his deputy had offered. After all, the reference had to be answered, with 'some explanation' other than 'we do not trust you'.[107]

It was the Ministry of States, however, where evidence was mounting that Patel's iron-grip was getting rusty. Having a hands-on Sardar deciding things on his own was one thing, having his mandarins exercise power-without-accountability quite another. Since September, it was being claimed that 'pressure' was mounted on certain states ministries in connection with the Congress presidential election. This was especially so about Rajasthan and PEPSU. Jainarain Vyas of Jodhpur was spoken to by Patel's secretary Shankar, who waved the stick of 'the case against him' and dangled the carrot of 'the Rajasthan ministry'. For Nehru, if Shankar spoke, it was 'improper', as most people naturally thought that he spoke on Patel's behalf.[108] Nehru then turned on the States Ministry and sketched its considerable unrepresentative prowess:

> It [has] the power to make and unmake ministries ... [in] 1/3rd of India.... [These] have no sanction of the people, they are not under the control of the Government of India as a whole.... Our cabinet knows very little of what is happening [in] ... Rajasthan, Madhya Bharat, Vindhya Pradesh, PEPSU.... It is inevitable that much is disposed of without your knowledge or with only a brief reference to you....[109]

Patel's officials prepared on 25 October 1950 a note for Nehru, which instead convinced him that 'policy' was being made in the secretariat. As Patel's health deteriorated, matters 'tended ... to be decided' by his *mulazims*, functioning 'without the normal checks'.[110] The prime minister suggested a cabinet committee to oversee the States Ministry, much as the foreign affairs committee. Afterwards, the maharaja of Rewa would confirm Nehru's impression of Menon et al., who relied on some local officer whom they appointed because he shared their prejudices and paranoias and served as a new yes-man to take their old-school dictation. In return, they made him 'a little man in a big place....'[111] From the last week of October 1950 to 1 December, this theme was at the heart of the last tussle of the duo. On 23 October, the ball was set rolling by Rafi Ahmed Kidwai, who informed Nehru that P. S. Krishna Pillai, the chief judge of Travancore-Cochin High Court, was retired on 21 January 1950 'illegally' and succeeded by C. Kunhiraman, a retired judge from Madras and then chairman of Travancore public service commission, 'who happened to be the uncle of V. P. Menon's wife'. Pillai was retired at 55, under the old state constitution, five days before the new all-India constitution would have come into force, under which he could have continued until 60. Kidwai did not mince his words when he wrote that 'our States Department thinks the Constitution … is not applicable to B and C class states….'[112]

The prime minister referred this matter to Gopalaswami Ayyangar, who met Pillai, who confessed that he did not want 'to antagonise people at the top', and Ayyangar felt that Pillai had agreed to retire because he was not sure how long he would be allowed to continue after 26 January 1950. It was the subsequent agitation against the appointment of Kunhiraman that made 'him see if he could not ask for some amends'.[113] On the same day, 30 October 1950, the Ministry of States issued a note that, by way of reorganising judiciary in five state unions, it had been decided to appoint retired or serving judges of provincial High Courts. Thus, PEPSU, Saurashtra, Madhya Bharat and Rajasthan got their chief justices, and thus also was explained Kunhiraman's retirement from Madras and reappointment in Travancore-Cochin. And then, the note threw light upon Pillai's retirement as an example of 'weeding out unsuitable personnel until … enquiry', for 'there was some discrepancy as regards the age of Pillai' and another judge Habib Muhammad. They were given the choice of either to face an enquiry or to retire, and Pillai had preferred to retire.

No sooner than this explanation could wash that a Pandora's box opened in Rajasthan, where the States Ministry was pursuing criminal charges against Jainarain Vyas, former and future chief minister of Jodhpur and Rajasthan.[114] It was striking because it was a 'double charge' for 'travelling allowances …', for which instead of a show-cause notice, Vyas was subjected to a police enquiry by a special officer, and Nehru was very interested in knowing who took all these decisions and with what motivations. After all, they were dealing with an old party colleague, and P. S. Rao, administrator of Jodhpur, could not be called upon to deal with him summarily. Five years ago, they would have criticised this procedure, which saw 'someone with an inquisitorial mind', a veiled dig at V. P. Menon, considering himself above ministers in these states. In nearby Vindhya Pradesh, Narbada Prasad Singh, another political colleague of 30 years standing, was being harassed by the States Ministry, which claimed that there was a solid case against him but could not share its details. These instances made the prime minister 'think of the Hyderabad cases as to how far [had] they [been] subjected to careful scrutiny….'[115] With Rajagopalachari too opining that cases against Vyas were not worth pursuing, adding that the machinery employed was 'inappropriate', and it 'cannot be sustained' judicially, Patel decided to withdraw them.[116]

The next case to come from Rajasthan was about the appointment of the chief justice there and the casual procedure adopted in the matter. By late November, Patel was rather unwell, and Nehru felt guilty at troubling him, but, equally, it was all-too-clear that officials were writing letters on Patel's behalf, 'perhaps without [his] even knowing'.[117] This instance was about the appointment of Justice K. N. Wanchoo, and again, it was not quite clear who took the initiative. The earliest letters were addressed by the Chief Justice of Allahabad bench to V. Shankar from 23 to 25 February 1950. These, in turn, referred to previous letters written by Shankar to him, while the next entry was a note of 28 February, from Shankar to civil servant N. M. Buch, in which Shankar referred to his 'previous conversations' with the Chief Justice of India and the Chief Justice of Allahabad and gave 'personal opinions' about various judges. For the prime minister, Shankar's opinion had 'no relevance', but it was not clear when he was 'speaking on behalf' of Patel, as Nehru found 'no mention' of Patel in these.

Subsequent papers indicated that Chief Justice Kania did not approve of Shankar's proposal that Wanchoo should be appointed, and President Prasad suggested the elevation of the acting chief justice of Rajasthan. Throughout the correspondence, there were 'repeated references' to Shankar as 'the deciding authority' until V. P. Menon entered this paper trail on 19 July, with a conversation with Kania in which the latter stated that he had no objection to Wanchoo but only to 'any additional remuneration' to be paid to him. The plot thickened with an entry of 4 November, in which Kania stood his ground, whereupon V. P. Menon went to see him, and, after this visit, Kania agreed to Wanchoo's 'provisional' appointment. Afterwards, it was discovered that this proviso could not be given effect to, as Patel himself wrote to Kania about it, and this extraordinary sequence of communications came to an end, with the prime minister and the law minister nowhere in the picture.[118]

Vallabhbhai Patel roused himself – 15 days from his death – to protect V. P. Menon and V. Shankar by claiming that 'oral instructions' had been given to them, to which, in an ironic role reversal, Nehru replied that 'the only thing that could remain in the office is the file....'[119] It was not that Patel did not remain characteristically vigilant in the one matter close to his weakening heart – that is, communists in India. Vladimir G. Sayadiants, the Soviet film promoter in Bombay, was the target of the Bombay government as well as Patel's Home Ministry. There was one complication here, namely that if he were expelled based on the 'judgement of police officers', then Indians abroad could be treated similarly.[120] By now, Patel was again in Bombay, and after seeing him off at the Palam aerodrome, Nehru had a talk with Rajagopalachari, with a view to decide to not trouble Patel for routine matters. With Rajagopalachari 'averse to any formal responsibility', it was decided that Nehru (home) and Gopalaswami Ayyangar (states) should step in. President Prasad agreed, and informing Patel about all this, Nehru expressed his hope to see him on the way to England for the Commonwealth conference in January 1951, with Rajagopalachari 'presumably agreeing to take up Home Affairs' then.[121]

Three days after this communication, at 9:37 a.m. on Friday, 15 December 1950, 'the hand of death fell on Sardar Patel', in the words of Jawaharlal Nehru. The prime minister's draft for the cabinet's statement was fulsome, as it distinguished between the 30 years before 1947, when he was one of the 'principal lieutenants' of Gandhi, and the three years after, when as deputy prime minister and in charge of two of the most important portfolios, in failing health, he continued, 'without rest or respite'. The one trait of Patel that Nehru highlighted more than once was 'his sense of discipline', which had allowed him to organise mass movements, and which enabled him to make 'a united India out of a welter of states'. He was 'irreplaceable', and the 'true and imperishable monument to his memory', for Nehru, was if people could follow his 'devotion to duty'.[122] Patel's devotees were also reportedly doing their duty to his memory and reputation. In an unverifiable report, G. K. Handoo, deputy director of the Intelligence Bureau, informed M. O. Mathai that meetings were held over 17–18 December, in which it was decided to destroy several papers in Patel's house by V. P. Menon (secretary, states), H. M. Patel (secretary, defence), C. C. Desai (secretary, commerce) and V. Shankar. They had been joined by Shavax Lal (secretary to president) and R. L. Gupta (secretary, food). This decision was mostly regarding the papers of States Ministry, as Home Secretary H. V. R. Iengar was, apparently, not 'a member of the "inner circle"'.[123]

The biggest question was to find the two sets of feet, which could step into Patel's shoes, and mutterings began within days, one of which was for Nehru to hold the combined portfolios of home and states until the general election, while he gave foreign affairs to Rajagopalachari. Another was that a cabinet committee called 'political affairs' should be created. The only thing on which there was unanimity across the party was to do away with the post of deputy prime minister. The other implication was that Nehru needed to take 'a little more detailed interest in Congress affairs …' wherein it was hoped that now Kripalani and others 'will not proceed with their Congress Democratic Front', while Nehru would also 'be able to bring back JP'.[124] In the event, Nehru met Rajagopalachari on 19 December 1950 and finalised portfolios that led to the latter becoming home minister and Ayyangar succeeding Patel as minister for states.

There was a third institutional legacy of the Sardar, namely as an unparalleled fund-raiser for the party. While this role of his had receded after the 1945–46 provincial elections, in 1950–51, there were three party accounts held at the United Commercial Bank, New Delhi – for Bengal relief fund, Punjab relief fund and the INA enquiry and relief committee – that stood in his name. After his death, they got transferred to the joint custody of his daughter Maniben and son Dayabhai. Maniben met Prasad, Nehru, Rajagopalachari and Morarji Desai in February 1951 to decide upon these. The Bengal relief fund, started after the Noakhali disturbances of August 1946, had a balance of INR 60,010, while the Punjab relief fund, started after the disturbances there in March 1947, had an amount of INR 1,10,714. It was decided to merge them for refugee relief under Congress president Tandon. The INA fund had a standing amount of INR 1,11,064, and there was yet another fund – Vithalbhai Trust for Congress' pre-1947 foreign propaganda – that had INR 1,39,733. These too were to be referred to Tandon. Patel had also managed a venture called the INA film fund that had emerged from the proceeds of the distribution of some 'Netaji Films'. The amount in this was INR 2,49,133, and it was agreed that 'half of the sum should be kept apart' for Bose's daughter, while the other half minus any expenses incurred should be paid to her immediately 'by a trust created by Maniben and Dayabhai, with the mother as the sole executor', and they should be invited to come to India. But the largest of the funds operated personally by Patel was the party's election fund, which, with its balance of INR 18,24,775, was to be kept aside. Finally, there was a personal fund in Patel's name, with an amount of INR 1,12,062, and Maniben Patel proposed that this should be given to the Bardoli Ashram vide a trust.[125]

NOTES

1   See Howard Spodek, 'Sardar Vallabhbhai Patel at 100', *Economic and Political Weekly* 10, no. 50 (1975): 1925–29, 1931–36; and Gandhi, *Patel*.
2   See Howard Spodek, 'Sardar Vallabhbhai Patel at 100', *Economic and Political Weekly* 10, no. 50 (1975): 1925–29, 1931–36; and Gandhi, *Patel*.
3   Sherman, *Nehru's India*, xvi–xvii.
4   26 June 1948, Nehru to Patel, File No. 10, JN (SG) Papers. For Patel's 'carrot-and-stick' style of disciplining provinces and inducing states, see Das, *Sardar Patel's Correspondence 1945–50 Vol. V* (1973).
5   4 July 1948, Patel's note on 'economic situation', File No. 43 (Part I), JN (SG) Papers.
6   16 August 1948, Nehru to Patel, File No. 10, JN (SG) Papers.

7   6 September 1948, Nehru to Patel, File No. 13 (Part I), JN (SG) Papers.

8   29 September 1948, Nehru to Iengar, File No. 13 (Part II), JN (SG) Papers. See Uditi Sen, 'Social Work, Refugees and National Belonging: Evaluating the "Lady Social Workers" of West Bengal', *South Asia: Journal of South Asian Studies* 44, no. 2 (2021): 344–61.

9   24 September 1948, Nehru to Khanna, File No. 13 (Part II), JN (SG) Papers.

10   Undated, November 1948, Nehru to Patel, File No. 15 (Part I), JN (SG) Papers.

11   17 November 1948, Nehru to Patel, File No. 15 (Part I), JN (SG) Papers.

12   17 September 1948, Nehru to Patel, File No. 13 (Part I), JN (SG) Papers.

13   25 September 1948, Nehru to Patel, File No. 13 (Part II), JN (SG) Papers.

14   19 November 1948, Nehru to Patel, File No. 15 (Part I), JN (SG) Papers.

15   28 and 29 September 1948, Nehru to Patel, File No. 13 (Part II), JN (SG) Papers.

16   3 October 1948, Nehru to Patel, File No. 14, JN (SG) Papers.

17   For Patel on Kashmir see Das, *Sardar Patel's Correspondence 1945–50 Vol. I* (1971).

18   15 October 1948, Patel to provincial premiers, File No. 14, JN (SG) Papers.

19   Manu Bhagavan, ed., *India, and the Cold War* (Chapel Hill: UNC Press, 2019), 1–18.

20   27 October 1948, Nehru to Patel, File No. 14, JN (SG) Papers. The next few quotes come from this letter.

21   Rakesh Ankit, *The Kashmir Conflict: From Empire to the Cold War, 1945–66* (London: Routledge, 2016).

22   See B. R. Rubin, 'The Civil Liberties Movement in India: New Approaches to the State and Social Change', *Asian Survey* 27, no. 3 (1987): 371–92.

23   8 November 1948, Nehru to Patel, File No. 15 (Part I), JN (SG) Papers.

24   5 December 1948, Nehru to Home Ministry, File No. 16 (Part I), JN (SG) Papers.

25   3 March 1949, Nehru's note to PMS, File No. 21 (Part I), JN (SG) Papers.

26   P. Kanungo, *RSS's Tryst with Politics: From Hedgewar to Sudarshan* (New Delhi: Manohar, 2002), 35–67.

27   3 March 1949, Nehru to Home Ministry and B. C. Roy, File No. 21 (Part I), JN (SG) Papers.

28   Bear, *Lines of the Nation*, 226–56.

29   5 March 1949, Patel's statement in Parliament, File No. 21 (Part I), JN (SG) Papers.

30   B. Pati, *South Asia from the Margins: Echoes of Orissa, 1800–2000* (Manchester: Manchester University Press, 2012), 138–58.

31   12 March 1949, Nehru to Patel, File No. 21 (Part I), JN (SG) Papers.

32   Dilip Mukerjee, 'Assam Reorganization', *Asian Survey* 9, no. 4 (1969): 297–311.

33   25 March 1949, Nehru to Sri Prakasa, File No. 21 (Part II), JN (SG) Papers. See H. Bhattacharya, *Radical Politics and Governance in India's Northeast: The Case of Tripura* (London: Routledge, 2018), ch. 7–8.

34   24 March 1949, Nehru to PPS, File No. 21 (Part II), JN (SG) Papers.

35   Neerja Singh, *Patel, Prasad and Rajaji: Myth of the Indian Right* (New Delhi: Sage, 2015), 121–79.

36   2 August 1949, Patel to Munshi, File No. 27 (Part I), JN (SG) Papers.

37   For Patel's role as party manager for the 1945–46 elections, see Das, *Sardar Patel's Correspondence 1945–50 Vol. II* (1972).

38   See K. C. Mahendru, *Gandhi, and the Congress Socialist Party, 1934–48: An Analysis of Their Interaction* (New Delhi: ABS, 1986).

39   Aditya Mukherjee, *Imperialism, Nationalism, and the Making of the Indian Capitalist Class, 1920–1947* (New Delhi: Sage, 2002), ch. 12.

40   3 August 1949, Patel's note, File No. 27 (Part I), JN (SG) Papers.

41   11 August 1949, M. O. Mathai's note, File No. 27 (Part I), JN (SG) Papers.

42   V. Krishna Ananth, *The Indian Constitution and Social Revolution: Right to Property since Independence* (New Delhi: Sage, 2015), ch. 1 and 2.

43   10 August 1949, Nehru's note, File No. 27 (Part II), JN (SG) Papers.

44   Menon, *The Story of the Integration of the Indian States*, 476–83.

45   9 August 1949, Patel to Nehru, File No. 27 (Part I), JN (SG) Papers. Singh, *Patel, Prasad and Rajaji*, 253–69.

46   11 August 1949, Nehru to Patel, File No. 27 (Part II), JN (SG) Papers.

47   For Patel's preference of merger of princely states via privy purses, see Das, *Sardar Patel's Correspondence 1945–50 Vol. VIII* (1973).

48   16 August 1949, Patel to Nehru, File No. 27 (Part II), JN (SG) Papers.

49   17 August 1949, Nehru to Patel, File No. 27 (Part II), JN (SG) Papers.

50   11 April 1949, Anand to Nehru, File No. 27 (Part II), JN (SG) Papers.

51   Aradhya Sethia, 'Where's the Party? Towards a Constitutional Biography of Political Parties', *Indian Law Review* 3, no. 1 (2019): 1–32.

52   For Patel's views on a republic India's membership of the British Commonwealth, see Das, *Sardar Patel's Correspondence 1945–50 Vol. VIII* (1973).

53   28 August 1949, Patel to Nehru, File No. 28, JN (SG) Papers.

54   24 October 1949, Nehru to Patel, Correspondences, Ayyangar Papers.

55   3 November 1949, Patel to provincial premiers, File No. 51 (Part I), JN (SG) Papers.

56   14 November 1949, Patel to premiers, File No. 51 (Part I), JN (SG) Papers. Godse was hung the next day.

57   Chakraborty, 'Political History of Merger of the Princely States', 161–207.

58   27 December 1949, Nehru to Patel, File No. 33, JN (SG) Papers.

59   See Subrata K. Mitra, *Governance by Stealth: The Ministry of Home Affairs and the Making of the Indian State* (New Delhi: Oxford University Press, 2021), 74–173.

60   6–7 February Nehru–Patel exchange, File No. 36 (Parts I and II), JN (SG) Papers. See A. U. Siddiqui, *Indian Freedom Movement in Princely States of Vindhya Pradesh* (New Delhi: Northern Book, 2004), 138–75.

61   12 February 1950, JP to Nehru, File No. 36 (Part II), JN (SG) Papers.

62   See Rani Dhavan Shankardass, 'Vallabhbhai Patel: His Role and Style in Indian Politics 1928–1947' (PhD thesis, SOAS, London, 1985).

63   20 February 1950, Patel to Nehru, File No. 37 (Part I), JN (SG) Papers.

64   15 February 1950, Nehru to Patel, File No. 37 (Part I), JN (SG) Papers.

65   21 February 1950, Patel to Nehru, No. 132/DPM/50, File No. 37 (Part I), JN (SG) Papers.

66   11 March 1950, Patel to chief ministers, No. 161/DPM/50, File No. 38, JN (SG) Papers.

67   4 March 1950, Nehru to Patel, File No. 38, JN (SG) Papers.

68   20 February 1950, Nehru to Patel, File No. 37 (Part I), JN (SG) Papers.

69   21 February 1950, Patel to Nehru (DO No. 126-DPM/50), File No. 37 (Part I), JN (SG) Papers.

70   21 February 1950, Nehru to Patel and Rajagopalachari, File No. 37 (Part I), JN (SG) Papers.

71   20 February 1950, Nehru to N. G. Ranga, File No. 37 (Part I), JN (SG) Papers.

72   21 February 1950, Nehru to Rajagopalachari, File No. 37 (Part I), JN (SG) Papers.

73   Raghavan, *War and Peace in Modern India*, 149–87.

74   18 April 1950, Patel to Nehru, File No. 42 (Part I), JN (SG) Papers.

75   18 April 1950, Nehru to Patel, File No. 42 (Part I), JN (SG) Papers.

76   19 May 1950, Nehru to Patel, File No. 44 (Part I), JN (SG) Papers.

77   18 May 1950, Rajagopalachari to Nehru, File No. 44 (Part I), JN (SG) Papers. See Rajmohan Gandhi, *Rajaji: A Life* (London: Penguin, 2010), ch. 19.

78   23–25 May 1950, Patel–Nehru exchange, File Nos. 44 (Part I) and 45 (Part I), JN (SG) Papers.

79   21 May 1950, Nehru to Patel, File No. 44 (Part I), JN (SG) Papers.

80   17 May 1950, Bhide to Saksena, File No. 44 (Part I), JN (SG) Papers.

81   25 May 1950, Nehru to Patel, No. 676-PM, File No. 45 (Part I), JN (SG) Papers. See Niraja Gopal Jayal, *Citizenship and Its Discontents: An Indian History* (Cambridge: Harvard University Press, 2013), 51–81.

82   25 May 1950, Nehru to Azad, No. 678-PM, File No. 45 (Part I), JN (SG) Papers.

83   4 and 5 June 1950, Patel to Nehru, File No. 46 (Part I), JN (SG) Papers.

84   5 June 1950, Nehru to Patel, File No. 46 (Part I), JN (SG) Papers.

85   4 June 1950, Nehru to Krishna Menon, File No. 46 (Part I), JN (SG) Papers.

86   26 June 1950, Nehru to Patel and Rajagopalachari, File No. 46 (Part I), JN (SG) Papers.

87   24 June 1950, Rajagopalachari to Nehru, File No. 46 (Part I), JN (SG) Papers. See Gandhi, *Rajaji*, ch. 14.

88   27 June 1950, Patel to Nehru, File No. 46 (Part I), and 6 July 1950, Nehru to Rajagopalachari, File No. 47 (Part II), JN (SG) Papers.

89   30 June 1950, Nehru to Patel, File No. 46 (Part II), JN (SG) Papers.

90   27 June 1950, Patel to Nehru, File No. 46 (Part I), JN (SG) Papers. See Christopher Snedden, *Independent Kashmir: An Incomplete Aspiration* (Manchester: Manchester University Press, 2021), ch. 5; and Hafsa Kanjwal, *Colonizing Kashmir: State-building under Indian Occupation* (Stanford: Stanford University Press, 2023), ch. 1.

91   29 June 1950, Nehru to Patel, File No. 46 (Part II), JN (SG) Papers.

92   3 July 1950, Patel to Nehru, No. 449-DPM/50, File No. 47 (Part I), JN (SG) Papers.

93   See Arudra Burra, 'Civil Liberties in the Early Constitution: The Crossroads and Organiser Cases', in *Human Rights in India*, ed. Satvinder Juss (London: Routledge, 2019).

94   11 July 1950, Nanda to Nehru, File No. 49 (Part I), JN (SG) Papers.

95   22 July 1950, Nehru's note, File No. 49 (Part I), JN (SG) Papers.

96   30 July 1950, Patel to Nehru, File No. 49 (Part II), JN (SG) Papers.

97   10 August 1950, Nehru to Patel, File No. 51 (Part I), JN (SG) Papers.

98   Narayani Basu, *V. P. Menon: The Unsung Architect of Modern India* (New Delhi: Simon & Schuster, 2020).

99   6 September 1950, Patel to Nehru, File No. 54 (Part II), JN (SG) Papers. See S. Maheshwari, 'Evolution of States in India', *Indian Journal of Public Administration* 22, no. 3 (1976): 307–29.

100 11 September 1950, Patel to Nehru, File No. 55 (Part I), JN (SG) Papers.

101 See R. S. Gae, 'Land Law in India: With Special Reference to the Constitution', *International and Comparative Law Quarterly* 22, no. 2 (1973): 312–28.

102 11 September 1950, Patel to Nehru, File No. 55 (Part I), JN (SG) Papers.

103 12 September 1950, Nehru to Patel, File No. 55 (Part I), JN (SG) Papers.

104 13 September 1950, Patel to Nehru, File No. 55 (Part II), JN (SG) Papers.

105 14 September 1950, Nehru to Patel, File No. 55 (Part II), JN (SG) Papers.

106 16 September 1950, Patel to Nehru, File No. 55 (Part II), JN (SG) Papers.

107 16 September 1950, Nehru to Patel, File No. 55 (Part II), JN (SG) Papers. See William Gould, Taylor C. Sherman and Sarah Ansari, 'The Flux of the Matter: Loyalty, Corruption and the Everyday State in the Post-partition Government Services of India and Pakistan', *Past and Present* 219, no. 1 (2013): 237–79.

108 Richard Sisson, *The Congress Party in Rajasthan: Political Integration and Institution-Building in an Indian State* (Berkeley: University of California Press, 1972), 204–39.

109 28 September 1950, Nehru to Patel, File No. 56 (Part II), JN (SG) Papers.

110 29 October 1950, Nehru to Patel, File No. 61 (Part II), JN (SG) Papers.

111 25 February 1951, Nehru to Ayyangar, File No. 74, JN (SG) Papers.

112 23 October 1950, Rafi Ahmed Kidwai to Nehru, File No. 61 (Part II), JN (SG) Papers.

113 30 October 1950, Ayyangar to Nehru, File No. 61 (Part II), JN (SG) Papers.

114 Sisson, *The Congress Party in Rajasthan*, 260–82.

115 29 October 1950, Nehru to Patel, File No. 61 (Part II), JN (SG) Papers.

116 7 November 1950, Rajagopalachari to Patel, and 9 November 1950, Patel to Nehru, File No. 62 (Part II), JN (SG) Papers.

117 21 November 1950, Nehru to Patel, File No. 64 (Part II), JN (SG) Papers. The next few quotes come from here.

118 See Abhinav Chandrachud, *The Informal Constitution: Unwritten Criteria in Selecting Judges for the Supreme Court of India* (New Delhi: Oxford University Press, 2014).

119 1–2 December 1950, Patel–Nehru exchange, File No. 66 (Part I), JN (SG) Papers.

120 1 December 1950, Nehru to Patel, File No. 66 (Part I), JN (SG) Papers.

121 12 December 1950, Nehru to Patel, No. 1953-PM, Correspondences, Ayyangar Papers.
122 16 December 1950, Nehru's draft, File No. 68 (Part I), JN (SG) Papers.
123 19 December 1950, Mathai to Nehru, File No. 68 (Part II), JN (SG) Papers.
124 19 December 1950, Mathai's note of Srinivasa Mallayya's views, File No. 68 (Part I), JN (SG) Papers.
125 25 February 1951, Nehru to Maniben Patel, File No. 74, JN (SG) Papers.

5

1951

THIS YEAR WILL 'TEST US TO THE UTTERMOST …'

The year 1951 is a somewhat overlooked year, sandwiched between the year of the republic and that of electoral democracy, with its overshadowed clearing of decks via, as this section shows, an interplay between pre-existing structures and their succeeding shapes. The first casualty of this was the Hindu Code Bill, which got kicked into the long grass given, as Nehru listed to Ambedkar, 'strong opposition, governmental reconstruction [and] Patel's death'.[1] A second were those Muslims of West Bengal, who had left before the Delhi Pact for either East Bengal or elsewhere in India and then returned afterwards. They had been promised and, in many cases, received grants of INR 200 by the state government to repair their houses, in lieu of their taken-away land and looted shops. An accompanying central loan for a sum between INR 500 and INR 750 for artisans/traders, like Hindu migrants from East Bengal, was, however, not forthcoming. A related and sensitive issue was with whom to arrange for this delivery, as B. C. Roy mistrusted old Khilafat leaders from Bengal and preferred 'the Jamiat'.[2] A third casualty was the government's grow-more-food campaign, which was overtaken by more than 5 million tons of import. Its concomitant tragedy was the unsustainable rural rationing and integrated controls, as the deficit had to be 'spread over the country'.[3] Indeed, it was not just food grains and essential items like sugar,[4] but even the newsprint situation that now needed 'control'.[5]

Control was also what the prime minister was seeking on the States Ministry now, especially on its treatment of Hyderabad. Receiving a file from it about services there, he found that one of its objectives was the 'dispersal' of Muslim officers to other parts of India and to replace them by people from Madras, Bombay and the Central Provinces. Nehru did not forget that New Delhi had entered Hyderabad by 'military occupation', and, two years and two months later, it had a 'civilian occupation'. Outsiders sent there had no ability in any of the languages but had a conqueror's attitude, and the so-called ministry was 'very communal in the Hindu sense'.[6] What was communal in a regional sense was 'the demand for more food' from Bombay, without regard to others.[7] B. G. Kher wrote strongly against the central insistence on self-sufficiency by 1952 and gave an 'ultimatum' on imports and controls. Nehru countered with 'sampling survey, river valley schemes [and] procurement machinery' and pleaded for 'cooperation'.[8] But with major irrigation projects like Damodar Valley, Hirakud and Bhakra-Nangal dams being stretched financially and causing 'retrenchment',[9] circumstances were distressing. In January 1951, the Madras state reduced its ration to 9 ounces, while seeking the centre's approval to increase rice content to 8 ounces, citing psychological danger, black market and comparisons with Orissa, Coorg, Madhya Pradesh and Travancore-Cochin.[10]

Altogether another kind of distress signal was coming from the States Ministry. Within ten days of Patel's death, the Gaekwad of Baroda became the first ruler to make a formal representation on 'sovereignty', a word that was never acknowledged by either New or Old Delhi. He was reminded that no government had treated the rulers 'so generously', for which 'Sardar Patel had to bring all the pressure....'[11] In contrast was the attitude of the nawab of Bhopal, who appealed about the harassing category of 'intending evacuees' for those Muslims in Bhopal who had, around August 1947, transferred money to Pakistan with no restrictions then. In most cases, future 'uncertainty' had caused these transfers, but, with new laws coming into force since, such persons were declared 'intending evacuees'. There was a lull in the custodians' activities around the Delhi Pact, but since then, show-cause notices were being served again. Hamidullah was at pains to confirm that 'almost every one of those who transferred money ... has no intention of leaving', despite 'the unfortunate attitude of the services'.[12]

Some steps away from the nawab was Prince Agha Khan, who prophesised to the prime minister that as 'national hatreds' were based on historic 'fear', '5 or 10 years hence there may be a Mahasabha government ... in Delhi'.[13] In February 1951, reports came on the Mahasabha's twin objectives, 'to drive away Muslims, to make Hindus anti-Congress', and riots took place around Hindu festivals 'by the story of ... cow-slaughter in areas where Muslims live in ... Bengal, UP, Bihar, Hyderabad'.[14] From the other end of the ideological spectrum, businesses and princes lived 'in fear' of a socialist government, and news came from Bihar that 28/41 communists had been in preventive detention since 26 February 1950.[15] Appeals were coming from the World Peace Congress for releasing them as well as for letting them hold public meetings. Unlike them, the one set of people whom even Nehru was keen to deny a political platform was the Naga National Council.[16] When the Assam governor, Jairam Doulatram, forwarded a letter from A. Z. Phizo, its president, it got a Patelite response from Nehru looking for 'reliable men in Nagaland ... there can be no question of their independence. But there might well be some question of autonomy'.[17]

On the other hand, he was also mindful that there was little 'sympathy' among the Assamese for the Nagas, as the educated rather wanted 'to boss over' them, and the state government reflected this 'aggressive policy'.[18] While Nehru let Bishnuram Medhi's government handle the situation, he demurred at any attempts to absorb areas and wanted these to have autonomy (land, customs) within limits (security, infrastructure). He compared the Nagas to the North-West Frontier tribes and, reminding Medhi of their 1948 Hydari-Bardoloi agreement, felt that to go back on it (as Bardoloi tried to do later) would be 'a breach of faith'. Simultaneously, though, he was clear that New Delhi would 'put down a rebellion ... followed by a constructive approach', which, however, also got caught with 'the intending Muslim settlers' in Assam.[19]

Meanwhile, across India, an 'election time' was on the anvil,[20] and so were election-minded acts. The UP government, after prolonged delays, passed their *zamindari* abolition bill, only for the High Court to stop it and start a contest between the parliament and the judiciary to be played out in the electoral arena to seek the mandate 'to change [the] Constitution'.[21] If institutions were up for re-inscription, then icons were up for grabs. When the Socialist Party was charged with 'misuse' of the national flag by the Congress during elections in the Mehrauli (Delhi State) notified area committee, the duty magistrate kept quiet, whereupon the socialist leaders demanded 'definite rules'.[22] The third electoral line to be drawn was along caste. In a typical example, 'Harijans' of Rohtak's Gandhi Ashram, led by Lal Chandi Gura, visited Nehru to complain about 'ill-treatment from Jat zamindars', as well as from the officials of Rohtak district who sided with the latter.[23]

Chandi Gura was not the only Gandhian disillusioned, as President Prasad found in his talks with Bhave, Mashruwala, Shrikrishnadas Jaju and Gopabandhu Chowdhuri at Wardha. They shared with him their 'embarrassment' with the government moving away from Gandhian programmes on centralisation, industrialisation, basic education (*nai talim*), prohibition and agricultural self-sufficiency. Only in the matter of Hindu–Muslim relations, they felt otherwise, and they conveyed to Nehru their message that non-alignment in foreign policy was 'only possible with economic planning on Gandhiji's lines'.[24] As a concession to them, G. L. Nanda produced a 'National Common Action Programme' on 20 February 1951, with headings like public cooperation under the Bharat Sewa Sangh, agricultural reconstruction under village production councils, Kisan Dals, registered cooperatives and cottage and small-scale industries.[25] But the pressing need of the hour was prompt imports, and New Delhi impressed upon its embassy in Washington in the frantic first week of February 1951 that cereals production was 'expected to fall short by at least 5 ½ million tons … 3.7 million tons can be paid with available funds … request [for rest] on special terms'.[26]

This American gift was to come with 'observers', with 'some say',[27] and Nehru was desperate for direct procurement of grain in Punjab and Western UP and distraught that food grains continued to 'flow into the black-market in Delhi',[28] as reports came about 'irregularity and corruption in purchase of fertilizers'.[29] This was especially bad as 'a private firm in Delhi … in charge of food distribution … controlled by 3 men, made 80 lakhs of rupees in 5 years….'[30] Meanwhile, ministries were asked to revise 'all capital works … reduce expenditure [and] think of … bamboo and thatched structures'.[31] Labour Minister Jagjivan Ram warned of a miners' strike as ration cuts fell 'most heavily' on them, and Rafi Ahmed Kidwai warned against raising 'the stamp fee of the inland letter, in view of the railway fares being raised'.[32] This enforced economising reduced quite a few ideas of the prime minister to nothing, including 'a film about the Ganga, the river of India'.[33] Then, he wanted the British firm Reed & Mallik 'to make prefabricated … hospitals', but their costs were prohibitive,[34] while, for penicillin from abroad, he wanted Tandon to take the 'lead'.[35] Around this time, what was finally given some lead was the States Ministry, when on 15 February 1951, the cabinet considered a resolution by Mukut Bihari Lal Bhargava and directed thus:

> PEPSU, Rajasthan and Hyderabad … elections should be held … Tripura and Manipur to be left … Cutch merged with Saurashtra … Bhopal would not be merged … for 5 years…. Vindhya Pradesh to be treated as Rajasthan [but with] greater [central] powers … Himachal Pradesh same [with] much greater powers … Bilaspur to merge with Himachal … Ajmer … with Rajasthan. Coorg should remain separate.[36]

The future of communities there was easier to direct than to determine the future of the Hindu Code Bill, which remained stuck in the parliament. Three days had been allotted for its reading, and the bill did not make much progress, leaving Dr Ambedkar discouraged about its chances before the general election.[37] Those opposed to the bill resorted to rules of procedure to stretch the debate, given the speaker's and the chief whip's support, and Ambedkar requested Nehru to allot '7/20 days' in the present session or ask the parliament to 'sit every evening between 5–7'. He demanded 'a time-limit on speeches', curtailing 'the power of the speaker on closure motion', as well as asking him to 'not [consider] every amendment'. The bill had been before the parliament 'for 3 years and 9 months', more than any other, and Nehru had issued a whip for every contentious bill except this one. Ambedkar called it 'a humiliation for a government with an enormous majority to be worsted by a despicable minority....'[38]

The prime minister was 'troubled' about obstructions, to avoid which he gave up key features, but remained wary of enforcing the issue, which he argued would 'create more difficulties'.[39] And so he did not go beyond admonishing Chief Whip Sinha, who was also delaying the Representation of the People Bill by making parliamentary motions. It was critical to enact this bill in this session, Nehru wrote to Ambedkar in a desperation of his own, otherwise 'our programme of elections will go to pieces',[40] even as the party was picking up pieces of defeat at places or/levels like municipal elections in Gujarat, where at Surat, out of 30 seats, 17 were won by a People's Party to Congress' 11, with the vice-president of Surat district Congress defeated, and at Baroda, where out of 45 seats, 18 were won by the Socialist Party and 9 by independents, to Congress' 21.[41] From nearby Sevagram, Vinoba Bhave was critiquing the government's inflexibility in grain procurement, revenue collection and price fixation, for which Mahtab, now the minister of commerce and industry, was emphasising 'regional self-sufficiency',[42] opposing Nehru's national planning preference.

Above all, it was being whispered in the corridors of the Congress that the 'unity' resolutions passed over 1950–51 had achieved 'nothing' between Nehru, Tandon and Kripalani. From P. C. Ghosh in Bengal to T. Prakasam in Andhra, regional satraps were restive, and the party was hoping to paper over these cracks by appointing a committee of Nehru, Rajagopalachari and Tandon to select the members of an election tribunal that would select the candidates for the elections. In February 1951, P. C. Ghosh left the party after 30 years, citing difficulties in making even 'moderate' changes. Ghosh's compatriot J. C. Gupta had been writing to the prime minister since November 1950 that the situation in Bengal was 'deteriorating', and, following Patel's death, it was essential for either Nehru or Azad to visit,[43] as the general feeling was that ministers had 'no grip on administration and economy'.[44]

As for corruption, in February 1951, a Delhi weekly, *Indian States*, re-published a copy of the trial balance sheet of a Dalmia company, which showed a loan entry of INR 10,000 to Jagjivan Ram to purchase a car upon becoming minister in the 1946 interim government. He had returned the money in June 1948, but for a labour leader to borrow money thus was not 'wise'.[45] Around this time, a question was asked in parliament about the travel allowance drawn by various ministers in 1950–51, and Rajagopalachari's answer revealed that the lowest withdrawals were made by Azad (INR 447), Neogy (INR 687), Mookerjee (INR 814), himself (INR 824), Baldev Singh (INR 840), Deshmukh (INR 947) and Nehru (INR 998).[46] Every question was being messaged towards the elections, as reports of the commissions of enquiry for West Bengal and Assam, set up under the April 1950 pact, showed. Justices Prasanta Bihari Mukherji, Abany C. Banerjee and M. A. Haque received 45,325 representations, examined 394 witnesses and declared 'that no case of abduction, rape or conversion was proved'. A separate commission of enquiry under Mukherji, Faiznur Ali and K. R. Barooah for Assam received 2,484 representations about the 125 Muslims and 22 Hindus killed and blamed 'the invasion by a vast horde of Muslim immigrants from East Pakistan [especially] Mymensingh'.[47]

The situation in neighbouring Bihar was pitiable in a different way. The Congress government there was divided into groups, with the state itself divided into spheres of influence. There were scandals of molasses, *sathiland* and a sense of 'concealed chaos'. Krishna Ballabh Sahay, the revenue minister and overlord of Chhota Nagpur division, celebrated his 52nd birthday on 31 December 1950 at Hazaribagh with 'a purse of 52,000', collected by government servants, a testimony to his influence as well as fund-raising role. R. K. Dalmia gave him INR 2 lakhs to start his paper *Rashtravani*, while provincial revenue came in like 'water unchecked' from the maintenance of *karamchari*s and went out to manage *zamindari*s. Old-timers recalled that in 1947, Gandhi had asked for Sahay's removal as minister to no avail, and they now found themselves either submitting to everything or going 'out of the Congress'.[48]

The problem was that provincial governments did not so much depend on a confidence vote in the legislature as on the 'sanction' of the Congress organisation, and, in view of the coming election, realignments were on that had 'little to do' with the old Congress.[49] This problem was worse in (princely) states where, for example, in Rajasthan, the Ministry of States was still involving ministers and ex-ministers in false charges. It was difficult to gauge who were the people's representatives and who were the state's, and discontented Congressmen were demanding the transfer of officers.[50] Madhya Bharat still had these official advisors, while in Rajasthan, in February 1951, the government restored to the *jagirdar*s the powers that had been taken away from them by the abolition ordinance of 1948.[51] That ordinance, forced through by Patel on the Venkatachar committee's recommendation, overruling his officials, had now fallen foul of the latter's executive order. A prominent camp in the party believed that this was done 'to strengthen jagirdars against the Congress' on the *zamindari* abolition issue.[52] This official *jagirdar* set-up had already seen the departure of Gandhian Hiralal Shastri from the chief ministership, and Nehru wrote to Ayyangar to get rid of this set-up,[53] which would eventually go when Jainarain Vyas became chief minister in April.

Rafi Ahmed Kidwai, who was tasked with this changeover, had planned for the *rajpramukh*, maharaja of Jaipur, to send for Vyas and ask him to form a ministry, but as the maharaja dragged his feet, Vyas felt that both he and Ayyangar's officials were opposed. Vyas had earlier incurred 'the hostility of Menon' on the abovementioned abolition of *jagirdari*, and as for the *rajpramukh*, there was the old tension between Jaipur and Jodhpur. Moreover, Ayyangar, backed by Nehru, insisted on having non-Congressmen and ex-rulers in the cabinet as independents. Vyas agreed to have one each of these but protested to Kidwai that the Congressmen were 'desperate'.[54] The prime minister was unimpressed that Jainarain Vyas, a Patel acolyte, had kept away from him and repeated his suggestion for a composite cabinet.[55] In response, Vyas sent Tika Ram Paliwal (CM, March–October 1952), Maniklal Verma (PM, Rajasthan, 1948–49) and Gokul Lal Asawa (PM, Rajasthan, 1948) to see Ayyangar. When they and Vyas resisted this 'imposition', Ayyangar offered the bait of removing officials.[56]

Old mavericks everywhere were becoming a liability. V. K. Krishna Menon's jeep scandal was now assuming proportions, which would see his departure from his post as India's envoy in London in 1952.[57] Nehru softened the blow to his friend by terming him a victim of 'unusual circumstances', but there was no way to sugar-coat the discomfiting admission that they were 'badly caught…', and he was committed to confirming 'the major facts to party at least'.[58] To that end, he had asked Deshmukh to investigate the contracts placed in London for the purchase of jeeps by Menon from a new contractor, Messrs Rovers, and not the old contractor, Anti-Mistant Ltd, which had been brought up by Narhari Rao (auditor-general) in October 1950, and since then had seen legislators demand action. Deshmukh's ministry came to the following findings:

> The contract had been badly worded and there was no provision for the inspection of vehicles … 155 found unsatisfactory … 1 ½ lakhs would be necessary to put them right. There was undue delay. We had already paid the contractor a sum of £ 172,110/-. Finance authorities were not consulted…. The Industries & Supply ministry were not consulted. Negotiations commenced in February 1948 when Chanda and Patel [went] to England for arms…. The H-C undertook to arrange [jeeps

while] the contract for rifles-ammunition was cancelled. From the same contractor we purchased steel to compensate....[59]

This scandal dogged Menon and, by extension, Nehru. On his part, Menon dug his heels and pivoted to a new agreement for (*a*) returning the government credit of 143,162 pounds sterling due, (*b*) supply of 1,007 new Jeeps type CJ 3A and delivery at 68 units per month, and (*c*) the involvement of WILLIS Overland, the manufacturer, with General James Marshal Cornwall as guarantor.[60] While Britain was thus proving a tricky territory, the commonwealth at large was transactional as usual – from exporting Australia and Canada to importing Southern Rhodesia. And the trade deadlock with Pakistan finally ended in February 1951 with an agreement under which Pakistan supplied raw jute, raw cotton and food grains while India supplied coal, steel, textiles and cement on the par value of the Pakistani rupee.[61]

Other agreements proved more difficult, including the festering wound of the permit system, this time afflicting the Pathans, former Khudai Khidmatgars, who had settled in Delhi and nearby but occasionally went back on business. Indian officials in Lahore treated them in temporary transit, as the Pakistani officials in Bombay were nudging some Pathans there towards an organisation called 'the Anjuman Pashtoon', with the problem being that the Indian officials either could not or did not 'distinguish' between the 'two groups of Pathans....'[62] Shortly thereafter, in June 1951, there was a scare around war-like manoeuvres of Indian army units, from Hyderabad to Rajouri, Alwar to Srinagar and Rajasthan to Poonch, which was in view of 'jihad' in Pakistan, combined with ceasefire violations, in Kashmir. The former was a reference to the arrest of Major-General Akbar Khan, activist Sajjad Zaheer and poet Faiz Ahmed Faiz, Goebbels in the words of Khub Chand, India's acting envoy, along with others for a coup. Khub Chand's reportage was so ridiculous that it claimed that Faiz and others would 'ask the nation to celebrate its deliverance from the un-Islamic muhajir ... Liaquat' by seeking a *fatwa*. Chand's colonial trope was that of UP *sahib*s versus the Punjabi army, his anti-communist trope was a maligning of Faiz and his Cold War trope was 'facilities to the US/UK' under Generals Douglas Gracey and Ayub Khan.[63] Mercifully, Nehru ignored it and simply told Cariappa that if Pakistan took any action in Kashmir, then 'we would carry the war into ... West Punjab ... so long as the war was won'.[64]

At another level, issues with both the Menons reflected the anomaly that there was still no established appointments committee of the cabinet.[65] A committee comprising Nehru, Patel and the minister concerned had been formed in June 1950 and dealt with 52 cases, but the ministries of railways, defence and external affairs had remained outside its remit. Now, Rajagopalachari wanted to uniformly apply it, but defence and external affairs continued to prefer their existing procedures. Nehru's secretary

M. O. Mathai pointed out the political advantage of an appointments committee as 'one way of straightening irregularities'.[66] When the prime minister resisted, Rajagopalachari conceded that service boards might continue, as well as 'political' appointments to labour tribunals, and embassies and so on.[67]

But this politics around key personnel did not compare with the party politics in East Punjab. The rift there between the Partap Singh Kairon-led state Congress and the Bhargava government had widened since Patel's death, who had brought about a compromise in September 1950. Kairon, who was the beneficiary then, had gone all out against Bhargava as Nehru made it clear that, in the coming election, the voice of the party would be more important. The prime minister knew that no government could 'function [without] party',[68] but this also meant that all kinds of elements started drifting to Kairon's side, starting with district elections, and Bhargava's hold became tenuous and the state politics bitter. Amritsar, Karnal and Gurgaon saw violence in district polls, not all of which could be attributed to the Akalis. On the language controversy, Scheduled Caste villagers were being told that 'they could get land if they declared Hindi as their mother tongue', and the local press 'carried venom'.[69]

Baldev's own Jalandhar district was emerging as the epicentre of this language controversy. Swaran Singh was reporting to him that (caste) Hindus were 'persuading the Harijan[s] to state that Hindi was their mother tongue', given the 'predominance of Hindus amongst the [census] enumerators....' He was blunt on the resentment this caused among the Sikhs but bashful about their 'peaceful boycott' of the Scheduled Castes, who were thus caught between the two sides. Quarrels broke out, arrests were made – '30–40% Harijans, remaining Jat Sikhs' – and despite Bhargava touring Jalandhar, the local press alternated between being 'poisonous' and 'playing with fire'.[70] It was serious enough for the Intelligence Bureau to have a deputy director devoted to this matter, as the social coercion and economic boycott of the Scheduled Castes by the Sikhs across Kapurthala, Sangrur, Bhatinda, Fatehgarh Saheb and Patiala were deteriorating into arson, harassment, migration and arrests of 'Harijans' (12) and Jat Sikhs (8). In Jalandhar district, 98 Jat Sikhs and 45 'Harijans' were arrested, as cases piled up, including murder. Gurdaspur, Hoshiarpur, Muktsar and Ferozepur were also affected, while in PEPSU, the Achhut Federation of Prithvi Singh Azad was protesting along with the Depressed Classes League at Patiala. The Harijan Sabha of Amritsar met and threatened a 'sweeper satyagraha', as did the Sweepers' Federation of Simla. Jumping on the bandwagon, the Hindu Mahasabha and the RSS set up a refugee camp at Amritsar, where N. C. Chatterjee warned the Sikhs with 'similar victimisation' elsewhere. When Master Tara Singh visited Patiala, Hindu refugees from Bahawalpur there started leaving.[71]

This quadrangular contest between or within the Akali Dal, the Kairon-led Congress party and Bhargava's government, overlain the social mosaic of Hindus versus Sikhs versus 'Harijans' versus refugees, the last being an overlapping category with the first three. At the apex, Nehru wished Kairon would not attack Bhargava, as if the Congress were still in opposition, for neither could they 'run a government without services' nor could they 'produce services suddenly'.[72] Whether it was the blowing language controversy or the brewing dispute over 'a betterment fee' for the land served by the Bhakra scheme, a modus vivendi was essential in the state, from where the recent Hansi incident had shocked Nehru. There the 'wife of a non-refugee, who was reported as carrying on with a refugee girl, was undressed and paraded through the streets by a crowd of refugees ...', and Trivedi feared 'large-scale bloodshed'.[73] The governor reported that Bhargava had directed a 'punitive tax on refugees', but the locals who saw the incident did not interfere either, and of the seventeen accused, all were granted bail as the victim was unable to identify the culprits, and Trivedi resisted 'withdrawing concessions from refugees'.[74]

Meanwhile, the prospect of a famine spreading like fire throughout the country was coming closer. The economic committee of the cabinet was receiving defective statistics of acreage and yield, and even these were showing a deficit of 2–4 million tons of rice.[75] This spectre was linked among the officials to a 'red scare', and in none other than B. N. Mullik, director of the Intelligence Bureau, who was touring in an arc from Telangana to Tripura.[76] After a visit to the latter in March, he produced a 19-page report, which Dharma Vira forwarded to Nehru with an accompanying note that 'if even half of what [he] says is correct, immediate and far-reaching measures will have to be taken'.[77] Mullik's report contained usual 'chapters' on the growth of the CPI there since its congress in Calcutta in March 1948, with obligatory verses on Pakistan, government shortcomings chiefly in intelligence, infrastructure and publicity, and a predictable security plan involving more arms for more men.

In the Intelligence Bureau's eyes at least, the shadows of the Cold War were lengthening in the national capital itself, with it being reported that the American Embassy was eyeing the *Times of India*, while the *Hindustan Standard* had been already weakened with the exit of its communist editor Rana Jung Bahadur Singh. In the Hindi press, it was rumoured that the daily *Pratap* was being paid INR 20,000 quarterly by the Americans through Dr Gokul Chand Narang, and journalists like Hansraj Rattan and R. L. Verma were also on their payrolls, writing for the Urdu daily *Tej*. The *Indian News Chronicle*, through its director Deshbandhu Gupta and staffer J. N. Sahni, was said to be another favourite of the embassy.[78] From the Home Ministry, meanwhile, Rajagopalachari refused permission to hold Saifuddin Kitchlew's All-India

Peace Congress in Delhi and denied entry to any foreign delegates elsewhere too. To Rajagopalachari, Kitchlew may have been a Congressman since the Rowlatt Act and Jallianwala Bagh massacre days, but the Peace Congress was 'a movement organised by the International Communist Party'.[79] Nehru was left to similarly cancel a cultural conference sponsored by the strange combine of K. M. Munshi and B. R. Ambedkar in Delhi, for otherwise it would have been embarrassing to explain the former refusal.[80]

In Delhi, election preparations were in swing too, and Asaf Ali, on the electoral rolls for over 30 years, found his and his father's names omitted, as he had sold his paternal property to the municipality. It was a 'sentimental shock' to him when his wife Aruna maintained a place in the constitution house and held bank accounts in New Delhi.[81] He had not exactly fit in as governor in Cuttack either, and Mahtab and his successor Nabakrushna Chowdhuri urged Rajagopalachari to make the tactical appointment of the maharaja of Mayurbhanj, as one-third of his state had been taken over from the bloc of eastern states, among whom the maharajas of Patna and Kalahandi were opposing the government. Rajagopalachari was inclined to send V. V. Giri, the trade unionist, who had been born in Berhampur, but Mahtab and Chowdhuri resisted this because 'of the Andhra–Oriya controversy'.[82]

These political jousts were overshadowed in March 1951, when President Rajendra Prasad accepted an invitation to re-open the re-built Somnath temple.[83] This infamous episode came up almost by stealth, in that the *jamsaheb*'s invitation to Prasad was buried among more important worries like his state Bihar having 'practically' no cloth and no food at a time of rising taxation, gathering discontent and slowing electoral preparations. Furthermore, the parliament had given an extension to the select committee on the critical People's Representation Bill until 31 March, and an unimpressed Prasad, calculating the number of days available in the budget session vis-à-vis the content of the bill and remembering the unhappy experience of the first attempt to pass it, which had already delayed the elections to November–December 1951, wondered whether there will be a general election in 1952. Much like the government's other promise of self-sufficiency in food by the same year and here, Prasad hinted at replacing Munshi. Amidst these issues, visiting Somnath was hardly tinged with any objection for him because it was the same as 'visiting Nizamuddin and Ajmer dargah, Jain temples, Sikh gurdwaras and Young Men's Christian Association'.[84] It was obviously not the same for Nehru, who too contextualised Prasad's visit within the grow-more-food campaign proceeding rather 'superficially', and when the select committee on voting rights was stuck in 'slow motion'.[85]

Prasad understood Somnath's 'historic significance', and that one implication of his 'association may be that some people may not like the idea of a temple, which was destroyed more than once by Muslim invaders of the time, being revived', but the line that he held to was statist as well as social in that it was 'not right to refuse the invitation [of] the *Rajpramukh* of the state who [was] also the chairman of the board of trustees [which had] two members of the central cabinet on it and perhaps also the Chief Minister'.[86] Nehru turned to Rajagopalachari for support, which was not forthcoming and, subject to the latter's advice, he left the matter to Prasad's discretion.[87] The other cultural matter that often saw presidential discretion remained the removal of 'deficiencies' in Hindi so that it may 'replace' English by 1965. Prasad was supported by an assortment of people in this, from speaker Mavalankar to Mauli Chandra Sharma of the Hindu Mahasabha, and he wished Nehru would allot this responsibility to some minister, as 15 months had gone since the new constitution, and Prasad felt that with no concrete steps taken, 15 years may not be enough.

The government's attention was rather on rising railway fares, raising fresh taxes and reinforcing preventive detention. The credit side of the ledger was also about to have the entry of the first Asian Games being held in Delhi,[88] while a commission on administration, headed by A. D. Gorwala, was to recommend appropriate ways and means.[89] Let alone attempt 'to try to regiment it',[90] Nehru found it difficult to regiment his party's legislators, no less than 43 of whom signed and sent a cable to the American Congress asking for food. And then one of them challenged him for placing 'the executive over the parliament … in the matter of contacting fellow legislators in other democracies', condemning it as a 'dangerous tendency towards a totalitarian national state'.[91]

If Nehru wished that Patel was around to deal with such impertinence, the latter's son wanted him to do something personal for him. Dayabhai Patel's business affairs were caught up with the evacuee property exchange since March 1950 and led to this 'direct approach' in March 1951.[92] This story of an exchange of his shares in Karachi Electric Supply Corporation with the mills at Ambernath, Bombay, belonging to Karim Brothers started before the latter were declared evacuees in December 1949 and saw, in May 1950, minister M. L. Saksena allowing it, pending their valuation. By the time this report came, there was a breakdown in negotiations with Pakistan, and this transaction could not go through. Meanwhile, Saksena was succeeded by Ajit Jain, while the Kher ministry was sympathetic to Dayabhai, with the proviso that he helped to rehabilitate refugees, as these mills were near the refugee township of Ulhasnagar. The complication was that the custodian in Bombay had agreed to lease out the mills to a refugee company, as the exchange of non-evacuee property in Pakistan with evacuee property in India was not allowed. Saksena's formula that 'Patel will transfer the mills to Bombay government for Rs. 50 lakhs [and] the Bombay government would then transfer [these] to the displaced persons' company, for Rs. 80 lakhs',[93] had Nehru's agreement on the condition that cash payment should be avoided. However, when this scheme was presented to the parties concerned, Karim backed out, and therefore, Jain ordered on 31 July 1950 that the allotment of the evacuee property may be made by the Bombay government as usual. With Vallabhbhai Patel assuring Jain that the case should be decided normally, the rehabilitation committee of the cabinet followed suit in refusing this individual exchange, and Jain was now disinclined to reopen the case. With Rajagopalachari's support, Nehru wrote to Dayabhai that in view of the expected 'objection from refugees', this was their 'unanimous opinion'.[94]

Around the same time, another son, that of Nizam Osman Ali Khan, was writing to Nehru on his personal issue, which was that New Delhi's proposed trust in Hyderabad for the jewellery of the nizam's family sought to 'deprive' him of his right as the elder son by introducing other members as equal 'co-sharers'. Reminding Nehru of his 'well-known hostility to [the] Laik Ali regime',[95] Azam Jah pointed out that this basis was not to be found in the history of Hyderabad, and the prime minister, peeved at such executive dispossession that had been a hallmark of the Ministry of States, wrote to Ayyangar. But his mind was more occupied by the fate of 5,000 teachers in the state who had lost their jobs and had been asked to learn Telugu or Marathi within two years if they wanted to resume. It would have been fairer 'to ask them to learn the language' simultaneously, and as others had been appointed in their place, it could only mean that they had been 'dismissed'. That 5,000 were unemployed meant 'about 25000 persons affected … open invitation to them to join the communists…'.[96] He was informed about this by Zain Yar Jung and Digambar Rao Bindu (state Congress), who claimed that Patel had overruled Azad on this.

Ayyangar promised to investigate this matter, but on the question of trust, he was as immovable as his predecessor. He pointed out that it involved jewellery worth about INR 12 crores, which was admitted as the nizam's private property in January 1950. Ayyangar added that this was a follow-up to the sale of gold or silver bullion, with its proceeds invested in central and state securities worth INR 27 crores. Of the remainder, '1/4th' each was allocated to the Prince of Berar and to the junior prince (Muazzam Jah), '1/16th' each to their sister and to the nizam's brother (Basalat Jah) and '3/16th' each to other sons, daughters and grandchildren. Given the notorious 'squander mania' of Azam Jah, this was in the government's interest, for the jewellery could 'fetch foreign exchange',[97] whose paucity was giving pause to the government accepting the American engineer Harvey Slocum's 'stiff terms' for the Bhakra project[98] and was leading the finance ministry to propose closing down the special police establishment dealing with corruption.[99]

Perennial economic concerns aside, what was foremost on the political agenda was the general election. Sukumar Sen informed the prime minister that if the government did not set in motion immediately the Representation of the Peoples Act, then neither would the bill get through parliament in that session nor would the election be held that year. Sen had also complained about states being 'dilatory' in their preparations, singling out UP and urging Nehru 'to expedite'.[100] It was not as if all was well with the election commission either. Both Asaf Ali and Mahtab had complained to Nehru that the delimitation work in Orissa had been 'thoroughly bad', with 'the whole object [being] to deprive the tribal people of proper constituencies....'[101] Not that there were many proper conditions anywhere else, for the two states or provinces closest to the capital, East Punjab or States Union and Rajputana or Rajasthan, were communally aflame. Refugees from Bahawalpur at the Rajpura camp, which Nehru had been involved in setting up, were being harassed as 'intruders', even as the tug of war between different groups continued, with its brunt being borne by the Scheduled Castes, in the tussle between the Harijan Sewak Sangh and *jathedars* across Sangrur, Fatehgarh Sahib and Barnala, and on their self-declaration in the census as Ramdasias or Balmikis, with 'practically all the officials involved'.[102]

In neighbouring Rajasthan, Jainarain Vyas and Hiralal Shastri groups remained at each other's throats, obstructing any 'unity ministry'.[103] In March 1951, on Abu Road, an incident escalated between Congress workers and the district collector, which brought to surface this instability. The former requested the latter to allow sales of wheat and sugar in the lead-up to the festival of Holi. While refusing the request, the official reportedly uttered *tum Marwari chor ho*. When party workers demanded an apology and threatened a *gherao* of his bungalow, the official left for Mount Abu with his family. The public burnt his effigy, and the official returned and ordered arrests of ten of those involved. Consequently, the public pelted Abu Road police station with stones. This brought forth lathi charge and firing, which left one person dead. With matters getting out of hand, Gokulbhai Bhatt, former chief minister of Sirohi state, came visiting. Interestingly, much of the ire was against the then Bombay government's police having a 'free hand',[104] in shades of the Rajasthan–Gujarat tussle over Mount Abu.

Elections though were not contested by officials, and at the top of the Congress party, the situation remained unsettled. In the first eight days of March, Kripalani and Nehru exchanged six letters after a breakdown in the Tandon–Kripalani correspondence, which could not produce anything beyond Tandon rejecting Kripalani's 'demand for enquiry' into his own election and 'appointment of [new] general secretaries',[105] while demanding the dissolution of Kripalani's group. Nehru offered small steps 'to lessen misunderstandings' but 'not a large-scale ... enquiry' in Tandon's election.[106] For Kripalani, a few 'sample enquiries' conducted by 'impartial office-bearers' would have been enough, but the prime minister, without Tandon's support, could only respond with a homily like 'we have to choose between lesser evils'.[107] This left Kripalani with little option but that they may leave with 'mutual goodwill', as without reform in the Congress, 'parties [were] inevitable'.[108]

In the meantime, cases that were a 'public scandal' continued before the custodian of evacuee property.[109] In one instance, with one month's notice, all petitions were dismissed when, with 'one sharer, however small his share, [going] to Pakistan, the whole property was seized', and in another, facing a four-year delay in adjudication, 'five persons in Delhi ... sent the keys of their properties to the custodian' and left for Pakistan,[110] thereby becoming evacuees which the state had deemed them to be.[111] By now, what was also assuming scandalous proportions was the census proceedings, especially from Punjab. From Amritsar, Udham Singh Nagoke was recalling that in 1931 and 1941 too, the question of mother tongue had been contentious, and Khan Ahmad Hussain Khan, the 1931 census superintendent, had observed that 'the figures of Hindustani [were] swollen at the expense of Punjabi', while in the 1941 census the figures were left 'untotalled' with the census commissioner recommending that these 'questions be dropped' in future.[112] Now in 1951, Nagoke charged that 'thousands speaking Punjabi everyday have been made to return Hindi as their mother-tongue' and demanded that 'New Delhi declare Punjabi as the language of the Punjab and PEPSU'.[113]

The prime minister and the home minister admitted that 'census in present conditions ... cannot be relied upon',[114] but they ruled out an enquiry fearing 'more passion' while reassuring Nagoke that the government would not accept this census' result in Punjab on the language question.[115] In turn, they were mindful of ejectment notices to almost 5,000 tenants across villages in Ferozepur, Hissar, Rohtak and Ambala in favour of 'in-comers' from Pakistan. Together with floods in summer, drought in winter and a major locust attack in spring, this worsened the winter crop procurement in Punjab for 1950–51, and Trivedi reported the statistical and sentimental scene in the province:

> We lent 78,500 tons of wheat to [New Delhi with] the intention to [get it] in January-April.... Now, we have been allocated 20,000 tons in March.... Our wheat stocks [are] about 60,000 tons; the offtake is 32,000.... People have begun to blame us.... You had to borrow [and] now we have trouble.[116]

At a time, when public opinion was the 'sole foundation' for government,[117] a clash followed between Hindus and Sikhs in the streets of Ludhiana on 24 March, which began with a provocative Arya Samaj procession, bricks thrown at it, and a following free-for-all, leaving many injured and many hours of curfew imposed.[118] The sights and sounds coming from other states tried to keep pace with Punjab. From Bihar, when a dissident legislator, Ram Narain Singh, complained to Tandon, the chief minister defended himself and his revenue minister in terms familiar.[119] Sinha termed the charges vague, excavated Patel's clean chit to himself and K. B. Sahay, cited some cases as being *sub judice*, explained Sahay's 'public purses' as 'the best method' for the party's touch with the masses and revealed that the 'son of Ram Narain Singh's brother-in-law' was involved in Sahay's fund collection, thereby discrediting him. Meanwhile, the state that had struggled to abolish *zamindari* had nonetheless created a machinery of *karamcharis* meant to take over their estates, when the judiciary allowed it, and INR 74 lakhs were already spent on it. On another charge that the state's aboriginal welfare budget was INR 12 lakhs, without much to show for it, Sinha replied that this budget was approved by the noted Gandhian A. V. Thakkar, and, out of this amount, INR 3 lakhs went to Adimjati Seva Mandal, of which President Prasad was the president. And then S. K. Sinha went on the offensive. Claiming that in his violent speeches, Ram Narain Singh had 'advocated that Sahay should be shot', he recommended Singh's prosecution.[120]

From Madras, this question of actionability under the new constitution was being given more dimensions as Chief Minister P. S. Kumaraswamy Raja denounced the state judiciary as 'hostile' towards the executive because the Madras High Court granted bail to the communist leader A. K. Gopalan. Justices Satyanarayana Rao and Raghava Rao were sympathetic to Gopalan and critical of the government, while for Raja the judiciary ought to be more a collaborator of the executive than a custodian of individual rights. In Gopalan's case, the judges found that 'the non-mention of the period of detention in the order' vitiated it, going against the Supreme Court's interpretation and the subsequently amended Preventive Detention Act of 22 February 1951. In a dramatic sequence, that very day being fixed for judgement in Gopalan's application, the judges refused to accept the new act as not yet authenticated and held his detention invalid. Raja was aghast, for could the judges not 'have adjourned the matter ... should they not ... as but another limb of the State, wait for the authenticated copy of the new act?'[121] Challenging the court, state officials re-arrested Gopalan a few minutes after his release, under a fresh order, this time with the period specified. He again applied to the High Court, and the same bench held the government for 'contempt of court', terming Gopalan's re-arrest 'a conspiracy' and riling up Raja with this 'judicial indecency'. These proceedings, which spanned the famous first amendment of the constitution, were 'unusual', especially the hasty re-arrest of Gopalan.[122]

From UP, on the other hand, it was the old social bone that was still stuck in the throat of the new state. It was reported that the Afghanistan team to the Asian Games had visited Aligarh Muslim University, where they were 'abused', which to many was proof that, four years after the Partition and despite a 'nationalist' vice-chancellor in Dr Zakir Hussain, 'the bulk of the students and professors … cherish the Muslim League ideals'.[123] UP was difficult, as ever, to govern, and in a bizarre incident, on 23 March 1951, a car carrying the Thai minister Luang Phinit-Akson and his family was smashed in Agra by three students at Rajput College, injuring the minister and his daughter, but the police would not register a case. When Nehru visited Agra two days later, the district magistrate claimed ignorance.[124] Neighbouring Central Provinces was a similar case. An old Marathi partyman from Nagpur gave a colourful account of Pandit Shukla's government's harsh treatment of its opposition, while promoting mouth-piece papers *Nagpur Times* and *Nawabharat*, and formulised the social hierarchy thus: 'Shuklas, Tiwaris and Dubeys are ruling over our province under the name of Congress'.[125]

From West Bengal, too, it was an old fault line that was tearing up the Congress party, as three of its legislators resigned after making complaints regarding census operations in Manbhum, where 'a dozen enumerators were compelled … to write down mother-tongue of the people as Hindi'.[126] This was a lingering symptom of a long territorial struggle since 1911, when some parts were tagged to the new state of Bihar.[127] Prominent Congressmen and liberals like Tej Bahadur Sapru, Parmeshwar Lal, Sachchidananda Sinha, Deep Narayan Sinha, Mohd. Faqruddin and Nand Kishore Lal had all argued for sub-regions like (*a*) Purnea or Malda to be divided, with the east of the Mahananda River to Bengal and the western portions to Bihar, (*b*) the Bengali tracts in Santhal Parganas to be given to Bengal and (*c*) in Chhota Nagpur, Manbhum and Dhalbhum for Bengal and the rest of Singhbhum for Bihar. By 1951, this territorial dispute was tangled with the language column of the ongoing census, thereby leading to calls for the former to be settled first before the latter could be recognised.[128] Similarly, in neighbouring Assam, the government had stopped rehabilitation loans to displaced persons who had migrated to the state before 31 December 1949 because of a tussle with New Delhi on the sharing of these,[129] even though, unlike Bihar or Madras, rice production there worked out at '23 ½ oz. per head', and President Prasad was puzzled as to 'why should there be so much scarcity and black-marketing?'[130]

On the other side of the country, in commercial Bombay, corruption was thriving as parliamentarian Mudgal, editor of the weekly *Indian Market*, agreed to canvass support for the Bullion Association on prohibition of option business, levy of stamp duties and others for a sum of INR 20,000.[131] That this was being done at a time of acute food shortage was merely incidental. In late March, New Delhi overruled the Kher ministry in deciding that the retail prices of food grains in the four large industrial cities of the province should be fixed by the finance ministry 'at Rs. 16/- per maund for wheat, Rs. 17/12 for rice and Rs. 11/3 for milo' with central subsidy, thereby relieving the resources of Bombay government.[132] Under the revised scheme introduced in January 1951, prices in Calcutta and Madras were not increased, whereas prices in Delhi and Bombay were raised, and Kher demanded '4 lakhs tons wheat, 1 lakh ton rice, 50,000 tons milo', with a heavy central subsidy.[133]

On the industrial side, a team from the Ministry of Works, Production and Supply visited the Sindri fertiliser factory on 7 March 1951, to find it at 'standstill'. This was not entirely surprising, for the estimates committee on Sindri had observed in March 1949 that 'government machinery is unsuitable to manage commercial enterprises' and a public corporation should be established. This recommendation was repeated in December 1950, and K. C. Neogy was offered its chairmanship. He declined, terming it 'bureaucratic management' camouflaged as 'a corporation', and it was suggested that a high official from business circles should be appointed in the prime minister's secretariat to run it. For now, the general manager of Sindri, B. C. Mookerjee, did not enjoy the power 'to appoint foremen', and there was no sign of immediate production, although Brigadier Cox, the engineer attached, claimed full production by November. To the visitors, this appeared impossible, and it was re-emphasised to a reluctant Nehru to have someone recruited from 'high commercial circle....'[134]

That this forging of a new India was stuck was only one-half of the administrative challenges, the other being that aspects of the old India refused to go away. An example comes from March 1951, when the annual list of persons considered 'undesirable' by the government for passports was prepared. It was the same list as from May 1946 and contained names which were 'objectionable to British authorities' then but were 'esteemed citizens of India' now.[135] It also contained names of students abroad, with prominent parents in India, names like Dr Shelvankar, who worked for the Ministry of External Affairs; Subhas Chandra Bose's follower A. C. N. Nambiar, India's counsellor at Berne; and Sarojini Naidu's brother Virendranath Chattopadhyay, who had died in 1937. Another instance came from the former princely states, whose reorganisation remained a stop-start affair:

> Vindhya Pradesh and Himachal Pradesh [HP] to have a legislature
> & ministers, Cutch [and] Saurashtra to be administered by a Chief-
> Commissioner and two more counsellors, Tripura, Manipur & Bhopal
> [same as Cutch] but Bhopal to be merged with Madhya Bharat [after] five

years, Bilaspur to be merged with HP, Delhi to be divided between Old and New with different corporations and a co-ordinating council, Ajmer & Coorg to be ultimately merged with the neighbouring territory....[136]

All this paled, however, in front of the happenings in Hyderabad, from where the selected parliamentarians protested Speaker Mavlankar's ruling that the then parliament was 'no place to ventilate the grievances of Hyderabad or like states'.[137] Padmaja Naidu and her five colleagues catalogued their woes, starting with their short-term nominations, for elections had been promised in Hyderabad in 1950. When these were postponed until the general election, their presence in the assembly-turned-parliament as public representatives was neutered by Mavalankar. This was Patel's favoured position, and after his death, the state Congress urged V. P. Menon to address this anomaly, but, by late March 1951, their 'anomalous position' was worsening, and they no longer felt 'justified to sit in parliament'.[138]

Denying speech to people's representatives was one thing, detaining and taking lives of people altogether another, as allegations continued that communists under arrest in Hyderabad were 'taken into jungle and shot'. Rather inadvertently, two cases – one in the Supreme Court and the other in the Hyderabad High Court – lifted the lid on this situation. In the former, the brother of a detenue had filed a habeas corpus petition, and the Hyderabad government replied that 'while attempting to escape, the detenue was shot dead in October 1949'. In the second case, the High Court was informed that the same thing had happened at the same time and another family had been 'kept in dark for more than 19 months....'[139] These cases pointed to more such undisclosed ones, as Ayyangar conceded,[140] before providing their details. The name of the person at the centre of the petition was Rangachari, who was shot dead on 29 October 1949 at Borgumpad, while being transported to Warangal from Hyderabad, along with two others, Raj Reddy and Srinivas Reddy, among whom Raj Reddy was also shot dead, while Srinivas Reddy was returned to Hyderabad jail. He was later convicted and sentenced to death but escaped. Nehru was now sceptical enough to wonder whether the man was shot 'at some late stage ... perhaps because of the habeas corpus petition....'[141]

April 1951, the month in which the first general election was originally planned for, began with the country's prime minister and the Congress party's president confabulating on the deteriorating situation, especially across East Punjab or PEPSU, Rajasthan or Bihar and Bombay. The common threads in these places were that their food supply was drying up while their government and the party deemed the other as 'ineffective'.[142] Within six months, both persons would go through a routine of resignation and return, but for now they were locked in an equal combat wherein one's anxiety was met by the other's alarmism, and both blamed the other for 'losing hold' on the public on three instances: 'food and other controls, rehabilitation of refugees and the Hindu Code Bill....'[143] While serious issues like not having enough jute, rubber or cotton to barter with the Soviet Union for wheat[144] coexisted with sensational matters like the parliament discussing the travelling allowances of ministers during 1950–51 (Nehru, INR 48,640; Patel, 17,757; and Azad, 1,363),[145] and symbolic ones like the 'possibility of UK capital being invested in India for a steel plant',[146] the spring of 1951 was all about East Punjab, as it moved down the road to become the first state to have president's rule. It started with the Congress Parliamentary Board (CPB) holding an emergency meeting to discuss the demand of 32 legislators there for a no-confidence motion in the Bhargava ministry.[147]

In early April, Trivedi produced a six-point memorandum for the home ministry, which elaborated upon the existence of groups in the Congress organisation around Bhargava, Sachar, Nagoke, Baldev Singh and Kairon. In his criticisms of Bhargava, Kairon had an ally in Lala Jagat Narain, the editor of *Hind Samachar*, with both charging the ministry of 'partiality and ... communalism'. With Hindu–Sikh relations nosediving over Hindi-Punjabi and the Scheduled Castes being caught in this crossfire, Giani Kartar Singh and Prithvi Singh Azad were out to defend their respective communities. All this was exacerbating the cost of living, incomplete rehabilitation and tenants' troubles and led to a no-confidence motion on 3 April 1951. The governor ended with weighing the two alternatives, either installing a composite ministry under Bhargava or invoking Article 356. The former was tried with Sachar, and therefore Trivedi thought that 'the public would welcome' the latter.[148] It was advantageous administratively as well, and this script would play out in June, but not without efforts at political compromise.

In the meantime, on 3 April 1951, in a speech in parliament, Padmaja Naidu finally let off some steam about the conditions in Hyderabad.[149] She was clear-eyed about the former feudal state and its poor peasantry, further hobbled by its famine zones, from which the Razakars drove almost 4 lakh people into neighbouring provinces in 1947–48. However, the administration since September 1948 did not much change their situation either, composed as it was of outsiders of 'low mental and moral stature....' For example, Gulbarga, one of the four districts that saw the most violence following the nizam's surrender, had a civil administrator who 'openly preached and practiced the most savage communalism', and when he was removed, 'he was received at Sholapur station by RSS men, who hailed him as a martyr in the noble cause of establishing Hindu rule'. In Hyderabad city itself, there were officials who continued with communal discrimination in services, which had left over a lakh unemployed, including 'about 30,000 because of jagirdari abolition [and]

25,000 because of state army's disbandment'. Consequently, the largest entry in Hyderabad's budget was law and order, which rose from '71.14 lakhs to 5.22 crores in last 5 years' as police numbers increased from 1,000 to 40,000, with one-third of these coming from outside, ostensibly to counter communism.

This atmosphere left little difference between communist methods and the Indian state, and Naidu spoke of 'entire villages subjected to sadism' because one villager was suspected of harbouring a communist. A 'power to kill communism' had been bestowed upon officials, while there was 'communal tension, unemployment, shortage of food, cloth, house'. For Naidu, what was needed was reform, industries and irrigation, as she pointed out that the finance ministry gave INR 32 crores to the Tungabhadra project in Mysore, while the Godavari valley project could do with INR 5.25 crores. Further, there was an 'unjust subvention' for Hyderabad to compensate for the revenue gap arising out of financial integration after three 'abnormal years', as well as a fear of famine with food procurement falling short by 50,000 tons.

Naidu's was not a solitary voice. Three days later, lawyer-politician Walter Monckton, former representative of the nizam, informed Nehru that he had been requested by persons interested in Telangana defendants to petition for pardon or commutation. Monckton refused the request but added that given these men were between 18 and 25 years of age and were sentenced to death back in August 1949,[150] leniency might be considered. Equally, Naidu drew criticism from closer home. Khub Chand, the acting envoy in Pakistan, complained that her 'condemnation' was reported there as 'corroboration'.[151] In contrast, Nehru hoped that, while exaggerated and injudicious, Naidu's 'powerful indictment' would 'shake up things'.[152] Gopalaswami Ayyangar followed-up when the 12 Telangana prisoners condemned to death appealed to the president for mercy. As the minister concerned, Ayyangar remarkably thought 'the killing of communists in police encounters … a more effective deterrent' and, notwithstanding the Supreme Court's decision that the sentences by the High Court of December 1949 were final, arranged the cases under two revealing heads:

(1) The denial of a right of appeal to the prisoners from the judgement of the HC to the judicial committee … [by] the new constitution [though] they presented a petition 5–6 days before 25 January 1950. Subsequently, their right to approach the SC was denied, because the offence was committed before the [new] constitution. These prisoners have been [thus] blocked from asserting the right, which they possessed before Hyderabad became part of India, or from invoking a similar right after Hyderabad became part. (2) The delay that has occurred … it is hardly comforting … that while the HC's judgement could not be appealed

against [under] the [new] constitution, the sentences confirmed by that judgement could be executed now.[153]

Khub Chand and other envoys of India did not have to answer for officials acting only in Hyderabad, though. From Bhopal, the case of Aizazuddin Khan (Bombay Educational Service Class I, 1929) was a representative affair. Khan's services were borrowed in August 1948 by the then government of Bhopal on a permanent basis as director of public instruction. In October 1949, after its accession, the post of education secretary was merged with that of home secretary by the chief commissioner, Bhopal, and Khan's post was retrenched on 15 November, and he retired with a proportionate pension. In May 1950, Azad asked B. G. Kher to take him back in his parent cadre, but Kher replied that Khan's transfer to Bhopal was permanent, and another officer had been appointed in Bombay. A month later, Vallabhbhai Patel assured Azad that if it was not possible to accommodate Khan in Bhopal, then he would be paid compensation. Soon, however, it became known that while in November 1949, Khan was made redundant, in June 1950, the chief commissioner had asked for the sanction of a new post of chief inspector of schools. And then Azad saw a letter of 25 March 1950 from the chief commissioner, N. Bonarji, to Bombay's education secretary, in which Bonarji made the reason plain: 'Aizazuddin would not have proved suitable in Bhopal.... The communal bias in this State must be changed so as not to operate against the majority'.[154]

Meanwhile, in East Punjab, delimitation of constituencies was producing several complaints from the Sikhs that where the Scheduled Castes were 'entitled to a full seat', they were not given any, and where they were 'entitled to three seats, they [were] given four'.[155] There was also gerrymandering going on, and the Sikhs threatened an agitation, forcing Nehru to caution Sukumar Sen. At the same time, an 'anti-cow-slaughter-movement' was gaining ground, being promoted not only by the usual suspects but by 'Congress quarters also' and a deputation met party president Tandon, who advised them to 'organise sufficient public opinion'.[156] No amount of Congress resolutions was effective on this undertow of the party, even as food problems persisted from Madras to Bihar and no food arrived from America or Soviet Russia. Now, the three-year period of 'truce' in labour relations was also coming to an end, and of special concern were the railway workers, who had been without any proportional increase in their dearness allowance for over two years. K. Santhanam, the minister of state for transport and railways, pleaded for finding ways and means, for it was not only JP's All-India Railwaymen's Federation but also the railway workers' federation affiliated to the Congress that was 'raising demands'.[157] But there was one kind of demand that could not be indulged. In April 1951,

Pratap Singh Rao Gaekwad (ruler of Baroda since 1939) was stripped of all his rights, privileges and privy purse, with V. P. Menon producing an eight-page dossier containing eightfold charges ranging from 'disreputable life' to disloyalty and treason.[158]

It was not so much the *what* of this incident but the *how* of it that caused concern among rulers, and Hamidullah, the nawab of Bhopal, drafted a note to President Prasad pointing out that with no enquiry held, this action was taken without giving Pratap Singh a chance to defend himself. Hamidullah argued that if the princes were 'citizens' then the Supreme Court's jurisdiction should be extended to them. Menon's sweeping chargesheet also indicated that ex-rulers had no 'right to participate in politics' and Hamidullah sought clarification on this.[159] In the event, after meeting Nehru, he decided not to send this letter, and instead, Gaekwad wrote to Prasad explaining himself on the 'vague' government's charges.[160] Afterwards, Maharani Shantadevi did the rounds in New Delhi 'seeking forgiveness', agreeing to a committee of management under V. T. Krishnamachari to not leave India and to resign at any time the government desired.[161]

In mid-April 1951, Tandon and Nehru made another intervention in the worsening Punjab crisis, with the aim of reconstructing Bhargava's ministry and strengthening its Congress numbers, at the expense of the Akali group. Trivedi met Bhargava, who told him that he could add Kairon and Chaudhuri Krishna Gopal Dutt to the cabinet, but he did not want 'to displease' Giani Kartar and Ishar Singh. As regards Prithvi Singh Azad, Bhargava wanted to 'retain him' and Trivedi felt that the only reason for this was that there was 'no other equally suitable Scheduled Caste legislator'.[162] The caste question was then undergoing a metamorphosis in Madras, where chief minister P. S. Kumaraswamy Raja was urging affirmative action in services. This required a constitutional amendment, which needed parliamentary agreement, and Raja was advised to 'frame an order within the terms of articles 15 [and] 16 (4)....'[163] Raja was not the only one bringing this issue up. On 15 April 1951, a day after he turned sixty, Dr Ambedkar delivered a speech in which, referring to the East Punjab/PEPSU census, he declared that the present government had done 'very little or nothing for the Scheduled Castes' compared to their British predecessors.[164] The person who took on Ambedkar was the home minister when H. V. Kamath brought up Ambedkar's speech in the parliament and Rajagopalachari stood up and, without consulting Ambedkar, who was present in the house, dismissed it as 'baseless allegations'. A hurt Ambedkar accepted his 'breach of joint responsibility' but also articulated his feelings in highly personal terms: 'You may be a *superior being* in your own and in the eyes of some. In mine, you are no more than a colleague ... you owe me an apology'.[165]

Ambedkar got a quick response but no apology, as Rajagopalachari replied that his comment was 'only to defend' the government. Nor was there any apology from V. K. Krishna Menon, whose jeep purchase scandal was gathering speed with H. N. Kunzru and B. Shiva Rao among parliamentary critics, Karanjia's *Blitz* printing 'leaks' from Bombay and Ananthasayanam Ayyangar heading a committee of enquiry.[166] The only person who seemed to be apologising all around was Jawaharlal Nehru. To M. A. Rauf, his envoy in Burma, who had sought Indian nationality for their common friend from Allahabad in the 1920s, Mohamed Hussain, Nehru regretted his inability to oblige. He was prepared to let Hussain stay in Allahabad for as long as he liked, but as a Pakistani citizen, for 'he had accepted Pakistan nationality'.[167] Burma was important because, along with then Siam and Vietnam, it comprised the nearby trinity to which New Delhi turned for rice, given 'unacceptable' American conditions.[168]

With the general election now a matter of months away, Sampurnanand and Rafi Ahmed Kidwai came to discuss the deteriorating food and law-and-order situation, though they knew that narrow communal and caste considerations will dominate it. They brought up a recent UP district election in which a 'non-Thakur' group won, and their five members were elected, only to be killed by the 'Thakur group'. The AICC was meeting in early May 1951, and, on its side-lines, feeling 'somewhat haunted' by the Tandon-led CWC,[169] Nehru wanted to meet separately with Dr B. C. Roy, Pandit G. B. Pant, B. G. Kher, Nabakrushna Chaudhuri and Anugraha Narayan Singh. By now, Kidwai was with Kripalani, and they were still insisting on an enquiry into Tandon's election, citing the case of Andhra, where Kripalani's majority was 'converted into a minority by restraining, through a court injunction, 23 delegates'.[170] The reconstructed Somnath temple's inauguration, though, was an issue that had no difficulty getting the majority support within the state. When one minority voice, K. M. Panikkar (the Indian ambassador in China), complained to another, Jawaharlal Nehru, that Indian embassies were being 'asked to collect the waters of distant rivers and twigs from various mountains' by the Somnath trust for the ceremony, the latter instructed him to ignore these appeals. Beyond that, all he could do was 'to tone down the effects of [Prasad's] visit....'[171] Panikkar was aghast and had articulated his anxieties, as under:

> The idea seems to be to wipe out symbolically the invasions of Mahmud and to gather up the broken threads of history from that time, as if the last 1,000 years were a kind of hiatus in the evolution of India.... Where is one to stop? Is the Kutub Minar to be pulled down and the stones, which came from temples used for restoring the shrines? Is Aurangzeb's tomb in Banares to be pulled down and Kashi Vishwanath restored to

original glory? This is the state of mind that leads straight to RSS and the desire to revive the *Hindupada padisahi* in India.... There could be nothing more disastrous ... than for us to consider that the period of history following the Muslim invasions is something which we should endeavour to forget ... the living humanism of India comes from [then], from Mira, Ramanand and Tulsidas, from Kabir, Nanak ... these are the real founders of the India of today [that] our '*somnathists*' desire to forget.[172]

In response, K. M. Munshi made it plain that Somnath, according to 'our' religious literature, was 'the principal' among the *jyotirlings*; its consecration required 'the soil of different countries, the water of rivers and oceans and twigs from certain mountains', the *jamsaheb* had written to several embassies and 'most of the material [had] arrived'.[173] The Saurashtra government had spent INR 5 lakhs on the ceremony at a time when expenditure on education and health was stopped.[174] On the other hand, was the matter that could be said to be the sole preserve of New Delhi, namely the Nehru–Liaquat Pact, and an annual review claimed its overall effect thus: 'April 1950–February 1951: 27.7 lakh Hindus came to India from East Bengal, while 21.7 lakh left India; 11.5 lakh Muslims came to India from East Bengal, while 10.7 lakh left India'.[175] It is instructive to pit a personal tale against the state's statistical claims: one Mrs Khawaja wanted an insurance company to advance her money against her property only to be told that the company had been advised that every Muslim is a 'presumptive evacuee', and they were not prepared to oblige unless either Mrs Khawaja or the property to be mortgaged are 'exempted'. When she applied for an exemption, it was refused without any reason, and when this case reached the prime minister, he simply sighed that 'life is not worth living in this country for any Muslim....'[176] He could have added, especially in former princely pockets like Bhopal and Hyderabad, and even if hitherto engaged in state services, as the discharged soldiers of Bhopal and Hyderabad were rendered unemployed without any release benefit, with the defence ministry 'still waiting' to decide.[177]

Both states had their relief funds confiscated but not spent on their demobilised soldiers when compared to the post-1945 demobilisation of the Indian army.[178] Soldiers in Bhopal 'without a single pie [were] in sheer desperation migrating to Pakistan', with V. P. Menon 'unable [or unwilling] to discuss this matter'.[179] Hamidullah's woes were only beginning as a circular had been issued that 'Muslims employed in the services should be got rid of progressively ...' to be replaced by 'Sindhis and UP men', and Viswanathan, the chief commissioner, was well-known for his association with the RSS and Hindu Mahasabha.[180] It got worse when it appeared that 500/770 demobilised soldiers had opted 'not to serve' in India and thus were not entitled to compensation. But they had exercised this option at an uncertain time, and the fact that they 'did not go to Pakistan [meant] that they did not seriously think of [it]' then.[181] It was not that only Muslim princely states were shoddily treated. In PEPSU, matters were being handled by Congress general secretary M. L. Gautam, as the proposed chief minister, Colonel Raghbir Singh, had a partisan reputation and was being considered, perhaps precisely because of that. Nehru remembered that 'the Akalis had taken part in the old agitation against the Maharaja …', but with Raghbir Singh in charge, he doubted their future cooperation.[182]

Further, in mid-April 1951, despite the prime minister's reservations, the East Punjab government decided to appoint M. S. Randhawa as commissioner, Jalandhar. This followed in the wake of the appointment of Sardar Divendra Singh as collector, Gurdaspur, from where the Praja Parishad of Jammu was reportedly functioning. Divendra Singh had been assistant district magistrate, Amritsar, in 1947, and Nehru remembered his culpability there, but on Randhawa's appointment, Trivedi had accepted Bhargava's advice, for 'Sardar Patel gave him a good chit [in] Delhi, disagreeing with the Chief-Commissioner [Sahibzada Khurshid] that Randhawa was incapable of bringing to bear unbiased judgement on communal matters'.[183] For one more time, Patel had thwarted Nehru, and the latter continued doing what he did best, namely protecting individuals from the state. Another illustration comes from the case of Feroze-ud-Din of Calcutta and his request for a passport for Japan. His application was rejected by the West Bengal government, which sent a copy of an adverse intelligence report to New Delhi. When Nehru went through the case, he found that the whole thing rested on this 'highly unsatisfactory' note, which stated that it was an 'offence on his part, to attend a Khilafat Committee meeting to condole the death of Mahatma Gandhi'.[184]

Other 'undesirable' activities mentioned were his presiding over 'a meeting for the advancement of Urdu' and attending 'a meeting of the Jamiat', and ironically, these undercut the one serious charge made in the note that he held 'pro-Pakistan views and was selected to do espionage work', albeit without any proof. Feroze-ud-Din was a cousin of Khan Bahadur Mohammad Jan, 'a prominent nationalist Muslim', but recently, the Delhi custodian had been looking into certain money transfers made by Feroze-ud-Din to Pakistan and terming him as 'an intending evacuee' although no evacuee laws applied to Bengal. All in all, there was little cause for a refusal of passports for trade purposes in Japan, but evacuee laws remained troublesome for the rehabilitation ministry, from which Ajit Jain resigned in April 1951. These resisted correction in the name of service protection, but rejecting Jain's letter, Nehru stressed that it was 'not an officer who decides [but] the minister'.[185]

But the police and intelligence continued to produce their reports too. After the aforementioned tour of B. N. Mullik to Tripura, he was now visiting the districts of Krishna, Guntur and Kurnool in Andhra and produced an eight-page report on the communist movement there that focused on the activities of their leaders – C. Rajeshwar Rao (Krishna), M. Basavapunnaiah (Guntoor), D. Venkateswar Rao (Telangana) and P. Sundarayya (Nellore) – all of whom were reportedly 'urging the Chinese way'.[186] Mullik argued for an 'offensive spirit' on the Bastar–Hyderabad–Madras frontier to prevent 'the development of the Nallamalla range as a liberation base'.[187]

Around this time, the IT investigation commission finally submitted its report on the Dalmia-Jain group of cases, in which it arrived at the astonishing conclusion that their 'concealed income' over a period of eight years (1939–47) was only INR 4.58 lakhs, when up to 1939, their 'concealment was estimated at Rs. 128 lakhs'.[188] Meanwhile, the famine-prone country continued crookedly, with the central government limited in its ability to procure directly, while state governments either would not or could not. What they could and did was try to maintain law and order, with the latest incident coming from Cooch Behar, where hunger-marchers were fired. With people angry at rice selling at INR 60 per maund, the officials forced the issue, while Nehru wanted an enquiry announced and food made available. Dr B. C. Roy did not need an enquiry to convey the salient facts of Cooch Behar, whose population of roughly 6.5 lakhs was staring at a deficit of 10,000 tons. Around 20,000 urban dwellers were getting 'modified rationing', and this disparity made people angry. Hunger marches and strikes were organised, and the opposition parties – Forward Bloc, Hindu Mahasabha and the socialists – got involved in the situation, which boiled over on 21 April, when lathi charge was resorted to on a crowd of 1,500 who retaliated with brickbats and acid bulbs and suffered firing, which killed 5, including 2 women and 1 child, and wounded 33, and left many among the police injured.[189]

With Gandhian methods under attack, his followers were meeting in Hyderabad in a Sarvodaya Sammelan held over 9–11 April 1951, attended by a quarter of its 4,000 members and addressed by notables like Vinoba Bhave, Shankarrao Dev, J. C. Kumarappa, Dharam Adhikari, Gopa Bandhu Chawdhry, Kaka Kalelkar, S. R. Shastri, Hari Upadhaya, Sarla Sarabhai, Anna Sahasrabhuday and R. K. Patil. The major issues discussed were food, cloth, corruption in controls and 'Harijan problems'. The Hyderabad state and Congress proved more hospitable than both Gujarat and Andhra groups, who had declined to be hosts, given Patel's 'unfavourable opinion' about *Sarvodaya*. The state government gave INR 10,000, while the party provided 400 volunteers. While it passed no resolutions,[190] Bhave stressed making villages self-sufficient, Patil emphasised tightening controls and

Bhave viewed with equanimity participation in electoral campaigning by Sarvodaya workers.

The delegates from Bombay, Gujarat and Maharashtra were critical of Bhave becoming a gatekeeper,[191] and to his aim of a Lok Seva Sangh, they posited their ambition of entering the Lok Sabha. Bhave also had personal differences with Kalelkar and Kumarappa,[192] although he was much more popular. On the other hand, among the conspicuous absentees were J. B. Kripalani, P. C. Ghosh and Rajendra Prasad, who was touring nearby but did not deign to drop in. Nehru sent a message, which Bhave read out, followed by his own views of the Nehru government: critical of its education, food and economic policies and supportive of its foreign and internal defence endeavours. Bhave was condemnatory of the Congress ministers though, his advice being to vote for the better candidate. The heir – of another kind – to the Mahatma, Vinoba Bhave had come to Hyderabad on foot, after a tour of 360 miles covering 85 villages from Wardha, and he was going next to the Telangana areas. He should have continued to Madras, from where a governmental challenge was arising to a Gandhian solution to caste.

P. S. Kumaraswamy Raja was seeking an amendment to the constitution to continue with Madras state's old 'communal ratio', which was an anathema to the Brahmins, who formed 'about 3% of the population' but enjoyed a 'monopoly [of] government service'.[193] Before 1950, claims of other communities were met by this formula in 'initial recruitment', but the new constitution frowned upon such concessions. As things stood, 60 per cent of seats in medical and engineering colleges were headed the 3 per cent way. Such being the position, the special provision in Article 16 (4) providing for reservation of appointments in government service became 'meaningless'. Under the much-maligned Madras formula, out of every 14 appointments, two were for the Scheduled Castes and two for the backward classes. Now, under Articles 14–15, these were deemed discriminatory, and Raja wanted 'to reserve 4 seats for Harijans and backward classes', while resisting lumping 'several communities under one "backward class" in the language of article 16 (4)'. He recommended his amendments as 'necessary' for 'can the Brahmin community hope to face perpetually the heartburning of the ... majority?'[194]

Meanwhile, the Brahmins in the central and provincial governments were preparing to face, what to them was, the hostility of America on food imports. When Nehru wrote to his seniormost chief ministers, Shukla and Pant, to lower expectations of American food grains, given its accompanying 'conditions', the latter expressed his 'disgust', while seeking a re-clamp of control on items like gram, for 'rationing in eastern UP and hill districts'.[195] This conditions–controls contradiction was easier to articulate than its cultural counterpart, which finally landed on the prime minister's desk when the *jamsaheb* of Nawanagar invited him on 22 April 1951 for the Somnath ceremonies.[196]

It was one thing to courteously decline a maharaja, quite another to curtly declaim to K. M. Munshi, the cabinet colleague who had spearheaded this reopening. When in a cabinet meeting on 23 April, Nehru sought to distance his government from the event,[197] Munshi gave chapter and verse of the 'association of the administration of Junagadh, the Saurashtra government and the Government of India with the reconstruction of the Somnath Temple'.[198] On 13 November 1947, Vallabhbhai Patel and N. V. Gadgil accompanied the *jamsaheb* to Prabhas, within days of India's takeover of Junagadh. There it was publicly announced by Patel that 'the Government of India had decided to rebuild the temple and instal the shrine'. The *jamsaheb* and the Junagadh administration followed with donations, while the latter also gave 5,000 acres of land. While Patel's States Ministry thereafter took steps to implement this decision, on 13 December 1947, it was the Standing Committee of Works, Mines and Power Ministry of Gadgil that deputed architects. Subsequently, Gandhi instructed Patel to raise funds publicly, and the idea of government finance was dropped.

On 25 December 1947, the Ministry of States requested the Junagadh authorities 'to lease out' an area surrounding the temple to enable a 'seaside resort, raising of the monument at Dehotsarga … a university and a model agricultural/cattle farm'. On 23 January 1949, a conference was held at Jamnagar by Patel, with the *jamsaheb*, Gadgil, U. N. Dhebar (premier, Saurashtra), Samaldas Gandhi, administrator Junagadh and the regional commissioner in attendance. A Somnath trust was finalised there, with New Delhi and Saurashtra both having two representatives each. Munshi himself had prepared the trust's deed. After Junagadh's merger with Saurashtra, an advisory committee was set up by the states and works, mines and power ministries, which included Dr J. C. Ghosh, a town planning expert and the director-general of the archaeological survey of India. On 18 October 1949, Patel approved the trust and its committees and appointed Gadgil and Rege (regional commissioner-Saurashtra) to it, alongside B. M. Birla and Munshi. The Saurashtra government nominated the *jamsaheb* and Samaldas Gandhi as its representatives. On 22 November 1949, the Ministry of States sought the Saurashtra government's execution of the trust, which came through before the new constitution came into force on 26 January 1950.

The temple's reconstruction had embarked at an initial cost of INR 3 lakhs, and Patel 'was to have performed the ceremony', and so Munshi felt that they should redeem his pledge. The Saurashtra government was spending money on pilgrim infrastructure, and Munshi was going to wear it as a badge of honour that 'the Government of India … formulated the scheme, and created the agency for its implementation' and, even more so, his own involvement.[199] His historical novels, especially *Jaya Somnath*, held a vivid hold on his imagination, and he assured Nehru that 'the "collective sub-conscious" of India is happier with the reconstruction of Somnath ... than with many other things that we are doing....' Finally, returning to the *jamsaheb*'s letter for 'ceremonial requirements', requesting Indian diplomats for natural tokens, Munshi told Nehru that his ministry was informed that if an envoy found it 'difficult or unwise' to oblige, 'he said so' and that even Panikkar 'wrote that he would send some of these things'. If all this was not enough, then there was one final word from Munshi: 'I cannot value freedom if it uproots our millions from the faith, with which they look upon our temples'.[200] Given such strong sentiments, the prime minister instructed R. R. Diwakar to 'tone down' our radio broadcast of what happens at Somnath.[201]

This however was not the only history lesson that Nehru was getting that month. The controversy around Dr Ambedkar's claim that the post-1947 government had done less than the British for the Depressed Classes was refusing to go away, fanned as its fires were by the *Indian News Chronicle* in New Delhi. Ambedkar was forced to explain himself and began by recalling the Scheduled Castes Welfare Association in the capital, for which, back in 1942–43, he had got some land on the mutiny memorial road. However, it was only over 1949–50 that the association was able to collect enough to hold a foundation stone-laying ceremony, which they wanted Ambedkar to perform. It was there that he had made his speech, in which he had also said that 'before 1942, the British Government did [only for] Muslims, Indian Christians and Anglo-Indians and aboriginal classes'. It was his memorandum as the labour member that saw the then-viceroy Linlithgow sanction 'Rs. 3 lakhs annually for the education of Scheduled Caste students in foreign countries ...' and reserve '8 1/3 % (subsequently 12 1/3%) in the central services', but after 1947, this was discontinued, and its successor scheme had remained 'in abeyance'.[202] Ambedkar reminded Nehru that the Scheduled Castes were oppressed 'in villages [across] the Punjab, UP and Andhra', with newspapers 'never' publicising this, and recalled how when '40 Scheduled Caste men started a fast unto death at Rajghat last year ... no newspaper took notice'. Arguing that sympathetic Hindus 'will not shoulder the responsibility', he lamented that in refugee rehabilitation no place was given to the Scheduled Castes because 'they were not agriculturalist'; instead, if they held any land, it was taken away from them 'to be given to Sikh and other Hindu refugees'.[203]

Away from this benighted immediate past, the immediate future too was somewhat blighted. With American food imports in limbo, New Delhi had been in talks with the Soviet Union for a barter arrangement. The Soviets wanted raw jute, while India was offering shellac, given the trade deadlock with Pakistan. Subsequently, the Soviets indicated that they could give '100 thousand tons of wheat [for] shellac, jute, tea and tobacco' and agreed to provide part of the shipping, quoting the same price at which they had sold wheat to Egypt (USD 98), when 'New York prices were $101.5'.[204] If food was pricey, then so was medicine, with Health Minister Amrit Kaur and Nehru trying to set up a penicillin-producing factory, procuring finance from the WHO or a British agency.[205] Unsurprisingly, alternative voices like Sri Prakasa, in an address to *vaidyas*, favoured Ayurveda. Kaur critiqued that Ayurvedic or Unani systems had remained 'static' and called their practitioners 'mostly quacks'. She was peeved that, first, because of Tandon's statements, people were not getting their children vaccinated against cholera, and now Sri Prakasa was talking like this. Kaur listed the services and the countries, including Pakistan, where modern medicine was on its way, though she added that 'research in ancient systems' was welcome as 'pre-clinical sciences'.[206] This mention of Pakistan was not gratuitous, given that such comparisons were then drawn across the board. When parliamentarian Balkrishna Sharma asked for all government servants from Sindh to be 'absorbed', Nehru replied that the standards there were 'generally low'.[207]

On the other hand, in India, Muslims with competence had their integrity questioned, no matter how high or low and not only from non-Muslims. M. N. Masood, Azad's private secretary, was being reported for carrying on 'Pakistani propaganda', not only from intelligence sources but also from persons like T. M. Zarif (chairman, All-India Muslim Convention). Nehru asked Azad to make Masood face Zarif, who had also similarly charged Maulana Hifzur Rehman. For Zarif, the test for nationalist Muslims was if anything they wrote, spoke, or did caused 'communal trouble' and/or was quoted in Pakistan approvingly.[208] This was not the only formula current. The Congress' formula for resolving the East Punjab crisis, 'proportionate representation', threatened to wreck Bhargava's cabinet.[209] It was clear that the existing set-up could not carry on and either New Delhi nominated a ministry from the top or devised a method to have it named from the bottom. A mechanism was sought by which Bhargava could continue, as the party members were to 'elect a panel of 10 out of which the Parliamentary Board will select 6'.[210] If Bhargava did not agree, then he was to be replaced, even if it was a gamble on getting 'intriguing men [with] more tactics than talent'.[211]

1951 Is 'Not 1947 ...'

Food continues [as] our primary occupation – popular ministry(s) in Rajasthan [and] PEPSU – representation of the peoples bill, delimitation of constituencies [and] amendment to remove the judicial interpretation of Fundamental Rights ... social measures relating to land held up ... [as will be] our general elections....[212]

Thus wrote the prime minister to the chief ministers at the start of what turned out to be the penultimate session of the assembly parliament in May 1951, and this section follows closely the duality of popular politics and state response. His government was besieged by problems, while personally he was on the verge of losing Rafi Ahmed Kidwai, whose 'reputation of being a successful intriguer' with Tandon was overtaking his resources of goodwill with Nehru.[213] This was a threefold crisis, for Kidwai's 'influence' on Nehru was being resented by not just Tandon but also Rajagopalachari and Gopalaswami Ayyangar. On his part, Nehru hoped that Kidwai and Kripalani will not 'precipitate action',[214] as this was a time when there was no shortage of other action, not least on the frontier with Pakistan. As relations with the neighbour deteriorated again, the defence ministry wished to wait before demobilising.[215] From the other frontier, the Naga question worsened as Nehru was clear that if they chose plebiscite, then coercion would follow.[216] Already reports of atrocities in neighbouring Manipur were coming from the visiting civil servant E. P. Moon:

> Under-trials of all ages and sexes ... in crowded verandahs with so-called communists and lunatics ... cases pending over a year ... penned in tiny cells [under] the Kumaon regiment.... How can you have a satisfactory administration when neither SP, DC, let alone CC, can talk to the people?[217]

At a notch below all this, Baldev Singh was involved in the political prospects of Giani Kartar Singh, who was on his way out of the re-jigged ministry, to be replaced by a member of his group, Narotam Singh, who was not as 'intensely communal'.[218] With the Sachar–Kairon group closing ranks, this left the Nagoke group's incumbent, Ishar Singh Majhail plagued by corruption charges, but this was hardly unique. The IT investigation commission report on Surajmull Choteylal of Calcutta's hessian trade and the vice-chair of McLeod & Co. (tea and jute) found him aided by J. R. Walker, ex-jute controller, and Mandhata Singh, ex-*dewan* of Bikaner. His concealed income was INR 45.60 lakhs, attracting a penalty of INR 42 lakhs.[219] Meanwhile, in the Congress too, political prospects inside the working committee and the central cabinet were up for grabs, with Kripalani telling Mahtab that the cabinet should not include those 'like Ambedkar and Syama Prasad ... [who] had opposed our struggle for independence'.[220] Mahtab's solution lay in the following procedure:

There is the [Tandon-led] selection board to select candidates.... There should be another set of candidates selected by a committee to be nominated by [Nehru] ... many of the candidates will be common.... If [Nehru's] selections are accepted then the Congress organisation also will be reformed.... Naturally [Nehru] will be expected to organise the elections, which means finance and campaigning....[221]

Mahtab discussed this plan with Kidwai and Rajagopalachari, but what if the Tandon side did not accept Nehru's selections? The prime minister would have 'to stand aside' then. All this seems fantastic, but it was a possibility fed by the divide that separated Nehru from his peers, nowhere more starkly than in his own province. In an episode that speaks volumes about the then UP government, Dr Tara Chand, historian and advisor in the union education ministry,[222] complained regarding certain textbooks in the state, whose Education Minister Dr Sampurnanand was first dismissive of it and then defensive about it. Arguing that Azad would agree with him that Indian secularism was not anti-religious, Sampurnanand explained it as a transcendental 'tradition'. His parallel was with Iran, where people were Muslims 'today' but were 'proud' of the old Iranian kings and heroes, and the Indian Muslim must be taught to regard the heroes of ancient India likewise. To Tara Chand's point that in this pantheon, Rana Pratap and Shivaji were controversial inclusions, Sampurnanand claimed the impossibility of finding patriots among 'Indian non-Hindus'.[223]

The minister turned next to legends like Dadhichi and Harishchandra and bizarrely asked for 'Indian Muslims, who could be classed' similarly. Interestingly, the three non-Hindus on his list were the Parsi politician Dadabhai Naoroji (1825–1917), Mughal emperor Akbar (1542–1605) and the Adil Shahs of Bijapur (15th–17th centuries).[224] Sampurnanand reported that he had instructed to include 'separate' chapters dealing with Muslim leaders as desired by Dr Tara Chand, while to Chand's claim that Rajendra Prasad should be considered 'a Hindu' leader, he responded that then 'Azad will have to be treated as a purely Muslim leader'. Sampurnanand then asked what was embarrassing about the following lines in a poem on Azad that had been included: 'who showed a new path to the Muslim public, who taught it to rise above the walls of religion and brought to every house the great message of Bapu that the country is higher than religion and humanity is higher than the country'.[225]

He was willing to delete them and was agreeable to inserting Eid alongside Holi or Diwali. The fact that it was not there in the first place is revealing, while contending that there was no reference to incarnation in a poem in Basic Reader Part V, whose problematic line reads as follows: 'where all were men of pure character and incarnations of virtues. ...' The poem was 'in praise of the

Motherland', and Sampurnanand challenged 'anyone [with] any knowledge of Hindi to interpret ... in any other way'. Then he turned to the next objection, that 'the cover of *Naya Khilauna* carries the picture of a girl with the image of *Ganesh Ji* in her hand'. To Sampurnanand's eyes, it was a boy, a girl and a toy elephant, for gods were 'not carried' irreverently. Saving the most serious stuff for last, he came to the book *Vishwa Itihas*, in which he conceded that 'the passage dealing with Prophet Mohammad should not have found place' but claimed that in UP, books for the higher secondary classes were 'prescribed by the Intermediate Board'. He had 'ordered its removal' much like he had ordered the removal of *Hans Mayur*, 'a book to which ... the Jain community took exception'.[226]

Teaching others was on many people's minds in those first years. Speaker Mavalankar waxed eloquent on training parliamentarians, given innate 'distrust of men in power', and asked for empowering the ministry for parliamentary affairs in preparing a legislation programme in advance. He wished for more whips (the House of Commons had eleven), wanted stricter time allocation and a steering and rules committee. Mavalankar concluded with the tricky suggestion of 'formation of groups ... with different ideological approach' to facilitate debate and the clear expectation that before the first general election, 'the house will have to sit for longer periods'.[227] Equally, Mavalankar urged to go slow on 'revolutionary' bills like *zamindari* abolition, where he was not willing 'to rely on the parliament', but the Congress could not risk 'a wall of judicial interpretation' either.[228]

Far away from these parliamentary nitty-gritties, A. Z. Phizo and the Naga nationals were seeking their plebiscite. Phizo informed the former governor of Assam, Sri Prakasa, that since the death of Gandhi, they had 'a feeling of distrust', and they were 'going to take a voluntary [vote] on May 16'.[229] With even processions prohibited, officials of the Naga Hills district, under the Assam government, were taking a hard line, and on such matters, Nehru mixed sympathy with suppression, admitting the difficulty 'to combine [these] approaches'.[230] The Assam government did not spare much consideration and resisted missionaries as well as a minister of social services for hill tribes.[231] New Delhi did sanction a special grant of INR 10 lakhs for Naga Hills, for the disbursal of which it was felt desirable to bring in Phizo. What was more difficult was the situation of the Marwari merchants allegedly 'ousted from Kohima [to] Dimapur' and claims on the latter, as the Nagas were demanding 'a portion of ... Nowgong'.[232] In early May 1951, Phizo delivered a speech at Kohima, while governor Doulatram was on a tour confirming the government's diminishing design on Dimapur.[233]

Other provinces too were mired in such territorial matters. From Bombay, B. G. Kher brushed aside any concerns on Dang district, hilly and

forested 660 square miles,[234] which had been administered by the collector
of Marathi-speaking Khandesh (1830–1901), before being switched over
to the collector of Gujarati-speaking Surat (1901–33), from when it was
administered by the political agent under the Baroda princely state until
1947. Since independence, it has been under Surat. In October 1949,
the then collector of this district of 18,000 voters (out of a chiefly tribal
population of 47,000) suggested Dang's inclusion with Surat on account of
its recent administrative past, though Marathi was recognised as the official
language there in May 1949. A year later, a delimitation committee decided
that Dang should be joined with Marathi-speaking Nasik, and Kher refused
to reconsider the matter, busy as he was in 'suppressing' a food riot, in the
Abu Road area, of Gandhians like Gokulbhai Bhat, against whom police
cases were slapped.[235]

From the Central Provinces, Pandit R. S. Shukla was upset that Union
Minister Mahtab had visited without informing him and fixed his programme
without involving him. But Shukla did not stop with a complaint and went
on to arrest 1,653 persons, nearly all of whom were tried and convicted on
the same day for a strike by handloom weavers, whose agitation, he claimed,
Mahtab's visit had rejuvenated. Mahtab had indeed addressed the strikers, and
Nehru could not help but ask Shukla 'if such large-scale arrests and summary
convictions had happened only five years ago, what would they have done?'
Regardless, the Shukla government followed up with collecting apologies,
realising fines and dispersing protest processions,[236] though Shukla knew that
well-known Congressmen like Dr Punjabrao Deshmukh were supportive
and had asked Mahtab to talk to the strikers. One Congress legislator among
those arrested was still in prison, and Shukla's strongarm action set a template
in terms of showing little regard for 'legitimate' grievances and excessive
regard for their exploitation by 'opponents'. Meanwhile, Shukla's governor,
Congressman Mangaldas Pakvasa, wanted all food portfolios to be empowered
with the Preventive Detention Act, special courts and punishments like
whipping, for 'election time magnifies discontent'.[237] A month later, in a small
postscript to this episode, Nehru met R. B. Kumbhare, president of the state's
weavers' congress, and was informed that those weavers who had struck were
being penalised by the vindictive government in being 'given far less yarn than
others'.[238]

Amidst such satraps as well as the party's 'parlour politics', reports continued
to come of 'riots planned before elections given Congress' corruption'.[239] In
mid-May 1951, a note prepared on 'Congress Unity' described the prevailing
situation as Nehru being 'inclined towards Kripalani', Tandon 'doing his best
to persuade N. G. Ranga' and JP meeting Kidwai for 'a common front'.[240]
Between the plotting by Kidwai on one side and Tandon on the other

remained the question 'of finding the proper formula'.[241] Around this time, when JP's Socialist Party sought to present a petition to President Prasad, Nehru and Rajagopalachari saw this too as an 'election campaign',[242] but as processions were disallowed in Delhi then, this was also a law-and-order issue. Iengar set out the legal position that in February 1951, the ban from public meetings in Delhi was lifted only to be re-imposed in March, but in May, the chief commissioner had let it lapse, for there had not been much trouble. Iengar disagreed and preferred the Punjab Public Safety Act, under which processions (of more than five persons) could be banned. Iengar had in mind not just the socialists but also the *kisan* procession on 3 June by Hind Kisan Panchayat and Hind Mazdoor Sabha, and he wondered about the 'practical limits' in physically stopping it, namely 'lathi-charge, tear-smoke or further', with his view being that 'demonstrations ... have no place in the capital, ...'.[243] But this was not 1942, and Iengar, then home secretary, Bombay, was no more rounding up Gandhi and others during the Quit India movement.[244] Now, the latter were his political bosses, and their position was that there should not be a ban on public meetings or processions 'unless peculiar circumstances arise', and that at best 'a limited area' in the vicinity of the Raisina hill should be kept 'out of range'.[245]

After all, these processions were expected to be led by JP, the hero of 1942, and Nehru did not mind the protestors marching right up to the Rashtrapati Bhavan, albeit under police watch and arresting afterwards some important persons in case of a breach of peace. Rajagopalachari concurred, and they advised Prasad to see JP, who had assured that they would not lower the president's dignity. However, they were not so sanguine about Master Tara Singh-led Sikh contingent's participation in JP's procession.[246] For time hung 'heavy' in that summer of 1951 in terms of a constitution already on the precipice of amendments, crucial meetings of a party on the verge of a split, continued wait for the American food grains as well as the Soviet despatch, the prevailing malnutrition in Bihar and Madras despite campaigns and – above all – a rising air of apprehension about parliamentary powers in press, judiciary, party and public, which was about the two matters of press laws and land reforms.[247]

In East Punjab, while the peculiar ministry formation was still meandering amidst the hitherto dominant Bhargava group, the rising claims of the Sachar–Kairon group and the proportional precedents from 1949,[248] an altogether different kind of exercise was being undertaken on the streets of Bombay city. Dr Gardner Murphy, an American studying social psychology, was visiting India for his research on 'social tensions'. One small set of its data collection was done under the direction of C. N. Vakil of Bombay University. In this, among the Hindus, 21 out of 71 respondents were indifferent towards all parties, while of the remaining, 'about 50% preferred Congress, 25% Socialist Party, 12.5% Hindu Mahasabha and 1% Communist Party'. Only 10 out of 71 respondents were indifferent to leaders, and 60 per cent of the rest chose Nehru, with 10 per cent recalling the late Vallabhbhai Patel. Among the refugees, 18 respondents were indifferent, while of the remaining, '50 preferred Hindu Mahasabha, 17 Congress, 4 Socialist Party and 3 Communist Party'. With almost 25 respondents being indifferent to leaders, 31 gave their vote of confidence in Nehru, while 15 remembered Patel. Among Muslim respondents, 7 expressed indifference, 24 liked Congress, 13 Muslim League, 10 Socialist Party and 3 Communist Party, while for leaders, 47 preferred Nehru.[249] This exercise also offered some conclusions about everyday life then, which were marked by:

> Low standard of living – rising prices – refugees in barracks – strong stereotypes of each other [with] different groups not in vital, day-to-day, and intimate contact with one another – distinction between religious and social practices – state secularism but communities predominantly religious....[250]

There was another survey done that summer, as a Delhi School of Economics' group of four students, one lecturer, and one researcher went to north Bihar to visit '35 villages' and meet residents of '21 other villages' in the districts of Saran, Muzaffarpur, Darbhanga and Purnea. This was a flood-prone area with a great density of population, which then saw a 'failure of all three crops', and the food shortage was worse as one moved 'from the west to the east'. Conversely, prices became higher, and with about 3,000 fair price shops (for rations of 8–12 ounces) for approximately 61 lakh people, of whom 40 per cent were landless labourers and small farmers, the group recommended supplies of '1,00,000 tons a month', emphasising that 'there should be more consciousness in the country of the Bihar food situation'.[251]

There were more imports promised, following a deal with China for milo and purchase from the international wheat agreement. As to 'how safe' this made the country's food position, the answer seemed to be 'safe till September 1951 [barring] unexpected interruption....'[252] This saw New Delhi reject the Punjab government's proposal regarding control of gram. Governor Trivedi was anxious that as their wheat surplus disappears, they will require central assistance if not allowed to control gram and maintain price parity with wheat. Prior to August 1950, the controlled rate of gram was below that of wheat, but upon decontrol, the market price of gram rose higher, seeing farmers switch to it, and in May 1951, only 10,600 tons of wheat were collected. The decision regarding Punjab was also puzzling because there was control of gram in Rajasthan and UP.[253]

Apprehensions of the future on food supply and party ideology came together in the 'personal fears' of Dr Syed Mahmud, minister for development and transport, Bihar, and a comrade of Nehru from the early 1920s. Now at a distance from him, Mahmud was distressed that those who commanded a majority of the party would get Congressmen 'of their persuasion' to be elected. Mahmud also felt that these persons considered Nehru 'indispensable' but not his 'policies', whereas these were indispensable for 'the fate of 40 million (Muslims)'. Therefore, he urged a 'reshuffling' of the election machinery while envisaging a cross-party coalition, as the CPI had 'no axe of their own to grind' and the Socialist Party were former colleagues. Otherwise, as there was 'not much chance of Muslims being returned ... will it not be better for [them] to stand aloof?'[254] The prime minister would be more hands-on with the party in the second half of 1951, but, for now, he had his back to the wall on multiple fronts, one of which was the constitutional amendment regarding the freedom of the press. When Deshbandhu Gupta (president, All-India newspaper editors' conference) shared concerns about it, Nehru called the amendment a practical step in an 'intervening' period.[255]

Gupta, Shiva Rao, Devadas Gandhi and R. N. Goenka cautioned him on 21 May 1951 that these powers constituted an 'invitation' to parliament to 'abridge' the freedom of the press,[256] as the word 'reasonable' qualifying 'restrictions' in all other clauses of Article 19 was absent in Clause (2), which applied to the press and appeared to them for an 'indefinite' period. Nehru responded by conceding the word 'reasonable' and by making all laws under Article 19 (2) 'justiciable'. In turn, Gupta and others brought up N. V. Gadgil's outburst against the press in a party meeting, where Home Minister Rajagopalachari was presiding, and asked, 'what protection can the papers critical of ministers, who administer press laws day-to-day, expect from them?'[257] Gadgil had also opined that those editors or managers who got government advertisements should be included in the category of those who might be disqualified. Nehru allowed Gupta, Goenka, Shiva Rao and S. C. Mazumdar, all newspapermen who were also Congressmen, to move amendments and vote on it differently. But once these were lost, they were expected to 'vote ... with the party'.[258] After the amendment's passage on 2 June 1951, he wrote to the chief ministers that

> sedition should have no place in our statute book but law dealing with racial and communal hatred [should] ... press controlled by a handful of people ... be careful in [acting] without reference to us except [for] vulgarity and defamation ... pre-censorship should not be indulged....[259]

There was another decision that was coming to a head now, and here it was the government in Bombay that wanted the prime minister to act in accordance with them. It was about the removal from India of Vladimir G. Sayadiants, director of Soviet film distributors, after his visa had expired on 12 May 1950. This case became something of a test case about the attitudes of Nehru and Patel towards Soviet cultural policies in India.[260] Since November 1949, the Intelligence Bureau's report on the Russian had not been good, but Nehru had prevailed upon Patel because the Soviet embassy intervened to let him stay until 20 November 1950, with the provision of a three months' notice. Then, in November–December 1950, Patel and the Kher ministry went after Sayadiants, given that he had a loss-making business and yet he was living well. Now, the Bombay government reported that Sayadiants had 'not ceased contacting communist individuals'[261] and sent a report by the Nagpur police in April 1951. For Rajagopalachari, this was akin to a misuse of 'hospitality', and he was against extension.

Nehru was 'tired' of the Bombay government, for whom whether Sayadiants did 'something or not', he was 'suspect'. The prime minister knew that Sayadiants had gone to Nagpur and 'met local communists', but this was hardly objectionable, for 'it must be presumed that he is a communist or pro-communist', and he saw Sayadiants' 'telephonic conversations [and] his two communist clerks' in a similar vein. As for the other charge against Sayadiants, the show put together by the Soviet Cine Art Committee, Nehru was himself present there, along with the chief justice of Bombay. By 'this approach … no Russian can be allowed to enter India', as nothing substantial was found against Sayadiants except 'suspicion … trained previously from another point of view'.[262] But if Kher and Rajagopalachari did not approve, then he could go.

A proud Rajagopalachari was not having this 'disgust' from the prime minister, and he pushed Nehru 'to give his definite view … that foreign nationals do not establish political contacts with groups … against government'.[263] Nehru conceded the point but added that it was 'a matter of evidence' and not 'a certain prejudice' or of 'vague data [yet] firm conclusions….'[264] What did not leave India with Sayadiants was this difference of opinion between their ministries. In June 1951, a British ex-MP, Platts-Mills, saw his visa application rejected, given the precedent of Crowther (a British scientist), who too was associated with the Peace Council. Platts-Mills was also associated with a representation about the Telangana accused, and Nehru told Rajagopalachari that he should have allowed visas for both. Any number of Labour, or for that matter Conservative, MPs fell into this category of association with the World Peace Council,[265] and many were 'associated' with India's independence movement. The only 'valid objection' could be 'if a person is dangerous … expression of views is not enough'.[266]

Anyway, at the top of domestic issues were the states of Bihar and Punjab, to the extent that Kumaraswamy Raja complained that New Delhi was 'ignoring' Madras' food problem only to receive a cheque of INR 25,000.[267] The issue with Bihar, however, was not simply food; it was the constitution amendment bill, which validated the ministry's land reforms, and Nehru urged Sinha to 'proceed cautiously', especially with the maharajas of Darbhanga and Ramgarh, whose cases the first amendment affected.[268] He met Kameshwar Singh of Darbhanga and Syam Nandan Sahay, landlord from neighbouring Muzaffarpur, and they appeared 'anxious to cooperate', and the prime minister deemed it 'worthwhile to isolate the troublesome' raja of Ramgarh.[269] Anyhow, by the end of June 1951, there were rumours that the Congress ministry would be 'unfair with zamindars' and would create its own favoured clients.[270]

As for Punjab, elections to the state ministry were followed by elections to the state tribunal (to select candidates for the general election), where eight members (including one Sikh, Giani Gurmukh Singh Musafir) were elected from the Kairon group, while all the candidates of Bhargava's group, including himself, like Ishar Singh Majhail, Comrade Ramkishen and Prithvi Singh Azad, were defeated. But Bhargava still commanded a majority in the state assembly, and Trivedi thought that 'the situation should be allowed to drift', though in the 'the long-term', this 'might alienate' the Sikhs from the Congress.[271] In early June, 33 Bhargava group legislators met at Ambala to express confidence in their leader, and Baldev Singh came there. He was helping Giani Kartar close ranks with Bhargava against Sachar–Kairon and Nagoke groups. This led Trivedi to identify the following ministry: 'Bhargava, Kartar Singh, Swaran Singh, Parkash Kaur, Captain Ranjit Singh, Sri Ram Sharma and Prithvi Singh Azad'.[272] Among these, Ranjit and Sharma represented the region of present-day Haryana. Neither of them was from the Jat community, and Trivedi wanted Sher Singh. As the two sides dug their heels in, president's rule looked imminent.[273]

No wonder then that this period was christened as one of 'myths, scandals and crimes' by that inveterate Nehru-baiter, Baburao Patel, editor of the Bombay-based magazine *Filmindia*, who made the arch comment that 'Pandit Jawaharlal Nehru, who can make millions do what he wants, cannot somehow control a hundred key men around him'.[274] Listing the 'main skeletons' in Nehru's 3.5-year-old cabinet as questions to be answered at the election, Patel spared no one, from Krishna Menon to K. M. Munshi: 'Jeep, Jute, Sugar, Prefab, Fertilizers, Rice, Wheat, Tractors, Textile, Tube-wells, Collieries, Damodar Valley, Sindri Factory, Bokaro Thermal Station, Grow-More-Food, *Vanamahotsav*, Embassies and Prohibition'.

Before that, there was one nagging question that had to be answered, which was if participation of a government servant in the activities of the RSS made him 'liable to disciplinary proceedings' and whether it should debar a candidate from future employment. This was raised, most recently, by the defence ministry in March, and the home ministry's assessment was that the activities of the organisation since the removal of the ban were not seriously objectionable. Nevertheless, the political position was still 'fluid', and association with it was considered liable for departmental action. Those dismissed in 1948–49 for this were to remain so, but for future employment, it was decided not to debar them for being in the RSS 'drills and meetings', when 'in school or college'.[275] This was not the only front on which the home ministry was holding forth. It subsumed the special development grant for the Naga Hills within the money sanctioned for Assam, thereby cutting down any hopes of autonomy for the former.[276] How to spend money, however, was not a question only in the further reaches of the country. It was at the forefront of governmental discussions in New Delhi itself, where the planning commission was ready with a draft of the first plan. JP visited them to offer his critique, as his party had proposed to have a ceiling of 30 acres on agricultural holdings and offered rehabilitation allowances instead of compensation for proprietary rights.

The commission had its own softer threefold aim, 'cooperative village management, farming societies [and] registered farms (above 60 acres)', and JP contrasted his preference for social justice over the commission's stress on production. On controls and price policy, JP said that the government should prioritise the availability of industrial products required by agriculturalists. On incomes policy, the socialists wanted the maximum gap to be '1 : 10' and proposed a ceiling of INR 1,000 per month for the salaries of ministers, president and others. Another target of the economy for JP was the princes' privy purses, as he urged them to move towards a large-scale nationalisation of banks–insurance––industries–trade, even if 'run on business principles....' Nanda tried to outdo JP's Gandhism with his own and argued that nationalisation without compensation would be 'forceful', to which JP responded that his main aim was to create an 'atmosphere of austerity', essential for planning. Finally, JP had a point to make on the optics of the draft plan in that it 'might be used for elections ... as government's main achievement'.[277]

This external challenge to the party in question was feeble, though, compared to the internal churnings going on in it. K. D. Malaviya, a Kidwai follower from UP, wanted corrupt Congress leaders to be dealt with while reducing the Patelite reliance on 'conceited services' in favour of Congress volunteers. For Malaviya, this 'transitional' time needed direct action, and showing the overlap between organisational corruption and legislative restrictions, he narrated events from Lucknow, where 'three boys were threatened under Section 107 because in a public meeting they threw a rotten egg or tomato on the Civil Supplies Minister, C. B. Gupta'.[278] Similarly, in Kanpur, when an effigy of Gupta was taken out, arrests followed, and a departing Malaviya warned Nehru against 'top-heaviness', even as the prime minister was preferring the planning commission to the economic committee of the cabinet, so as to pitch people's needs against industry's profits. But Commerce Minister Mahtab did not blush and explained that the price of unginned cotton was not determined by the agriculture ministry, while the planning commission's proposed price structure put together agricultural and industrial labour. On the availability of cloth, the 'famine' of December 1950 was 'over', thanks to rationing, decreasing exports and imports from America and Pakistan, but these must continue, otherwise 'textile production will collapse about October', given the capital's cloth requirement itself.[279]

Fed up with his ministers and fobbed off by his partymen, Nehru forced the issue in June 1951 by resigning from the CPB, with the 'final blow' being the situation in East Punjab. He withdrew from those 'entangled' policies, where he was 'not wholly seized with the subject' and felt that they functioned 'more and more as the old British Government, only with less efficiency', while relying 'more on official agencies....'[280] Ironically, the seniormost officials were not happy either. The Comptroller and Auditor-General V. Narahari Rao, with 34 years of service behind him, traced the 'gradual' transfer of power from the reforms of 1920 to the rules of 1935 and the constitution of 1950, when it was 'impossible' to punish an official.[281] The implicit bureaucratic inertia of the late 1940s was overtaken, momentarily, by the infusion of the first Five-Year Plan's preliminary outline. On 2 June 1951, the planning commission circulated the first glimpse of the INR 1,350 crores (centre's share, 680; states, 670) plan,[282] with its major expenditures as under:

> Centre: irrigation & power – 160 crores, railways – 150, rehabilitation – 77, communications – 67, industries – 46, education – 41, roads – 32, agriculture – 26, housing – 11, health – 10. States: irrigation & power – 265, agriculture – 165, health – 67, education – 64, roads – 48, labour/backward classes – 17, industries – 12, cottage – 9, housing – 7.

Among the central government's responsibilities were loans for four multipurpose river valley schemes, refugee rehabilitation, the construction of a new capital for Punjab and food production. INR 400 crores were to come from the current revenue receipts of centre and states, and, of the remaining, the railways were expected to finance their expenditure. For the rest, a scheme of 'fresh taxation (158), public loans (95), small savings (293) and economies in administration (45)' was laid out. This left scope for deficit financing to the tune of INR 225–250 crores, which were to be compensated by releases of sterling balances from London.[283] For the private sector, INR 135 crores were earmarked, out of which there was some central assistance (40–45), but the major share (80–95) was to be raised from the capital market. Major industrial targets were electricity, steel, cement, aluminium and paper or newsprint. More importantly, the food or cash crop production targets were as under:

Food grains 100,000 tons to 650,000 tons by 1955–56 – this plus import of 30 lakh tons [could raise] consumption per adult per day to 14.50 ounces by 1955–56. [This was still less than the pre-war all-India average of 15.80 ounces over 1936–39]. *Deficit provinces* in 1949–50 [were] … all except Madhya Pradesh, Orissa, and Punjab, [while] expected surplus provinces in 1955–56 [were] … all except Bombay and Madras. *Deficit states* in 1949–50 [were] … all except Madhya Bharat and PEPSU, [while] expected surplus states in 1955–56 [were] … all except Kashmir, Mysore, Rajasthan, and Travancore-Cochin.

Energised by this first sight of the product of his cherished institution, Nehru prepared himself to take on the CWC over 10–13 July at Bangalore and, afterwards, in September.[284] He had given up on Kripalani returning to the party and was himself out of the CPB, which, consequently, had asked Bhargava to resign. Explaining the Punjab crisis to President Prasad, the prime minister brought up the open opposition of 'the party', deteriorating work and unsatisfactory law and order, but, above all, the 'failed' attempts to form a composite ministry.[285] In these circumstances, Article 356 was the only option, which was announced on 20 June 1951. The president may have signed on this proclamation, but he was not satisfied, given that Bhargava had resigned not because he lost confidence of the assembly but 'in obedience' to the CPB. Prasad argued that this was similar to Kripalani's resignation from the Congress presidentship in 1947 and pointed out that Trivedi's complaints had not been against Bhargava's ministry but against its opponents, but no action was taken against them. Prasad had observed the 'impracticable' instruction asking the groups to select names for ministership and did not mince his words, calling it 'an emergency … artificially created.…'[286] The prime minister was taken aback and claimed that 'the ministry, supported by Congress party, was controlled by non-Congress elements [in its] artificial majority'.[287] Dismissing the Kripalani parallel, he charged Bhargava with not being active on corruption charges and promised that the rule by Article 356 would not continue for long with the election close. To Trivedi, Nehru admitted that the situation was 'possible to criticise, from the democratic point of view', but argued that it was necessary 'to give the province a shock'.[288]

And then he was off to Bihar, where he discussed the Kosi project in the first pages of a saga that was the sorrow of north-east Bihar.[289] Kosi's floods obsessed the minds of people there, but the prime minister was also overwhelmed by the large sum involved: 'Rs. 177 crores in 7 stages'. Nepal and Bihar governments pledged INR 2 crores each, but New Delhi could only afford the first stages, without the dam, for 20–60 per cent flood protection, and anyway, not in 1951–52. But the prime minister wanted some public work generating rural employment from October, and there was some 'vague talk by Americans for a loan'.[290] A reluctant G. L. Nanda preferred, instead, the Gandak project, as more viable and useful, but Nehru wanted to 'go ahead with the first two stages [with] two crores from Nepal'.[291] In response, feeling 'undermined', C. D. Deshmukh threatened resignation and, showing extended finances and suggesting ruffled egos, refused money to a project whose technical soundness was not yet ascertained.[292]

Money and morals were in conflict everywhere. The gurdwara at Pulbangash, Delhi, was coming 'in the way' of a market scheme in western UP, 'agriculturalist Brahmin ex-soldiers' from the frontier province were still at their camp, while refugees in Hyderabad faced ejections from their rented camps during monsoon[293] as the state continued in free-fall with the recent closure of Madrassa Nizamyah.[294] When Jamiat-Ulema, Delhi, passed resolutions on its political prisoners, for Patel too had promised 'a generous policy', Nehru admitted that it was 'unbecoming to be so vengeful', even as people were calling for a name change of Osmania University and for a promotion of Hindi and Telugu in place of Urdu. The prime minister resolved to keep the name, the university's central control and continue 'Urdu, in its simpler Hindustani version'.[295] But Hindi in Nagari was already an 'essential subject for anyone who wishes to function in India/on behalf of India'.[296]

A week after the planning commission released the outline of the first plan, the election commission fixed 'elections for November/December' 1951.[297] Bihar and Orissa preferred January–February 1952 but agreed to November–December. Madras had proposed the first three weeks of December, then suggested January–February, but accepted the end of December. Punjab had suggested early elections for the 6,000+ voters in Lahaul and Spiti in July–August, the first three weeks of October for Himachal and November–December otherwise. Faced with these variances, Sukumar Sen felt that the elections ought to be between early October and December, for if they went into January 1952, then it would not be possible to reconvene for the budget session before the end of March. On the other hand, if elections were to be held earlier, then the present parliament must end by 15 September for the new parliament to start from 15 March. Sen hoped that they would not need to go further, for he recalled that when elections had been proposed for summer 1951, most states had declined, given the 'harvesting season' and 'hot climate', and as Nehru wondered about the middle-of-November to middle-of-January window,[298] Sen offered it, while listing detailed suggestions from all states:

Part A states: Assam (December 5, 19 and 29), Bihar (3–15 December), Bombay (1st week of December), Madhya Pradesh (19 Nov–20 Dec), Madras (first three weeks of December), Orissa (15–30 Nov, 10–20 Dec), Punjab (26 Nov–21 Dec, L & S-July-Aug), UP (Ballia district-last week of November. *Information in respect of other districts awaited*), West Bengal (21 Nov–15 Dec). *Part B* states: Hyderabad (four weeks from 7 November), Madhya Bharat (2nd–4th weeks of Dec), Mysore (3–17 Dec), PEPSU (November), Rajasthan (Oct-Dec), Saurashtra (Nov), Travancore-Cochin (2nd week of Nov–2nd week of Dec). *Part C* states: Ajmer (3rd week of Nov), Bhopal (15–31 Dec), Bilaspur (last week of Nov), Coorg (26–29 Nov), Delhi (1st week of Nov), Himachal (1st three weeks of October and Chamba earlier), Kutch (3rd–4th week of Nov), Manipur (1–15 November), Tripura (1st–4th week of Dec), Vindhya Pradesh (15–31 Dec).

It is not difficult to discern why different states were not exactly enthusiastic at the prospect of elections. Rajasthan, for instance, continued in turmoil. The 'popular' ministry of Jainarain Vyas remained unhappy at the Ministry of States. Their predecessor, the 'official' regime of C. S. Venkatachar, had brought outsiders into the services, and Venkatachar had not relinquished control over expenditure. This was an interwar dyarchy,[299] with civil servants, 'encouraged by the adviser', disregarding ministers and the inspector-general of police 'ignoring the Chief Minister', who in a tit-for-tat held up the appointment of Menon, former personal assistant of Venkatachar, and it was being asked across Part B and Part C states if the position of regional commissioner was 'really necessary'.[300]

The answer, for places like Naga Hills and Manipur, was an unambiguous yes,[301] and Nehru trusted this set-up so much that in late June 1951, he claimed 'that the Naga question [had] passed the critical stage'.[302] He was checked by E. P. Moon's report on the neighbouring Manipur, where in November 1950, N. M. Buch too had found 'administrative labefaction'.[303] Moon sketched a remarkable scene of an area where policemen were 'arrested' by villagers, 'popular' ministers were 'penned' in their houses by the public and corruption ruled the roost, causing heavy arrears of work, shortage of yarn and feeding the emergence of 'a determined communist Irabat Singh' (Hijam Irabot, 1896–1951). With incompetent local staff and 'foreigner' officers, civil and criminal cases and revenue appeals dating back to 1946, a 'hopeless' PWD, Moon warned that 'the humdrum work consequent on integration' was not done, and if the Manipuris appeared to have an 'intense xenophobia', that was justifiable.[304]

New Delhi held the ground on the back of a Gurkha force, and Moon was clear that any solution lay in either absorbing Manipur in Assam or absorbing Manipur in a 'new Northeast Frontier State … having a joint cadre with Assam', with the second option politically more palatable and the first administratively easier. If devolution was thus edgy, then development was expensive. Outside the capital, Imphal, there were 'scarcely any buildings-roads-bridges', but

Manipur had received only 10 out of its 'Rs. 40 lakhs at integration'. If this was owed, then so was war compensation, albeit whatever was 'distributed' unevenly between the hill areas and the valley was causing 'corruption'. Part C states like Manipur were at a 'great disadvantage', and who would risk elections there? And so, reluctant state ministries, complaining cabinet members, a reproving president and a hard-line parliamentary board completed the prime ministerial roster by the end of June 1951. With little response to the public appeal for 'food gifts for Bihar and Madras', except from the Kashmir government and the East Punjab governor,[305] at least, statistics poured out from the planning commission, which released the distribution of its outlay of INR 1,493 crores from 1951 to 1956 as under:

> Agriculture: 192.54 (12.9%), Irrigation/power: 450.66 (30.2%), Transport/communication: 388.57 (26.1%), Industry: 100.99 (6.7%), Social services: 252.47 (16.9%), Rehabilitation: 79 (5.3%); Share of central and state governments: Central government – 734 crores, Part A states – 559, Part B – 171, Part C – 28; Regional development in the first part of the plan: *Part A* states: Assam (12.5 crores), Bihar (55.5), Bombay (121), MP (43.5), Madras (137), Orissa (15), Punjab (15.5), UP (91), WB (69); *Part B* states: Hyderabad (40.5 crores), Madhya Bharat (23), Mysore (36.5), PEPSU (8), Rajasthan (15), Saurashtra (21.5), Travancore-Cochin (26); *Part C* states: Ajmer (1.61 crores), Bhopal (3.67), Bilaspur (.42), Coorg (.53), Delhi (6), HP (4.48), Kutch (2.68), Manipur (1), Tripura (1.5), Vindhya Pradesh (6.24).[306]

Among the people to be tasked with realising this plan, one who would not get a chance was Dr Gopichand Bhargava,[307] for Jawaharlal Nehru had decided to draw a line under the government of 1947–51 as he prepared to take on Purushottamdas Tandon in Bangalore by putting together a survey of 'the last 3–4 years' in a 17-page note to the AICC.[308] In this stock-tacking, the boxes ticked were rather understandable: 'communal menace', relief and rehabilitation, Kashmir and economic stagnation. These had been met by the old bureaucracy with its new departments. This 'unwieldy' administration was overshadowed, however, by the 'attention' given to the constitution and the planning commission, and now there were spectres of 'regional famine' and 'sectional loyalties'. Alongside, there was a secularism of 'flabbiness', a struggle to abolish *zamindari* and a stymied industrial bill. Education and health remained neglected, while corruption, customs and conventions resisted legislation. Above all, the Congress party itself stared at the question, 'Was it 'to function [with the] sole aim [to] somehow to win an election?'[309]

About this, in late June 1951, the election commission asked if the CPI could be invited to an all-party conference for allotting party symbols. From

Iengar to Nehru, all baulked at the prospect, supported by Vellodi from Hyderabad, but queried by Trivedi from Simla, as the party was unlawful in some states but not in others. On 10 March 1951, Rajagopalachari, in a parliamentary statement, said that the CPI stood for violent upheaval, and he awaited crime reports from Telangana, Madras, Assam and elsewhere to show otherwise. Then, in May 1951, Home Secretary Iengar observed that he could not see how the government could recognise a party 'under directions from outside' and wanted to maintain the status quo.[310] Rajagopalachari put his ministerial imprimatur on his mandarin's position and concluded that the time was not 'ripe for inviting the CP to meetings of the EC....'[311] With many areas of communist activities being under the Ministry of States, Gopalaswami Ayyangar too chimed in by adding that there were 'communists ... engaged in lawful pursuits' and, 'if they group themselves ... they cannot obviously be refused'.[312] Nehru discarded this possibility and determined that 'the CP should not be invited.... The only right course is to recognise the Congress, the Socialist Party, the new Praja Party, the Hindu Mahasabha'.[313]

If these were the four parties of governmental choice to contest the upcoming election, then in the meantime, three governments, between them, could not do more than contemplate an upcoming project. The government of Nepal 'implied' that it had set INR 2 crores aside for the Kosi project, while the Bihar ministry sought loan for its own 'petty scheme', even as New Delhi's experts were evaluating stages without the expensive dam. Stage one could produce electricity (Kathmandu was especially interested in this), railways and roadways, and barrage and houses, thereby employing '5000–20,000 people', and stage two promised irrigation, thus controlling floods, but with neither the finance ministry nor the planning commission keen, and correspondents covering Bihar's famine and flood were asking why not 'attract American help'.[314] In the meantime, requests from Patna continued for a milo subsidy as well as a grant for agriculturalist or landless labourers. Milo was being centrally subsidised in Bombay city, Ahmedabad, Poona, Sholapur and Bangalore/ Mysore city, whereas *jowar* was being subsidised in Madhya Bharat.[315] By now, the May 1950 loan for land improvement had been disbursed, and so Nehru's hopes for Kosi hinged on Kathmandu.[316] The other place where money and land intertwined in this manner was East Punjab, where the governor's rule was tackling the ministerial problem of 'ejectment of tenants'.[317] The Sacher–Kairon combine was urging Trivedi for amendments to the security of tenure act 1950, with retrospective effect:

> [L]imit lowered to 50 standard acres, (ii) if any landlord wants to sell land occupied by a tenant for the last 4 years, the tenant should have the first priority, (iii) if any tenant has occupied land for 6 years, he should have the option to purchase it, (iv) rent should not be more than 1/4 of

the produce or the rent fixed in 1948–49, whichever is less, (v) tenure of the tenant should be 5 years....[318]

Trivedi's view was that (i) and (v) were 'sound' suggestions, and he could agree to (ii) and (iii) with modifications, but (iv) was 'controversial', and his choices were to stand still and upset the politicians or to go ahead and risk upsetting the landlords. He would rather the parliament legislated for the province, but he knew that the only option was to issue orders according to party preference. Kairon and Giani Gurmukh Singh Musafir met him on 21 July, and Nehru asked Trivedi to go ahead on (i) and (v), but also (ii) and (iii), as Kairon emphasised that there had been 8,000 ejections, '2000 in Hissar district alone', in the past year.[319] In mid-July, giving an account of his first month of direct administration, the governor counted the number of corrupt officials terminated (80), black-marketeers detained (30) and irregularities regularised. He was reversing Bhargava's nominations to local bodies and re-introducing the *zaildari* system while ordering enquiries into the yarn corporation. Trivedi's governance challenges also included 'grow-more-food', Chandigarh and Bhakra, as wheat procurement in 1951 was running low, '150,000 tons as against expected 2.25 lac'.[320]

The prime minister wanted him to go further and order enquiries into any specific charges against ex-ministers like Ishar Singh Majhail and Prithvi Singh Azad.[321] All this was straightforward compared to the awkward matter of Master Tara Singh, who seemed to have shifted the fulcrum of his activities to Patiala with his defiance of the ban on public meetings there. The PEPSU government risked looking 'foolish' if it took no action, but the said meeting was held in a gurdwara and if the Master was arrested, it could be risky. Neither Rajagopalachari nor Nehru rushed to take this decision, even as Iengar remained anxious.[322] This was soon overtaken by a far bigger anxiety when none other than President Rajendra Prasad, convinced that 'Pakistan is seriously preparing for a show-down', after the departure of the UN's Graham Mission to Kashmir and before the constituent assembly elections there, impressed upon Nehru certain suggestions made to him by Baldev Singh and General Cariappa. Prasad held that the time had come 'to stock petrol', to build-up 'semi-military, Home Guards', and to interrogate the 'services and loyalty' of 'nationals of Pakistan [working] in essential industries' in India. Giving the example of Jamshedpur, where 'Muslims from Eastern Bengal' worked, Prasad wanted them interned and added that 'there are many who have one leg in Pakistan and the other in India.... In times of tension, such families should choose one side....'[323]

Prasad urged Nehru to let people know the seriousness of the situation at the upcoming Congress session, and Baldev Singh and Cariappa had given him a memorandum in view of their feeling that the retrenchment of 50,000 men had encouraged Pakistan, seeking a decision on whether in the event of war, fighting was to be restricted to Jammu and Kashmir or action would be taken in West and East Pakistan. Having averted a near-war on the two Bengals a year ago, Nehru was not going to ratchet up the deteriorating situation now. He had conferred with the defence chiefs, visited Kashmir recently and ordered moving an armoured division from Meerut to the Punjab border, but he was 'surprised' at Cariappa insinuating that a decision had not been taken as to 'whether the fighting … is to be confined to Kashmir', when Nehru had 'clearly stated repeatedly that it will not be so'.[324]

And so, on the eve of leaving for Bangalore, Nehru informed the chief ministers that if Pakistan attacked, then there would be 'an extension of conflict', even as this scare was already spreading and there was a spurt in migration from East to West Bengal.[325] Assam, meanwhile, was facing floods in 1951 after the earthquake in 1950, but the state government's relief work was hampered by an 'outsider' chief secretary, A. D. Pandit of UP, who did not want to extend his tenure, demoralised by the 'Assamese-Bengali trouble'.[326] Pandit had been sent there in September 1950 by Nehru, as Vallabhbhai Patel had foisted upon Medhi an inspector-general of police, K. R. Chaudhuri. When Governor Doulatram confirmed Pandit's reluctance, a disapproving prime minister recalled his dissatisfaction with the Assam secretariat.[327] To Medhi though, he wrote not about giving work to Pandit but about not giving 'prominence' to Phizo and told him to prepare for polls, to 'begin about 3 January [1952]',[328] despite West Bengal and Assam joining Bihar and Madras in the frontline of food receivers.[329]

Nehru accepted that the bureaucratic procedure for collecting food grains and converting them into cash to be sent to the respective district magistrates had turned out to be complex,[330] but it was not as if the private sector was helping, and when the Roy ministry proposed to purchase the Oriental Gas Company from Messrs Soorajmull Nagarmull & Co., the latter had a tax liability of INR 2.34 crores. Deshmukh told Nehru that it will take 40 years to recover the amount, while pointing out that Calcutta was unable to finance their road development project for the year.[331] If Roy's financial priorities seemed skewed, then New Delhi's appeared unequal. Pandit Shukla was unhappy that the planning commission had not allotted an iron and steel factory to the Chhattisgarh division of his state, and in its lieu, he sought a factory to manufacture newsprint at Nepa Nagar, as his government had got the technical aspects drawn up from America.[332]

Further south, the Madras ministry of P. S. Kumaraswamy Raja had passed a government order on college admissions in June 1951, which was being termed communal. Raja clarified that it was within constitutional provisions, as it reserved 15 per cent of the seats for Scheduled Castes and Scheduled

Tribes, with the proviso that if qualified students were not available, then the rest will come from the 'general pool' and 25 per cent of the seats for Backward Classes, regardless of religious denomination. This was an old classification comprising 148 communities in the Madras presidency for educational fee concessions, with only one change, namely the inclusion of 'Harijan' Christians. If anything, this affirmative action should have been more,[333] as the 'general pool' remained untouched, and Raja shared a letter censuring its inadequacy by one Congress legislator: 'The population of [Madras] was 5 crores and 70 lakhs … Harijans: 80 lakhs, Backward Classes: 3 crores, Others: 1 crore and 90 lakhs. While 15% seats for 80 lakhs was just, 25% for 3 crores was not....'[334]

At the other end, in East Punjab, the Dayanand Anglo-Vedic schools' managing committee was up in arms against what it called an 'ill-conceived' policy on languages of instruction by the state. On the 'supreme importance' of teaching Hindi, it decided that in its schools, Panjabi-in-Gurmukhi would be 'optional' from class V, while the non-Punjabis in the state were to be turned to Hindi 'as early as possible'. Further, it instructed its schools to exercise 'vigilance' over local bodies' and Khalsa schools if they did not make provisions thus. Finally, it urged its tutors to create 'public opinion' so that students desired to be taught 'undeterred by pressure'.[335] Next-door PEPSU's 'popular' chief minister found it difficult to get along with his 'official' advisor, given the 'non-cooperative' attitude of his police chief. Simultaneously, the Sikh leaders looked 'towards' Tara Singh, convinced that there was 'no chance' of a Congress ticket.[336] Nehru assured Raghbir otherwise and asked Ayyangar to replace Bhide. Like Vyas, Raghbir complained about outsider officers, and like Raghbir, Vyas was struggling with *jagirdars*; both felt aggrieved at the States Ministry.[337]

Also feeling aggrieved was JP, who complained to G. L. Nanda that the planning commission was not 'working for the nation [but] for a party', to which Nanda replied that the commission was meeting all parties' representatives – except the CPI – and reminded JP of their talks of 14 May and 4 June 1951. In addition, the commission had discussed its agrarian and industrial programmes with his colleagues Ramnandan Mishra and Asoka Mehta. The issue at the heart of JP's charge was that the commission had made the draft outline available to the Congress before the latter drew up its electoral manifesto, leading Nanda to admit that 'it was important that the biggest political party should make up its mind in the light of the plan' and hoped that JP should 'not think the worse of it simply because [of this]'.[338] Nehru was not that bashful. Writing to the chief ministers after the adoption of the party's election manifesto in Bangalore, he made his satisfaction evident at the 'leading organisation in India' adopting the 'same line' as the planning commission, thereby strengthening JP's point. But the big statement that was dominating conversations in the second half of July 1951 was that of Nehru's Pakistani counterpart Liaquat Ali Khan, who warned against Indian troop movements. In turn, Nehru repeated that an 'attack on Kashmir would result in war', although he was more concerned about people getting 'excited', Hindus in East Pakistan exiting and the 'illegal' forthcoming railway strike.[339] Meanwhile, the defence ministry was outlining expansive plans for recruitment and retention, recall and raising of units, well exceeding the defence budget.[340]

Simultaneously, ministers were pushing back at the press' 'anti-state' activities. When in June 1951, central ministries were told that enquiries should be held to meet newspaper allegations, Food Minister K. M. Munshi retorted that many publications made statements without evidence, and when asked for facts, editors like Karaka would reply that those were for the minister to find. In an episode, Mubarak Mazdoor, a left-wing Congressman of yore with a 'shady reputation', offered rice from China, and when ambassador Panikkar refused to entertain him, Mazdoor publicly criticised Panikkar. Munshi was unwilling to consider such charges, without which *Atom*, or *Blitz*, or *Current*, would not have been published, and he would rather not respond.[341] He had support from Rajagopalachari, who was pro-active on related matters. The home minister successfully advised Nehru against meeting communist leaders, given that there was no real change in them. Down the chain of command, M. K. Vellodi in Hyderabad was upset about his interviews with communist leaders being 'misinterpreted', and Rajagopalachari was mistrustful until the latter gave 'practical evidence' of non-violence in, at least, Telangana, where, in the week 11–18 July, the police report showed '11 murders'.[342]

Two weeks earlier, the home secretary, while processing the Bombay ministry's request 'to impound the passport of Mirajkar, a communist', had remarked that he had thought of S. S. Mirajkar as a 'moderate', but the Intelligence Bureau had reported otherwise, convincing him that any 'shift of opinion is ... tactical'.[343] His minister obviously 'agreed',[344] and the prime minister acquiesced 'in preventing any leading communist from going abroad', conceding that 'a list of such persons be prepared'.[345] Still, though Nehru held the CPI guilty of crimes, he reminded Rajagopalachari that it could never have caused the communal situation that existed in Punjab and Delhi in 1947. Bringing up recent speeches delivered in the capital 'by Hindu communal leaders ...', he pointed out that his ministers met 'these people ... in a friendly way' but not the communists. Similarly, if the Intelligence Bureau was at pains to show the latter's Soviet contacts, then it also had evidence that the former received 'indirect support and sympathy' from American and British officials. And yet, only the Russians and the Chinese were kept under 'a close watch' because of an 'innate bias'. Then, there were some ex-rulers whose 'mischief' could only come from the right-wing, and this whole matrix was 'tolerated largely by a positive or an unconscious element of communalism in many of us....'[346]

Every so often, an example would appear, as in late July 1951, when N. V. Gadgil asked the prime minister if it would 'not be a good thing informally' to call the leaders of the Akali Sikhs, Hindu Mahasabha and the RSS and 'impress upon them the desirability of restraint?'[347] As for the bias against communism, it was best revealed in the regular rejection of applications for passport, especially in Bombay, where it was enough for the ministry to go by police reports that would mention 'facts' like the applicant was 'said to be a member of the Students' Federation and of the Scheduled Castes Youth Conference' or 'secretary of the Municipal Kamgar Union', which encouraged the sweepers' strike in 1949.[348] Meanwhile, within the party, the ministerial duo of Kidwai and Ajit Jain resigned from the cabinet after the Bangalore session, but Nehru re-drafted their press statement, leaving their party's future open. His words reveal impatience with Tandon while buying a short-lived truce: '[Nowhere] in the world the president of an organisation is the very anti-thesis of [the government] that the organisation stands for....'[349]

Tandon was not impressed by the 'personal references'; Nehru admitted to the existing 'mess of their being in government and opposing the Congress';[350] and it became impossible for Kidwai to carry on in government in late July 1951.[351] At this delicate intersection of party and government personnel stood the planning commission, whose publication of the Gorwala Report caused ripples in both directions. Gadgil was one of those asking whether, in the first place, Gorwala's appointment was within its 'terms of reference'. Calling it a 'stick' for the government's critics, he used it to beat at 'the status' of the commission and asked if the home ministry was 'consulted' before publishing this critical report. The prime minister, who also chaired the commission, had no qualms defending his decision, as like other such reports, this one too did 'not bind government' but just bolstered 'public discussion'.[352] Gadgil's ministry was then amidst a fertiliser scandal. The issue was that when tenders were invited, Binny Corporation of Calcutta was one among the 38 concerns submitting bids, and 'at the last moment, they sent an amended tender, which was just below the lowest....'[353]

But, with considerable public costs and private profits involved, Deshmukh's ministry seemed to have let the matter pass, and a rare chief minister who was happy at the Gorwala report was the fellow civil servant Vellodi, who gave supporting illustrations. When the Kher–Desai combine in Bombay had sought 'a dry belt' in their neighbourhood, Vellodi had opposed citing his economic committee's warning against a 'pursuit of fads'.[354] This committee too had been presided over by Gorwala, and the Bombay ministers had not been pleased. Vellodi concluded, a touch self-servingly, that the major calamity that had befallen post-1947 was 'the metamorphosis of the civil servant into a quasi-politician',[355] with attendant 'chicanery', clientelism and corruption. Rajagopalachari deflected these comments in his inimitable manner by observing that 'we cannot get any conceivable set-up than what we have....'[356]

Ministers like Sri Prakasa wanted Gorwala's report to be classified. Gadgil had alerted him to Gorwala's remarks on the working of their ministries, and the former connected the shock of this report with that of the Hindu Code Bill. Notwithstanding the legislature's nod to proceed with the Hindu Code Bill, Sri Prakasa cautioned that the rest of the programme will be choked, before concluding archly that 'the present parliament is self-constituted ... for the sole purpose of framing the constitution.... We had to carry on ... to fill a vacuum [but] radical changes should be left over to a properly constituted legislature'.[357] The prime minister stood his ground over the Gorwala report, while on the Hindu Code Bill, he argued that 'a pending bill' would give 'a greater handle' to their opponents in the election.[358] As for Mavalankar, he indeed was proving an immovable object, not only on this subject but also on controls, which to him were impossible to administer. Equally, the idea that as speaker he should keep quiet was 'intolerable' to him, and, echoing Rajagopalachari, Mavalankar concluded that 'in our present set-up, [it was] difficult to [have] the British ideal'.[359]

One other area where the British way of doing things was faltering was the Naga Hills. Once again, it was Sri Prakasa, ex-governor of Assam, who bluntly articulated the connection between this eastern edge of the state and its south-western sector. He was sure that slowly all the Hindus of East Bengal will leave, notwithstanding the Nehru–Liaquat Pact, and, instead of finding ways to stem or reverse this movement, Sri Prakasa wanted to focus on spreading them among various states, with expenses paid by the centre. Now, with 'an eye on the vote', Bishnuram Medhi had told him that they did not want more refugees or, failing that, they did not want more refugees with publicity.[360] The Assam government had to meet the movement of '45 lakhs [Bengali] Hindus in 4 districts of Rangpur, Mymensingh, Sylhet and Tipperah' in their adjoining areas, and they must 'become Assamese'.[361]

It was a variation on this theme that the Nagas were being told by Sri Prakasa's successor, Jairamdas Doulatram, and the central commissioner for Scheduled Castes and Tribes, Laxmidas Shrikant. Predictably, to Shrikant, the person coming from New Delhi, Doulatram, the person in Shillong, appeared to be 'giving too much prominence to Phizo'.[362] Shrikant also felt that too much money had been given to the Naga Hill districts at the expense of Manipur. Both Doulatram and Shrikant submitted their reports to President Prasad, contrasting the courteous Nagas with a challenging Phizo. Doulatram had announced New Delhi's sanction of INR 30 lakhs for war damages, as well as a special grant of INR 10 lakhs while assuring the Nagas that 'their land would not be taken', and after his travels that took him far beyond Kohima, Doulatram noted, as evidence of his benevolent paternalism, that the 'Naga Hills people have no clear conception of ... independence.... Social contact on an equal basis [and] accelerated welfare programme can bind us....'[363]

This reasonableness was undercut by Shrikant reporting to the president that the two grants could be utilised better and complaining that Medhi's ministry was sidelined. Pointing out that the Naga Hills district was after all one of six tribal districts in the region, and the only one without its council, Shrikant recommended having this election. President Prasad recalled that Sri Prakasa too had stressed similarly and wanted Nehru and Rajagopalachari to 'lay down policy' via the Assam ministry,[364] whose commissioner, S. J. Duncan, declared on 24 July 1951 that Phizo was 'responsible' for the Japanese invasion during the World War and if the Nagas insisted on plebiscite, then they should go to him for war compensation. When Phizo complained about this absurd charge, Nehru replied that regardless, there could be 'no ... plebiscite'.[365] India's 'state-making' in Nagaland was on,[366] even as other crises like Bengal's refugee and Bihar's Kosi showed few signs of being on the mend.

On the last day of July, A. N. Khosla produced an 11-page-long report on the Kosi project, in which calling the region the 'worst flood and silt affected area' across India, Khosla traced its origins and commented on its bleak future. Viceroy Wavell had visited the Kosi area in 1945 and authorised investigations for flood control. Khosla had followed in January 1946, suggested a multipurpose project and took its report to Kathmandu subsequently, where the matter remained stuck till April 1950, when the Nepalese premier visited New Delhi, leading to an advisory committee. Nearly 70 lakhs were spent on surveys in cooperation with the American Bureau of Reclamation, but in December 1950, the Bihar government submitted a report on their Gandak project, which Khosla termed 'inadequate' and 'presumptuous', as neither Lucknow nor Kathmandu were consulted. With concerns that Nepal's interest 'may lapse', Khosla suggested 'a diversion dam ... in 2 years with 4 crores'.[367]

That nothing happened in 1951 was due to a strange war-scare gripping much of the government, fed by India's acting envoy in Pakistan, Khub Chand, who, while requesting the removal of records or personnel from Karachi, fancifully claimed that an invasion 'on the traditional capital of Muslim India',[368] without formal declaration, in three acts: ceasefire violations, stage-managed uprising in Kashmir and armed *jihad*. Nehru was unimpressed at Chand having 'too much imagination' and, instructing him and his officials to stay where they were, until the new high commissioner, Dr Mohan Sinha Mehta, arrived, lambasted Chand's proposal of 'exchanging diplomats [with

Pakistan] in Colombo'.[369] Soon, however, support came for Khub Chand's position from Calcutta, as Dr B. C. Roy complained that the soldiers allotted to Bengal were much less than in Punjab, and claiming that his counterpart was recruiting, Roy revealed his government's semi-military pioneer corps of 8,000 volunteers.

The prime minister's response was a mixture of caution, and consolation, as he shared his information that if war came, it would not be in Bengal. While glad for Roy's volunteers, Nehru urged him to not panic. Having refused to evacuate the East Punjab border, he was not expecting war but worried about a warlike atmosphere in which 'refugees might attack Muslims' and the state might arrest suspects pre-emptively. West Bengal's high numbers of preventive detentions were already an example, and, warning Roy against relying solely on the 'policeman-view', he wanted a 'close watch on the Hindu communal organisations'.[370] Roy went ahead and did the exact opposite. Informing Nehru that he was preparing for civil defence, he asked for aid, insisting that New Delhi was taking 'things easy' and declaring 'the problem of East Bengal … more difficult than … West Punjab'.[371] In turn, the prime minister cautioned that 'steps [of] readiness also [led] to greater tension'.[372]

It was not just Roy though, for Baldev Singh was 'greatly worried' if Liaquat had 'something up his sleeves'.[373] Singh had got a draft produced on Pakistan's plans in Kashmir for a meeting of the military brass on 14 August 1951 at Western Command Headquarters. If things were threatening to get out of hand, then this was not due to a lack of trying on the prime minister's part. On 29 July, he addressed a large public meeting in Delhi, where he juxtaposed the 'clenched fist' of Pakistan with the Ashoka Chakra. His worries were, as ever, more internal than external. Given that the last parliamentary session before the first election was to begin on 6 August 1951, the picture of India was that of 'a caste-ridden country', and while 'there may be Muslims who cannot be trusted, the dangerous element will be the Hindu communal element'.[374] To his envoys abroad, he wrote about exchanging telegrams with Liaquat being 'better than declaring war', though the government and the party functioned 'differently'.[375]

But no one else was on the horizon, as Kripalani's Praja Party already seemed to be lost, JP's Socialist Party had made little mark, and it was Nehru and not Tandon who held the people. As for the 1945–46 batch of parliamentarians and their legislative programme, President Prasad had his own ideas, as he desired the finance commission's inclusion in his address, wanted to mention the imposition of Article 356 in East Punjab and disapproved the reference to the Hindu Code Bill.[376] The prime minister pushed back on the latter, as he had prevailed upon his parliamentary opponents, to let the bill be tabled during this session. In return, the disputed bits were to be taken up later.

To a sceptical Dr Ambedkar, Nehru wrote tactfully that he was keen to finish first 'with the ordinances, part C states bill, industry bill' and was prepared to make the parliament sit 'till at least October'.[377] More serious was Prasad's mention of the word 'jehad' in his address, which both Rajagopalachari and Nehru resisted, at a time when the India–Pakistan trade was finally moving, with coal and coke changing hands for jute and cotton.[378] Meanwhile, routine challenges continued. Three hundred refugees of the Palwal camp, next door to Delhi, gathered at Nehru's residence in the first week of August, 'complaining' against an allowance of 'Rs. 50',[379] regardless of family numbers.

Simultaneously, from Moscow, the Indian embassy was reporting the Soviet officials bringing up the CPI in their conversations. Ambassador Radhakrishnan was telling them that the objection was to the 'communist hostility to religion and its violent methods' while conveying the home ministry's conditions of commitment to 'parliamentary means....'[380] Nehru met a communist legislator from Bengal who claimed that they were being 'hunted' and they could stop 'provided they would not be shot ...', leaving an uneasy prime minister asking Ayyangar, 'how are we to deal with these people?'[381] He was clearer on not letting any political party have specific facilities from the information and broadcasting ministry for election broadcasts, as this hinged on giving airtime to recognised parties, which though reopened the recognition question for the CPI and Nehru did not know 'where to draw the line'.[382] By now, the CPI had a 'clear political line', which had come from conversations in Moscow in March 1951, when Stalin had plainly observed to S. A. Dange and others that 'the government of Nehru is not as unsteady as it seems.... Do not think that the government being a sham will fall'.[383]

Finally, among the states, the only one under governor's rule was arresting people under preventive detention, as Trivedi disliked 'the difficulty of obtaining ... convictions in a court of law'. This was accompanied by an anti-corruption drive in faction-ridden departments and taking care of Bhargava's transfers or appointments, restructuring and irregularities, like refusing advertisements to *Hind Samachar* (editor Lala Jagat Narain, secretary of the Pradesh Congress) and *Prabhat* (Tara Singh's paper), all of which had created, what Trivedi called, 'gangs of Rai Sikhs, Virks, Jats and Brahmins'. On the upside, the Bhakra–Nangal project's technical report and betterment fee bill were finalised, 1,78,000 tons of wheat and 20,000 tons of gram were procured and a tenants' protection bill was finalised. For a frontier state, East Punjab seemed relatively calm, and Trivedi merely mentioned 'some civil defence in border towns', as his intelligence unit was more interested in reporting that Giani Kartar Singh was joining hands with General Mohan Singh of the Forward Bloc, 'with the support of Baldev Singh'.[384]

NOTES

1   19 December 1950, Nehru to Ambedkar, File No. 68 (Part II), JN (SG) Papers.
2   19 December 1950, Roy to Nehru, File No. 68 (Part II), JN (SG) Papers.
3   21–22 December 1950, Nanda to Nehru, File No. 68 (Part II), JN (SG) Papers.
4   23 December 1950, Cabinet meeting, File No. 69 (Part I), JN (SG) Papers.
5   20 December 1950, Nehru to Sri Prakasa, File No. 68 (Part II), JN (SG) Papers.
6   23 December 1950, Nehru to Ayyangar, File No. 69 (Part I), JN (SG) Papers.
7   27 December 1950, Nehru to Maharaj Singh, File No. 69 (Part I), JN (SG) Papers.
8   25 December 1950, Nehru to Kher, File No. 69 (Part I), JN (SG) Papers.
9   31 December 1950, Nehru to S. N. Mozumdar (Chairman, DVC), File. No. 69 (Part II), JN (SG) Papers. Hart, *New India's Rivers*, 136–44, and 203–22.
10   23 January 1951, Madras government to F&A, New Delhi, File No. 71 (Part I), JN (SG) Papers.
11   31 December 1950, Nehru to Gaekwad of Baroda, File No. 69 (Part II), JN (SG) Papers.
12   27 December 1950, Hamidullah to Nehru, File No. 69 (Part II), JN (SG) Papers.
13   25 January 1951, Aga Khan to Nehru, File No. 72 (Part I), JN (SG) Papers.
14   7 February 1951, Nehru to chief ministers, File No. 72 (Part II) and 19 February 1951, Nehru to Rajagopalachari, File No. 73 (Part II), JN (SG) Papers.
15   25 January 1951, Patna–New Delhi exchange, File No. 71 (Part I), JN (SG) Papers. See Niloufer Bhagwat, 'Institutionalising Detention without Trial', *Economic and Political Weekly* 13, no. 11 (1978): 510–13.
16   Sajal Nag, 'Nehru and the Nagas: Minority Nationalism and the Post-Colonial State', *Economic and Political Weekly* 44, no. 49 (2009): 48–55; and U. Misra, 'The Naga National Question', *Economic and Political Weekly* 13, no. 14 (1978): 618–24.
17   25 January 1951, Nehru to Doulatram, File No. 71 (Part I), JN (SG) Papers.
18   4 February 1951, Nehru to Doulatram, File No. 72 (Part I), JN (SG) Papers.
19   2–3 February 1951, Nehru to Medhi, File No. 72 (Part I), JN (SG) Papers. See Sajal Nag, 'Nehru and the North-East' (NMML Occasional Paper, [History and Society], New Series 75), 1–57.
20   I borrow this term from Badri Narayan.
21   1 February 1951, Nehru to chief ministers, File No. 72 (Part I), JN (SG) Papers. See Reeves, 'The Congress and the Abolition of Zamindari in Uttar Pradesh'.
22   5 February 1951, Note by Rup Narain, Secretary (Socialist Party), File No. 73 (Part II), JN (SG) Papers.
23   5 February 1951, Nehru to Bhargava, File No. 72 (Part I), JN (SG) Papers.
24   7 February 1951, Nehru to chief ministers, File No. 72 (Part II), JN (SG) Papers. See B. Hettne, 'The Vitality of Gandhian Tradition', *Journal of Peace Research* 13, no. 3 (1976): 227–45.
25   20 February 1951, Nanda's note, File No. 73 (Part II), JN (SG) Papers.
26   5 February 1951, New Delhi to Washington, File No. 72 (Part I), JN (SG) Papers.

27   13 February 1951, Nehru to Deshmukh, File No. 73 (Part I), JN (SG) Papers.

28   4 February 1951, Nehru to Munshi, Pant and Bhargava, File No. 72 (Part II), JN (SG) Papers.

29   8 February 1951, Nehru to Munshi, File No. 72 (Part II), JN (SG) Papers.

30   10 February 1951, Nehru to PPS, File No. 72 (Part II), JN (SG) Papers.

31   6 February 1951, Nehru to PPS, File No. 72 (Part II), JN (SG) Papers.

32   13 February 1951, Nehru to Munshi, and 24 February 1951, Nehru to Deshmukh, Files No. 73 (Part I) and 74, JN (SG) Papers.

33   6 February 1951, Nehru to filmmaker John, File No. 72 (Part II), JN (SG) Papers.

34   12 February 1951, Nehru to Deshmukh, and 15 February 1951, Gadgil to Nehru, File No. 73 (Part I), JN (SG) Papers.

35   11 and 12 February 1951, Nehru to Tandon and Deshmukh, File No. 73 (Part I), JN (SG) Papers.

36   15 February 1951, Meeting of the Cabinet (Case No. 26/6/51), File No. 73 (Part I), JN (SG) Papers.

37   Runi Datta, 'Emancipating and Strengthening Indian Women: An Analysis of B. R. Ambedkar's Contribution', *Contemporary Voice of Dalit* 11, no. 1 (2019): 25–32.

38   15 February 1951, Ambedkar to Nehru, File No. 73 (Part II), JN (SG) Papers.

39   19 February 1951, Nehru to Ambedkar, File No. 73 (Part II), JN (SG) Papers.

40   27 February 1951, Nehru to S. N. Sinha and Ambedkar, File No. 74, JN (SG) Papers.

41   21 February 1951, Note from Mridula Sarabhai, File No. 74, JN (SG) Papers.

42   25 and 26 February 1951, Nehru to Mahtab and Munshi, File No. 74, JN (SG) Papers.

43   20 January 1951, J. C. Gupta to Nehru, and 23 February 1951, Ghosh to Nehru, File No. 75, JN (SG) Papers.

44   28 February 1951, Note on AICC and Nehru to Deshmukh/Munshi, File No. 74, JN (SG) Papers.

45   23 February 1951, Nehru to Rajagopalachari and 28 February 1951, Nehru to Jagjivan Ram, File No. 74, JN (SG) Papers.

46   21 February 1951, File No. 74, JN (SG) Papers. Conversely, the biggest travellers were Mahtab (INR 13,767), Kidwai (INR 11,169), Keskar (INR 10,333) and Jagjivan Ram (INR 8,127).

47   File No. 74, JN (SG) Papers.

48   24 February 1951, Ram Narain Singh to Tandon, File No. 74, JN (SG) Papers.

49   27 February 1951, Nehru to Bhargava, File No. 74, JN (SG) Papers.

50   14 February 1951, Kidwai to Nehru, File No. 75, JN (SG) Papers.

51   Myron Weiner, ed., *State Politics in India* (Princeton: Princeton University Press, 1968), 321–98.

52   28 February 1951, Kidwai to Nehru, File No. 74, JN (SG) Papers.

53   27 February 1951, Nehru to Ayyangar, File No. 74, JN (SG) Papers.

54   6 March 1951, Kidwai to Nehru, File No. 76 (Part I), JN (SG) Papers.

55   6 March 1951, Nehru to Kidwai, File No. 76 (Part I), JN (SG) Papers.

56   2 March 1951, Vyas–Ayyangar–Nehru exchange, File No. 76 (Part I), JN (SG) Papers.

57   Jairam Ramesh, *A Chequered Brilliance: The Many Lives of V. K. Krishna Menon* (Delhi: Penguin, 2019), ch. 12.

58   27 February 1951, Nehru to Krishna Menon, File No. 74, JN (SG) Papers.

59   21 February 1951, Deshmukh to Nehru, File No. 74, JN (SG) Papers.

60   3 March 1951, Krishna Menon to H. M. Patel, File No. 76 (Part I), JN (SG) Papers.

61   28 February 1951, Nehru to G. M. Huggins, File No. 74, JN (SG) Papers.

62   28 February 1951, Nehru to Subimal Dutt, File No. 74, JN (SG) Papers.

63   11 March 1951, Chand to K. P. S. Menon, Subimal Dutt and Dharma Vira, File No. 75, JN (SG) Papers.

64   7 July 1951, Nehru–Cariappa Meeting (No. 15555/A/MO3), File No. 71 (Part II), JN (SG) Papers.

65   15 February 1951, Rajagopalachari to Nehru, File No. 75, JN (SG) Papers.

66   19 February 1951, Mathai to Nehru, File No. 75, JN (SG) Papers.

67   8 March 1951, Rajagopalachari to Nehru, File No. 76 (Part II), JN (SG) Papers.

68   2 March 1951, Nehru to Baldev Singh, File No. 76 (Part I), JN (SG) Papers.

69   8 March 1951, Baldev Singh to Nehru, File No. 75, JN (SG) Papers. See Mehar Singh Gill, 'Politics of Population Census Data in India', *Economic and Political Weekly* 42, no. 3 (2007): 241–49.

70   6 March 1951, Swaran Singh to Baldev Singh, File No. 75, JN (SG) Papers.

71   15 March 1951, P. V. Bhaskaran (IB) to Iengar, V. P. Menon and Dharma Vira, File No. 75, JN (SG) Papers.

72   1–2 March 1951, Nehru to Kairon, File No. 76 (Part I), JN (SG) Papers.

73   1–2 March 1951, Nehru to Bhargava and Trivedi, File No. 76 (Part I), JN (SG) Papers.

74   11 March 1951, Trivedi to Nehru, File No. 76 (Part II), JN (SG) Papers.

75   3 March 1951, Note by Vishnu Sahay, File No. 75, JN (SG) Papers.

76   See H. Bhattacharya, 'Communism, Nationalism and Tribal Question in Tripura', *Economic and Political Weekly* 25, no. 39 (1990): 2209–14.

77   14–15 March 1951, Mullik's report, File No. 75, JN (SG) Papers. See D. P. Chaya, 'Proximity or Sycophancy? The Relationship between Intelligence and Policy in the Nehruvian Era, 1947–64', *South Asia: Journal of South Asian Studies* 45, no. 4 (2022): 621–36.

78   27 March 1951, K. Sankaran Nair to P. N. Haksar, File No. 75, JN (SG) Papers. See Paul M. McGarr, 'Quiet Americans in India: The CIA and the Politics of Intelligence in Cold War South Asia', *Diplomatic History* 38, no. 5 (2014): 1046–82.

79   1 March 1951, Rajagopalachari to Nehru, File No. 76 (Part I), JN (SG) Papers.

80   16 March 1951, Nehru to Munshi, File No. 77 (Part I), JN (SG) Papers.

81   22 March 1951, Asaf Ali to Nehru, File No. 75, JN (SG) Papers.

82   22 March 1951, Ali to Rajagopalachari, File No. 75, JN (SG) Papers. V. P. Menon was sent there in 1952.

83 See Romila Thapar, *Somanatha: The Many Voices of a History* (London: Verso, 2005), 195–225.

84 2 March 1951, Prasad to Nehru, File No. 76 (Part I), JN (SG) Papers.

85 2 March 1951, Nehru to Prasad, File No. 76 (Part I), JN (SG) Papers.

86 10 March 1951, Prasad to Nehru, File No. 76 (Part II), JN (SG) Papers.

87 11 March 1951, Nehru to Rajagopalachari, File No. 76 (Part II), JN (SG) Papers. Singh, *Patel, Prasad and Rajaji*, 70–121.

88 See M. K. Singh Sisodia, 'India and the Asian Games: From Infancy to Maturity', *Sport in Society: Cultures, Commerce, Media, Politics* 8, no. 3 (2005): 404–13.

89 B. C. Mathur, 'Administrative Reforms', *Indian Journal of Public Administration* 31, no. 3 (1985): 548–60.

90 2 March 1951, Nehru to chief ministers, File No. 76 (Part I), JN (SG) Papers.

91 3 March 1951, P. Y. Deshpande to Nehru, File No. 76 (Part I), JN (SG) Papers.

92 3 March 1951, Dayabhai Patel to Nehru, File No. 76 (Part I), JN (SG) Papers.

93 8 March 1951, Jain to Nehru (No. 735/PSMR), File No. 76 (Part II), JN (SG) Papers.

94 9 March 1951, Nehru to Dayabhai Patel, File No. 76 (Part II), JN (SG) Papers.

95 4 March 1951, Azam Jah to Nehru, File No. 76 (Part I), JN (SG) Papers.

96 28 February 1951, Nehru to Ayyangar, File No. 76 (Part I), JN (SG) Papers. See Afsar Mohammad, *Remaking History: 1948 Police Action and the Muslims of Hyderabad* (Cambridge: Cambridge University Press, 2023).

97 9 March 1951, Ayyangar to Nehru, File No. 76 (Part II), JN (SG) Papers.

98 4 March 1951, Trivedi to Nehru, File No. 76 (Part I), JN (SG) Papers.

99 6 March 1951, Nehru's note, File No. 76 (Part I), JN (SG) Papers.

100 6 March 1951, Nehru to Dharma Vira, File No. 76 (Part I), JN (SG) Papers.

101 11 March 1951, Nehru to Dharma Vira, File No. 76 (Part II), JN (SG) Papers. See U. K. Singh and A. Roy, *Election Commission of India: Institutionalising Democratic Uncertainties* (Oxford: Oxford University Press, 2019), ch. 1.

102 6 March 1951, Nehru to Ayyangar, File No. 76 (Part I), JN (SG) Papers.

103 8 March 1951, Nehru to Ayyangar, File No. 76 (Part I), JN (SG) Papers.

104 24 March 1951, R. S. Agrawal to Nehru, File No. 78 (Part II), JN (SG) Papers.

105 27 February 1951, Kripalani to Tandon, File No. 76 (Part I), JN (SG) Papers.

106 1–2 March 1951, Kripalani–Nehru exchange, File No. 76 (Part I), JN (SG) Papers.

107 5 March 1951, Kripalani–Nehru exchange, File No. 76 (Part I), JN (SG) Papers.

108 8 March 1951, Kripalani to Nehru, File No. 76 (Part I), JN (SG) Papers. See Weiner, *Party Politics in India*, 98–116.

109 9 March 1951, Nehru to Azad and Jain, File No. 76 (Part II), JN (SG) Papers.

110 15 March 1951, Nehru to Jain, File No. 77 (Part I), JN (SG) Papers.

111 24 March 1951, Nehru to Jain, File No. 78 (Part I), JN (SG) Papers.

112 W. W. M. Yeatts, 'The Indian Census of 1941', *Journal of the Royal Society of Arts* 91, no. 4634 (1943): 182–94.

113 6 March 1951, Nagoke to Nehru, File No. 76 (Part II), JN (SG) Papers. See L. M. Khubchandani, 'A Demographic Typology for Hindi, Urdu, Panjabi

Speakers in South Asia', in *Language and Society: Anthropological Issues*, ed. W. C. McCormack and S. A. Wurm (The Hague: Moulton, 1979), 183–94.

114   10 March 1951, Nehru to Nagoke, File No. 76 (Part II), JN (SG) Papers.

115   16–18 March 1951, Nagoke–Nehru correspondence, File No. 77 (Part I), JN (SG) Papers.

116   9 March 1951, Nehru to Bhargava and Trivedi to Nehru, File No. 76 (Part II), JN (SG) Papers.

117   18 March 1951, Nehru to Bhargava, File No. 77 (Part I), JN (SG) Papers.

118   26 March 1951, Bhargava to Nehru, File No. 78 (Part I), JN (SG) Papers.

119   See Ramashray Roy, 'Intra-Party Conflict in the Bihar Congress', *Asian Survey* 6, no. 12 (1966): 706–15.

120   12 and 18 March 1951, Sinha–Nehru correspondence, File No. 76 (Part II), JN (SG) Papers.

121   13 March 1951, Kumaraswamy Raja to Nehru, File No. 76 (Part II), JN (SG) Papers. See P. K. Tripathi, 'Preventive Detention: The Indian Experience', *American Journal of Comparative Law* 9 (1960): 219.

122   18 March 1951, Nehru to Raja, File No. 77 (Part I), JN (SG) Papers. See Kalyani Ramnath, 'ADM Jabalpur's Antecedents: Political Emergencies, Civil Liberties, and Arguments from Colonial Continuities in India', *American University International Law Review* 31 (2016): 209.

123   14 March 1951, B. V. Keskar to Nehru, File No. 76 (Part II), JN (SG) Papers. See Laurence Gautier, 'Crisis of the "Nehruvian Consensus" or Pluralization of Indian Politics? Aligarh Muslim University and the Demand for Minority Status', *Samaj* 22 (2019), accessed 12 May 2024, https://doi.org/10.4000/samaj.6493.

124   26 March 1951, Nehru to Pant, File No. 78 (Part I), JN (SG) Papers.

125   19 February 1951, Chief Editor *Chavhata Weekly* to Nehru, File No. 78 (Part I), JN (SG) Papers.

126   15 March 1951, Arun Chandra Guha to Nehru, File No. 77 (Part I), JN (SG) Papers.

127   See Hugh McPherson, 'The Indian Province of Bihar and Orissa: Its History, Physical Features, and Land Problems', *Scottish Geographical Magazine* 47, no. 1 (1931): 1–19.

128   Medha Bhattacharya, 'Linguistic Minorities and Strategic Mobilisation in Eastern India: Bengali-Biharis During the Era of Linguistic Territorialism (1935–57)', *The Indian Economic and Social History Review* 60, no. 3 (2023): 275–300.

129   16 March 1951, Nehru to Bishnuram Medhi, File No. 77 (Part I), JN (SG) Papers.

130   23 March 1951, Prasad to Nehru, File No. 78 (Part I), JN (SG) Papers.

131   15 March 1951, Kher to Nehru, File No. 77 (Part I), JN (SG) Papers.

132   22 March 1951, Cabinet meeting (case no. 71/14/51), File No. 78 (Part I), JN (SG) Papers.

133   26 March 1951, Kher to Nehru, File No. 78 (Part I), JN (SG) Papers.

134 17 March 1951, B. Das (MP) to Nehru, File No. 77 (Part I), JN (SG) Papers. Stephen Merrett, 'The Growth of Indian Nitrogen Fertilizer Manufacture: Some Lessons for Industrial Planning', *Journal of Development Studies* 8, no. 4 (1972): 395–410.

135 17 March 1951, Nehru's note, File No. 77 (Part I), JN (SG) Papers. See Kalathmika Natarajan, 'The Privilege of the Indian Passport (1947–1967): Caste, Class, and the Afterlives of Indenture in Indian Diplomacy', *Modern Asian Studies* 57, no. 2 (2023): 321–50.

136 15 March 1951, Cabinet's decision, File No. 77 (Part I), JN (SG) Papers.

137 23 March 1951, Nehru to Rajagopalachari, File No. 78 (Part I), JN (SG) Papers.

138 20 March 1951, Padmaja Naidu, Kashinath Rao Vaidya, Shridhar Vaman Naik, Bakar Ali Mirza, Annarao Ganamukhi and Puli Ramaswamy to S. N. Sinha, File No. 78 (Part I), JN (SG) Papers.

139 26 March 1951, Kidwai to Nehru, File No. 78 (Part I), JN (SG) Papers.

140 31 March 1951, Ayyangar to Nehru, File No. 78 (Part II), JN (SG) Papers.

141 File No. 79 (Part I), JN (SG) Papers. For two contextual readings, see A. Murali, ed., *Putchalapalli Sundarayya: An Autobiography* (New Delhi: National Book Trust, 2009); and Sujata Gidla, *Ants Among Elephants: An Untouchable Family and the Making of Modern India* (New York: Faber & Faber, 2017).

142 30 March 1951, Nehru to Tandon, File No. 78 (Part II), JN (SG) Papers.

143 6 April 1951, Tandon to Nehru, File No. 79 (Part I), JN (SG) Papers.

144 Undated, late-March 1951, New Delhi to Moscow, File No. 79 (Part I), JN (SG) Papers.

145 31 March 1951, Deshmukh to Rajagopalachari and 4 April 1951, Rajagopalachari to Nehru, File No. 79 (Part I), JN (SG) Papers.

146 5 April 1951, Cabinet meeting (case no. 97/17/51), File No. 79 (Part I), JN (SG) Papers.

147 31 March 1951, Nehru to Bhargava, File No. 78 (Part II), JN (SG) Papers.

148 3 April 1951, Trivedi's memorandum, File No. 79 (Part I), JN (SG) Papers.

149 3 April 1951, Naidu's speech, File No. 79 (Part II), JN (SG) Papers. The next few quotes come from here.

150 6 April 1951, Monckton to Nehru, File No. 80 (Part I), JN (SG) Papers.

151 6 April 1951, Khub Chand to Subimal Dutt, File No. 79 (Part II), JN (SG) Papers.

152 6 April 1951, Nehru to Ayyangar, File No. 80 (Part I), JN (SG) Papers.

153 19 April 1951, Ayyangar's note, File No. 81 (Part I), JN (SG) Papers.

154 9 April 1951, Azad to Nehru, File No. 79 (Part II), JN (SG) Papers.

155 10 April 1951, Nehru to Sen, File No. 79 (Part II), JN (SG) Papers. See Singh, 'A Century of Constituency Delimitation in India'.

156 11 April 1951, MHA/IB report, File No. 80 (Part I), JN (SG) Papers.

157 7 April 1951, Santhanam to Nehru, File No. 79 (Part II), JN (SG) Papers.

158 10 April 1951, File No. 80 (Part I), JN (SG) Papers.

159 16 April 1951, Hamidullah to Nehru, File No. 80 (Part II), JN (SG) Papers.

160 File No. 81 (Part I), JN (SG) Papers.

161 24 April 1951, Ayyangar's note, File No. 82 (Part I), JN (SG) Papers.

162 11–18 April 1951, Nehru–Trivedi exchange, File Nos. 80 (Part I) and 81 (Part I), JN (SG) Papers.

163 11 April 1951, Nehru to Raja, File No. 80 (Part I), JN (SG) Papers. See Satish Deshpande, 'Reservation and the Republic: One Constitution, Two Amendments and Seven Decades', *Social Change* 49, no. 3 (2019): 512–18.

164 16 April 1951, Nehru to Ambedkar, File No. 80 (Part III), JN (SG) Papers.

165 21 April 1951, Ambedkar to Rajagopalachari, File No. 81 (Part II), JN (SG) Papers.

166 File No. 80 (Part I), JN (SG) Papers.

167 12 April 1951, Nehru to Rauf, File No. 80 (Part I), JN (SG) Papers.

168 12 April 1951, Cabinet Meeting (case no. 107/18/51), File No. 80 (Part I), JN (SG) Papers.

169 13 April 1951, Nehru to Roy, Pant, Kher, Chaudhuri and Sinha, File No. 80 (Part I), JN (SG) Papers.

170 15 April 1951, Kripalani and Kidwai to Nehru, File No. 80 (Part III), JN (SG) Papers.

171 17 April 1951, Nehru to Panikkar, File No. 80 (Part III), JN (SG) Papers.

172 21 March 1951, Panikkar to Nehru, File No. 80 (Part III), JN (SG) Papers.

173 18 April 1951, Munshi to Nehru, File No. 81 (Part I), JN (SG) Papers.

174 22 April 1951, Nehru to Munshi, File No. 81 (Part II), JN (SG) Papers.

175 Undated, April 1951, Review Note, File No. 81 (Part I), JN (SG) Papers.

176 19 April 1951, Nehru to Ajit Jain, File No. 81 (Part I), JN (SG) Papers.

177 19 April 1951, Nehru to Baldev Singh, File No. 81 (Part I), JN (SG) Papers.

178 19 April 1951, Nehru's note (No. 2627-PM), File No. 81 (Part I), JN (SG) Papers. See Daniel Marston, *The Indian Army, and the End of the Raj* (Cambridge: Cambridge University Press, 2014), 239–80.

179 19 April 1951, Hamidullah to Nehru, File No. 81 (Part I), JN (SG) Papers.

180 18 April 1951, Nehru to Ayyangar, File No. 81 (Part I), JN (SG) Papers. See Geeta Thatra, 'Differentiated Rehabilitation and the Geographies of Unfreedom in Post-Colonial Bombay', *Journal of Sindhi Studies* 7, no. 2 (2022): 1–40.

181 See C. Jaffrelot and L. Gayer, eds., *Muslims in Indian Cities: Trajectories of Marginalisation* (London: Hurst, 2012).

182 18 April 1951, Nehru to Ayyangar, File No. 81 (Part I), JN (SG) Papers.

183 18 April 1951, Nehru–Trivedi exchange, File No. 81 (Part I), JN (SG) Papers.

184 19 April 1951, Nehru's note, File No. 81 (Part I), JN (SG) Papers.

185 21 and 24 April 1951, Nehru to Jain, File Nos. 81 (Part II) and 82 (Part I), JN (SG) Papers.

186 See P. Sundarayya, *Telangana People's Struggle and Its Lessons*, Part II (Calcutta: Ganashakti, 1972); and, J. A. Curran (Jr.), 'Dissension among India's Communists', *Far Eastern Survey* 19, no. 13 (1950): 132–36.

187 18 April 1951, Mullik's note, File No. 81 (Part II), JN (SG) Papers.

188 20 April 1951, Deshmukh to Nehru, File No. 81 (Part II), JN (SG) Papers.

189 22–23 April 1951, Nehru–Roy exchange, File Nos. 81 (Part II) and 82 (Part I), JN (SG) Papers.

190   13 April 1951, Report on the Sammelan, File No. 82 (Part I), JN (SG) Papers.

191   See Taylor C. Sherman, 'A Gandhian Answer to the Threat of Communism? Sarvodaya and Postcolonial Nationalism in India', *Indian Economic and Social History Review* 53, no. 2 (2016): 249–70.

192   See Venu Madhav Govindu and Deepak Malghan, *The Web of Freedom: J. C. Kumarappa and Gandhi's Struggle for Economic Justice* (New Delhi: Oxford University Press, 2016).

193   22 April 1951, Kumaraswamy Raja to Nehru, File No. 82 (Part I), JN (SG) Papers.

194   L. Brennan, J. McDonald and R. Shlomowitz, 'Caste, Inequality and the Nation-state: The Impact of Reservation Policies in India, c. 1950–2000', *South Asia: Journal of South Asian Studies* 29, no. 1 (2006): 117–62.

195   23–25 April 1951, Nehru–Pant (with Shukla and others) exchange, File No. 82 (Part I), JN (SG) Papers.

196   24 April 1951, Nehru to D. R. Jadeja, File No. 82 (Part I), JN (SG) Papers.

197   23 April 1951, Cabinet meeting (case no. 131/20/51), File No. 82 (Part I), JN (SG) Papers.

198   24 April 1951, Munshi to Nehru, File No. 82 (Part I), JN (SG) Papers. The next few quotes come from here.

199   V. B. Kulkarni, *K. M. Munshi: Builders of Modern India* (New Delhi: Publications Division, 1959).

200   24 April 1951, Munshi to Nehru, File No. 82 (Part I), JN (SG) Papers.

201   28 April 1951, Nehru to Diwakar, File No. 82 (Part II), JN (SG) Papers.

202   25 April 1951, Ambedkar to Nehru, File No. 82 (Part I), JN (SG) Papers. This para quotes from here.

203   Roy, *The Partition of India*, 112.

204   13–19/20 April 1951, Gundevia to Menon, File No. 82 (Part II), JN (SG) Papers.

205   Sunil Amrith, *Decolonizing International Health: India and Southeast Asia, 1930–65* (London: Palgrave Macmillan, 2006), 99–120.

206   25 April 1951, Kaur to Prakasa, File No. 82 (Part II), JN (SG) Papers.

207   27 April 1951, Nehru to Balkrishna Sharma, File No. 82 (Part II), JN (SG) Papers.

208   27 April 1951, Zarif to Nehru and 28 April 1951, Nehru to Azad, File No. 82 (Part II), JN (SG) Papers.

209   30 April 1951, Munshi to Nehru, File No. 82 (Part II), JN (SG) Papers.

210   28 April 1951, Nehru to Trivedi, File No. 82 (Part II), JN (SG) Papers.

211   28 April 1951, Gadgil to Nehru, File No. 82 (Part II), JN (SG) Papers.

212   2 May 1951, Nehru to chief ministers, File No. 83 (Part I), JN (SG) Papers.

213   4 May 1951, Kidwai to Nehru, File No. 83 (Part I), JN (SG) Papers. See Pran Chopra, *Rafi Ahmad Kidwai: His Life and Work* (Agra: S. L. Agarwala, 1960), 110–26, and 143–57.

214   6–7 May 1951, Kidwai–Nehru exchange, File No. 83 (Part II), JN (SG) Papers.

215   6 May 1951, Baldev Singh to Nehru, File No. 83 (Part II), JN (SG) Papers. Wilkinson, *Army, and Nation*, 86–123.

216 9 May 1951, Nehru to Jairamdas Doulatram, File No. 84 (Part I), JN (SG) Papers. See Sanjib Baruah, *In the Name of the Nation: India and Its Northeast* (Stanford: Stanford University Press, 2020), ch. 4.

217 22 April 1951, Moon's report, File No. 84 (Part I), JN (SG) Papers.

218 8 May 1951, Trivedi to Nehru, File No. 83 (Part II), JN (SG) Papers.

219 8 May 1951, Deshmukh to Nehru, File No. 83 (Part II), JN (SG) Papers.

220 10 May 1951, Kripalani to Mahtab, File No. 84 (Part I), JN (SG) Papers.

221 11 May 1951, Mahtab (DO No. 107/HM/Res) to Nehru, File No. 84 (Part I), JN (SG) Papers.

222 See Tara Chand, *Influence of Islam on Indian Culture* (Oxford: Oxford University Press, 1922).

223 See Khushwant Singh, *A History of the Sikhs: 1469–1838* (Oxford: Oxford University Press, 1963); and Kate Brittlebank, *Tiger: The Life of Tipu Sultan* (New Delhi: Juggernaut, 2016), for examples.

224 On Bijapur, see Manan Ahmed Asif, *The Loss of Hindustan: The Invention of India* (Cambridge: Harvard University Press, 2020).

225 12 May 1951, Sampurnanand to Nehru/Azad, File No. 84 (Part I), JN (SG) Papers. This paragraph and the next quote from this letter. See William Gould, 'Contesting Secularism in Colonial and Postcolonial North India between the 1930 and 1950s', *Contemporary South Asia* 14, no. 4 (2005): 481–94.

226 For UP as 'the postcolonial "heartland"', see Gyanesh Kudaisya, *Region, Nation, 'Heartland': Uttar Pradesh in India's Body Politic* (New Delhi: Sage, 2006), Part IV.

227 28 March 1951, Mavalankar to Nehru (No. D.901/51), File No. 84 (Part II), JN (SG) Papers.

228 16 May 1951, Nehru to Mavalankar, File No. 84 (Part II), JN (SG) Papers.

229 8 May 1951, Phizo to Sri Prakasa, File No. 84 (Part II), JN (SG) Papers.

230 13–14 May 1951, Nehru to Doulatram and J. N. Hazarika, File No. 84 (Part II), JN (SG) Papers.

231 19 May 1951, Nehru to B. Das, File No. 85 (Part I), JN (SG) Papers.

232 22 May 1951, Nehru to Doulatram, File No. 85 (Part II), JN (SG) Papers.

233 16 May 1951, Phizo's speech and 29 May 1951, Doulatram to Nehru, File No. 87 (Part I), JN (SG) Papers.

234 See Oliver Godsmark, *Citizenship, Community, and Democracy in India: From Bombay to Maharashtra* (Abingdon: Routledge, 2018), ch. 3.

235 12–19 May 1951, Kher–Nehru exchange, File Nos. 84 (Part II) and 85 (Part I), JN (SG) Papers.

236 13 May 1951, Nehru to Shukla, File No. 84 (Part II), JN (SG) Papers.

237 15 May 1951, Pakvasa to Nehru, File No. 85 (Part I), JN (SG) Papers.

238 23 June 1951, Nehru to Shukla, File No. 89 (Part I), JN (SG) Papers.

239 14 May 1951, Nehru to Tandon and 15 May 1951, Nagoke to Nehru, File No. 84 (Part II), JN (SG) Papers.

240 16 May 1951, File No. 84 (Part II), JN (SG) Papers.

241 16 May 1951, Chaman Lall to Nehru, File No. 85 (Part I), JN (SG) Papers.

242 17 May 1951, Nehru to Prasad, File No. 85 (Part I), JN (SG) Papers.

243 21 May 1951, Iengar's note, File No. 85 (Part II), JN (SG) Papers.
244 Indira Patel and Bipin Patel, eds., *Snapshots of History: Through the Writings of HVR Iengar* (Mumbai: Ananya, 2002).
245 23 May 1951, Nehru to Rajagopalachari and Prasad, File No. 86 (Part I), JN (SG) Papers.
246 25 and 28 May 1951, Nehru to Rajagopalachari, File Nos. 86 (Part I and Part II), JN (SG) Papers. See Javed Iqbal Wani, *Sovereign Anxiety: Public Order and the Politics of Control in India, 1915–1955* (New Delhi: Cambridge University Press, 2023), 1–40.
247 17 May 1951, Nehru to chief ministers and 18 May 1951, Nehru to Rajagopalachari, File No. 85 (Part I), JN (SG) Papers.
248 19 May 1951, Trivedi to Nehru, File No. 85 (Part I), JN (SG) Papers.
249 See Hilal Ahmed, 'Researching India's Muslims: Identities, Methods, Politics', *Journal of Ethnographic Theory* 10, no. 3 (2020): 776–85.
250 16 May 1951, Vakil to Nehru, File No. 85 (Part II), JN (SG) Papers.
251 19 May 1951, V. K. R. V. Rao's note on 'the Bihar Food Crisis', File No. 85 (Part II), JN (SG) Papers.
252 22 May 1951, Vishnu Sahay's note on 'import position', File No. 85 (Part II), JN (SG) Papers.
253 23 May 1951, Trivedi to Nehru, File No. 86 (Part I), JN (SG) Papers.
254 20 May 1951, Mahmud to Nehru, File No. 85 (Part II), JN (SG) Papers. See Papiya Ghosh, 'Writing Ganga-Jamni: In the 1940s and After', *Social Scientist* 34, nos. 11/12 (2006): i–xx.
255 20 May 1951, Nehru to Gupta, File No. 85 (Part II), JN (SG) Papers. See Arudra Burra, 'Freedom of Speech in the Early Constitution: A Study of the Constitution (First Amendment) Bill', in *The Indian Constituent Assembly*, ed. Bhatia.
256 21 May 1951, Gupta to Nehru, File No. 85 (Part II), JN (SG) Papers.
257 25 May 1951, Gupta to Nehru, File No. 86 (Part I), JN (SG) Papers.
258 25 May 1951, Nehru to Gupta and 30 May 1951, Nehru to Sinha, File Nos. 86 (Part I) and 87 (Part I), JN (SG) Papers.
259 2 June 1951, Nehru to chief ministers, File No. 87 (Part I), JN (SG) Papers.
260 Gautam Chakrabarti, 'From Moscow with Love: Soviet Cultural Politics across India in the Cold War', *Safundi* 20, no. 2 (2019): 239–57.
261 1 November 1950, Iengar to Mathai, File No. 62 (Part I), JN (SG) Papers.
262 30–31 May 1951, Rajagopalachari's and Nehru's notes, File No. 87 (Part I), JN (SG) Papers.
263 1 June 1951, Rajagopalachari's note, File No. 87 (Part I), JN (SG) Papers.
264 1 June 1951, Nehru's note, File No. 87 (Part I), JN (SG) Papers.
265 See Günter Wernicke, 'The Unity of Peace and Socialism? The WPC on Cold War Tightrope between the Peace Struggle and Intra-systematic Communist Conflicts', *Peace and Change* 26, no. 3 (2001): 332–51.
266 25 June 1951, Nehru to Rajagopalachari, File No. 89 (Part II), JN (SG) Papers.
267 1 June 1951, Nehru to Kumaraswamy Raja, File No. 87 (Part I), JN (SG) Papers.

268   1 and 5 June 1951, Nehru to S. K. Sinha, File No. 87 (Parts I and II), JN (SG) Papers.

269   6 June 1951, Nehru to Sinha, File No. 87 (Part II), JN (SG) Papers. See Stephen Henningham, 'Bureaucracy and Control in India's Great Landed Estates: The Raj Darbhanga of Bihar, 1879 to 1950', *Modern Asian Studies* 17, no. 1 (1983): 35–57.

270   23 June 1951, Nehru to Sinha, File No. 89 (Part I), JN (SG) Papers.

271   1 June 1951, Trivedi to Nehru, File No. 87 (Part I), JN (SG) Papers.

272   7 June 1951, Trivedi to Nehru, File No. 88 (Part I), JN (SG) Papers.

273   S. C. Arora, *President's Rule in Indian States: A Study of Punjab* (New Delhi: Mittal, 1990), 71–92.

274   May 1951, 'Festival of Crime', File No. 88 (Part I), JN (SG) Papers.

275   6 June 1951, MHA memorandum (23/10/51-Ests.) on MoD letter no. 1059-O/D (GS) dated 7 March 1951, File No. 87 (Part II), JN (SG) Papers. See Jean A. Curran (Jr.), 'The RSS: Militant Hinduism', *Far Eastern Survey* 19, no. 10 (1950): 93–98.

276   Undated, June 1951, Doulatram to Nehru (No. GAL/407/51), File No. 88 (Part I), JN (SG) Papers.

277   4 June 1951, JP's meeting with the Planning Commission, File No. 88 (Part I), JN (SG) Papers.

278   9 June 1951, Malaviya to Nehru, File No. 88 (Part I), JN (SG) Papers. Brass, *Factional Politics in an Indian State*, 167–203.

279   8–9 June 1951, Nehru–Mahtab exchange, File No. 88 (Part I), JN (SG) Papers.

280   9 June 1951, Nehru to Rajagopalachari, File No. 88 (Part I), JN (SG) Papers.

281   7 June 1951, Rao's note on 'discipline amongst government servants', File No. 88 (Part I), JN (SG) Papers.

282   2 June 1951, 'The Five-Year Plan – a Preliminary Outline', File No. 88 (Part I), JN (SG) Papers.

283   Marcelo de Paiva Abreu, 'Britain as a Debtor: Indian Sterling Balances, 1940–53', *Economic History Review* 70, no. 2 (2017): 586–604.

284   13 June 1951, Nehru to Radhakrishnan and Azad, File No. 88 (Part II), JN (SG) Papers.

285   15 June 1951, Nehru to Prasad, File No. 88 (Part II), JN (SG) Papers.

286   18 June 1951, Prasad to Nehru, File No. 89 (Part I), JN (SG) Papers.

287   21 June 1951, Nehru to Prasad, File No. 89 (Part I), JN (SG) Papers.

288   24 June 1951, Nehru to Trivedi, File No. 89 (Part II), JN (SG) Papers.

289   M. G. Untawale, 'The Political Dynamics of Functional Collaboration: Indo-Nepalese River Projects', *Asian Survey* 14, no. 8 (1974): 716–32.

290   21 June 1951, Nehru to Nanda, File No. 89 (Part I), JN (SG) Papers.

291   25 June 1951, Nanda–Nehru exchange, File No. 89 (Part II), JN (SG) Papers.

292   29 June 1951, Deshmukh to Nehru, File No. 90 (Part I), JN (SG) Papers.

293   23 June 1951, Nehru to Ayyangar, Pant and PPS, File No. 89 (Part I), JN (SG) Papers.

294   Undated, June 1951, Azad to Nehru, File No. 88 (Part II), JN (SG) Papers.

295 23 June 1951, Nehru to Ayyangar, File No. 89 (Part I), JN (SG) Papers. Sherman, *Muslim Belonging in Secular India*, 147–73.

296 25 June 1951, Nehru to Deputy Minister, MEA, File No. 89 (Part II), JN (SG) Papers.

297 9 June 1951, Nehru's note, File No. 89 (Part II), JN (SG) Papers. See R. L. Park, 'India's General Elections', *Far Eastern Survey* 21, no. 1 (1952): 1–8.

298 13 June 1951, Notes by Sen and Nehru, File No. 89 (Part II), JN (SG) Papers.

299 See Stephen Legg, 'Dyarchy: Democracy, Autocracy, and the Scalar Sovereignty of Interwar India', *Comparative Studies of South Asia, Africa and the Middle East* 36, no. 1 (2016): 44–65.

300 24 June 1951, Raj Bahadur to Nehru and 25 June 1951, Nehru's note, File No. 89 (Part II), JN (SG) Papers.

301 See Bethany Lacina, 'The Problem of Political Stability in Northeast India: Local Ethnic Autocracy and the Rule of Law', *Asian Survey* 49, no. 6 (2009): 998–1020.

302 25 June 1951, Nehru to Doulatram, File No. 89 (Part II), JN (SG) Papers.

303 See H. S. Singh, 'Socio Religious and Political Movements in Modern Manipur 1934–51' (PhD Thesis, JNU, Delhi, 2011).

304 24 June 1951, Ayyangar to Nehru, File No. 89 (Part II), JN (SG) Papers.

305 25 June 1951, Nehru to Sri Prakasa and chief ministers, File No. 89 (Part II), JN (SG) Papers.

306 File No. 90 (Part I), JN (SG) Papers.

307 26 and 29 June 1951, Bhargava–Nehru exchange, File No. 90 (Part I), JN (SG) Papers.

308 4 July 1951, Nehru to Tandon, File No. 90 (Part II), JN (SG) Papers.

309 2 July 1951, Nehru's 'Report to the AICC', File No. 90 (Part II), JN (SG) Papers.

310 27 June 1951, Iengar's note, File No. 90 (Part II), JN (SG) Papers.

311 1 July 1951, Rajagopalachari's note, File No. 90 (Part II), JN (SG) Papers. See Antony R. H. Copley, *The Political Career of C. Rajagopalachari, 1937–1954* (New Delhi: Macmillan India, 1978), 237–306.

312 4 July 1951, Ayyangar's note, File No. 90 (Part II), JN (SG) Papers.

313 6 July 1951, Nehru to Iengar, File No. 90 (Part II), JN (SG) Papers.

314 4 July 1951, Nehru's note, File No. 90 (Part II), JN (SG) Papers. Hart, *New India's Rivers*, 255–70.

315 5–9 July 1951, Nehru–Sinha exchange, File Nos. 91 (Part I) and 92 (Part I), JN (SG) Papers.

316 20 July 1951, Nehru to C. P. N. Singh and 21 July 1951, Nehru to Nanda, File No. 92 (Part I), JN (SG) Papers.

317 S. S. Gill, 'Changing Land Relations in Punjab and Implications for Land Reforms', *Economic and Political Weekly* 24, no. 25 (1989): A79–A85.

318 6 July 1951, Trivedi to Nehru, File No. 90 (Part II), JN (SG) Papers.

319 21 July 1951, Nehru to Trivedi, File No. 92 (Part I), JN (SG) Papers.

320 13 July 1951, Trivedi to Nehru, File No. 92 (Part I), JN (SG) Papers.

321 20 July 1951, Nehru to Trivedi, File No. 92 (Part I), JN (SG) Papers.

322　7 July 1951, Iengar's note, File No. 91 (Part I), JN (SG) Papers. See Grewal, *Master Tara Singh in Indian History*, part II, ch. 18.

323　7 July 1951, Prasad to Nehru, File No. 91 (Part I), JN (SG) Papers.

324　7 July 1951, Nehru to Prasad, File No. 91 (Part I), JN (SG) Papers. See S. Raghavan, 'Soldiers, Statesmen, and India's Security Policy', *India Review* 11, no. 2 (2012): 116–33.

325　7 July 1951, Nehru to chief ministers, File No. 91 (Part I), JN (SG) Papers.

326　18 July 1951, Iengar to B. N. Kaul, File No. 92 (Part I), JN (SG) Papers.

327　19 July 1951, Nehru to Doulatram, File No. 92 (Part I), JN (SG) Papers.

328　Undated, July 1951, Nehru to Bishnuram Medhi, File No. 92 (Part II), JN (SG) Papers.

329　6 July 1951, Mashruwala to Nehru, File No. 92 (Part II), JN (SG) Papers.

330　22 July 1951, Nehru to Mashruwala, File No. 92 (Part II), JN (SG) Papers.

331　14 July 1951, Deshmukh to Nehru, File No. 92 (Part I), JN (SG) Papers.

332　20 July 1951, Shukla to Nehru, File No. 92 (Part I), JN (SG) Papers. See N. Tyabji, 'The Politics of Industry in Nehru's India', *Economic and Political Weekly* 50, no. 35 (2015): 97–103.

333　See A. Deshpande, 'Quest for Equality: Affirmative Action in India', *Indian Journal of Industrial Relations* 44, no. 2 (2008): 154–63.

334　6 July 1951, Kumaraswamy Raja to Nehru, File No. 92 (Part II), JN (SG) Papers.

335　21 July 1951, Kartar Singh to Nehru, File No. 92 (Part II), JN (SG) Papers.

336　24 July 1951, Nehru to Ayyangar, File No. 92 (Part II), JN (SG) Papers.

337　22 July 1951, Nehru to Ayyangar and 27 July 1951, Vyas to Nehru, File Nos. 92 (Part II) and 93 (Part II), JN (SG) Papers.

338　Undated, July 1951 (after the AICC session), Nanda to JP, File No. 92 (Part I), JN (SG) Papers. See S. Mehrotra and S. Guichard, eds., *Planning in the 20th Century and Beyond: India's Planning Commission and the NITI Aayog* (Cambridge: Cambridge University Press, 2020), 23–43.

339　22 July 1951, Nehru to chief ministers, File No. 92 (Part II), JN (SG) Papers.

340　Undated, July 1951, Defence Committee's paper, File No. 92 (Part II), JN (SG) Papers.

341　22–23 July 1951, Munshi to Nehru, File No. 92 (Part II), JN (SG) Papers.

342　24 July 1951, Rajagopalachari to Nehru, File No. 92 (Part II), JN (SG) Papers.

343　6 July 1951, Iengar's note, File No. 92 (Part II), JN (SG) Papers.

344　13 July 1951, Rajagopalachari's note, File No. 92 (Part II), JN (SG) Papers.

345　22 July 1951, Nehru's note, File No. 92 (Part II), JN (SG) Papers.

346　25 July 1951, Nehru to Rajagopalachari, File No. 93 (Part I), JN (SG) Papers.

347　26 July 1951, Gadgil to Nehru, File No. 93 (Part I), JN (SG) Papers.

348　1 August 1951, Nehru to Rajagopalachari, File No. 94 (Part I), JN (SG) Papers.

349　21 July 1951, Nehru to Kidwai, File No. 92 (Part II), JN (SG) Papers.

350　22–23 July 1951, Nehru to Tandon, File No. 92 (Part II), JN (SG) Papers.

351　30–31 July 1951, Kidwai–Nehru correspondence, File No. 94 (Part I), JN (SG) Papers.

352　29 July 1951, Gadgil–Nehru exchange, File Nos. 93 (Part I and Part II), JN (SG) Papers.

353 2 August 1951, Nehru to Deshmukh, File No. 94 (Part I), JN (SG) Papers.

354 See De, *A People's Constitution*, 32–76; and H. M. Patel, ed., S*ay Not the Struggle: Essays in Honour of A. D. Gorwala* (New Delhi: Oxford University Press, 1976).

355 4 August 1951, Vellodi to Nehru, File No. 94 (Part II), JN (SG) Papers.

356 9 August 1951, Rajagopalachari to Nehru, File No. 95 (Part I), JN (SG) Papers. Arudra Burra, 'The Cobwebs of Imperial Rule', *Seminar* 615 (2010): 79–83.

357 9 August 1951, Sri Prakasa to Nehru, File No. 95 (Part I), JN (SG) Papers.

358 10 August 1951, Nehru to Sri Prakasa, File No. 95 (Part I), JN (SG) Papers.

359 24 July 1951, Mavalankar to Nehru, File No. 93 (Part II), JN (SG) Papers.

360 See Akunthita Borthakur and Ritu Thaosen, 'Rethinking the Line System in Assam and Its Politics', *Proceedings of the Indian History Congress* 73 (2012): 545–52.

361 25 July 1951, Sri Prakasa to Nehru, File No. 93 (Part II), JN (SG) Papers.

362 28 July 1951, Nehru to Doulatram, File No. 93 (Part II), JN (SG) Papers.

363 16 July 1951, Doulatram to Prasad, File No. 93 (Part II), JN (SG) Papers.

364 25 July 1951, Prasad to Nehru, File No. 93 (Part II), JN (SG) Papers.

365 30 July and 7 August 1951, Phizo-Nehru exchange, File No. 95 (Part I), JN (SG) Papers.

366 See D. Naorem, 'Japanese Invasion, War Preparation, Relief, Rehabilitation, Compensation and "State-making" in an Imperial Frontier (1939–1955)', *Asian Ethnicity* 21, no. 1 (2020): 96–121.

367 31 July 1951, Khosla's report, File No. 93 (Part II), JN (SG) Papers.

368 26 July 1951, Khub Chand to B. N. Chakravarty, File No. 94 (Part I), JN (SG) Papers.

369 1 August 1951, Nehru to G. S. Bajpai, File No. 94 (Part I), JN (SG) Papers.

370 30 July–1 August 1951, Roy–Nehru exchange, File No. 94 (Part I), JN (SG) Papers.

371 1 August 1951, Roy to Nehru, File No. 94 (Part I), JN (SG) Papers.

372 3 August 1951, Nehru to Roy, File No. 94 (Part I), JN (SG) Papers.

373 10 August 1951, Baldev Singh to Nehru, File No. 95 (Part I), JN (SG) Papers. See Raghavan, *War and Peace in Modern India*, 188–215.

374 1 August 1951, Nehru to chief ministers, File No. 94 (Part I), JN (SG) Papers.

375 3–4 August 1951, Nehru to Pandit, File No. 94 (Part I), JN (SG) Papers.

376 2 August 1951, Nehru to Rajagopalachari, File No. 94 (Part I), JN (SG) Papers.

377 10 August 1951, Nehru to Ambedkar, File No. 95 (Part I), JN (SG) Papers.

378 3 August 1951, Nehru to Prasad, File No. 94 (Part I), JN (SG) Papers.

379 4 August 1951, Nehru to Jain, File No. 94 (Part II), JN (SG) Papers.

380 5 August 1951, Gundevia to K. P. S. Menon, File No. 94 (Part II), JN (SG) Papers.

381 5 August 1951, Nehru to Ayyangar, File No. 94 (Part II), JN (SG) Papers.

382 4 August 1951, Nehru to Rajagopalachari, File No. 94 (Part II), JN (SG) Papers.

383 See *Revolutionary Democracy*, XXV (2), September 2020 and XXVI (1) April 2021, 181.

384 7 August 1951, Trivedi to Nehru, File No. 94 (Part II), JN (SG) Papers.

Epilogue

In August 1951, the person responsible for the food ministry as well as, often, providing food for thought, K. M. Munshi was a troubled man. Unburdening himself at some length to the prime minister, Munshi roamed far and wide: from the 'oppressive' India–Pakistan relation and our 'timid' people, because of the government's 'weak policy', to the unsympathetic international situation. His frustration's chief causes though were that cabinet colleagues were not entirely 'in confidence' of Nehru and that there was a need for effective publicity. Munshi was sorry that the information and broadcasting ministry lacked a 'purposive education of *self-righteous* public opinion', whether internally in Telangana, where forces were fighting communists 'who pose as harmless politicians', or externally. Munshi had visited three countries – England, America and then-Burma – in the last two years and found the external affairs ministry's publicity wanting. Munshi concluded his quasi-war cry with a characteristic passage: 'Indians abroad [are] our best advertisers.... Modern publicity has become a thing of art and money, and we must stoop to conquer....'[1]

Mirroring the Prologue, this extended Epilogue attempts to delineate the path to the people's court and its accompanying electoral politicking, which in turn paved the way from 'agitation' to 'construction'.[2] Mohanlal Saksena, former central minister for refugee rehabilitation, and future parliamentarian, put his finger on the pulse of party politics at this time in a spirited exchange with Rafi Ahmed Kidwai, who had given a call to Congressmen to leave. Saksena, a legislator in UP since the 1920s, posited Kidwai's 'exhortation' with

Nehru's 'call to remain united' and pointed out to Kidwai the problem in his position, which was that his 'grouse' was against party organisation, while having 'full faith' in the leadership of Nehru. Instead of leaving, if Kidwai stayed and helped the latter, it would have been politically sounder. For, as Saksena asked, were 'the dissident Congressmen ... morally superior'?[3]

Before Tandon's election in 1950 and before the departure of the Congress Socialists in 1948, the CWC had as many members from the left as from the right, and Saksena could see Kripalani's Krishak Mazdoor Party becoming irrelevant in the electoral battle between those 'who are out to dislodge [Nehru] ... [those] who pay lip homage to him [and] those who, while swearing by him ... forswear his advice'. Saksena concluded by reminding Kidwai that he too had resigned from ministership in 1950 but had chosen to stay on in the party, as 'the exigencies of elections' will take over. As indeed they were, as none other than Purushottamdas Tandon realised, on 6 August 1951, he read from Nehru a letter of resignation from the CWC and CPB, which could split the party. At this juncture, two (or six) months away from elections, it was imperative to have him within the party's leadership, and therefore Tandon offered to resign. Preferring words like 'drifts', 'fade', 'drive', 'fit', 'decay' and 'risks' in their exchange, Nehru reiterated feeling 'out of tune', disavowed any reasons for Tandon to go and deplored winning elections but losing 'soul'.[4]

It was an ironical situation in which much of the government seemed to consider an external war likely, while its head felt embattled on the internal fronts of party psychology and public morale. Nehru had less reasons to expect the sequence of invasion-partial defeat than communal invocation-tension, even though he called for care regarding strategic spots and was prepared for an 'all-out war'.[5] At this time, Kanji Dwarkadas, a Bombay-based lawyer, Home Rule activist and labour legislator, would travel in India, make notes of his meetings and, in two of his extended visits abroad, spread his impressions among his friends. In New Delhi, he met Nehru, Munshi, Iengar, Bajpai, Joint Secretary (Labour) Subramaniam and Housing Commissioner Koenigsberger. In Bombay, where he met Kher, Morarji Desai, Governor Maharaj Singh, Mayor S. K. Patil, Food Minister Dinkar Desai, Housing Minister Jivraj Mehta, Chief Secretary Bhatt, Home Secretary Daheja, Labour Secretary Joshi and Housing Commissioner C. R. Desai, he was happy to note that all these were '100% pro-American'.[6]

Giving special attention to Morarji Desai because he was in the six-member CPB, which was to select Congress candidates for the elections, Dwarkadas prophesised that Desai would be chief minister soon and that he would challenge Nehru. Desai told Dwarkadas that he was confident of 'getting 70–75% Congress majorities ... except in West Bengal, East Punjab, PEPSU and Rajasthan' – that is, the two partitioned regions and two princely unions. From Bombay, Dwarkadas flew to London, where he met Prime Minister Clement Attlee, journalists Rushbrook Williams (*The Times*) and Kingsley Martin (*New Statesman*), former civil servants Percival Griffiths and Frederick James, Nehru baiters Louis Fischer and C. P. Ramaswamy Aiyar, Nehru supporters the Mountbattens and, at the India House, V. K. Krishna Menon and Dharma Vira. He assured Attlee that Nehru was not a communist, and if he left, 'the right-wing Congress, conservative [and] communal parties' would come.

On Congress politics, when Dwarkadas informed Krishna Menon that Nehru, Tandon, Morarji Desai, Patil and two others constituted the CPB, Menon commented that Nehru was in a 'minority of one', albeit not with any adverse effect on the party's electoral prospects, for as Dwarkadas argued with Kingsley Martin, Kripalani had 'hesitated too long', while Nehru saw 'the danger of a split'. Back in India, echoing Desai's concerns about state assemblies, an example came from East Punjab in mid-August, when an ex-Congress legislator fired a sweeping note on the now-defunct ministry based on his survey conducted across ten districts in 1949–50. It focused on Gopichand Bhargava, Prithvi Singh Azad, Giani Kartar Singh and their acts of patronage. Azad, formerly a 'modest preacher' of Arya Samaj or Hindu Mahasabha, now owned 'a house outside Kharar, worth thousands....'[7]

Bhargava's largesse appeared directed towards his brother Thakur Das Bhargava, lawyer-parliamentarian, who owned a sugar mill and a woollen mill and whose son Anand Prakash's firm had 'a monopoly' in arms-licences in Hissar, held 'a depot' of petrol-kerosene-food, was a member of the municipality or rehabilitation committee, had a brother in Loharu state's gram stocks' export-business and a licence for Agmark ghee. Anand Prakash was also a member of the RSS. Bhargava's other clients seem to be in the fields of truck permits, *khaddar* and paper manufacturing, iron quota and potatoes. He had revoked the arrest warrant of legislator Seth Sudarshan, the 'king of iron & steel' in the state. As for the Giani, he had sanctioned 170 applications for arms by Sikhs in Hissar, in comparison to '2 by Hindus', and while holding agriculture and transport portfolios, his profiteering had been the talk of the town. A variation on this theme was Lala Hans Raj Kundra, a prominent Congressman of Sialkot, being appointed deputy superintendent of police, in which capacity he 'extorted' Muslims in Jalandhar in lieu of evacuee property.

There were others too. Legislator Dev Raj moved goods without permits and bribed the police. Legislator Kabul Singh, belonging to Govindpur, Jalandhar, was 'not a refugee but got a palatial house, garden, lands left by a well-known Muslim evacuee lawyer worth 3 lacs....' Sardar Gopal Singh Qaumi made money in the allotment committee of houses or shops,

Chaudhury Krishna Gopal Dutt, ex-finance minister, 'gave cloth quota worth 12 lacs from Karnal Cloth Association to 6 refugees from Gujranwala', while Chaudhury Kartar Singh, legislator since 1937, cultivated Baldev Singh and made money 'from Delhi to Hoshiarpur'. This mixture of wild and watchful corruption was not restricted to the partitioned Punjab. In neighbouring UP, Congress stalwarts C. B. Gupta and Dr Sampurnanand had been collecting money from sugar mills, prompting a short notice question in the parliament, which fell upon the official-minister C. D. Deshmukh to field, and the politically correct answer was provided by the prime minister himself: 'payments made are not free from Income-Tax ... [there was] nothing illegal in a company [contributing] according to rules'.[8]

That may have been so in the parliament and the press, but privately, Sampurnanand and Gupta had unflattering tales to tell.[9] In the third week of June 1951, Tandon informed Sampurnanand that Padmapat Singhania had discussed contributing to the Congress election fund, and now Sampurnanand should speak with Jackson, acting head of a group of European businesses in India, as the European group felt 'embarrassed' to contribute. Jackson assured the latter that they were 'solidly behind' the Congress and that Singhania had suggested that they should give '8 lakhs'. To this, Sampurnanand responded, 'money had lost its value',[10] and asked Jackson to find out from European businesses in Calcutta how much contribution they were making there and follow suit; after all, at home they gave money to the Conservative Party. As for Gupta, he had been present in April 1951, when K. K. Birla and Rameshwar Nevatia saw Pant at Lucknow and offered their 'services from the sugar industry'. On 1 July, Birla rang Gupta to confirm about others and met him with Hari Raj Swarup, president of the Indian Sugar Mills Association, who also asked 'whether there were any chances for non-Congressmen to seek election on the support of Congress'.[11] Gupta replied in the affirmative, if they were like Chaudhury Mukhtar Singh (Bulandshahr) and H. N. Kunzru (Allahabad).

Even as such planning was picking up pace for the next parliament and government, the present arrangement lingered on. After food, the major matter of maladministration was the 'delay' in issuing licences for the import of cloth and other essential items. Between January and June 1951, the government received 117,440 applications, with Commerce Minister Mahtab claiming the disposal of 'all but 5186'. Comparatively, a year ago, the number of pending applications was 65,340, largely because of an adverse balance of trade, subsequent currency devaluation and the consequent trade deadlock with Pakistan, which saw the cancellation of the 'open general license' for many items. Still, anything from 6 to 8 weeks was being taken on each application, and Mahtab initiated 'proceedings against 22 officers'.[12]

This delay was hardly comparable to that on the passage of the Hindu Code Bill, and the crisis in the party, which was joined by the possibility of an unhappy and unwell Rajagopalachari leaving in mid-August 1951, but the prime minister had made up his mind now.[13] With the party situation deteriorating, both cancelled their trip to Srinagar, instead going to a Congress meeting on 8 September, where Tandon resigned and Nehru replaced him the following day, bringing the curtains down on a year-long drama. Throughout this period, they had remained at odds, persuaded by others (Azad, Rajagopalachari and Patel), agreed on the party's decline, differed on what was 'responsible' for it, and formed 'certain notions' about each other.[14]

Now that he had combined the posts of party president and prime minister, in addition to his chairmanship of the planning commission and ministership of external affairs, Jawaharlal Nehru was in the saddle to gallop towards his decade in Indian politics, the challenges of which were already all around him. From Madras, P. S. Kumaraswamy Raja wrote about Swami Sitaram, or Potti Sriramulu, who had conveyed his intention to undertake a fast unto death for an Andhra province. Replying to Raja that the party's election manifesto referred to linguistic states, and recalling his, Patel's and Sitaramayya's 1948 committee and thereafter the Pannalal committee appointed by Patel, both of which concluded against linguistic units, he nevertheless expressed his 'readiness [for] Andhra', but not when Sriramulu desired, which was before 2 October 1951, a year before this enforced sequence of events took place.[15]

Like the road to this state reorganisation was not straightforward, the road to Nehru's consolidation of the party had turns that were not taken. One of these was brought up by Dr B. C. Roy, who said that given that the Congress organisation and administration must cooperate, a way forward was for Nehru to propose the new CWC. Roy was worried that with Maulana Azad following Nehru, this meant 'a cleavage between the Congress and a representative Muslim', and he wondered if, without them, 'they will have long discussions about cow-killing and monkey-killing'.[16] But how was the prime minister to propose the CWC personnel without becoming party president? Writing as much to the Calcutta strongman, Nehru refused Roy's 'patch-work' solution for a 'dual leadership' and accepted that his 'mistake … was to defer for too long'.[17] This was much like the fate of some important bills in progress through the legislature. S. N. Sinha, the parliamentary affairs minister, was reporting the near postponement of matters like the Banaras and Aligarh Universities Act, Part C States Bill, disqualification of members, the Press and Industries Bill and the Punjab Bill, let alone the Hindu Code Bill. Against this background, the 'only way' forward was for the latter to be considered first and 'with some speed'.[18]

There were some things, however, which seemed over and above the party or the parliament. One such was the Intelligence Bureau, which, in early August 1951, intercepted a letter written by the daughter of Major-General Anis Ahmad Khan to 'someone in Pakistan'. Khan, a rare Muslim officer of such seniority in the Indian army, had been serving as director-general of supplies and transport since 1949.[19] His tenure was until 1953, and there was a reference in the letter 'about the correspondents coming together' after that. Baldev Singh asked if the letter should be ignored 'as that of a child' or whether 'they are her parents' views....' At the time of Khan's appointment, Singh had expressed 'doubts', and now Rajagopalachari chimed in that these were 'difficult to ignore', with the defence minister 'very reluctant'.[20] The prime minister prevailed, and Khan completed his tenure, albeit leaving for Pakistan afterwards.[21] Meanwhile, after 15 August 1951, reports came in of 'panic' and 'exodus' in Amritsar, and Trivedi was asked to go there amidst claims that New Delhi 'paid no attention to the Sikh gurdwaras in Pakistan'.[22] It was a time when the government was unable to pay attention to so many things that it wished to. For instance, the prime minister would have preferred to buy Scindia ships in view of the rising costs of shipping. Instead, Deshmukh, supported by Rajagopalachari, decided to do otherwise, leaving Nehru to feel further that their economic policy benefited 'vested' interests. Ayyangar, Mahtab and Deshmukh had decided the price at which to sell the ships with no buyers around when the undertaking was made, but the market changed after the outbreak of the Korean War and demand for ships rose, giving an advantage to the Scindias. Deshmukh understood that Nehru's reaction was more due to his 'frustration' that they had been 'unable to do more' in economic terms since 1947.[23]

This economic frustration was joined by 'foggy politics' on legislation like the Part C States Bill, which was to bring democracy to these princely areas, and the Press Bill, which was taking some democracy away from the whole country. Outside, the All-India Railwaymen's Federation had decided to postpone their announced strike for the time period deemed 'critical' for India–Pakistan relations, which ended with the shock assassination of Liaquat Ali Khan on 16 October 1951. Ten days later, the first votes were cast for the general election. This time period also saw 'leading Muslims [pledge] loyalty' to the country, the 'first ship carrying [American] food [reach] Bombay', and now the question remained, 'how to bring about communion between ... adventurist slogans [and] the so-called practical man?'[24] An answer came on 20 August 1951 from an unusual source, which was akin to a voice from beyond the grave.

Maniben Patel wrote a rare letter to her father's comrade, weighing in on the affairs of the party that they had commanded in a duopoly. It was at once a letter beseeching the prime minister and one reproaching him. Maniben started by recalling Nehru's visit to her a week after Vallabhbhai Patel had died, promising her that 'if there will be anything I can do, I will do it' – sentiments that had strengthened her.[25] She had visited New Delhi on 11 August to attend the CWC meeting, where she learnt about Nehru's resignation from it. Having spoken since with Azad and S. N. Sinha, she was writing to ask what had happened since the Bangalore session in July for Nehru to do so. To her, it appeared that from Nasik in September 1950 to Ahmedabad in January 1951, and from Delhi in May to Bangalore in July, all of Nehru's resolutions had been accepted. At the provincial level, his wish to remove the Bhargava ministry in East Punjab had been granted, even if his desire to have early elections in West Bengal was thwarted by Roy. Maniben then referred to Nehru's *raj-hat* when the nation's reins were in his hands, while tracing the Congress' trajectory from everybody's Bapu (Gandhi) to her 'Bapu Ji' (Patel) and to Nehru, their 'heir'.

Starting with Shanmukham Chetty's resignation in 1948 and ending with Rafi Ahmed Kidwai's in 1951, she noted that all such episodes were about personal acceptability. Touching upon the uneasy moments in the Nehru–Patel relations, she put together Nehru's feelings that Patel 'wanted' to replace him, with the 14-year-older, and in poorer health, Patel telling him that he was only continuing to 'lighten [Nehru's] burden'. In any case, since December 1950, politically speaking, there had been 'none older' to Nehru in the Congress. Moving to some issues next, Maniben turned to the question of control of essential items – a matter of 'difference of opinion' between Patel and Nehru, involving Gandhi, since 1946–47 – and asked why 'after 5 years of government', the controls had made 'the masses unhappy'. She agreed with Nehru that 'no practical work' was being done for almost a year now and concluded this personal letter with another political reminiscence, when she reminded the prime minister that upon Tandon's election in September 1950, he had told Patel, 'If I resign now everything will be steady by elections. To resign then will not be good'. With the country on the cusp of elections, she asked how resigning was 'appropriate now'.

If Jawaharlal Nehru was taken aback by this personal entreaty, then another setback was the personal treaty with Nepal on the Kosi project. Ambassador C. P. N. Singh wrote from Kathmandu that he had not been able to ascertain if and when New Delhi would receive the amount promised. When General Subarna, the finance minister, gave a 'discouraging' reply, Singh had asked the Maharaja, who would not confirm in writing.[26] The prime minister however had more pressing matters closer home, as on and from 15 August 1951, Old Delhi saw trouble 'in connection with animal slaughter'.[27] On enquiry it was found that 'some Muslims had slaughtered some buffalo calves', while 'mischief-makers' spread the rumour about cows, with some troublemakers even getting 'a cow to be killed'. Apart from the public sentiment involved, this slaughter in private houses was 'undesirable', if uninspected by local municipalities, but with people objecting to regulated slaughterhouses, the chief commissioner's hands were tied.[28] Old and New Delhi were indeed heating up with public meetings, before the party lines deepened in October 1951, with the formation of the Bharatiya Jana Sangh, blessed by the RSS and the Hindu Mahasabha, and the merger of the Krishak Mazdoor and Socialist Party into the Praja Socialist Party.[29]

Sri Prakasa was approached by Maulichand Sharma, formerly of the Congress, then the Hindu Mahasabha and presently of the Punjab–Delhi Jana Sangh, with close ties with the RSS, to address a meeting in Daryaganj on Janmashtami. Sharma and Sri Prakasa went back some way, given their shared existence in the Hindi sphere of north Indian politics, but Sri Prakasa was committed to a similar event at Model Town on the same day. Jagjivan Ram was approached next by Sharma's deputation, which gave him to understand that this 'purely religious' meeting was under the auspices of a dozen organisations, but he declined when he was informed that the RSS was among this dozen.[30] S. N. Sinha followed suit, promising to attend first and then withdrawing when Nehru's secretary M. O. Mathai conveyed to him the 'implications'. N. V. Gadgil left for Bombay, but all were instructed to issue a statement distancing themselves from this overlap between the centre ground and the right-wing.[31] It embarrassed none on either side except the prime minister, who considered empowering the chief commissioner in view of the 'political situation' for the next six months.[32] In those days, what else could control the national capital? As Health Minister Amrit Kaur put it:

> Delhi state should be under central administration. We might have given Delhi 8 seats in the central parliament instead of 4 and we should have agreed to a corporation like Bombay for Old Delhi … [Despite] all our efforts, perhaps only 2–3 [Muslims] will be returned in the municipal elections. I doubt if even 1 comes into the Delhi legislature. Zuberi has gone to Pakistan. Naseem is also thinking of going. They feel there is no hope for their children. No Muslims are left in the police … the strength of the RSS alarms me. All the refugees are disgruntled and think that way.[33]

If, however, this need could only be met by the centre, then its cost was going to be prohibitive. In terms of governmental irregularities too, be it on licences or tenders, from East Punjab to Madras, if the requirements could only be met by the union, then little could stem favouritism – as when the Bihar governor complained to President Prasad about the textile scarcity in the state. In addition to its food scarcity, cloth supplies to Bihar during 1951 were fluctuating, leading to high prices. Patna's 'distribution machinery' faced 'complaints against control' as well as about 'their handling of cloth meant for Nepal'.[34] The enforcement directorate was focusing on the open border being used by exporters to sell export-oriented cloth at home for profit, as well as importers bringing in cloth and yarn from Nepal and selling them for profit, with both sets obliterating cloth marks and stamping fresh prices, up to '2½ times more'.[35] It was some consolation that across this open border, lives, homes, lands and cattle were not grabbed or attacked, like in Bengal, with consequent communal excitement.[36] In this milieu, President Rajendra Prasad dropped a 2,000-word objection note on 15 September 1951 to the potential passing of the Hindu Code Bill. Unable hitherto to give public expression to his views on the matter since being elevated to his present position, now that the matter was in the legislative domain, Prasad entered the fray so that Nehru was not surprised later. His expansive note laid bare this issue's multiple fault-lines:

> [1] The present Parliament is not competent to enact such a measure
> ... [2] The revolutionary changes contemplated have never been placed
> before the electorate ... [3] The measure is of a discriminatory nature
> ... [4] There is no reason why ... a uniform code for all should not be
> sought....[37]

Prasad then went on to illustrate 'the greatest latitude' in the Hindu law 'under custom ...' and concluded with the ominous proposal 'to watch the measure', to reserve his 'right to examine' but, more than that, to 'take appropriate action ... with the dictates of my conscience'. Nehru was quick to make it plain to Prasad that 'the President has no power to go against the Parliament'; while regarding the latter's 'disapproval' of the bill, the prime minister's defence was a mixture of principled commitment and procedural consideration. On 'the competence of the present Parliament', Nehru pointed out that Mavalankar had decided, and now it was not open to 'even the President' to challenge that decision. About the bill's 'revolutionary' character, Nehru disagreed and called it a 'very moderate measure', though he conceded that 'in view of the heavy business and the short time', it was 'decided to concentrate on passing ... Part II of the Bill ... dealing with Marriage and Divorce' and no further.[38]

On 25 September 1951, a note was circulated in the cabinet by the prime minister's secretariat, signed by Nehru, after having consulted Attorney-General Setalvad and Krishnaswami Aiyar (advocate-general, Madras, 1929–44) on the question of the president's powers. Both assured him that the president 'cannot act independently' of the advice of the cabinet, and any such action would lead to their resignation. In exactly one month from

Rajendra Prasad's voice thus contained within the chamber of presidential powers, Rajagopalachari resigned his home ministership and left for Madras, citing ill-health but also indicating some ill-will with Nehru on their old trope of containing communalism versus communism. Four days earlier, on 21 October 1951, the Telangana peasants' armed struggle had been withdrawn by the communists,[39] and the Bharatiya Jana Sangh had come into being,[40] thereby making the line-up for the upcoming electoral race complete.[41]

> [Nehru] ... had the practical aim of modernising India ... but had no illusions about [it].... He complained of the reluctance of his subordinates to accept responsibility. He could lay down guidelines but could not occupy every stage in the chain of command....[42]

This book ends where many of independent India's political histories begin, with the coming together of the first general election (1951–52), the first Five Year Plan (1951–56) and the first presidency of the Congress party by the prime minister (1951–54).[43] This onset of Nehruvianism is a lodestar of liberal nation-building, a bulwark against the Cold War outside and communitarian wars inside, even if it may be as much mythological or mythical as real.[44] Judith M. Brown's 2003 'life' of Nehru deals with this period, showing how 'a prime minister can create networks ... among leaders rooted in state politics, in order to achieve government and ... social and economic change'.[45] Much earlier, Michael Brecher showed this 'democracy at work', but before that there was an interim government of ambiguity and equivalence, throughout which Nehru's 'way of being prime minister was' that 'he fought against rather than adapting to and working the political system as it was emerging after 1947'.[46]

In March 1951, the Congress trinity of Jawaharlal Nehru, Chakravarti Rajagopalachari and Rajendra Prasad were sharing with each other their (a) 'apprehension' about elections stuck in 'slow motion', (b) worries about the 'superficial' grow-more-food campaign, (c) concerns around 'additional' taxation in that year's budget and (d) the 'bad general situation'.[47] It was against this bleak background that the president attended the reopening of the rebuilt Somnath temple, perhaps with a prayer for propitious times. Nine months later, an exultant Nehru was surveying a successful election bar exception(s); maybe Prasad's prayers were answered.[48] The party lined up behind its new president and the principal vote winner, with those like S. K. Patil collecting funds and those like Sri Prakasa contributing to it. Finding himself in an unfamiliar role in his first election without Gandhi and Patel, the prime minister was touched by the latter sending a cheque for INR 5,000 and drew the contrast with those who feel that 'by having gone to jail', they have obliged the country. He offered Sri Prakasa party presidency, as they 'could cooperate with the greatest ease'.[49]

For now, the freshly mandated prime minister, firmly cast in his role, mused about his flock, its voting, and sought to take lessons from the results, where the 'opportunist' socialists and the too-little-too-late Bharatiya Jana Sangh were the biggest sufferers.[50] Then, there were the communists, who proved to be neither adventurists nor pushovers, especially in regions like Travancore-Cochin and Madras. This left the Congress, for which the 'conservative sections' of the country had voted more than any others. Its taking over of the colonial state apparatus and subsequent electoral success enabled it to continue with enhanced legitimacy, prevail upon internal conflicts and further institutionalise governance. In the postcolonial world, comparatively speaking, this was no mean achievement, warts and all.[51]

Hostilities across provinces and states were deeper than depicted here, and Nehru knew that, but for his 'tremendous tour, the result would have been worse'. Underneath the campaign rhetoric were pending promises like those for land reform. What could his favoured Five Year Plans offer the people in their stead? The planning commission's deputy, G. L. Nanda, was offering his Bharat Seva Sangh as a vehicle for constructive work. The other side of this coin was resetting the administrative 'machinery', as in West Bengal, where the most 'conservative' government in India saw things done with 'speed', if the 'big man' wanted it. Envious of this, the prime minister was also mindful of the inherent authoritarianism, though, so far as the party was concerned, it was one of 'ruts, cliques and bossdom',[52] if now 'with a definite platform'.[53] Although Sri Prakasa was unhappy at the 'pseudo-socialism enveloping' the country,[54] in latter-day echoes of pseudo-secularism, the shift has been from a cherished unity in diversity to a concocted 'unity in purity'.[55]

The 1947–51 government thus provides many a site where contradictions coexist – for example, the parts A, B and C states, despite the lightning rods at the top. Structural divisions, at different levels, were somehow sought to be fused together, and the breaches never quite widened, be it the domestication of the CPI or the politicisation of the RSS, while the gaps were filled, often with force. Most political crises are twofold, about legitimacy and authority. From the late 1940s to 40 years later, there were cycles of ebb and flow in this regard, contained in words like Partition, Coalition, Emergency, Mandal-Mandir and Liberalisation, but the central presence of the first lines drawn cannot be entirely erased. That 1947–51 period rewired a state-dominated, socially hierarchical and class-stratified country with a communalised consciousness – traits that have only metamorphosed since. Take, for instance, this old-new project of 'defining Indian nationalism by historicizing India's nationhood'.[56]

Ultimately, this book has tried to outline a time period of transitional governance in independent India's political history, reading from recently made available prime ministerial papers. It has aimed to give a bird's-eye view of the interim government of that period and its principles, problems and policies. The chronicle approach adopted, tracking as many events as they happened, shows a dense sequence in the hope of conveying something of the constant flux that governance in that period was. The many moments narrated here show how difficult it was to decide upon the big issues then, let alone to solve them. The range and strength of challenges made any conclusive impact difficult to achieve in those first, unsettled years. While employing the prime ministerial gaze, the narrative has widened to take in multi-sited, party-political and socio-economic scenes, which even from this singular vantage appear so plural. Thus, to survey those first five years in the light of the last ten has been both salutary and sobering.

NOTES

1   7 August 1951, Munshi to Nehru, File No. 95 (Part I), JN (SG) Papers.
2   Brecher, *Nehru*, viii.
3   8 August 1951, Saksena to Kidwai, File No. 95 (Part I), JN (SG) Papers. This and the next quote are from here.
4   9 August 1951, Tandon–Nehru exchange, File No. 95 (Part I), JN (SG) Papers.
5   9 August 1951, Nehru to chief ministers, File No. 95 (Part I), JN (SG) Papers.
6   31 July 1951, I. J. Bahadur Singh to Bajpai, File No. 95 (Part II), JN (SG) Papers. The next few quotes come from this letter enclosing Dwarkadas' notes.
7   11 August 1951, Duni Chand to Nehru, File No. 95 (Part II), JN (SG) Papers. The next few quotes come from this note.
8   13 August 1951, Nehru to Deshmukh, File No. 95 (Part II), JN (SG) Papers.
9   See William Gould, 'From Subjects to Citizens? Rationing, Refugees, and the Publicity of Corruption over Independence in UP', *Modern Asian Studies* 45, 1 (2011): 33–56.
10   13 August 1951, Sampurnanand's note, File No. 95 (Part II), JN (SG) Papers.
11   13 August 1951, Gupta's note, File No. 95 (Part II), JN (SG) Papers.
12   10 August 1951, Mahtab's note, File No. 95 (Part I), JN (SG) Papers.
13   13 and 18 August 1951, Nehru to Abdullah, File Nos. 95 (Part II) and 96 (Part I), JN (SG) Papers.
14   3 November 1950, Tandon to Nehru [in Hindi, translation mine], File No. 62 (Part I), JN (SG) Papers.
15   15 August 1951, Nehru to Kumaraswamy Raja and Rajagopalachari, File No. 95 (Part II), JN (SG) Papers. See R. S. Mantena, 'The Andhra Movement, Hyderabad State, and the Historical Origins of the Telangana Demand: Public Life and Political Aspirations in India, 1900–56', *India Review* 13, no. 4 (2014): 337–57.
16   15 August 1951, Roy to Nehru, File No. 96 (Part I), JN (SG) Papers.

17   17 August 1951, Nehru to Roy, File No. 96 (Part I), JN (SG) Papers.

18   15 August 1951, Nehru to Ambedkar and 16 August 1951, Nehru to Sinha, File No. 96 (Part I), JN (SG) Papers.

19   See Omar Khalidi, 'Ethnic Group Recruitment in the Indian Army: The Contrasting Cases of Sikhs, Muslims, Gurkhas and Others', *Pacific Affairs* 74, no. 4 (2001–02): 529–52.

20   16 August 1951, Baldev Singh to Nehru, File No. 96 (Part I), JN (SG) Papers.

21   8 August 1951, P. V. Bhaskaran (IB) to Iengar, File No. 96 (Part I), JN (SG) Papers. See Sebastian Schutte, 'Politics or Prejudice? Explaining Individual-Level Hostilities in India's Hindu–Muslim Conflict', *International Interactions: Empirical and Theoretical Research in International Relations* 45, no. 4 (2019): 666–92.

22   17 August 1951, Nehru to Trivedi, File No. 96 (Part I), JN (SG) Papers.

23   16–17 August 1951, Deshmukh–Nehru exchange, File No. 96 (Part I), JN (SG) Papers.

24   19 August 1951, Nehru to chief ministers, File No. 96 (Part I), JN (SG) Papers.

25   20 August 1951, Maniben Patel to Nehru [translated from Hindi], File No. 96 (Part I), JN (SG) Papers. This and the next paragraph draw upon this letter.

26   8 August 1951, Singh to Nehru, File No. 96 (Part II), JN (SG) Papers. Harry Blair, 'Identity, Dignity, and Development as Trajectory: Bihar as a Model for Democratic Progress in Nepal? Part I. Bihar's Experience', *Commonwealth and Comparative Politics* 56, no. 1 (2018): 103–23; Harry Blair, 'Identity, Dignity, and Development as Trajectory: Bihar as a Model for Democratic Progress in Nepal? Part II. Nepal's Promise', *Commonwealth and Comparative Politics* 56, no. 2 (2018): 216–33.

27   See Ian Copland, 'Cows, Congress and the Constitution: Jawaharlal Nehru and the Making of Article 48', *South Asia: Journal of South Asian Studies* 40, no. 4 (2017): 723–43.

28   22 August 1951, Nehru to MHA, File No. 96 (Part II), JN (SG) Papers.

29   See Boris Niclas-Tolle, *The Socialist Opposition in Nehruvian India 1947–1964* (Frankfurt: Peter Lang, 2015).

30   P. Friedlander, 'Reassessing Religion and Politics in the Life of Jagjivan Rām', *Religions* 11, no. 5 (2020): 224.

31   Bruce Graham, *Hindu Nationalism, and Indian Politics: The Origins and Development of the Bharatiya Jana Sangh* (Cambridge: Cambridge University Press, 1990), 43–52.

32   Undated, August 1951, Mathai's note to PMS, File No. 96 (Part II), JN (SG) Papers.

33   23 August 1951, Amrit Kaur to Nehru, File No. 96 (Part II), JN (SG) Papers.

34   23 August 1951, Nehru–Mahtab exchange, File No. 96 (Part II), JN (SG) Papers.

35   27 July 1951, Mahtab to A. N. Sinha, File No. 96 (Part II), JN (SG) Papers.

36   2 November 1950, Nehru to Roy, File No. 62 (Part I), JN (SG) Papers.

37   15 September 1951, Prasad's note, Correspondences, Sri Prakasa Papers (I-III Instalments). The next few quotes are from here. See also Saumya Saxena,

Divorce and Democracy: A History of Personal Law in Post-Independence India (Cambridge: Cambridge University Press, 2022), 35–92.

38   15 September 1951, Nehru to Prasad, Correspondences, Sri Prakasa Papers (I-III Instalments).

39   P. Sundarayya, 'Telangana People's Armed Struggle, 1946–1951. Part One: Historical Setting', *Social Scientist* 1, no. 7 (1973): 3–19.

40   Baxter, *The Jana Sangh*, 54–80; and Weiner, *Party Politics in India*, 177–98.

41   Werner Levi, 'India's Political Parties', *Far Eastern Survey* 20, no. 17 (1951): 169–72.

42   A. J. Ayer, *More of My Life* (Oxford: Oxford University Press, 1985), 155.

43   See Guha, *India after Gandhi*, Part 2 – 'Nehru's India'; and Benjamin Zachariah, *Nehru* (London: Routledge, 2004), 169–252.

44   See Zachariah, *Nehru*, xxiii; Sherman, *Nehru's India*; and V. Krishna Ananth, *India since Independence: Making sense of Indian Politics* (New Delhi: Pearson, 2010), 37–50.

45   Judith M. Brown, '"Life Histories" and the History of Modern South Asia', *American Historical Review* 114, no. 3 (2009): 587–95.

46   Brown, '"Life Histories"', 591; Brecher, *Nehru*, 448–508.

47   2 March 1951, Nehru to Prasad, File No. 82, Rajagopalachari Papers (V Instalment).

48   For this period, see S. Gopal, ed., *Selected Works of Jawaharlal Nehru, Second Series 2, Volume 17 (November 1951–March 1952)* (New Delhi: Teen Murti House, 1995).

49   11 November 1951, Nehru to Sri Prakasa, Correspondences, Sri Prakasa Papers (I-III Instalments).

50   Brecher, *Nehru*, 426–47.

51   R. L. Park, 'Indian Democracy and the General Election', *Pacific Affairs* 25, no. 2 (1952): 130–39.

52   26 January 1952, Nehru to Deshmukh, File No. 23, C. D. Deshmukh Papers (I Instalment).

53   13 January 1952, Nehru to Sri Prakasa, Correspondences, Sri Prakasa Papers (I-III Instalments).

54   16 February 1952, Sri Prakasa to K. N. Katju, Correspondences, Sri Prakasa Papers (I-III Instalments).

55   See Michael Gottlob, 'India's Unity in Diversity as a Question of Historical Perspective', *Economic and Political Weekly* 42, no. 9 (2007): 779–89.

56   Sheth, *At Home with Democracy*, 37.

Bibliography

Primary Sources

Nehru Memorial Museum and Library, New Delhi

C. Rajagopalachari Papers.
C. D. Deshmukh Papers.
Diwan Chaman Lall Papers.
Gopichand Bhargava Papers.
Jagdish Prasad Papers.
Jawaharlal Nehru (post-1947) Papers (JN SG).
N. Gopalaswami Ayyangar Papers.
R. M. Deshmukh Papers.
Sri Prakasa Papers.

National Archives of India, New Delhi

Ministry of Home Affairs.

Published Material

Abreu, Marcelo de Paiva. 'Britain as a Debtor: Indian Sterling Balances, 1940–53'. *Economic History Review* 70, no. 2 (2017): 586–604.

Agnihotri, R. K. 'Constituent Assembly Debates on Language'. *Economic and Political Weekly* 50, no. 8 (2015): 47–56.

Ahmed, Hilal. 'Researching India's Muslims: Identities, Methods, Politics'. *Journal of Ethnographic Theory* 10, no. 3 (2020): 776–85.

Alam, Javeed. 'State and the Making of Communist Politics in India, 1947–57'. *Economic and Political Weekly* 26, no. 45 (1991): 2573–83.

Alexandrowicz, C. H. 'Personal Liberty and Preventive Detention'. *Journal of the Indian Law Institute* 3, no. 4 (1961): 445–58.

Alonso, Isabel H. *Radio for the Millions: Hindi-Urdu Broadcasting Across Borders.* New York: Columbia University Press, 2023.

Alpes, Maybritt Jill. 'The Congress and the INA Trials, 1945–50: A Contest over the Perception of "Nationalist" Politics'. *Studies in History* 23, no. 1 (2007): 135–58.

Ambagudia, J. 'Scheduled Tribes, Reserved Constituencies and Political Reservation in India'. *Journal of Social Inclusion Studies* 5, no. 1 (2019): 44–58.

Amrith, Sunil. *Decolonizing International Health: India and Southeast Asia, 1930–65.* London: Palgrave Macmillan, 2006.

Ananth, V. Krishna. *India since Independence: Making Sense of Indian Politics.* New Delhi: Pearson, 2010.

———. *The Indian Constitution and Social Revolution: Right to Property since Independence.* New Delhi: Sage, 2015.

Anderson, Walter, and Shridhar Damle. *The Brotherhood in Saffron: The Rashtriya Swayamsevak Sangh and Hindu Revivalism.* New Delhi: Penguin, 2019.

Anil, P. *Another India: The Making of the World's Largest Muslim Minority, 1947–77.* London: Hurst, 2023.

Ankir, R. 'Bureaucracy, Community, and Land: The Resettlement of Meos in Mewat, 1949–50'. *Journal of Social History* 54, no. 1 (2020): 306–29.

———. 'De-linking "the Two Rupees": Devaluation Dilemma and Economic Divergence in the Decolonised Subcontinent, September 1949–February 1951'. *Modern Asian Studies* 57, no. 3 (2023): 918–39.

———. *India in the Interregnum: Interim Government September 1946–August 1947.* New Delhi: Oxford University Press, 2019.

———. 'In the Hands of a "Secular State": Meos in the Aftermath of Partition, 1947–49'. *Indian Economic and Social History Review* 56, no. 4 (2019): 457–88.

———. *The Kashmir Conflict: From Empire to the Cold War, 1945–66.* London: Routledge, 2016.

Ansari, Sarah, and William Gould. *Boundaries of Belonging: Localities, Citizenship and Rights in India and Pakistan.* Cambridge: Cambridge University Press, 2019.

Arora, S. C. *President's Rule in Indian States: A Study of Punjab.* New Delhi: Mittal, 1990.

Asif, Manan Ahmed. *The Loss of Hindustan: The Invention of India.* Cambridge: Harvard University Press, 2020.

Ayer, A. J. *More of My Life*. Oxford: Oxford University Press, 1985.

Bakshi, S. R. *Govind Ballabh Pant: The True Gandhian*. New Delhi: South Asia Books, 1991.

Balasubramanian, Aditya. *Toward a Free Economy: Swatantra and Opposition Politics in Democratic India*. Princeton: Princeton University Press, 2023.

Bandyopadhyay, Sekhar. *Decolonization in South Asia: Meanings of Freedom in Post-independence West Bengal*. New York: Routledge, 2009.

———. 'Freedom and Its Enemies: The Politics of Transition in West Bengal, 1947–1949'. *South Asia: Journal of South Asian Studies* 29, no. 1 (2006): 43–68.

———. 'The Story of an Aborted Revolution: Communist Insurgency in Post-independence West Bengal, 1948–50'. *Journal of South Asian Development* 3, no. 1 (2008): 1–32.

Bandyopadhyay, Sekhar, with Anasua Basu Ray Chaudhury. 'Partition in Bengal: Re-visiting the Caste Question, 1946–47'. *Studies in History* 33, no. 2 (2017): 234–61.

Baru, Sanjaya. *The Political Economy of Indian Sugar: The Political Economy of Sugar in India—State, International and Structural Change*. Oxford: Oxford University Press, 1990.

Baruah, Sanjib. *India against Itself: Assam and the Politics of Nationality*. Philadelphia: PENN Press, 1999.

———. *In the Name of the Nation: India and Its Northeast*. Stanford: Stanford University Press, 2020.

Basu, Aparna. *Mridula Sarabhai: Rebel with a Cause*. New Delhi: Oxford University Press, 1996.

Basu, Narayani. *V. P. Menon: The Unsung Architect of Modern India*. New Delhi: Simon & Schuster, 2020.

Baxter, Craig. *The Jana Sangh: A Biography of an Indian Political Party*. Philadelphia: University of Pennsylvania Press, 1969.

Bear, L. *Lines of the Nation: Indian Railway Workers, Bureaucracy, and the Intimate Historical Self*. New York: Columbia University Press, 2007.

Bekker, K. 'Land Reform Legislation in India'. *Middle East Journal* 5, no. 3 (1951): 319–36.

Benichou, Lucien D. *From Autocracy to Integration: Political Developments in Hyderabad State (1938–1948)*. New Delhi: Orient Longman, 2000.

Bhagavan, Manu, ed. *India and the Cold War*. Chapel Hill: University of North Carolina Press, 2019.

Bhagwat, Niloufer. 'Institutionalising Detention without Trial'. *Economic and Political Weekly* 13, no. 11 (1978): 510–13.

Bhargava, G. S. *Bhim Sen Sachar: An Intimate Biography*. New Delhi: Har Anand, 1997.

Bhatia, Udit, ed. *The Indian Constituent Assembly: Deliberations on Democracy*. London: Routledge, 2018.

Bhattacharya, H. 'Communism, Nationalism and Tribal Question in Tripura'. *Economic and Political Weekly* 25, no. 39 (1990): 2209–14.

———. *Radical Politics and Governance in India's Northeast: The Case of Tripura*. London: Routledge, 2018.

Bhattacharya, Medha. 'Linguistic Minorities and Strategic Mobilisation in Eastern India: Bengali-Biharis During the Era of Linguistic Territorialism (1935–57)'. *Indian Economic and Social History Review* 60, no. 3 (2023): 275–300.

Bhavnani, Nandita. *The Making of an Exile: Sindhi Hindus and the Partition of India*. New Delhi: Tranquebar Press, 2014.

Biswas, R. *R. A. Kidwai: Bridging Region and Nation: A Political Biography*. Chennai: Notion Press, 2020.

Blair, Harry. 'Identity, Dignity, and Development as Trajectory: Bihar as a Model for Democratic Progress in Nepal? Part I. Bihar's Experience'. *Commonwealth and Comparative Politics* 56, no. 1 (2018): 103–23.

———. 'Identity, Dignity, and Development as Trajectory: Bihar as a Model for Democratic Progress in Nepal? Part II. Nepal's Promise'. *Commonwealth and Comparative Politics* 56, no. 2 (2018): 216–33.

Borthakur, Akunthita, and Ritu Thaosen. 'Rethinking the Line System in Assam and Its Politics'. *Proceedings of the Indian History Congress* 73 (2012): 545–52.

Bose, S. K. *Sarat Chandra Bose: Remembering My Father*. Kolkata: Netaji Research Bureau, 2014.

Brass, Paul R. *Factional Politics in an Indian State: The Congress Party in Uttar Pradesh*. Berkeley: University of California Press, 1965.

Brecher, Michael. *Nehru: A Political Biography*. Oxford: Oxford University Press, 1959.

Brennan, L., J. McDonald and R. Shlomowitz. 'Caste, Inequality and the Nation-state: The Impact of Reservation Policies in India, c. 1950–2000'. *South Asia: Journal of South Asian Studies* 29, no. 1 (2006): 117–62.

Brittlebank, Kate. *Tiger: The Life of Tipu Sultan*. New Delhi: Juggernaut, 2016.

Brown, Judith M. '"Life Histories" and the History of Modern South Asia'. *American Historical Review* 114, no. 3 (2009): 587–95.

Burra, Arudra. 'Civil Liberties in the Early Constitution: The Crossroads and Organiser Cases'. In *Human Rights in India*, edited by Satvinder Juss, 1–34. Abingdon: Routledge, 2019.

———. 'The Cobwebs of Imperial Rule'. *Seminar* 615 (2010): 79–83.

———. 'The Indian Civil Service and the Nationalist Movement: Neutrality, Politics and Continuity'. *Commonwealth and Comparative Politics* 48, no. 4 (2010): 404–32.

Carnall, G. *Gandhi's Interpreter: A Life of Horace Alexander*. Edinburgh: Edinburgh University Press, 2010.

Chakrabarti, Gautam. 'From Moscow with Love: Soviet Cultural Politics across India in the Cold War'. *Safundi* 20, no. 2 (2019): 239–57.

Chakraborty, Biman. 'Political History of Merger of the Princely States: A Study of Cooch Behar'. PhD thesis, University of North Bengal, Darjeeling, 2001.

Chand, Tara. *Influence of Islam on Indian Culture*. Oxford: Oxford University Press, 1922.

Chandavarkar, R. *Imperial Power and Popular Politics: Class, Resistance and the State in India, 1850–1950*. Cambridge: Cambridge University Press, 1998.

Chandrachud, Abhinav. *The Informal Constitution: Unwritten Criteria in Selecting Judges for the Supreme Court of India*. New Delhi: Oxford University Press, 2014.

Chatterji, Joya. *The Spoils of Partition: Bengal and India, 1947–1967*. Cambridge: Cambridge University Press, 2007.

Chatterji, P. K. *Syama Prasad Mookerjee and Indian Politics*. New Delhi: Foundation, 2022.

Chaya, D. P. 'Proximity or Sycophancy? The Relationship between Intelligence and Policy in the Nehruvian Era, 1947–64'. *South Asia: Journal of South Asian Studies* 45, no. 4 (2022): 621–36.

Chopra, Pran. *Rafi Ahmad Kidwai: His Life and Work*. Agra: S. L. Agarwala, 1960.

Copland, Ian. 'Cows, Congress and the Constitution: Jawaharlal Nehru and the Making of Article 48'. *South Asia: Journal of South Asian Studies* 40, no. 4 (2017): 723–43.

———. 'The Further Shores of Partition: Ethnic Cleansing in Rajasthan in 1947'. *Past and Present* 160, no. 1 (1998): 203–39.

———. *The Princes of India in the Endgame of Empire, 1917–1947*. Cambridge: Cambridge University Press, 1997.

Copley, Antony R. H. *The Political Career of C. Rajagopalachari, 1937–1954*. New Delhi: Macmillan India, 1978.

Crouch, Harold A. *Trade Unions and Politics in India*. Bombay: Manaktala, 1966.

Curran (Jr.), Jean A. 'Dissension among India's Communists'. *Far Eastern Survey* 19, no. 13 (1950): 132–36.

———. 'The RSS: Militant Hinduism'. *Far Eastern Survey* 19, no. 10 (1950): 93–8.

D'Souza, Rohan. 'Damming the Mahanadi River: The Emergence of Multi-purpose River Valley Development in India (1943–46)'. *Indian Economic and Social History Review* 40, no. 1 (2003): 81–105.

Das, Durga, ed. *Selected Correspondences of Sardar Patel, 1945–50, Vols. I–X.* Ahmedabad: Navajivan, 1971–74.

Datla, Kavita. 'A Worldly Vernacular: Urdu at Osmania University'. *Modern Asian Studies* 43, no. 5 (2009): 1117–48.

———. *The Language of Secular Islam: Urdu Nationalism and Colonial India.* Honolulu: University of Hawaii Press, 2013.

Datta, Runi. 'Emancipating and Strengthening Indian Women: An Analysis of B. R. Ambedkar's Contribution'. *Contemporary Voice of Dalit* 11, no. 1 (2019): 25–32.

De, Rohit. 'Between Midnight and Republic: Theory and Practice of India's Dominion Status'. *International Journal of Constitutional Law* 17, no. 4 (2019): 1213–34.

———. 'Rebellion, Dacoity, and Equality: The Emergence of the Constitutional Field in Postcolonial India'. *Comparative Studies of South Asia, Africa and the Middle East* 34, no. 2 (2014): 260–78.

———. *A People's Constitution: The Everyday Life of Law in the Indian Republic.* Princeton: Princeton University Press, 2018.

De, Rohit, and Ornit Shani. 'Assembling India's Constitution: Towards a New History'. *Past and Present* 263, no. 1 (May 2024): 205–48.

Deshpande, A. 'Quest for Equality: Affirmative Action in India'. *Indian Journal of Industrial Relations* 44, no. 2 (2008): 154–63.

Deshpande, S. 'Reservation and the Republic: One Constitution, Two Amendments and Seven Decades'. *Social Change* 49, no. 3 (2019): 512–18.

Dubey, Abhay Kumar. 'Hindi and the Politics of Status: Official/National—Anatomy of a Double Sector Discourse'. 2021, 1–73. https://abhaykumardubey.com/wp-content/uploads/2021/08/Politics-of-Hindis-Status-latest-1.pdf. Accessed 12 May 2024.

Duncan, Ian. 'The Politics of Liberalisation in Early Post-Independence India: Food Deregulation in 1947'. *Journal of Commonwealth and Comparative Politics* 33, no. 1 (1995): 25–45.

Engerman, David C. *The Price of Aid: The Economic Cold War in India.* Cambridge: Harvard University Press, 2018.

Fahey, David M., and Padma Manian. 'Poverty and Purification: The Politics of Gandhi's Campaign for Prohibition'. *The Historian* 67, no. 3 (2005): 489–506.

Framke, M. 'The Politics of Gender and Community: Non-Governmental Relief in Late Colonial and Early Postcolonial India'. In *Gendering Global*

Humanitarianism in the Twentieth Century Practice, Politics and the Power of Representation, edited by E. Moller, J. Paulmann and K. Stornig, 143–66. London: Palgrave Macmillan, 2020.

Franda, Marcus F. *West Bengal and the Federalizing Process in India*. Princeton: Princeton University Press, 1968.

———. 'The Organizational Development of India's Congress Party'. *Pacific Affairs* 35, no. 3 (1962): 248–60.

Friedlander, Peter. 'Reassessing Religion and Politics in the Life of Jagjivan Rām'. *Religions* 11, no. 5 (2020): 224.

Furber, H. 'The Unification of India, 1947–1951'. *Pacific Affairs* 24, no. 4 (1951): 352–71.

Gadbois (Jr.), George H. *Supreme Court of India: The Beginnings*. New York: Oxford University Press, 2018.

Gae, R. S. 'Land Law in India: With Special Reference to the Constitution'. *International and Comparative Law Quarterly* 22, no. 2 (1973): 312–28.

Gandhi, Rajmohan. *Patel: A Life*. Ahmedabad: Navajivan, 1990.

———. *Rajaji: A Life*. London: Penguin, 2010.

Gautier, Laurence. 'Crisis of the "Nehruvian Consensus" or Pluralization of Indian Politics? Aligarh Muslim University and the Demand for Minority Status'. *Samaj* 22 (2019). https://doi.org/10.4000/samaj.6493. Accessed 12 May 2024.

Geva, Rotem. *Delhi Reborn: Partition and Nation Building in India's Capital*. Stanford: Stanford University Press, 2022.

———. 'Torn Between the Nation and the World: D. F. Karaka and Indian Journalism in the Second World War'. *Modern Asian Studies* 57, no. 5 (2023): 1459–94.

Ghosh, Arunabha. 'Jharkhand Movement in West Bengal'. *Economic and Political Weekly* 28, nos. 3/4 (1993): 121–27.

Ghosh, Papiya. 'Writing Ganga-Jamni: In the 1940s and After'. *Social Scientist* 34, no. 11/12 (2006): i–xx.

Ghosh, Subhasri, ed. *The 1947 Partition in The East: Trends and Trajectories*. Abingdon: Routledge: 2022.

Gidla, Sujata. *Ants Among Elephants: An Untouchable Family and the Making of Modern India*. New York: Faber & Faber, 2017.

Gill, Mehar Singh. 'Politics of Population Census Data in India'. *Economic and Political Weekly* 42, no. 3 (2007): 241–49.

Gill, S. S. 'Changing Land Relations in Punjab and Implications for Land Reforms'. *Economic and Political Weekly* 24, no. 25 (1989): A79–A85.

Godsmark, Oliver. *Citizenship, Community, and Democracy in India: From Bombay to Maharashtra*. Abingdon: Routledge, 2018.

Goel, S. 'Tales of Restoration: A Study of the Evacuee Property Laws'. *Studies in History* 36, no. 2 (2020): 251–79.

Gopal, Sarvepalli, ed. *Selected Works of Jawaharlal Nehru, Second Series 2, Volume 17 (November 1951–March 1952)*. New Delhi: Teen Murti House, 1995.

Gottlob, Michael. 'India's Unity in Diversity as a Question of Historical Perspective'. *Economic and Political Weekly* 42, no. 9 (2007): 779–89.

Gould, William. *Bureaucracy, Community, and Influence in India: Society and the State, 1930s–1960s*. London: Routledge: 2010.

———. 'Contesting Secularism in Colonial and Postcolonial North India between the 1930 and 1950s'. *Contemporary South Asia* 14, no. 4 (2005): 481–94.

———. 'From Subjects to Citizens? Rationing, Refugees, and the Publicity of Corruption over Independence in UP'. *Modern Asian Studies* 45, no. 1 (2011): 33–56.

———. *Hindu Nationalism and the Language of Politics in Late Colonial India*. Cambridge: Cambridge University Press, 2004.

Gould, William, Taylor C. Sherman and Sarah Ansari. 'The Flux of the Matter: Loyalty, Corruption and the Everyday State in the Post-partition Government Services of India and Pakistan'. *Past and Present* 219, no. 1 (2013): 237–79.

Govindu, Venu Madhav, and Deepak Malghan. *The Web of Freedom: J. C. Kumarappa and Gandhi's Struggle for Economic Justice*. New Delhi: Oxford University Press, 2016.

Graham, Bruce. *Hindu Nationalism and Indian Politics: The Origins and Development of the Bharatiya Jana Sangh*. Cambridge: Cambridge University Press, 1990.

Grewal, J. S. *Master Tara Singh in Indian History: Colonialism, Nationalism, and the Politics of Sikh Identity*. New Delhi: Oxford University Press, 2018.

Guha, Ramachandra. *India after Gandhi: The History of the World's Largest Democracy*. London: Pan Macmillan, 2008.

Gupta, Saumya. 'India in the Interregnum: Interim Government, September 1946–August 1947, Delhi: OUP, 2019'. *Indian Economic and Social History Review* 58, no. 4 (2021): 563–65.

Guyot-Rechard, Berenice. 'Reordering a Border Space: Relief, Rehabilitation, and Nation-building in North-eastern India after the 1950 Assam Earthquake'. *Modern Asian Studies* 49, no. 4 (2015): 931–62.

Haider, S. M. 'Social Organisation of the Refugees in Bhopal State'. *Sociological Bulletin* 6, no. 1 (1957): 61–71.

Haines, D. *Rivers Divided: Indus Basin Waters in the Making of India and Pakistan*. Oxford: Oxford University Press, 2017.

Hart, Henry C. *New India's Rivers*. Hyderabad: Orient Longman, 1956.

Hasan, Mushirul. '"Congress Muslims" and Indian Nationalism, Dilemma, and Decline, 1928–1934'. *South Asia: Journal of South Asian Studies* 8, nos. 1/2 (1985): 102–20.

———. *A Nationalist Conscience: M. A. Ansari, the Congress, and the Raj*. New Delhi: Manohar, 1987.

Henningham, S. 'Bureaucracy and Control in India's Great Landed Estates: The Raj Darbhanga of Bihar, 1879 to 1950'. *Modern Asian Studies* 17, no. 1 (1983): 35–57.

Hettne, Björn. *The Political Economy of Indirect Rule: Mysore 1881–1947*. London: Curzon Press, 1978.

———. 'The Vitality of Gandhian Tradition'. *Journal of Peace Research* 13, no. 3 (1976): 227–45.

Hossain, Ashfaque. 'The Making and Unmaking of Assam–Bengal Borders and the Sylhet Referendum'. *Modern Asian Studies* 47, no. 1 (2013): 250–87.

Jaffrelot, Christophe, and L. Gayer, eds. *Muslims in Indian Cities: Trajectories of Marginalisation*. London: Hurst, 2012.

Jaiswal, Shivangi. 'Labour Ministers, State and the Prism of Law, 1942–52'. *South Asia Chronicle* 8 (2018): 233–56.

Jana, Arun K. 'Confronting the "Congress System" in West Bengal: Electoral Strategies of the CPI in the 1950s'. *Journal of Political Studies* 12 (March–October 2016): 1–20.

Jannuzi, F. T. *Agrarian Crisis in India: The Case of Bihar*. Austin: University of Texas Press, 1974.

Jayal, N. G. *Citizenship and Its Discontents: An Indian History*. Cambridge: Harvard University Press, 2013.

Jha, Dhirendra. *Gandhi's Assassin: The Making of Nathuram Godse and His Idea of India*. New Delhi: Penguin, 2022.

Jha, Dhirendra, and Krishna Jha. *Ayodhya: The Dark Night—The Secret History of Rama's Appearance in Babri Masjid*. New Delhi: HarperCollins, 2016.

Jha, M. 'Nehru and Civil Liberties in India'. *International Journal of Human Rights* 7, no. 3 (2003): 103–15.

Jha, Sadan. *Reverence, Resistance and Politics of Seeing the Indian National Flag*. Cambridge: Cambridge University Press, 2016.

Kalia, Ravi. *Bhubaneswar: From a Temple Town to a Capital City*. Carbondale; Edwardsville: Sothern Illinois University Press, 1994.

Kamtekar, I. 'A Different War Dance: State and Class in India 1939–1945'. *Past and Present* 176, no. 1 (2002): 187–221.

Kana, S. 'Voluntarism in Partition's Aftermath: The Faridabad Story'. *Contemporary South Asia* 31, no. 1 (2023): 1–18.

Kanjwal, Hafsa. *Colonizing Kashmir: State-building under Indian Occupation.* Stanford: Stanford University Press, 2023.

Kanungo, P. *RSS's Tryst with Politics: From Hedgewar to Sudarshan.* New Delhi: Manohar, 2002.

Kashyap, Subhash C. *Dada Saheb Mavalankar, Father of Lok Sabha: His Life, Work and Ideas, A Centenary Volume.* New Delhi: Lok Sabha Secretariat, 1989.

Kaur, Ravinder. 'Narrative Absence: An "Untouchable" Account of Partition Migration'. *Contributions to Indian Sociology* 42, no. 2 (2008): 281–306.

———. *Since 1947: Partition Narratives among Punjabi Migrants of Delhi.* New Delhi: Oxford University Press, 2007.

Khan, Yasmin. 'The Arrival Impact of Partition Refugees in Uttar Pradesh, 1947–52'. *Contemporary South Asia* 12, no. 4 (2003): 511–22.

Khalidi, Omar. 'Ethnic Group Recruitment in the Indian Army: The Contrasting Cases of Sikhs, Muslims, Gurkhas and Others'. *Pacific Affairs* 74, no. 4 (2001–02): 529–52.

Khubchandani, L. M. 'A Demographic Typology for Hindi, Urdu, Panjabi Speakers in South Asia'. In *Language and Society: Anthropological Issues,* edited by W. C. McCormack and S. A. Wurm, 183–94. The Hague: Moulton, 1979.

Khusro, A. M. *Economic and Social Effects of Jagirdari Abolition and Land Reforms in Hyderabad.* Hyderabad: Osmania University Press, 1958.

King, Robert D. 'Language Politics and Conflicts in South Asia'. In *Languages in South Asia,* edited by Brij B. Kachru, Yamuna Kachru and S. N. Sridhar, 311–24. Cambridge: Cambridge University Press, 2008.

———. 'The Poisonous Potency of Script: Hindi and Urdu'. *International Journal of the Sociology of Language* 150 (August 2001): 43–59.

Klingensmith, Daniel. *'One Valley and a Thousand': Dams, Nationalism, and Development.* New Delhi: Oxford University Press, 2007.

Kochanek, Stanley A. *Business and Politics in India.* Berkeley: University of California Press, 1974.

———. *The Congress Party of India: The Dynamics of a One-Party Democracy.* Princeton: Princeton University Press, 1968.

Kohli, Manorama. *From Dependency to Interdependence: A Study of Indo-Bhutan Relations.* New Delhi: Vikas, 1993.

Kudaisya, G. *Reorganisation of States in India: Text and Context.* New Delhi: NBT, 2014.

———. *Region, Nation, 'Heartland': Uttar Pradesh in India's Body Politic.* New Delhi: Sage, 2006.

Kudaisya, M. '"A Mighty Adventure": Institutionalising the Idea of Planning in Post-colonial India, 1947–60'. *Modern Asian Studies* 43, no. 4 (2009): 939–78.

Kulkarni, V. B. *K. M. Munshi: Builders of Modern India*. New Delhi: Publications Division, 1959.

Lacina, Bethany. 'The Problem of Political Stability in Northeast India: Local Ethnic Autocracy and the Rule of Law'. *Asian Survey* 49, no. 6 (2009): 998–1020.

Legg, S. 'Dyarchy: Democracy, Autocracy, and the Scalar Sovereignty of Interwar India'. *Comparative Studies of South Asia, Africa and the Middle East* 36, no. 1 (2016): 44–65.

Leonard, J. G. 'Politics and Social Change in South India: A Study of the Andhra Movement'. *Journal of Commonwealth Political Studies* 5, no. 1 (1967): 60–77.

Levi, Werner. 'India's Political Parties'. *Far Eastern Survey* 20, no. 17 (1951): 169–72.

Lockwood, D. *The Indian Bourgeoisie: A Political History of the Indian Capitalist Class in the Early Twentieth Century*. London: Bloomsbury Academic, 2020.

Mahendru, K. C. *Gandhi and the Congress Socialist Party, 1934–48: An Analysis of Their Interaction*. New Delhi: ABS, 1986.

Maheshwari, S. 'Evolution of States in India'. *Indian Journal of Public Administration* 22, no. 3 (1976): 307–29.

Maingi, B. 'Politics of Minority Communities of Punjab: A Case Study of the Namdhari Sikhs'. *Proceedings of the Indian History Congress* 69 (2008): 1243–53.

Mantena, R. S. 'The Andhra Movement, Hyderabad State, and the Historical Origins of the Telangana Demand: Public Life and Political Aspirations in India, 1900–56'. *India Review* 13, no. 4 (2014): 337–57.

Marston, Daniel. *The Indian Army and the End of the Raj*. Cambridge: Cambridge University Press, 2014.

Masani, Z. *Radical Nationalism in India, 1930–42: The Role of the All-India Congress Socialist Party*. DPhil thesis, University of Oxford, UK, 1976.

Mathur, B. C. 'Administrative Reforms'. *Indian Journal of Public Administration* 31, no. 3 (1985): 548–60.

Matthews, David J. 'Urdu Language and Education in India'. *Social Scientist* 31, nos. 5/6 (2003): 57–72.

Mayer, Albert, and R. L. Park. *Pilot Project, India: The Story of Rural Development at Etawah, Uttar Pradesh*. Berkeley: University of California Press, 1958.

McGarr, Paul M. '"Quiet Americans in India": The CIA and the Politics of Intelligence in Cold War South Asia'. *Diplomatic History* 38, no. 5 (2014): 1046–82.

McPherson, Hugh. 'The Indian Province of Bihar and Orissa: Its History, Physical Features, and Land Problems'. *Scottish Geographical Magazine* 47, no. 1 (1931): 1–19.

Mehrotra, Santosh, and S. Guichard, eds. *Planning in the 20th Century and Beyond: India's Planning Commission and the NITI Aayog*. Cambridge: Cambridge University Press, 2020.

Mendes, S. S. 'Jawaharlal Nehru and the Liberation Struggle of Goa'. *Proceedings of the Indian History Congress* 67 (2006–07): 549–55.

Menon, Dilip M. *Caste, Nationalism and Communism in South India Malabar 1900–1948*. Cambridge: Cambridge University Press, 2008.

Menon, Nikhil. *Planning Democracy: Modern India's Quest for Development*. Cambridge: Cambridge University Press, 2022.

Menon, V. P. *The Story of the Integration of the Indian States*. Bombay: Orient Longman, 1956.

Merrett, Stephen. 'The Growth of Indian Nitrogen Fertilizer Manufacture: Some Lessons for Industrial Planning'. *Journal of Development Studies* 8, no. 4 (1972): 395–410.

Metcalf, B. D. *Husain Ahmad Madani: The Jihad for Islam and India's Freedom*. London: Simon & Schuster, 2012.

Mills, R. H. 'India's Food Crisis'. *Far Eastern Survey* 28, no. 10 (1959): 145–49.

Misra, M. *Business, Race, and Politics in British India, c. 1850–1960*. Oxford: Clarendon Press, 1999.

Misra, U. *Burden of History: Assam and the Partition—Unresolved Issues*. New Delhi: Oxford University Press, 2018.

———. 'The Naga National Question'. *Economic and Political Weekly* 13, no. 14 (1978): 618–24.

Mitra, Subrata K. *Governance by Stealth: The Ministry of Home Affairs and the Making of the Indian State*. New Delhi: Oxford University Press, 2021.

Mohammad, Afsar. *Remaking History: 1948 Police Action and the Muslims of Hyderabad*. Cambridge: Cambridge University Press, 2023.

Moore, R. J. *Making the New Commonwealth*. Oxford: Clarendon Press, 1987.

Mujumdar, N. A. 'Minimum Wages in Agriculture'. *Indian Journal of Agricultural Economics* 12, no. 4 (1957): 67.

Mukerjee, Dilip. 'Assam Reorganization'. *Asian Survey* 9, no. 4 (1969): 297–311.

Mukherjee, Aditya. *Imperialism, Nationalism, and the Making of the Indian Capitalist Class, 1920–1947*. New Delhi: Sage, 2002.

Mukherjee, Anit. *The Absent Dialogue: Politicians, Bureaucrats, and the Military in India*. New Delhi: Oxford University Press, 2019.

Murali, A., ed. *Putchalapalli Sundarayya: An Autobiography*. New Delhi: National Book Trust, 2009.

Nag, Sajal. 'Nehru and the Nagas: Minority Nationalism and the Post-Colonial State'. *Economic and Political Weekly* 44, no. 49 (2009): 48–55.

———. 'Nehru and the North-East'. NMML Occasional Paper (History and Society), New Series 75: 1–57.

Namakkal, J. *Unsettling Utopia: The Making and Unmaking of French India*. New York: Columbia University Press, 2021.

Naorem, D. 'Japanese Invasion, War Preparation, Relief, Rehabilitation, Compensation and "State-making" in an Imperial Frontier (1939–1955)'. *Asian Ethnicity* 21, no. 1 (2020): 96–121.

Natarajan, K. 'The Privilege of the Indian Passport (1947–1967): Caste, Class, and the Afterlives of Indenture in Indian Diplomacy'. *Modern Asian Studies* 57, no. 2 (2023): 321–50.

Nayar, B. R. *Minority Politics in the Punjab*. Princeton: Princeton University Press, 1966.

Newbigin, E. *The Hindu Family and the Emergence of Modern India: Law, Citizenship and Community*. Cambridge: Cambridge University Press, 2013.

Niclas-Tolle, Boris. *The Socialist Opposition in Nehruvian India 1947–1964*. Frankfurt: Peter Lang, 2015.

Noorani, A. G. 'Vande Mataram: A Historical Lesson'. *Economic and Political Weekly* 8, no. 23 (1973): 1039–43.

———. *The Destruction of Hyderabad*. London: Hurst, 2014.

Overstreet, G. D., and M. Windmiller. *Communism in India*. Berkeley: University of California Press, 1959.

Pai, Sudha. 'Politics of Language: Decline of Urdu in Uttar Pradesh'. *Economic and Political Weekly* 37, no. 27 (2002): 2705–08.

Pandit, Aishwarya. *Claiming Citizenship and Nation: Muslim Politics and State-Building in North India, 1947–1986*. New Delhi: Routledge India, 2022.

Park, R. L. 'Indian Democracy and the General Election'. *Pacific Affairs* 25, no. 2 (1952): 130–39.

———. 'India's General Elections'. *Far Eastern Survey* 21, no. 1 (1952): 1–8.

Patel, H. M., ed. *Say Not the Struggle: Essays in Honour of A. D. Gorwala*. New Delhi: Oxford University Press, 1976.

Patel, Indira, and Bipin Patel, eds. *Snapshots of History: Through the Writings of HVR Iengar*. Mumbai: Ananya, 2002.

Pati, Biswamoy. *South Asia from the Margins: Echoes of Orissa, 1800–2000*. Manchester: Manchester University Press, 2012.

Pernau, M. *Passing of Patrimonialism: Politics and Political Culture in Hyderabad 1911–1948*. New Delhi: Manohar, 2000.

Perumal, N. *Economic Ambassador: The Life and Work of Dr Sir R. K. Shanmukham Chetty*. Coimbatore: Popular, 1954.

Piramal, Gita. *Business Legends*. New Delhi: Penguin, 1998.

Potter, David C. 'Jawaharlal Nehru and the Indian Civil Service'. *South Asia Research* 9, no. 2 (1989): 128–44.

———. *India's Political Administrators: From ICS to IAS*. Oxford: Oxford University Press, 1996.

Prasad, M. *A Gandhian Patriarch: A Political and Spiritual Biography of Kaka Kalelkar*. Bombay: Popular, 1965.

Purushotham, Sunil. *From Raj to Republic: Sovereignty, Violence, and Democracy in India*. Stanford: Stanford University Press, 2021.

———. 'Internal Violence: The "Police Action" in Hyderabad'. *Comparative Studies in Society and History* 57, no. 2 (2015): 435–66.

———. 'Jawaharlal Nehru, Indian Republicanism, and the Commonwealth'. In *Commonwealth History in the Twenty-First Century*, edited by Saul Dubow and Richard Drayton, 143–59. London: Palgrave Macmillan, 2020.

Qasmi, Ali Usman. *The Ahmadis and the Politics of Religious Exclusion in Pakistan*. London: Anthem Press, 2014.

Raghavan, Pallavi. *Animosity at Bay: An Alternative History of the India–Pakistan Relationship, 1947–1952*. New York: Oxford University Press, 2020.

Raghavan, Srinath. 'Soldiers, Statesmen, and India's Security Policy'. *India Review* 11, no. 2 (2012): 116–33.

———. *War and Peace in Modern India*. London: Palgrave Macmillan, 2010.

Revolutionary Democracy XXV, no. 2 (September 2020) and XXVI, no. 1 (April 2021).

Rai, Alok. *Hindi Nationalism*. Hyderabad: Orient Longman, 2001.

Rai, Satya M. *Partition of the Punjab: A Study of Its Effects on the Politics and Administration of the Punjab (I) 1947–56*. Bombay: Asia Publishing House, 1965.

Ramaswamy, Deepa. 'Making a Self-Reliant Citizen: Technocracy, Rural Redevelopment and the Etawah Pilot'. *Journal of Planning History* 22, no. 1 (2022): 68–82.

Ramesh, Jairam. *A Chequered Brilliance: The Many Lives of V. K. Krishna Menon*. New Delhi: Penguin, 2019.

Ramnath, Kalyani. 'ADM Jabalpur's Antecedents: Political Emergencies, Civil Liberties, and Arguments from Colonial Continuities in India'. *American University International Law Review* 31 (2016): 209.

Rao, M. S. A. Rao. 'Caste and the Indian Army'. *Economic and Political Weekly* 16, no. 35 (1964): 1439–43.

Reeves, Peter. 'The Congress and the Abolition of Zamindari in Uttar Pradesh'. *South Asia: Journal of South Asian Studies* 8, nos. 1/2 (1985): 154–67.

Robinson, Francis. *Jamal Mian: The Life of Maulana Jamaluddin Abdul Wahab of Farangi Mahall, 1919–2012*. Karachi: Oxford University Press, 2018.

Roy, Haimanti. *Partitioned Lives: Migrants, Refugees, Citizens in India, and Pakistan, 1947–65*. New Delhi: Oxford University Press, 2013.

Roy, R. 'Intra-Party Conflict in the Bihar Congress'. *Asian Survey* 6, no. 12 (1966): 706–15.

Rubin, B. R. 'The Civil Liberties Movement in India: New Approaches to the State and Social Change'. *Asian Survey* 27, no. 3 (1987): 371–92.

Rudolph, Lloyd I., and Susanne H. Rudolph. 'Generals and Politicians in India'. *Pacific Affairs* 37, no. 1 (1964): 5–19.

Said, Edward. *Culture and Imperialism*. New York: Vintage, 1993.

Sajjad, M. *Muslim Politics in Bihar: Changing Contours*. New Delhi: Routledge, 2014.

Sarangi, Asha, and Sudha Pai, eds. *Interrogating Reorganisation of States: Culture, Identity and Politics in India*. Abingdon: Routledge, 2020.

Sarkar, Tanika. 'Birth of a Goddess: "Vande Mataram", "Anandamath", and Hindu Nationhood'. *Economic and Political Weekly* 41, no. 37 (2006): 3959–69.

Saxena, Saumya. *Divorce and Democracy: A History of Personal Law in Post-Independence India*. Cambridge: Cambridge University Press, 2022.

Schendel, Willem van. *The Bengal Borderland: Beyond State and Nation in South Asia*. London: Anthem Press, 2004.

Schutte, Sebastian. 'Politics or Prejudice? Explaining Individual-Level Hostilities in India's Hindu–Muslim Conflict'. *International Interactions: Empirical and Theoretical Research in International Relations* 45, no. 4 (2019): 666–92.

'Selected Works of Jawaharlal Nehru'. Jawaharlal Nehru Memorial Fund. https://nehruselectedworks.com/. Accessed 21 December 2023.

Sen, Uditi. *Citizen Refugee: Forging the Indian Nation after Partition*. Cambridge: Cambridge University Press, 2018.

———. 'Social Work, Refugees and National Belonging: Evaluating the "Lady Social Workers" of West Bengal'. *South Asia: Journal of South Asian Studies* 44, no. 2 (2021): 344–61.

Sengupta, Anwesha. '"They Must Have to Go Therefore, Elsewhere": Mapping the Many Displacements of Bengali Hindu Refugees from East Pakistan, 1947 to 1960s'. *Public Arguments* 2, Occasional Paper (January 2017): 5–26.

Sengupta, A., and R. Sharma, eds. *Appointment of Judges to the Supreme Court of India: Transparency, Accountability, and Independence.* New Delhi: Oxford University Press, 2018.

Sethia, Aradhya. 'Where's the Party? Towards a Constitutional Biography of Political Parties'. *Indian Law Review* 3, no. 1 (2019): 1–32.

Shani, Ornit. *How India Became Democratic: Citizenship and the Making of the Universal Franchise.* Cambridge: Cambridge University Press, 2018.

Shankardass, Rani Dhavan. 'Vallabhbhai Patel: His Role and Style in Indian Politics 1928–1947'. PhD thesis, SOAS, London, 1985.

Sharma, Chetna. 'National Register of Citizens Assam, India: The Tangled Logic of Documentary Evidence'. *Journal of Immigrant and Refugee Studies* 22, no. 1 (2024): 225–37.

Shastri, Vanita. 'The Political Economy of Policy Formation in India: The Case of Industrial Policy, 1948–1994'. PhD thesis, Cornell University, Ithaca, 1995.

Sherman, Taylor C. 'A Gandhian Answer to the Threat of Communism? Sarvodaya and Postcolonial Nationalism in India'. *Indian Economic and Social History Review* 53, no. 2 (2016): 249–70.

———. 'From "Grow More Food" to "Miss a Meal": Hunger, Development, and the Limits of Post-Colonial Nationalism in India, 1947–1957'. *South Asia: Journal of South Asian Studies* 36, no. 4 (2013): 571–88.

———. *Muslim Belonging in Secular India: Negotiating Citizenship in Postcolonial Hyderabad.* Cambridge: Cambridge University Press, 2015.

———. *Nehru's India: A History in Seven Myths.* Princeton: Princeton University Press, 2022.

Sheth, D. L. *At Home with Democracy: A Theory of Indian Politics.* Edited with an introduction by Peter Ronald deSouza. London: Palgrave Macmillan, 2018.

Siddiqui, A. U. *Indian Freedom Movement in Princely States of Vindhya Pradesh.* New Delhi: Northern Book Centre, 2004.

Siegel, Benjamin R. *Hungry Nation: Food, Famine, and the Making of Modern India.* Cambridge: Cambridge University Press, 2018.

Singh, C. P. 'A Century of Constituency Delimitation in India'. *Political Geography* 19, no. 4 (2000): 517–32.

Singh, Gursharan, *History of PEPSU: Patiala and East Punjab States Union, 1948–1956.* New Delhi: Konark, 1991.

Singh, H. S. 'Socio Religious and Political Movements in Modern Manipur 1934–51'. PhD thesis, JNU, Delhi, 2011.

Singh, Khushwant. *A History of the Sikhs: 1469–1838.* Oxford: Oxford University Press, 1963.

Singh, Neerja. *Patel, Prasad and Rajaji: Myth of the Indian Right*. New Delhi: Sage, 2015.

Singh, U. K., and A. Roy. *Election Commission of India: Institutionalising Democratic Uncertainties*. Oxford: Oxford University Press, 2019.

Sinha, Chitra. *Debating Patriarchy: The Hindu Code Bill Controversy in India (1941–1956)*. Oxford: Oxford University Press, 2012.

Sinha, Rita, and Ramu Manivannan, eds. *Basawon Sinha: A Revolutionary Patriot (1909–1989): A Commemorative Volume*. New Delhi: Kamala Sinha, 1999.

Sisodia, M. K. Singh. 'India and the Asian Games: From Infancy to Maturity'. *Sport in Society: Cultures, Commerce, Media, Politics* 8, no. 3 (2005): 404–13.

Sisson, Richard. *The Congress Party in Rajasthan: Political Integration and Institution-Building in an Indian State*. Berkeley: University of California Press, 1972.

Snedden, C. *Independent Kashmir: An Incomplete Aspiration*. Manchester: Manchester University Press, 2021.

———. 'What Happened to Muslims in Jammu? Local Identity, "The Massacre of 1947" and the Roots of the "Kashmir Problem"'. *South Asia: Journal of South Asian Studies* 24, no. 2 (2001): 111–34.

Som, Reba. 'Jawaharlal Nehru and the Hindu Code: A Victory of Symbol over Substance?' *Modern Asian Studies* 28, no. 1 (1994): 165–94.

Spodek, Howard. 'Sardar Vallabhbhai Patel at 100'. *Economic and Political Weekly* 10, no. 50 (1975): 1925–29, 1931–36.

Sundarayya, P. 'Telangana People's Armed Struggle, 1946–1951. Part One: Historical Setting'. *Social Scientist* 1, no. 7 (1973): 3–19.

———. *Telangana People's Struggle and Its Lessons*, Part II. Calcutta: Ganashakti, 1972.

Suradkar, Santosh. '*Mukti Kon Pathe*? Caste and Class in Ambedkar's Struggle'. *Economic and Political Weekly* 52, no. 49 (2017): 61–68.

Talbot, Ian, and G. Singh. 'Punjabi Refugees' Rehabilitation and the Indian State: Discourses, Denials and Dissonances'. *Modern Asian Studies* 45, no. 1 (2011): 109–30.

———, eds. *Region and Partition: Bengal, Punjab, and the Partition of the Subcontinent*. Oxford: Oxford University Press, 1999.

———. *The Partition of India*. Cambridge: Cambridge University Press, 2009.

Talbot, Ian, and D. S. Tatla, eds. *Epicentre of Violence: Partition Voices and Memories from Amritsar*. New Delhi: Permanent Black, 2006.

Tewari, Saagar. 'Kasht-nivarak Thakkar Bapa: Samaj seva ko samarpit jeevan par ek vihangam drishti'. *Pratiman* 5, no. 10 (2017): 278–96.

Thapar, Romila. *Somanatha: The Many Voices of a History*. London: Verso, 2005.

Thirumali, I. 'The Political Pragmatism of the Communists in Telangana, 1938–48'. *Social Scientist* 24, nos. 4/6 (1996): 164–83.

Thatra, Geeta. 'Differentiated Rehabilitation and the Geographies of Unfreedom in Post-Colonial Bombay'. *Journal of Sindhi Studies* 7, no. 2 (2022): 1–40.

Tripathi, D., and J. Jumani. *The Concise Oxford History of Indian Business History*. New Delhi: Oxford University Press, 2007.

Tripathi, P. K. 'Preventive Detention: The Indian Experience'. *American Journal of Comparative Law* 9 (1960): 219.

Tyabji, Nasir. *Forging Capitalism in Nehru's India: Neocolonialism and the State, c. 1940–1970*. New Delhi: Oxford University Press, 2015.

———. 'The Politics of Industry in Nehru's India'. *Economic and Political Weekly* 50, no. 35 (2015): 97–103.

Untawale, M. G. 'The Political Dynamics of Functional Collaboration: Indo-Nepalese River Projects'. *Asian Survey* 14, no. 8 (1974): 716–32.

Vagale, L. R., B. M. Bhuta and M. S. V. Rao. 'Faridabad: A Critical Study of the New Town'. *Ekistics* 10, no. 59 (1960): 156–65.

Virdee, Pippa. *From the Ashes of 1947: Reimagining Punjab*. Cambridge: Cambridge University Press, 2018.

Wani, Javed Iqbal. *Sovereign Anxiety: Public Order and the Politics of Control in India, 1915–1955*. Cambridge: Cambridge University Press, 2023.

Weiner, Myron. *Party Politics in India: The Development of a Multi-Party System*. Princeton: Princeton University Press, 1957.

———, ed. *State Politics in India*. Princeton: Princeton University Press, 1968.

Wernicke, Günter. 'The Unity of Peace and Socialism? The WPC on Cold War Tightrope between the Peace Struggle and Intra-systematic Communist Conflicts'. *Peace and Change* 26, no. 3 (2001): 332–51.

Wilkinson, Steven I. *Army, and Nation: The Military and Indian Democracy Since Independence*. Cambridge: Harvard University Press, 2015.

Yadav, Nomita. 'Other Backward Classes: Then and Now'. *Economic and Political Weekly* 37, nos. 44/45 (2002): 4495–4500.

Yeatts, W. W. M. 'The Indian Census of 1941'. *Journal of the Royal Society of Arts* 91, no. 4634 (1943): 182–94.

Zachariah, Benjamin. *Nehru*. London: Routledge, 2004.

Zamindar, Vazira Fazila-Yacoobali. *The Long Partition and the Making of Modern South Asia: Refugees, Boundaries, Histories*. New York: Columbia University Press, 2007.

Index